ANYTHING YOU ASK

Anything You Ask

Colin Urquhart

HODDER AND STOUGHTON
LONDON SYDNEY AUCKLAND

*This Colin Urquhart Omnibus edition first published 1995
by Hodder and Stoughton, a Division of Hodder Headline PLC*
0 340 64315 3

10 9 8 7 6 5 4 3 2 1

British Library Cataloguing in Publication Data
A record for this book is available from the British Library

Anything You Ask

Copyright © 1978 by Colin Urquhart.
First published in a single volume 1978 by Hodder and Stoughton

The right of Colin Urquart to be identified as the author of this
work has been asserted by him in accordance with the Copyright,
Designs and Patents Act 1988.

Printed and bound in Great Britain by
Cox & Wyman Ltd, Reading, Berks

Hodder and Stoughton
A Division of Hodder Headline PLC
338 Euston Road
London NW1 3BH

In thanksgiving for
the precious gift of
the Holy Spirit, who
inspires faith within
God's children.

Acknowledgments

My thanks are willingly expressed to all whom God has used to encourage faith in Him in my life. My prayer is that this book will be used by Him to build faith in others – and I know God will answer that prayer!

I praise the Lord for my wife, Caroline, and my children, Claire, Clive and Andrea. I am thankful for all their love and the encouragement they have given me in writing this book. My thanks also to Vivienne who has done all the typing, to Maureen for all her help, and to George whose helpful suggestions have been greatly appreciated.

The Biblical references in this book are taken from the Revised Standard Version, with the exception of the quotations from Nehemiah, chapter 9.

Contents

1

An Unbelievable Promise?

WE WERE SITTING having a leisurely cup of coffee when we heard screams. One of the boys came rushing into the kitchen: "Dad, there's been an accident." Charles didn't wait to hear any more. He ran out of the house and across the yard, closely followed by Joyce.

Caroline and I were staying with Charles and Joyce and their family, while I was ministering for a few days in Cornwall. On the previous evening I had been speaking about the prayer promises of Jesus and what it means to pray with faith, knowing that God is going to answer you.

We were already praying when Charles carried ten-year-old Joanna into the room. In the garage the children had been melting down lead to pour into moulds, to make gifts for Christmas. One of them dropped a cold piece of metal into the container causing some of the molten mixture to fly into Joanna's face.

Some of the liquid lead had gone into both eyes. Can you imagine the effect of molten lead on eyes?

It took her mother nearly forty minutes to remove all the pieces of metal. During that time we all prayed, silently and aloud, with Joanna and for her. But all the time we thanked the Lord that there would be no damage to the eyes, and praised Him for His healing.

Joanna was obviously in considerable distress, so once the metal had been removed from her eyes, we asked the Lord to give her a good sleep, so that she would not suffer from prolonged shock after such an experience.

She slept, and at 5 p.m. was downstairs having tea with us. Her eyes were not even blood-shot! And it was subsequently confirmed that she had suffered no damage to them at all.

That is our loving heavenly Father answering the prayers of His children.

Will He Answer Me?

Nearly everyone prays – at least occasionally. When they are feeling desperate enough. When things get so black, that God is the last resort.

For Christians, prayer is a way of life – or supposed to be. Yet for many it is a dull routine; for others an exercise that lacks power or reality.

"Does God really hear me?"

"Why doesn't He answer?"

Such questions are the symptom of a deeper unrest:

"Does God love me?"

"How can I be sure that He does?"

'Does He care about my problems?"

These and other uncertainties make it almost impossible to pray with faith, with the conviction and expectancy that God will answer. Many feel so desperate about their inadequacy in prayer that the cry of their hearts echos that of Jesus' disciples: "Lord, teach us to pray."

The Promise of Jesus

Jesus told His disciples: "If you ask anything in my name, I will do it" (John 14: 14). If you ask ANYTHING!

And the promise He gives: "I WILL do it." Not, "I may do it", or "I might", or "I can", or "I could". "I WILL DO IT."

At first sight those words seem so far from reality, as to be unbelievable. Yet Jesus said them and many like them, teaching that God wants to give you "ANYTHING YOU ASK".

When I ask church-going people if they pray, most say that they do. But if I go on to enquire if God does whatever they ask of Him, there is usually an embarrassed silence or even laughter at the very suggestion. People seem to be saying: "Oh we pray, but fancy expecting God to do everything we ask!"

And yet that is precisely what Jesus promises. Many of the things He says about prayer demonstrate that He knows His Father to be a generous Giver, One who loves His children so dearly that He *wants* to give to them.

This makes it even more remarkable that many Christians do not appear to believe that He is willing to give them whatever they ask. Some seem more concerned with discovering reasons why God should not give to them and meet their needs. Reasons, or excuses.

Jesus wants us to be an asking people. And when we pray He wants us to know that we can expect to receive *whatever* we ask.

He wants His Church to be a FAITH-FULL people! He is longing to see the faith that will release His giving into their lives. He does not want to speak words of promise that are disbelieved; for He is the faithful God, who keeps His Word. He always has, and He always will.

Here are three questions to ask yourself:

"How can I see the promise of Jesus fulfilled in my life?"

"How can I know that if I ask Jesus ANYTHING He WILL do it?"

"How can I pray and obtain positive results?"

The Roof on the Building

The answer to such questions is like the roof on a building. You have to construct the building before you can put the roof on. And before you construct the building, you need a firm foundation, the words of Jesus:

> Everyone who comes to me and hears my words and does them, I will show you what he is like: he is like a man building a house, who dug deep, and laid the foundation upon rock; and when a flood arose, the stream broke against that house and could not shake it, because it had been well built (Luke 6: 46–48).

When your life is built securely on faith in the words of Jesus, it does not matter what storm breaks, what difficulties you are confronted with or how desperate things become. For you will see Him bringing you through to peace, joy and victory over all such oppressive circumstances. You will know that the One to whom we pray is the God who is faithful. "I will not fail you or forsake you" (Josh. 1: 5).

However, Jesus warns:

> But he who hears and does not do them is like a man who built a house on the ground without a foundation; against which the storm broke, and immediately it fell, and the ruin of that house was great (Luke 6: 49).

People often believe they have faith, only to discover how fragile that faith is when put under pressure. They have never 'dug deep' and laid the foundation of their lives on rock. When the going grows tough they no longer know what to believe, or who to believe, let alone how to pray. The idea that they can ask Jesus for anything *and receive it* seems totally impossible.

Digging Deep

We are going to dig into the Bible to lay a firm foundation that will never move, no matter what pressures we come under. We are going to 'dig deep' so that God can inspire within us a faith that will not be shaken.

Your words of faith: "IF YOU ASK ANYTHING IN MY NAME, I WILL DO IT."

At the end of every chapter, you will be given some words of faith from the Bible. They are words God is speaking to *YOU*. Say them to yourself over and over again until they become part of you.

2

A Righteous Man

GOD WANTS A people for Himself. His own people. A people who belong to Him. Not because He is possessive, but because He wants to give to them. A people to love.

However, the rebellion, the sinfulness and disobedience of men had made it impossible for them to enjoy the relationship with God that He intended. Neither had they been able to receive all that He had wanted to give them. This grieved God.

> The Lord saw that the wickedness of man was great upon the earth, and that every imagination of the thoughts of his heart was only evil continually. And the Lord was sorry that he had made man on the earth, and it grieved him to his heart (Gen. 6: 5–6).

So God decided to "blot out man whom I have created". One man, Noah, "found favour in the eyes of the Lord". He is described as "a righteous man, blameless in his generation": the only man to be in right standing with God.

Although "the earth was corrupt in God's sight, and the earth was filled with violence", He would not condemn any righteous man to death. Noah alone was concerned to be a man of God, and his faithfulness was rewarded. God wanted to save His people; everybody else was too busy doing his own thing to worry about Him or His salvation.

Out of the relationship that he had with God, Noah heard his command to build an ark. God is going to "bring a flood of waters upon the earth, to destroy all flesh in which is the breath of life from under heaven; everything that is on the earth shall die" (Gen. 6: 17).

This does not sound like a God of love speaking; more like a God of destruction! And yet in the midst of this destruction God is to show His willingness to love and to save. His purpose is not to destroy but to give life. But, like you, God wants to see the end of all that is evil and unloving in His creation. He is the God of justice and as Paul was to write thousands of years after the story of Noah, "the wages of sin is death". God shows man the dreadful, awful consequences of rebellion, sin, disobedience and selfishness. They inevitably end in destruction, instead of the love, joy and peace that God wants to give to all His people.

A Binding Agreement

So to Noah, His faithful servant, God says:

> I will establish my covenant with you, and you shall come into the ark, you, your sons, your wife, and your sons' wives with you. And of every living thing of all flesh, you shall bring two of every sort into the ark, to keep them alive with you (Gen. 6: 18–19).

Here God introduces the idea of establishing a 'covenant' with Noah. A covenant is an agreement, a legal contract, a solemn pledge, a bargain, even. God does not *have* to make any such agreement; He chooses willingly to do so.

First, Noah must be obedient to what God tells him to do. "Noah did all that the Lord had commanded him" (Gen. 7: 5).

God, for His part, delivers Noah and his family from the flood and then establishes with His servant this covenant that He had promised.

> I establish my covenant with you, that never again shall all flesh be cut off by the waters of a flood, and never

again shall there be a flood to destroy the earth (Gen. 9: 11).

God gives Noah His word, which He will never break. And the rainbow is taken as the sign, the continual reminder, of this covenant. From God's early dealings with man we know He willingly commits Himself to a covenant, to making and remembering the everlasting covenant, "which I have established between me and all flesh that is upon the earth" (Gen. 9: 17).

The terms of this early covenant are simple. God promises not to repeat the destruction of the flood. He has demonstrated the awful consequences of rebellion, sin and disobedience, and in the deliverance of Noah and his family, He has shown His love and faithfulness to save those who are righteous in His sight and obey Him.

Above all, God shows that He is not afraid to pledge Himself to a binding covenant or agreement with man – a word that cannot be broken!

Where You Stand

Today God still wants a people for Himself, His own people. And He wants you to be one of those people, someone who knows that he or she belongs to Him. He wants you to be His, so that out of His love for you He can give to you to meet every need in your life.

Like Noah, you are surrounded by so much destruction and violence, and it may be that you cannot understand how God can love His creation, or why He doesn't do more to end the world's problems.

You may be conscious of anger and rebellion in your heart towards God, because you believe He has given you a rough deal. You may feel so full of guilt that you cannot see how you can ever get right with God, or why He should want to give you anything.

You may have been a Christian for years, and yet you have never 'broken through' in your prayers; you have not come to that place of knowing that God is going to answer you.

God wants to show you that He does love you; He cares about you so much that He wants to meet you in every area of need in your life. He wants you to be free of anger, guilt and doubt. He wants you to be free to love Him, to pray with faith, knowing that your prayers will be answered.

In this book, He is going to teach you how to believe and trust Him, how to pray and receive the answers you need. He wants you to be one of His covenant people, enjoying His faithfulness and generosity, even when things seem at their most desperate.

Noah's Faith

Noah was a man of great faith. Out of personal relationship with God, he hears the Lord and believes the words that are spoken to him.

Believing God means acting upon His words. Not simply hearing them or agreeing with them. Doing them! Putting them to work in your life.

> By faith Noah, being warned by God concerning events as yet unseen, took heed and constructed an ark for the saving of his household (Heb. 11: 7).

That faith was amply vindicated, as the events that followed were to prove.

If we are to pray with faith, knowing that ANYTHING we ask will be done for us and given to us by God, we will need to believe what God says, and be prepared to act upon His words. That should be easier for us than for Noah. He had to hear God for himself and believe that what he heard was indeed the voice of God, before acting upon those words. We have the benefit of the Bible: God's Word spoken to His people over thousands of years; the revelation of who He is and what His purposes are.

Whenever we want to hear God speak, we only have to turn to the pages of scripture and there we discover words that are far more remarkable than those spoken to Noah. For God's promise to all His convenant people today is: "If you ask anything in my name, I will do it."

And that is only a small part of what He promises in His abounding, loving, generosity!

Your words of faith: "HE DID ALL THAT THE LORD COMMANDED HIM."

3

The Father of Faith

WE MODERN PEOPLE like to deal with facts. Presents us with a set of facts and we know where we stand. We have become very suspicious of promises. We are too familiar with politicians who make enticing statements, which are at best fond hopes; at worse, deliberate deception.

From early childhood, we learn to distrust promises. Human beings find they are easy to make; much more difficult to keep. As we enter adult life, we enter a world not of promises, but of legal contracts, binding agreements, often with penalty clauses if the requirements are not met. Everything must be 'cut and dried'.

God, however, has chosen to work in the lives of His people, by asking them to believe a series of promises that He gives them. But He is no human politician, or well-meaning, but unreliable, parent. By contrast, He is faithful to His Word – always.

So faithful that He does not mind incorporating these promises into a legal contract, a covenant.

Abram

Now the Lord said to Abram, "Go from your country and your kindred and your father's house to the land that I will show you. And I will make of you a great nation, and I will bless you, and make your name great, so that you will be a blessing . . . " So Abram went, as the Lord had told him (Gen. 12: 1–4).

Abram was a nomad, without a book of scriptures to teach him or a church to instruct him. Yet, like Noah, out of the simplicity of his personal relationship with God, he hears the Lord speak. And he knows enough about God not to argue with Him. If God says: "Get up and go!" you get up and go!

That is a good example of faith. Not only hearing and believing what God says, *but being prepared to act upon it.*

God promises to bless Abram. That means that God will care for him, will give to him and enrich him. He will make of Abram 'a great nation' and a blessing to others.

Abram, for his part, has to obey God and believe the promises that he is given.

> By faith Abraham obeyed when he was called to go out to a place which he was to receive as an inheritance; and he went out, not knowing where he was to go (Heb. 11: 8).

He would need to trust that God would lead him and guide him, and fulfil the words of promise that He had spoken.

The Covenant

The Lord kept His Word and gave Abram a land of promise. But how could He make of him a great nation, when he had no children by his wife, Sarah?

God's answer was to make a covenant with him.

> When Abram was ninety-nine years old the Lord appeared to Abram, and said to him, "I am God Almighty; walk before me, and be blameless. And I will make my covenant between me and you, and will multiply you exceedingly." Then Abram fell on his face; and God said to him, "Behold, my covenant is with you,

and you shall be the father of a multitude of nations. No longer shall your name be Abram, but your name shall be Abraham ... I will make you exceedingly fruitful ... And I will establish my covenant between me and you and your descendants after you throughout their generations for an everlasting covenant, to be God to you and to your descendants after you" (Gen. 17: 1–7).

Such promises must have seemed almost impossible for this old man to believe. And yet who can stop God doing what He says He is going to do? Especially when the promises given are part of a covenant, a binding agreement between God and His people.

Abram, for his side of the agreement must "walk before me, and be blameless". To mark the establishing of the covenant relationship, he is given a new name, Abraham, which means, "father of a multitude". And the sign of this covenant with Abraham and his descendants was circumcision. By this act, they are to pledge themselves to obedience to God, to be His people; and God will be faithful to them, fulfilling the promises that He gives.

No Laughing Matter

Not that God has come to the end of His promises to Abraham. He says that his wife Sarah, is to bear him a son. What a laughable suggestion!

Abraham fell on his face and laughed, and said to himself, "Shall a child be born to a man who is a hundred years old? Shall Sarah, who is ninety years old, bear a child?" (Gen. 17: 17).

When Sarah later overheard the news she too laughed.

The Lord said to Abraham, "Why did Sarah laugh, and

say, 'Shall I indeed bear a child, now that I am old?' Is anything too hard for the Lord?" (Gen. 18: 13–14).

At first, the things that God promises may seem incredible. You will be tempted to treat them like the statements of politicians. If only they were true! How different life would be! It is only when you begin to act upon God's promises that you discover that they are true and THEY ARE FOR YOU! Human beings are fallible; they fail constantly. God is Almighty and never fails. "Is anything too hard for the Lord?"

Abraham and Sarah both thought God's promise to be beyond belief – at first. Then they had time to consider who had made the promise, the One who always keeps His Word:

> By faith Sarah herself received power to conceive, even when she was past the age, since she considered him faithful who had promised (Heb. 11: 11).

> The Lord did to Sarah as He had promised (Gen. 21: 1).

That is the remarkable thing about Noah and Abraham and Sarah. In God's dealings with them, they discovered Him to be the God who was faithful to His promises. He kept His Word, even when it seemed impossible. If God said it, IT WOULD HAPPEN.

Giving What is Precious

Isaac was born to Abraham and Sarah, as God had promised. But the testing of Abraham's faith was by no means over. Isaac was the one through whom God's great promises to Abraham's descendants would be fulfilled. Without him there would be no descendants. And yet God says to Abraham:

"Take your son, your only son Isaac, whom you love,

and go to the land of Moriah, and offer him there as a
burnt offering upon one of the mountains of which I
shall tell you." So Abraham rose early in the morning,
saddled his ass, and took two of his young men with
him, and his son Isaac; and he cut the wood for the
burnt offering, and arose and went to the place of which
God had told him (Gen. 22: 2–3).

Oh the quiet submission! What is the use of arguing with
Almighty God? Was He now going back on His word? No.
Never. Abraham knew that God would still keep His prom-
ises concerning his son.

By faith Abraham, when he was tested, offered up
Isaac, and he who had received the promises was ready
to offer up his only son, of whom it was said, "Through
Isaac shall your descendants be named." He considered
that God was able to raise men even from the dead
(Heb. 11: 17–19).

God had given His word. God had entered into covenant
with Abraham, a binding agreement that He would never
break. If Isaac was to be offered in sacrifice then God would
somehow raise him to life again so that His promises would
be fulfilled.

Such was Abraham's faith. Because he knew the faithfulness of God.

At the last moment, the angel of the Lord tells Abraham
not to harm Isaac and delivers this message:

"By myself I have sworn, says the Lord, because you
have done this and have not withheld your son, your
only son, I will indeed bless you, and I will multiply
your descendants as the stars of heaven and as the sand
which is on the seashore ... because you have obeyed
my voice" (Gen. 22: 16–18).

God is the God of promise. The faithful God. He keeps

His word, even when that seems impossible; even when the circumstances seem to point to the opposite.

Abraham showed himself to be a man of faith, because he didn't believe the circumstances, he didn't believe the facts as they appeared to him. He believed the words of God and the promises he had been given.

Paul tells the Romans that the promise of God is "to those who share the faith of Abraham, for he is the father of us all" (Rom. 4: 16). The "father of faith".

You do not need to be overwhelmed by the faith that Abraham displayed. God wants to teach you to believe His words and His promises, to apply them to the situation that confronts you. Time and time again, you will feel more inclined to believe the situation, to accept that the problem is insurmountable, that God's promises could not be for you, that He will not change the circumstances. You will be tempted to believe that your faith is insufficient to see God answer your prayers.

"Is anything too hard for the Lord?" God asked Sarah. Apply those same words to all the problems in your life. You can struggle to solve them and fail miserably, over and over again. Then the problems seem like immovable mountains.

Remember that Jesus said:

> If you have faith as a grain of mustard seed, you will say to this mountain, "Move from here to there", and it will move; and nothing will be impossible for you (Matt. 17: 20).

Faith the size of a tiny seed. A very little faith. God asks: "Is anything too hard for the Lord?" His Son says: "Nothing will be impossible for you" when you have that tiny seed of faith.

Your words of faith: "IS ANYTHING TOO HARD FOR THE LORD?"

4

My Own People

GOD NEVER FORGETS the promises that He gives His people.
The descendants of Abraham left the land that God had
given them during a time of famine and went to Eygpt.
While there they became a nation of slaves.

> And God heard their groaning, and God remembered
> his covenant with Abraham, with Isaac, and with
> Jacob. And God saw the people of Israel, and God
> knew their condition (Exod. 2: 24–25).

In His love for His people, God wants to set them free
from their bondage. He calls Moses to return to Egypt,
where he had been brought up in the Pharaoh's court. He
had fled the country after killing an Egyptian who was beat-
ing a Hebrew, "one of his own people".

The Lord says to Moses: "I have seen the affliction of my
people who are in Egypt . . ." (Exod. 3: 7). MY PEOPLE.
That phrase which is an indication of the special covenant
relationship that God had been prepared to enter into with
Abraham and his descendants. He would be *their* God; they
would be *His* people.

Moses, like countless others after him, thinks of all the
possible excuses for avoiding the responsible task that God
calls him to fulfil. The confrontations with Pharoah, the
plagues that were sent upon Egypt until its ruler agreed to
allow the Hebrews to leave the country, the Egyptians' pur-
suit and the miraculous crossing of the sea, these are all familiar enough. It is when Moses and the Hebrews had come
into the wilderness of Sinai, that God speaks to them again

of the covenant, of the binding agreement that is to exist between Him and His people.

> It is because the Lord loves you, and is keeping the oath which He swore to your fathers, that the Lord has brought you out with a mighty hand, and redeemed you from the house of bondage, from the hand of Pharaoh, king of Egypt (Deut. 7: 8).

The Covenant

Moses "went up to God" on Mt. Horeb, the holy mountain. Through him, the Lord says to His people:

> Now therefore, if you will obey my voice and keep my covenant, you shall be my own possession among all peoples; for all the earth is mine, and you shall be to me a kingdom of priests and a holy nation (Exod. 19: 5–6).

MY OWN PEOPLE. All the earth belongs to God and all the people in it: and yet He wants His OWN PEOPLE, who will be a holy nation, living for Him, obedient to Him. He wants them to receive all the blessing He desires to give in His generous love for them. "I will be your God, and you shall be my people."

What did God want of His people? What were they to do as their side of the covenant agreement?

God does not leave them in any doubt. He clearly and precisely gives to Moses the law, incorporating the Commandments by which they were to live. His people were to be obedient to the Law; then they would see fulfilled the rich promises that God had given them. He would be their God, to provide for them, to care for them, to heal them, to bless them. "MY OWN PEOPLE."

The immediate response of the Hebrews was: "All that

the Lord has spoken we will do, and we will be obedient"
(Exod. 24: 7). In this way they expressed their intention of
keeping their side of the covenant pact; they gave their
solemn promise to God.

The covenant was sealed with the blood of animals, which
was thrown on the altar and sprinkled over the people, with
the words: "Behold, the blood of the covenant which the
Lord has made with you in accordance with all these words"
(Exod. 24: 8).

Israel did not deserve to have the Lord as their personal
God, or to be His own people. The desire for the covenant
came from God, not from men.

> And he said, "Behold, I make a covenant. Before all
> your people I will do marvels, such as have not been
> wrought in all the earth or in any nation; and all the
> people among whom you are shall see the work of the
> Lord" (Exod. 34: 10).

God is not afraid to commit Himself to more and more
promises, for He has the power, the love and the faithfulness
to keep every one of them. They are set, however, firmly
within the context of the covenant. To see God's side of the
covenant fulfilled completely, they will need to be obedient
in fulfilling their side, of being a holy people who are living
to please God.

> You shall therefore keep all my statutes and all my
> ordinances, and do them (Lev. 20: 22).
> You shall be holy to me; for I the Lord am holy, and
> have separated you from the peoples, that you should
> be mine (Lev. 20: 26).

The Lord is saying: "You give your lives to Me, and I
promise that I will give Myself to you."

What an amazing offer! All that any man can offer to God
is a weak, sinful life. In exchange, God offers to him His life,

which is perfect love, joy, peace, healing, forgiveness and abundant provision.

> If you walk in my statutes and observe my commandments and do them, then I will give you your rains in their season, and the land shall yield its increase, and the trees of the field shall yield their fruit . . . (Lev. 26: 3–4).

God is concerned, not only with the spiritual lives of His people, but with their material needs and prosperity. He will fulfil His promises for these things, if they are obedient.

> I will give peace in the land, and you shall lie down, and none shall make you afraid (Lev. 26: 6).
> I will have regard for you and make you fruitful and multiply you, and will confirm my covenant with you . . . And I will make my abode among you, . . . And I will walk among you and will be your God, and you shall be my people (Lev. 26: 9, 11–12).

The wonder of it all! And yet God has something in store for all who believe in Jesus, that is far more wonderful.

God's Warning

But the Lord warns His people that if they fail to keep the covenant, if they are disobedient, the consequences will be dire. In love He wants to give to them and bless them; their disobedience stops the flow of that giving and blessing. So God will discipline His children for their own good, because of His love for them, so that once again they will be able to receive all that He has to give.

What if they do not submit to the Lord and return to obedience?

> And if by this discipline you are not turned to me, but

walk contrary to me, then I also will walk contrary to
you, and I myself will smite you sevenfold for your
sins. And I will bring a sword upon you, that shall
execute vengeance for the covenant; and if you gather
within your cities I will send pestilence among you, and
you shall be delivered into the hand of the enemy (Lev.
26: 23–25).

That does not sound quite so good. God will warn His
people before He allows these calamities to befall them; He
will give them the time and opportunity to repent, to return
to obedience to Him. For His purpose is not to afflict and
destroy His people, but to be their God, who will live among
them, providing and caring for them.

Yet for all that, when they are in the land of their
enemies, I will not spurn them, neither will I abhor
them so as to destroy them utterly and break my covenant with them; for I am the Lord their God; but I
will for their sake remember the covenant with their
forefathers (Lev. 26: 44–45).

God will never give up on His people! That is good news
for all of us. He has not given up on you. You may feel that
He is a million miles away, totally unconcerned about the
details of your life and the problems that you face. It may
appear to you that the only thing about God that you have
experienced is His discipline.

But He has made a covenant that He will not forget. He
warns Israel not to forget it either.

Take heed to yourselves, lest you forget the covenant of
the Lord your God, which he has made with you (Deut.
4: 23).

These words are so applicable today. Many Christians
suffer great difficulties because they forget the covenant

that God has made with them – not the covenant made with Moses, but the new and better one given by Jesus. Some do not understand that they are in covenant relationship with God, and that he wants to honour every promise in their lives. Others long for such a relationship and for an assurance of God's love for them. He told Israel:

> You will seek the Lord your God, and you will find him, if you search after him with all your heart and with all your soul. When you are in tribulation, and all these things come upon you in the latter days, you will return to the Lord your God and obey his voice, for the Lord your God is a merciful God; he will not fail you or destroy you or forget the covenant with your fathers which he swore to them (Deut. 4: 29–31).

The Lord will have mercy upon *you*. He will not fail *you* or destroy *you*. His purpose is to give you life, His own life. He wants to meet *you* right in the middle of the tribulation you experience. He wants you to understand the covenant He establishes with all who believe in Jesus. He wants you to remember that covenant, to live by it and see His faithfulness in loving you and giving His blessings to you.

As you read this book, you can "search after him with all your heart and all your soul". And you will find Him. Because Jesus promises that: "He who seeks finds" (Matt. 7: 8).

Your words of faith: "I WILL BE YOUR GOD AND YOU SHALL BE MY PEOPLE."

5

Dismal Failure

WHICH IS THE better way? Obedience to God, or disobedience? That is the question that faced Israel throughout her history.

> And because you hearken to these ordinances, and keep and do them, the Lord your God will keep with you the covenant and the steadfast love which he swore to your fathers to keep; HE WILL LOVE YOU, BLESS YOU, AND MULTIPLY YOU (Deut. 7: 12–13).

But continually Israel failed to keep the covenant; although God remained utterly faithful to His side of the agreement. When the people were obedient, the nation prospered materially and spiritually; when they were disobedient, the Lord disciplined them. If they did not repent, He had to resort to stronger methods to bring them to obedience.

Repeated Disobedience

In Nehemiah, Chapter 9, Ezra summarises a whole period of history under the covenant:

> You are the Lord, the God who chose Abram ... You found his heart faithful before you, and made the covenant with him to give his descendants the land ... and YOU HAVE FULFILLED YOUR PROMISE, FOR YOU ARE RIGHTEOUS (Neh. 9: 7–8).

He then traces briefly the deliverance from Egypt, the crossing of the Red Sea, how God led His people through the wilderness and gave them "right ordinances and true laws, good statutes and commandments" (v. 14).

> You gave them bread from heaven for their hunger, and brought water for them from the rock for their thirst, and told them to go in and possess the land you had sworn to give them (v. 15).

Then Ezra begins to draw out Israel's great sins of presumption and disobedience.

> But they and our fathers acted presumptuously and stiffened their necks, and did not obey your commandments; THEY REFUSED TO OBEY, and were not mindful of the wonders which you did among them; but they stiffened their necks and appointed a leader that they might return to their bondage in Egypt (vv. 16–17).

Israel might be prepared already to forsake the covenant, but God had no intention of doing so!

> BUT YOU ARE A GOD READY TO FORGIVE, GRACIOUS AND MERCIFUL, SLOW TO ANGER AND ABOUNDING IN STEADFAST LOVE. YOU DID NOT FORSAKE THEM (v. 17).

God was utterly faithful even in the face of their disobedience. "You in your great mercies did not forsake them in the wilderness" (v. 19). "You gave your good Spirit to instruct them" (v. 20). "They lacked nothing" (v. 21). And God led them to the land He had promised them.

Did that lead to thankfulness on the part of the people, a thankfulness shown by a renewed obedience to God? Not at all!

Nevertheless they were disobedient and rebelled against you and cast your law behind their back and killed your prophets, who had warned them to turn back to you (v. 26).

Another time of discipline was necessary:

Therefore you gave them into the hand of their enemies, who made them suffer; and in the time of their suffering they cried to you and you heard them from heaven; and ACCORDING TO YOUR GREAT MERCIES you gave them deliverers who saved them from their enemies (v. 27).

God's Endless Mercy

The mercy of God is so immense; His patience infinite. If He dealt with us as we deserved, we would all be judged and condemned. He doesn't want that; He wants to forgive. He wants to heal and restore His people.

Sadly, many do not come to know His mercy until their lives are in such a mess that they cry out to Him in desperation. In His love, God hears them and answers them. He is listening for that cry that comes from the heart. He is looking and waiting for that turning to Him, even as a last resort.

WHEN THEY TURNED AND CRIED TO YOU, YOU HEARD FROM HEAVEN, AND MANY TIMES YOU DELIVERED THEM ACCORDING TO YOUR MERCIES (v. 28).

Many times they sinned, rebelled and disobeyed. Many times they cried out to God in desperation. Many times He had mercy on them, forgave and restored them.

And many times they sinned again!

So the same sorry process of Israel's failure to live by the covenant is repeated over and over again. The only consolation in all this is to see the faithfulness of the Lord, never rejecting the cries of His people but always honouring His words of promise to them.

Knowing His faithfulness and mercy, Ezra prays to Israel's covenant God, 'our God'.

> Now therefore, *our* God, the great and mighty and terrible God, WHO KEEPS COVENANT AND STEADFAST LOVE, let not all the trouble seem little to you that has come upon us ... (v. 32).

At the same time, he acknowledges God's justice in the way He has dealt with His people.

> You are just in all that has come upon us, for you have dealt faithfully and we have acted wickedly (v. 33).

That is the great difference between God and men. He is always faithful. They are so often sinful, disobedient and faithless.

Ezra prays in a time of crisis. The people are prepared to return to the covenant that they had so often forsaken.

> Because of all this we make it a firm covenant and write it, and our princes, our Levites and our priests set their seal to it (v. 38).

But that was not to be the end of the nation's disobedience. Their covenant with God would be broken again, and again, and again.

His Mercy Endures for Ever

As you look back over your life, it may appear to you like the history of Israel, a story of repeated disobedience. He is still the God of mercy. You may think that your disobedience means that you cannot expect to receive anything from Him.

It is not His purpose to reject you, or condemn you. He wants you to know His forgiveness for all your sins, your failure and disobedience. It is that same gracious merciful and faithful God, who sent His Son to establish an even better covenant, with even better promises. He wants you to be part of that covenant. It does not matter how disobedient and sinful you have been, whether you feel a complete failure or whether your life is in a total mess. God will not reject you when you turn to Him. He welcomes the repentant sinner and orders heaven to rejoice over him.

Your words of faith: "YOU ARE A GOD READY TO FORGIVE, GRACIOUS AND MERCIFUL, SLOW TO ANGER AND ABOUNDING IN STEADFAST LOVE."

6

The Better Way

THERE HAD TO be a better way. But God did not abandon the idea of a covenant with His people. However, Israel's constant failure to keep the old covenant clearly indicated that an entirely new one was needed.

The New Covenant

In the prophecy of Jeremiah, God looks forward to the establishing of this new pact between God and man.

> Behold, the days are coming, says the Lord, when I will make a NEW COVENANT with the house of Israel and the house of Judah, NOT LIKE THE COVENANT WHICH I MADE WITH THEIR FATHERS when I took them by the hand to bring them out of the land of Egypt, MY COVENANT WHICH THEY BROKE, THOUGH I WAS THEIR HUSBAND, says the Lord (Jer. 31: 31–32).

God had been a faithful husband to Israel. He had entered into a covenant, a marriage contract with His people. But the nation had been like an adulterous wife, forever proving unfaithful, going in search of other gods, disobeying her husband, breaking His laws, deserting Him in favour of other pleasures. "Rejoice not, O Israel! Exult not like the peoples; for you have played the harlot, forsaking your God" (Hos. 9: 1). How will the new covenant be different?

But this is the covenant which I will make with the house of Israel after those days, says the Lord: I WILL PUT MY LAW WITHIN THEM AND I WILL WRITE IT UPON THEIR HEARTS; and I will be their God and they shall be my people. And no longer shall each man teach his neighbour and each his brother, saying, "Know the Lord", FOR THEY SHALL ALL KNOW ME, from the least of them to the greatest, says the Lord; for I will forgive their iniquity, and I will remember their sin no more (Jer. 31: 33–34).

"I WILL PUT MY LAW WITHIN THEM": Under the old covenant, the Law was written on tablets of stone given to Moses on the holy mountain. Under the terms of the new covenant, the law of God will be written on the hearts of His people. God would need to deal personally with each one of them to accomplish that.

"I WILL WRITE IT UPON THEIR HEARTS": The finger of God had written the Ten Commandments on stone. Only the hand of God could write His law on human hearts! "*I* will write it . . ." God says. Somehow God Himself would build His desires, His will and His purpose into those hearts.

"AND I WILL BE THEIR GOD, AND THEY SHALL BE MY PEOPLE": The old covenant promise is repeated. God still has the same intention. He wants a people for Himself; a faithful, loving people, who will live for Him and inherit all the promises that He has given. A people to whom He can give Himself. He will be their God, the faithful God who keeps His covenant and honours His words of promise.

"THEY SHALL ALL KNOW ME": Every one of the new covenant people will have a personal relationship with their God; they will "know the Lord". And that relationship will come about through the forgiveness of their sins: "I will remember their sins no more."

In the past, God spoke to the mass of His people through intermediaries like Abraham, Moses and the prophets. In the future, God will be able to speak directly to each one of His covenant people because "they shall all know me".

A Change of Heart

God would have to do something divine within His people, if they were to live in continual fellowship with Him. They would need 'new hearts', with the law of God written upon them. That calls for 'heart surgery' that only the heavenly hand can perform.

> A NEW HEART I WILL GIVE YOU, and a new spirit I will put within you; and I will take out of your flesh the heart of stone and give you a heart of flesh. And I WILL PUT MY SPIRIT WITHIN YOU, AND CAUSE YOU TO WALK in my statutes and be careful to observe my ordinances (Ezek. 36: 26–27).

"A NEW HEART I WILL GIVE YOU": God will take away the old heart, hardened against His purposes; the sinful, disobedient and selfish heart. Instead, He will give a brand new heart filled with His love, pulsating with His desires and turned towards His purposes.

A New Spirit

"A NEW SPIRIT I WILL PUT WITHIN YOU": Not only will God give a new heart that will desire obedience to Him; He will also make new the human spirit within His people. They will then have the inner resources to actually *be* obedient, to put into effect what the new heart desires.

"I WILL PUT MY SPIRIT WITHIN YOU": God will put His own Spirit, His own life, His own power, His own love, His own Being, HIMSELF, into His people. God will come and live in them, to *enable* them to be obedient.

When would God give His Spirit? With the establishment of the new covenant. In the time of Jeremiah and Ezekiel that is still a promise that awaits fulfilment. "I will put my Spirit within you, and you shall live and . . . you shall know that I, the Lord, have spoken, and I have done it." (Ezek. 37: 14).

This points, once again, to the fact that God will touch each life personally; He will live in every new covenant child of His. Each one will know that He has 'done it'.

"AND CAUSE YOU TO WALK in my statutes and be careful to observe my ordinances": Under the old covenant, God said: "You obey me and I will bless you. You do your part and I will do mine." That did not work because the people constantly failed to keep their side of the agreement.

Under the new covenant, God is saying. "I will live in you to enable you to do your part. I will do it in you. I will cause you to walk in my ways."

In other words, God is going to be the determining factor in BOTH sides of the agreement. When He left one side to men, there was continual failure. God knew there would be. He knew that the old covenant would not work and that one day He would need to send His own Son to establish the new one. But He had to prove to men that they were incapable of pleasing Him, of being obedient and faithful, if they depended only on their own human resources.

Under the new covenant there would not need to be continual failure, for God would be living within His people, enabling them to love, to obey and BELIEVE!

A New Marriage

A new kind of 'marriage' is envisaged. God will continue to be as He has always been, the righteous and just, loving, merciful and faithful Husband.

I will betroth you to me for ever; I will betroth you to

me in righteousness and injustice, in steadfast love, and
in mercy. I will betroth you to me in faithfulness, and
you shall know the Lord (Hos. 2: 19–20).

His 'wife' is to be like Him. A people who are righteous,
in right standing and relationship with Him. A just people,
who are loving, merciful and faithful to their God. How
Hosea longs for the time when the people will 'know' their
husband, will be bound in that new everlasting, marriage
covenant with Him!

Let us know, let us press on to know the Lord; his going
forth is as sure as the dawn; He will come to us as the
showers, as the spring rains that water the earth (Hos.
6: 3).

"*Know the Lord*"

Those words are for you: "Let us press on to know the
Lord." For the new covenant has already been established
and God wants you to be one of His people.

He wants to give *you* a new heart.

He wants to give *you* His Spirit.

He wants to cause *you* to walk in His ways.

He wants *you* to 'know' Him.

And He has made all this possible through His Son Jesus
Christ.

To try and please God in your own way will not make you
one of His new covenant people. You will never be able to
make yourself acceptable to Him, or work your ticket to
heaven. He doesn't want you to think that being a Christian
is living by a code of Biblical laws. A Christian is someone
who has a new heart, a new spirit, with the Holy Spirit of
God living within him or her. Someone who is 'betrothed' to
the Lord. Someone who inherits all the rich promises that
God has for His people.

As you seek Him, He will come to you "as the showers, as the spring rains that water the earth". He will bring an end to your harsh winter; He will water the parched earth of your life with "rivers of living water" – as you will see.

Your words of faith: "A NEW HEART I WILL GIVE YOU AND A NEW SPIRIT I WILL PUT WITHIN YOU."

The Separation Ended

THE PEOPLE OF Israel did not "know the Lord". Their sin, disobedience and rebellion separated them from God and from His purposes. That separation made it impossible for them to receive all the riches that He wanted to pour into their lives.

That separation had to be ended, at any cost. Even the death of the Son of God!

The Word Made Flesh

Jesus is the Word of God, the Word that existed before time began. God created through that Word. God spoke that Word from heaven to His people throughout the years of the old covenant. Some heard that Word for themselves; Noah, Abraham, Moses, Hosea, Jeremiah, Ezekiel, to name only a few. Others only heard that Word 'second-hand' through the revelation given to such men. And often that Word was deliberately ignored and disobeyed.

Under the new covenant, God wanted all His people to hear that Word for themselves, through His own Spirit living within them. Before the Spirit could come, the Word had to come in human flesh and then they could hear clearly what God was saying. They could hear directly, with no need for an intermediary. They could hear the promises that God wanted to fulfil in their lives.

The Word of God was coming to bring life to men, God's own life; to bring light into the darkness of the world, separated from fellowship with its Creator. God Himself was coming to live among His people!

Jesus described His own mission in these terms: "I came that they (men) may have life and have it abundantly" (John 10: 10). God's life, eternal life, "life in all its fullness". This is what God wants for His new covenant children: to know Him and to live His life.

To hear the words of Jesus was not enough to receive that life; these words had to be believed. To believe His words was to believe Jesus. To disbelieve His words was to disbelieve Jesus and the Father who sent Him.

> Truly, truly, I say to you, he who hears my word and believes him who has sent me, has eternal life; he does not come into judgment, but has passed from death to life (John 5: 24).

Would God's old covenant people accept Jesus? Would they believe His words and receive Him? Would they pass from the death of sin and disobedience into this new life?

> To *all* who received him, who believed in his name, he gave power to become children of God (John 1: 12).

To *all*, whether Jew or Gentile. All who received Jesus, who believed Him, were given power to become God's children. The old covenant relationship was between God and His people; the new covenant relationship is between a Father and His children, because those children 'know' Him.

Jesus came to reveal His Father by speaking His words and performing His works.

> The word which you hear is not mine but the Father's who sent me (John 14: 24).
> The Son can do nothing of his own accord, but only what he sees the Father doing; for whatever he does, that the Son does likewise. For the Father loves the Son, and shows him all that he himself is doing (John 5: 19–20).

The unity of relationship between the Father and the Son is obvious. Jesus is living in covenant with His Father, speaking His words and doing His works. This is what God envisages for all His covenant children; living in them by the power of His Holy Spirit; speaking through them His words of life; and doing in them His works of love.

So Jesus comes to lead men into the Kingdom of His Father. He teaches them to pray: "Thy kingdom come, thy will be done on earth, as it is in heaven." He demonstrates the life, the love and power of that kingdom, of God's reign in and among His people. He shows that God's will is all-important.

> I have come down from heaven, not to do my own will, but the will of him who sent me (John 6: 38).

That is the outworking of a 'new heart'; someone who does not want his own will, only that of his heavenly Father. That was to be finally tested in the Garden of Gethsemane, on the evening before the Crucifixion when Jesus prayed: "Father, if thou art willing, remove this cup from me; nevertheless not my will, but thine, be done" (Luke 22: 42).

The Cross

Just as the old covenant was sealed with the blood of animals, so the new would be sealed with blood; that of God's own Son, Jesus. On the night of His arrest, Jesus had taken the cup while eating with His disciples, and said:

> THIS CUP WHICH IS POURED OUT FOR YOU IS THE NEW COVENANT IN MY BLOOD (Luke 22: 20).

To establish this new covenant relationship with His children, God was having to pay the highest possible price. Why was such a price necessary? Would it not have been enough for Jesus to come and speak the Father's words to demonstrate His works of love and power? No, because the separation between God and His people had to be ended, so that they could enjoy true union and fellowship with Him. So that they could 'know' him. So that they could receive the Spirit that God had promised and the new hearts that He wanted to give. So that they could become children of God and know Him as 'Father'.

Man's sin, rebellion and disobedience made him worthy only of death, of being separated from God. Jesus took that death-sentence upon Himself. The Sinless One dies for the sinners. The One who lives in union with the Father dies for those who are separated from Him, so that, through His death, they might be restored to that union and fellowship that God desires to have with all His people. The One who lives with his Father dies to establish the new covenant between the Father and His children; between God and those who believe and receive His Son.

Crucified with Christ

And yet Jesus did far more than die for men on the Cross. He took all sinful humanity to die with Him.

> For the love of Christ controls us, because we are convinced that one has died for all; therefore all have died. And he died for all, that those who live might live no longer for themselves but for him who for their sake died and was raised (2 Cor. 5: 14–15).

He took the sin, the failure, the fears, the doubts, the anxieties, the oppression, the grief, the sorrow, the pains, the diseases and sickness of men upon Himself and crucified them. He put them to death. And His resurrection proved conquered.

But not only the negative aspects of our lives were taken to the Cross. Jesus took us as whole people, body, soul and spirit, and put us to death with Him that we might become new creatures, raised to a new life in Him and restored to fellowship with His Father.

> Therefore, if anyone is in Christ, he is a new creation; the old has passed away, behold, the new has come (2 Cor. 5: 17).

The old way of approaching God and relating to Him has gone, has passed away. The old covenant is a thing of the past. Now, with the blood of Jesus, the new has come. And God Himself has done it!

> All this is from God, who through Christ reconciled us to himself and gave us the ministry of reconciliation; that is, in Christ God was reconciling the world to himself, not counting their trespasses against them, and entrusting to us the message of reconciliation (2 Cor. 5: 18–19).

It is this message that the world still needs to hear; that, through Jesus, a man can be restored to fellowship with God. He can know God and become His child and live in a new relationship with Him. He can be given a new heart, and God will put His own Spirit within Him, and cause Him to walk in obedience to His ways.

You Were on the Cross

Jesus took *you* to the Cross. "He died for all." And that includes *you*! He took you to the Cross because He does not want you to be separated from His Father. He wants you to know that His Father loves you, accepts you as the person you are, and forgives everything in your life that has been opposed to His will for you.

You are not accepted by God because you deserve to be, or because you have worked hard for Him, to make yourself acceptable to Him; but because Jesus died *for you*. He suffered your death-sentence for you. He experienced separation from His Father, so that your separation from Him can end. He took all your sin and failure and crucified it. He took YOU and offered YOU to the Father, so that your life can belong to Him and be filled with His love and power. You can share the personal testimony of St. Paul:

> I have been crucified with Christ; it is no longer I who live, but Christ who lives in me; and the life I now live in the flesh I live by faith in the Son of God, who loved me and gave Himself for me (Gal. 2: 20).

You will be unable to live the new covenant life until you have grasped this fundamental truth: GOD LOVES YOU AND HAS ACCEPTED YOU, because Jesus died for you.

It is a waste of time to try to make yourself acceptable to Him, because you will never succeed and because Jesus has already done it for you. It does not matter how sinful, disobedient or rebellious you consider your past life to have been; you are still made acceptable to God through the Cross of Jesus Christ. He died for *all* sinners. With *all* their failure, *all* their sins, *all* their disobedience and rebellion against God.

You cannot make yourself a child of God.

You cannot make yourself part of the new covenant.

Only God can do that. And He has made it possible for YOU, through the blood of Jesus. "This cup is the new covenant in my blood."

All?

Does that mean that all men are saved? That all are part of the new covenant? That all know God as their Father and are restored to fellowship with Him?

No, obviously not! You only have to look around you to encounter many people who appear to know nothing of the salvation of God, or the new covenant; who are unfamiliar with God and may even profess not to believe in His existence, let alone know Him as Father and live their lives in fellowship with Him!

These blessings await all who come personally to the Cross and appropriate what Jesus has already done for them. There is no other way to a new covenant life, but the way of the Cross. "No one comes to the Father, but by me," says Jesus.

But for every one who comes, there is a new life, a new heart, a new Spirit, a new relationship with God, a new covenant with new promises.

Your words of faith: "I HAVE BEEN CRUCIFIED WITH CHRIST."

8

"Lord, I come"

"How CAN I become a child of God? How can I enter the new covenant, with God as my Father?"

"By coming to the Cross!" is the short answer. By accepting for yourself what Jesus has done there for you. How?

Here is a simple method. It is not the only way, but it is thorough. It will clear the way not only to 'know' the Lord but also to receive the answers to your prayers. So even if you already know the Lord Jesus in a personal way, this chapter will be important for you. For it is crucial to understand how you can approach God, knowing that He will give to you and do for you, what you ask.

God has chosen to relate to His people through a covenant relationship, because He wants to give Himself to them. A covenant, however, needs two parties.

The Lord says: "You give yourselves to me and I will give Myself to you. You will be MY people and I will be YOUR God."

Entering the new covenant involves giving yourself to God; not only your sins to be forgiven; but *all of you*. Either you belong to Him, or you belong to yourself. Either you are His or you are not. Either you are His child or you are lost.

If you are His child, then you have come to that place of acknowledging to yourself, to God and to the world, that your life is not your own to do with as you like. You belong to God. You are His!

All of You

Jesus didn't die for part of you, but for YOU. He didn't take bits and pieces of your life to the Cross. He took YOU to the Cross.

Any housewife will know that one of the highlights of the week is the trip around the supermarket! Every time the same routine is repeated. You take a basket or trolley and begin to collect your groceries, item by item. Having selected what you want, you come to the check-out. You place every item from your basket or trolley on the counter and, as you do so, the assistant rings up the price of each on the cash register.

When every item has been accounted for, the assistant rings up the total and asks you for the money. Once you have recovered from the shock of how much you have spent, you hand over the required amount. You have paid the price for all those goods. They no longer belong to the supermarket; they are now yours, so you have the right to pack them in your shopping bags and take them home with you.

You don't select two or three items and leave the rest for general distribution! You have paid for the lot, so you take the lot.

God has paid the price for every part of YOU. Jesus died for YOU – not just the dirty, unclean, unsavoury, sinful, imperfect, failing parts of you. He paid the price for you as a complete person. And you were expensive!

Coming to the Cross is acknowledging, therefore, that every part of you belongs rightly to God. "You were bought with a price" (1 Cor. 7: 23).

You were already His, before you even thought of coming to the Cross. Jesus paid the price for you before you were born. It may be that in the past you have not realised or acknowledged that your life belongs to God, that He has the perfect right to do with you as He pleases. That is nothing to be afraid of because His purpose is to give to you, to be your

Father and to fulfil all His promises in the life of His new covenant child.

A token acknowledgment that Jesus is Lord and Saviour is not enough to bring about the real changes in your life that will enable you, not only to relate to God as your father, but to believe Him to meet you in every need, to answer every prayer.

Make a thorough commitment of your life to God. Here is how you can do it.

A Letter to Jesus

Make time to be quiet on your own. Have with you pen and paper. First, pray a simple prayer like this: "Please, Lord, show me myself as I really am and all that needs to be given to you." Then begin to write down everything that comes to you. Don't expect to hear audible voices from heaven; God will use your mind to show you what needs to be given to Him.

When I do this myself, I write it in the form of a letter to Jesus. That is more personal than a list of items. Such a letter may begin like this:

> Dear Jesus,
>   I am offering you my life and this is what I am giving to you now.

You will need to write down both the negative and positive aspects of your life. I will list the kind of things that I mean, although when you write your letter, they will not necessarily come in the orderly way set out below. That does not matter. Nor do you need to write in beautiful English. God wants you to express what is in your heart.

A. THE NEGATIVE
My sins: Anything from the past that troubles you, even

things from childhood; your guilt and failure. Don't try to think of every sin you have committed; you would need a book for that, not a sheet of paper! The relevant things will come to mind.

My fears: Of people, of particular situations, of death, of the future, even your fear of giving your life to God. Don't try to psycho-analyse yourself, or impress the Lord with your knowledge of why you have such fears. Simply write them down to be given to Him.

My doubts: Doubt is spiritual disease, which you will never be able to resolve for yourself. Bring your doubts to Jesus that He might deal with them. Be honest with Him for only He can transform your doubting into believing.

B. THE POSITIVE

Many people bring the negative things to the Cross, when they first become Christians. However, many have never made a detailed offering of the positive side of their lives. Later we shall see how important this is.

My relationships: It is particularly important to give God any bitterness, resentment, or anger that you feel towards anyone, even if you have held on to these feelings for years because of hurt done to you by someone or several people. This is not always easy. In giving yourself to God, you are giving your feelings, the whole situation, with all the grief, sorrow, sadness and hurt that has resulted.

My marriage: Possessiveness can easily destroy relationships. Even your husband or wife belongs to God. Many marriages have been healed of deep tensions when the couple have acknowledged God's ownership of their lives and of each other.

My children: They are 'His' too. Often dangerously ill children have only begun to recover when their parents have 'given' them to the Lord, instead of holding on to them for themselves. God can take and fill, touch and heal, what is given into His hands.

My home and family life: God wants to fill your home with His love and praise. It will be a home where Jesus lives and wants to share His life.

My work: God is concerned about your working life. He wants you to prosper and know His enabling Presence wherever you are and in all that you have to do.

My time: Every day is a fresh gift from God, a day in which He can be honoured and praised in our lives; so the way in which we use the time God gives us is important.

My money and possessions: If Jesus has paid the price for you, then everything you are and everything that you have is rightly His – *even your money*. He is concerned, not only with how much you put in the offering on Sunday, but how you use all the finances and material resources that are His and that He makes available to you. Even under the old covenant, Israel only prospered when the nation was faithful to God in material giving to Him.

If you are already a Christian, it is important to give also:

My relationship with God: Your time for prayer, worship and studying His Word.

My life in the Body of Christ: If you belong to Jesus, you are part of His Body. He doesn't ask us to be 'independent' Christians, but "members one of another", sharing His life together. And remember, that church to which you belong is not yours to be run in your way. It is to become what God wants. So give it to Him. And give yourself to be used by Him to build up that Body in love and faith.

It will be obvious that the negative and positive sections are not exclusive. For example, in offering your time to God, you may become aware of ways in which you have been misusing it. That misuse will need God's forgiveness.

God is concerned that what you write comes from your heart; He is not interested in the neat way in which it is set out.

Why write these things down? For three reasons.

First: you will see clearly what you need to give to God, bad and good, in a way that is not possible by simply thinking about yourself.

Second: you will see yourself as you really are. That may not be very comfortable, for you may never before have been confronted with an overall picture of the awful truth about yourself.

Third: you will realise that the giving of yourself to God is not only something that you ought to do, or that He is wanting you to do. It is something you desperately need to do. Only He can accept you with all your mess (the sin, the failure, the doubts, and fears) and then transform you into someone filled with His love, His life and joy and peace; someone able to have his needs met, his body, soul and spirit healed, and his prayers answered.

"Come to Me"

What do you do with what you have written? One of two things.

Either: Get on your knees (if you are physically able to do that) and pour it all out to Jesus. Read it to Him. He is the One who said: "Come to me, all who labour and are heavy laden, and I will give you rest" (Matt. 11:28). That is a command: "Come to me". If you obey, His promise is that "you will find rest for your souls" (v. 29). You will find that He is gentle and loving and accepting.

Ask the Lord to forgive the sin, to set you free from the fears and resolve the doubts. Ask Him to heal you in any way that is necessary and to give you a completely new start to your life, with all the failure of the past forgiven, washed away by the cleansing blood of Jesus.

Ask Him for the precious gift of the Holy Spirit (see next Chapter).

And He will accept you, because the blood of Jesus has made you acceptable for fellowship with Him. He will forgive you. He will begin that work of salvation and healing in your life that is His plan for you. And He will give His own Spirit to live in you.

You will have a new heart and a new Spirit. You will be a child of the new covenant. And that means that all the promises of God are available to you.

Or: You may like to ask someone to pray through your letter with you. This should be someone whose confidence you can depend upon, and who exercises a ministry in the power of the Holy Spirit. It is not necessary to introduce this third person, but some people find it easier to receive assurance of God's forgiveness, or the healing power of Jesus, when there is someone to minister to them personally and to pray with them to be filled with the Holy Spirit.

God will answer your prayers and will give you the desire of your heart, whether you pray alone or with someone else.

God Wants to Give

Before you make this offering of yourself to God you may wish to read the next chapter about receiving the Holy Spirit. God wants you to give yourself to Him so that He can give Himself to you. He wants to fill you with His Spirit.

This is the way that He has chosen. We give to Him first, and then He gives to us. Later we shall see that this is a principle that runs through the teaching of Jesus: "The measure you give will be the measure you get, and still more will be given you" (Mark 4: 24).

God wants you to give Him your sins that He may give you His forgiveness.

God wants you to give Him your fears that He might set you free to trust and depend upon Him.

God wants you to give Him your doubts because He wants to give you a new believing heart and a new relationship with Him, knowing Him as your Father who loves you.

God wants you to give Him your relationships, that He may heal the wounds of past hurts and set you free to love and receive love from others.

God wants you to give Him your marriage, so that it can become a marriage filled with His love, where He is Lord, and a partner to you both.

God wants you to give Him your children, for He wants to be Lord of their lives and to give freely to them as He gives freely to you.

God wants you to give Him your home, so that He can fill it with His Presence and make it a place where people know the love of Jesus.

God wants you to give Him your work, so that He might cause it to prosper.

God wants you to give Him your time, because He wants to give to you as you learn to give to others.

God wants you to give Him your money and possessions, so that He can give back to you immeasurably more than you have given Him.

God wants you to give Him your relationship with Him, so that He can continue to give Himself, His riches, His blessings, His life and love and healing to you.

God wants you to give Him your life in the Body of Christ, in His Church, because through the love of His people He wants to give you joy in worship, fellowship and teaching.

YOU CAN NEVER OUTDO THE LORD IN GIVING!

We give of our poverty. He gives back to us out of His riches. We give to Him in our need. He gives Himself and His resources to meet those needs. We give, longing to be loved by God. He gives, longing to fill us to overflowing with His steadfast, perfect love.

We give ourselves. HE GIVES HIMSELF.

To me that is one of the greatest wonders of the Christian life. That God knows all about me, how weak and useless I am – and yet, He accepts me, He loves me and gives Himself to me.

What a God! What a Father to have!

Your words of faith: "IT IS NO LONGER I WHO LIVE, BUT CHRIST WHO LIVES IN ME."

The Holy Spirit

GOD WANTS TO give Himself to you. To live in you by putting His own Spirit within you. The Holy Spirit.

The promise God gives about the new covenant is:

> A new heart I will give you, and a new spirit I will put within you.
>
> I will put my Spirit within you.
>
> I will put my Spirit within you, and you shall live.

John the Baptist was "preaching a baptism of repentance for the forgiveness of sins" (Mark 1: 4). But He stated clearly that "after me comes he who is mightier than I" (Mark 1: 7). Of Him John promised:

> I have baptised you with water; but he will baptise you with the Holy Spirit (Mark 1: 8).

The word 'baptise' means to completely cover or 'submerge'. Those who came to John were submerged in water to show that God was washing away their sins.

Those who come to Jesus are not only to be submerged in water and cleansed of sin; they are also to be submerged in the Spirit of God and filled with His power and love. Jesus said:

> Truly, truly, I say to you, unless one is born of water and the Spirit he cannot enter the kingdom of God (John 3: 5).

Through the act of believing in Jesus, God gives us eternal

life, we are born of the Spirit and are given "power to become children of God" (John 1: 12).

> God so loved the world that He gave His only Son, that whoever believes in him should not perish but have eternal life (John 3: 16).

However, God's purpose is that we should not only be born of the Spirit, but that we should be submerged in the Spirit, enfolded completely by Him and filled to overflowing with His love, life and power.

The Counsellor

The disciples had become used to the physical presence of Jesus with them. The prospect of His imminent death caused them to be grief-stricken. Jesus assured them that they were not to be left to their own devices.

> I will pray the Father, and he will give you another Counsellor, to be with you for ever, even the Spirit of truth, whom the world cannot receive because it neither sees him nor knows him; you know him, for he dwells with you, and will be in you (John 14: 16–17).

They had known the work of the Spirit in Jesus's life and ministry and in the work that He had commissioned them to do in preaching the gospel of the kingdom of God and in healing the sick. The Spirit of Jesus, the Holy Spirit had been with them. Now the Lord gives the promise that the Spirit will be *in* them.

> But the Counsellor, the Holy Spirit, whom the Father will send in my name, he will teach you all things, and bring to your remembrance all that I have said to you (John 14: 26).

The Holy Spirit is the Counsellor, the Advocate, the One who will speak and act on our behalf. He is the Spirit of truth, who will teach us and declare the words of Jesus to us. That is of crucial importance.

If we are to believe His words and promises we will need the Holy Spirit to bring them to life for us. Only the Spirit can speak those words of Jesus to our hearts so that we believe them.

You can try hard to believe the words of Jesus and never make it. But when the Spirit declares them to you, He produces that inner 'knowing' that God means what He says and that He will do it. He will fulfil His promises.

> He will glorify me, for he will take what is mine and declare it to you (John 16: 14).

Rivers of Living Water

> Jesus stood up and proclaimed, "If any one thirst, let him come to me and drink. He who believes in me, as the scripture has said, 'Out of his heart shall flow rivers of living water'." Now this he said about the Spirit, which those who believed in him were to receive; for as yet the Spirit had not been given, because Jesus was not yet glorified (John 7: 37–39).

Out of these new hearts that God gives to His new covenant children, are to flow "rivers of living water". The Holy Spirit is not simply to fill our lives, but flow out from us. Not as a tiny trickling stream, nor even as a large river. As RIVERS. Rivers of love, life, joy, peace, power, forgiveness, healing and faith. Rivers of the life of Jesus.

But the Spirit of Jesus could not be given to live in God's people until Jesus had first given His life on the Cross, had been raised from the dead and had returned to be with His Father in heaven. He would receive glory, and those who believed in Him could then receive the Holy Spirit.

Jesus appeared to His disciples in His risen body.

> And while staying with them he charged them not to depart from Jerusalem, but to wait for the promise of the Father, which he said, "you heard from me, for John baptised with water, but before many days you shall be baptised with the Holy Spirit" (Acts 1: 4–5).

And Jesus told them what this would mean for them:

> You shall receive power when the Holy Spirit has come upon you; and you shall be my witnesses in Jerusalem and in all Judea and Samaria and to the end of the earth (Acts 1: 8).

"You shall receive *power* ..." In Luke's account of the Gospel we read:

> Behold, I send the promise of my Father upon you; but stay in the city until you are clothed with power from on high (Luke 24: 49).

To live as new covenant children is to live with God's power within us; it is to know Him as our Father, who loves us and cares for us. St. Paul says:

> Because you are sons, God has sent the Spirit of his Son into our hearts, crying, "Abba! Father!" So through God you are no longer a slave, but a son, and if a son then an heir (Gal 4: 6–7).

An heir of all the covenant promises of God, both in the Old and New Testaments!

Receiving the Spirit

Jesus tells us to ask the Father and He will give the Holy Spirit.

Ask, and it will be given you; seek, and you will find; knock and it will be opened to you. For everyone who asks receives, and he who seeks finds, and to him who knocks it will be opened. What father among you, if his son asks for a fish, will instead of a fish give him a serpent; or if he asks for an egg, will give him a scorpion? If you then, who are evil, know how to give good gifts to your children, how much more will the heavenly Father give the Holy Spirit to those who ask him! (Luke 11: 9–13).

From these words of Jesus notice that:

1. We are told to ask and are given the promise that "everyone who asks receives".

2. God is not going to give anything harmful. He wants to bless and give life, not destroy us.

3. Even earthly fathers know how to treat their children properly and give them the good things they need and want. How much more will our perfect heavenly Father give us what is good? In fact He gives the best. Himself. His Spirit.

4. God *wants* to give the Holy Spirit "to those who ask him".

Paul asks the Galatians: "Did you receive the Spirit by works of the law, or by hearing with faith?" (Gal. 3: 2). Trying to obey the commandments of God will not result in being filled with His power. Trying to please God with our own efforts will not earn us the right to be filled with the Holy Spirit.

No, the Spirit is "the promise of my Father", according to Jesus. You receive the gift by hearing that promise for yourself, by coming to Jesus and asking Him to fill you with the Holy Spirit, to release the "rivers of living water" in your life.

And God will give you His Spirit because He has promised to do precisely that. And He is faithful!

Three Warnings

1. Try to avoid any preconceived ideas of what it will be like to be filled or baptised with the Holy Spirit. Don't look at other people or their experiences and try to be like them. God will do a unique, personal work in your life which will be just right for you.

2. Jesus does not say that you need any particular gift or manifestation of the Spirit to prove that you have received. He simply promises, "Ask and you will receive." And He adds, "Everyone who asks receives." He doesn't say: "Everyone, except you!" He says, "Everyone who asks!"

3. Don't look for particular feelings or experiences. Some people do have 'an experience', but many don't especially at the time of asking. Some people are tempted to doubt that God has honoured His promise and given the gift, if they do not have 'an experience'. Often they turn themselves inside out, looking for some hidden sin that could be the cause of God's displeasure and the reason for withholding the gift, when their real problem is that they do not believe God's faithfulness in honouring His Word. The 'experience' follows the believing; it does not precede it! When we seek the fulfilment of God's promises in our lives, it is not only a question of asking, but believing as we ask.

Prepare First

Do not ask to be filled with the Holy Spirit until you have done what is suggested in the previous chapter. You need to come to the Cross, before you experience a personal Pentecost in your life.

Or, if you are already a Christian, come back to the Cross and renew that offering of your life, and then ask to be filled with that "power from on high". God will answer you because He loves you and will give you what He has promised through His son Jesus.

God's Continual Giving

From time to time in your Christian life, you will find that God is calling you back to the Cross, calling you to a fresh repentance, to a new turning of your life over to Him. It is wise not to delay in responding to the Lord. He only calls us to a new repentance because He knows that it is necessary and will prepare the way for a fresh outpouring of His Holy Spirit upon our lives, a new release of the "rivers of living water" within us.

The disciples were first filled with the Holy Spirit on the Feast of Pentecost (see Acts 2). It was not long afterwards they were praying together and asking God,

> "Grant to thy servants to speak thy word with all bold-ness, while thou stretchest out thy hand to heal, and signs and wonders are performed through the name of thy holy servant Jesus." And when they had prayed, the place in which they were gathered together was shaken; and they were all filled with the Holy Spirit and spoke the word of God with boldness (Acts 4: 29–31).

They were filled again! As with those first disciples, those 'rivers' need to keep flowing in our lives. God wants those 'rivers' to be constantly released to enable us to love, to serve, to believe.

Your words of faith: "I WILL PUT MY SPIRIT WITHIN YOU, AND YOU SHALL LIVE."

10
The Word

Do you want to believe God, so that He answers *your* prayers?

Believing Him, His Word and His promises, can only come about through the work of the Holy Spirit within you. Because you are filled with the Holy Spirit does not mean that you will automatically believe and see the answers to your prayers. But the Spirit will "teach you all things, and bring to your remembrance all that I have said to you" (John 14: 26). It is the role of the Spirit to declare the words of Jesus to you.

Rock

So when the Holy Spirit begins to operate in you, the words of scripture take on a new meaning. It seems that they are addressed personally to you; they have relevance in your life. Jesus said: "The words that I have spoken to you are spirit and life" (John 6: 63).

The words of Jesus are not only for the times in which they were spoken or when the books of the Bible were written. They are words of eternal life, of eternal meaning and significance. "You have the words of eternal life" (John 6: 68), Simon Peter says to Jesus. Jesus Himself said: "Heaven and earth will pass away, BUT MY WORDS WILL NOT PASS AWAY" (Matt. 24: 35).

That verse is gold-dust! Do you realise that the words of Jesus are more reliable and dependable than the ground you walk on? You don't expect that to give way beneath your

feet at any moment; and although there will come a time
when the earth will 'pass away', the words of Jesus will
never 'pass away'. They are for ever reliable and if we base
our lives on them, we are on the firm rock that Jesus speaks
of.

> Every one then who hears these words of mine and does
> them will be like a wise man who built his house upon
> the rock; and the rain fell, and the floods came, and the
> winds blew and beat upon that house, but it did not fall,
> because it had been founded on the rock (Matt.
> 7: 24–25).

Sand

If you are not on the rock, depending on the words of
Jesus, you are on sand – and that is disastrous. The sand can
consist of many different things:

The sand can be basing your life on the opinions of men,
or your own opinions even.

The sand can be believing your own ideas of God, instead
of what the Bible reveals about Him.

The sand can be depending upon having experiences of
God. The experiences are fine. But if they are the basis of
your faith, what happens when you have no experiences?
God seems remote and distant and everything comes crashing down about your ears.

The sand can be living to please yourself instead of living
for God and giving to others.

The sand can be always wanting to receive without giving
first.

And what does Jesus say about building on sand? He says
only a foolish man does that, and when the storm comes the
house crashes to the ground, "and great was the fall of it".

During the early years of my Christian life I was taught
that our reason was as important as the Bible. You came to

the words of scripture and applied your powers of reasoning to it. As a result, you only believed what you could rationally accept as true and were free to discard the rest.

The outcome was a relatively powerless life and ministry.

Then I began to see the Word with the eyes of the Spirit. I began to believe it instead of criticise it! I began to accept it, instead of pull it apart so that I needn't believe it.

And the outcome was a new life and a new ministry in which I have seen the power of God at work in ways that I never thought possible, but in ways that GOD PROMISES IN HIS WORD.

Believing the Word

When you believe the Word of God, what He says can be translated into action, God's action in your life and in His world around you. The Bible stresses the importance of hearing the words of God and believing them. In the Old Testament we read:

> Hold fast to my words with all your heart, keep my commands and you will have life (Prov. 4: 4 NEB).
> Hear, my son, and accept my words (Prov. 4: 10).

It is for our own welfare that God is concerned that we heed His words:

> My son, be attentive to my words; incline your ear to my sayings. Let them not escape from your sight; keep them within your heart. For they are life to him who finds them, and healing to all his flesh (Prov. 4: 20–22).

It is through the words of God that we will be given understanding of His ways:

> The unfolding of thy words gives light; it imparts understanding to the simple (Ps. 119: 130).

Thy word is a lamp to my feet and a light to my path
(Ps. 119: 105).

Being the Word of God in human flesh, the words of Jesus
are words of life:

He who hears my word and believes him who sent me,
has eternal life (John 5: 24).
The words that I have spoken to you are spirit and life
(John 6: 63).

When He prays to His Father, He says:

Thy word is truth (John 17: 17).

Therefore: "Man shall not live by bread alone, but by
EVERY WORD that proceeds from the mouth of God"
(Matt. 4: 4). His words that God speaks to His children.
And the Lord promises His disciples:

If you abide in me, AND MY WORDS ABIDE IN
YOU, ask whatever you will and it shall be done for
you (John 15: 7).

No wonder Paul says: "Let the word of Christ dwell in
you richly" (Col. 3: 16).

New Minds

God does not want us to waste our intellectual powers of
reasoning, so that we become 'mindless' Christians. God
wants our minds and our intellects to be given to Him in
order that they may become consecrated intellects; minds
through which God can reveal His wisdom, understanding
and truth. St. Paul tells us:

Be transformed by the renewal of your mind, that you may prove what is the will of God, what is good and acceptable and perfect (Rom. 12: 2).

Being a Christian involves a whole new way of thinking, no longer seeing situations with a typically human attitude but as God sees them. What for us seems an insurmountable problem, is an opportunity for Him to manifest His love and power.

There are so many situations that I encounter in which I cannot understand the purpose of God, why he should be allowing this particular set of circumstances to happen. I have to remind myself of the scripture:

For my thoughts are not your thoughts, neither are your ways my ways, says the Lord. For as the heavens are higher than the earth, so are my ways higher than your ways and my thoughts than your thoughts (Isa. 55: 8–9).

Our minds need a life-long retraining programme. But I have learned to trust my Father in heaven and to know that He never loses control of a situation.

Believing Jesus

We can be so thankful for the Bible, for the written Word of God reveals His thoughts and ways to us. If we are to see God answering our prayers then we will need to look closely at what Jesus says about praying and asking. We will need to pray in the way that He tells us, and see what He promises. Those promises reveal what is in God's mind, what it is that He desires to do in the lives of His children.

You cannot separate Jesus from His words. If you accept the authority of Jesus in your life, then you accept the authority of His words. If Jesus is your Lord, then His words are precious to you. They are "words of eternal life". They are "words of spirit and life". And it is to the Word that you will turn for the guidance and the answers that you need.

This is not to say that the Bible is the sole means of God's revelation to us. We have already seen how the Bible can seem to be a dead letter without the work of the Spirit. And Jesus promised that his truth would be revealed by the Spirit. The Word and the Spirit belong together.

When the Spirit speaks the words of Jesus to your heart, anything becomes possible.

Your words of faith: "HEAVEN AND EARTH WILL PASS AWAY, BUT MY WORDS WILL NOT PASS AWAY."

11

The God of Promise

GOD WORKS BY promise in the lives of His children. Within the old convenant, He proved faithful to his words. Every time His people obeyed Him and fulfilled their side of the covenant agreement, they saw the blessings and prosperity that He had promised.

> Blessed be the Lord who has given rest to His people Israel, according to all that He promised; not one word has failed of all His good promise which He uttered by Moses His servant (1 Kings 8: 56).

Under the new covenant He is still the God of Promise. Those who live by putting their faith in His words shall see fulfilled in their lives all that God promises to do and to give.

Living by Promise

The great men of faith in the Bible are those who believed the promises that God made to them. St. Paul writes of Abraham:

> No distrust made him waver concerning the promise of God, but he grew strong in his faith as he gave glory to God, fully convinced that God was able to do what he had promised (Rom. 4: 20–21).

To live by faith is to live by the promises of God!

It is not enough to believe that God makes promises; we are only living by faith if we are trusting God to fulfil His words in our lives.

A Christian believes *in* Jesus. He believes Him to be the Son of God, our Saviour and Lord.

That same Christian may believe *that* Jesus can do today, by His Spirit, the same things that He did in His physical body nearly two thousand years ago. He may believe, therefore, *that* Jesus can heal the sick and perform miracles.

That still does not mean that he is believing Jesus to do those things in response to his prayers. He is only exercising faith, in the way that Jesus teaches, when he not only believes in Jesus, or believes *that* Jesus can; but *when he believes Jesus to do what he asks of Him*! When he acts upon the promises of God.

Faith

Faith is not only believing *in* Jesus.

Faith is not only believing that Jesus can work today.

Faith is believing Jesus to do it: to meet the need, to answer the prayer, to change the situation, even if a miracle is needed to do so!

How can we have such faith? And how can we exercise it when we have it?

> Faith comes from what is heard, and what is heard comes by the preaching of Christ (Rom. 10: 17).
> Does he who supplies the Spirit to you and works miracles among you do so by works of the law, or by hearing with faith? (Gal. 3: 5).

You are not necessarily living by faith, if you walk around with a Bible underneath your arm saying: "This is the Word of God, and I believe it!"

If you really believe the Word, you'll put it to work in

your life and then you will see God doing the things that He says He will do, the things that He promises.

Faith is:

    Hearing what God says;

    Accepting or believing it;

    AND ACTING UPON IT.

All the Promises

St. Paul says of His brothers in Christ: "to them belong the sonship, the glory, the covenants, the giving of the law, the worship, and the promises" (Rom. 9: 4).

Christians are the sons of God. To them belong the *covenants* – in the plural. To them belong the promises. THE PROMISES OF BOTH THE OLD AND NEW TESTAMENTS.

Jesus does not annul the old promises that God had given to Israel; He came to confirm and fulfil them. But the new promises that Jesus gives are even better than the old ones! "The covenant he mediates is better, since it is enacted on better promises" (Heb. 8: 6).

St. Paul tells the Corinthians:

ALL THE PROMISES OF GOD FIND THEIR 'YES' IN HIM (2 Cor. 1: 20).

He came to confirm the old promises.

He came to give the new promises.

And His Father will honour all of them. That means that we will see them fulfilled in our lives WHEN WE BELIEVE THEM; when we have the FAITH to believe them!

Before we were Christians, we had no part in these promises.

Remember that you were at that time separated from Christ, alienated from the commonwealth of Israel, and strangers to the COVENANTS of PROMISE, having no hope and without God in the world (Eph. 2: 12).

Now that we are Christians, we are in fellowship with Christ and "the covenants of promise" are our inheritance. God desires to see His words fulfilled in our lives. He wants us to receive His gifts and see Him meeting our needs. "Believe me," God says to us, "and I will do what you ask."

We are warned not to "be sluggish, but imitators of those who through faith and patience inherit the promises" (Heb. 6: 12).

Note that both FAITH and PATIENCE will be needed.

Receiving the Promises

To read the promises does not mean that you will believe them, or even 'hear' them in a personal way.

When you have a particular need, you may turn to the Bible for help and discover many verses that are relevant to your situation, including several promises. The problem is how to believe them!

Sometimes the Holy Spirit does this for you immediately. The words seem to jump out of the page and into your heart. You may have read those same words countless times before; now they are for YOU.

But it is not always so easy. And God does not want His children to turn to His Word only when they have a particular need. He wants them to live by His promises continually, for only then will they be living by faith and trust in Him. Somehow the promises need to be living words deep within us. How can they be transferred from the head to the heart?

A Simple Method

Here is a simple method of storing the promises of God within you. It is the way that I have found most effective and powerful not only for myself, but for many others.

First: take one of the promises from either the Old or New Testament. As a covenant child of God you inherit them all!

Second: sit down quietly in a reasonably comfortable chair and be as relaxed as possible. Spend a few moments letting the tensions of the day flow out of your body and mind. Deliberately allow your muscles to slacken.

Third: take a minute or two handing over to God the things that are of concern to you, so that these will not get in the way of hearing and receiving what God is saying in His Word. This is *not* a time to sit down and think about your problems. Just let go of them for a few minutes. You may need to ask God to forgive you and you may need to forgive someone who has wronged or hurt you.

Fourth: take the promise that you have decided to use and repeat it slowly to yourself a number of times. If you are on your own, you may like to speak it aloud, but quietly. This often helps concentration. Don't try to work out the meaning of the words in your mind. 'Hear' God speak them to you, to your spirit. Repeat the promise over and over again. 'Receive' it. At first, you will only be able to spend a couple of minutes with the one sentence. As you become used to this method of prayer, you will be able to concentrate on the same sentence for a much longer period of time. It is better to spend a few minutes, two or three times a day, than trying to 'receive' for too long at any one time.

Nothing dramatic is going to happen. Often you may feel that nothing at all has happened. But as you persist with the same word of promise for a week or more, it becomes part of you, and of your inheritance as a child of your heavenly Father.

Your words of faith, "MY WORDS . . . ARE LIFE TO HE WHO FINDS THEM AND HEALING TO ALL HIS FLESH."

Footnote As a companion to this book, the author is at present preparing a series of daily meditations, using this method of prayer, and describing how to use the Word of God as a powerful means of healing for oneself and intercession for others. These meditations will be published shortly under the title *Listen and Live.*

12

Old Promises

THE PROMISES OF God speak to your situation. He always has a word to meet your need.

As you read the Bible, you may like to mark or underline the promises God gives. They will be much easier to find again, if you do.

The prophetic books of the Old Testament are particularly rich in promises. God has often had to discipline His people; but He always gives words of encouragement and promises of abundant blessing, if they will turn back to Him and be obedient to His commands.

For many years I have been 'receiving' the promises of God. Here are some that have come to mean a great deal to me, many taken from Isaiah, (40–55), which are full of promises.

God's Calling

You are ... my servant whom I have chosen, that you may know and believe me and understand that I am He (Isa. 43: 10).

Fear not, for I have redeemed you; I have called you by name, you are mine (Isa. 43: 1).

His Love that is so personal for each of His children:

You are precious in my eyes, and honoured, and I love you (Isa. 43: 4).

With everlasting love I will have compassion on you (Isa. 54: 8).

My steadfast love shall not depart from you, and my convent of peace shall not be removed (Isa. 54: 10).

Incline your ear, and come to me; hear, that your soul may live; and I will make with you an everlasting covenant, my steadfast, sure love (Isa. 55: 3).

His Strength when I am confronted with my weakness, which is often:

He gives power to the faint, and to him who has no might he increases strength (Isa. 40: 29).
They who wait for the Lord shall renew their strength (Isa. 40: 31).
I will strengthen you, I will help you, I will uphold you with my victorious right hand (Isa. 41: 10).

His Forgiveness, which is constantly needed:

I, I am He who blots out your transgressions for my own sake, and I will not remember your sins (Isa. 43: 25).
I have swept away your transgressions like a cloud, and your sins like mist (Isa. 44: 22).
I have taken your iniquity away from you, and I will clothe you with rich apparel (Zech. 3: 4).

His Presence, especially when confronted with a situation that seems impossible:

Fear not, for I am with you, be not dismayed for I am your God (Isa. 41: 10).
I, the Lord your God, hold your right hand, it is I who say to you, Fear not, I will help you (Isa. 41: 13).
My presence will go with you, and I will give you rest (Exod. 33: 14).
I will go before you and level the mountains (Isa. 45: 2).

His Faithfulness in bringing about the purpose that He has for my life and in honouring His Words:

> I will fulfil to you my promise ... I know the plans I
> have for you, says the Lord, plans for welfare and not
> for evil, to give you a future and a hope (Jer.
> 29: 10–11).
> My counsel shall stand, and I will accomplish all my
> purpose (Isa. 46: 10).
> I have spoken, and I will bring it to pass; I have pur-
> posed, and I will do it (Isa. 46: 11).

His Words of Encouragement when things are at their blackest:

> You will not be forgotten by me (Isa. 44: 21).
> I will be with you; I will not fail you or forsake you
> (Josh. 1: 5)
> Even to your old age I am He, and to grey hairs I will
> carry you. I have made, and I will bear; I will carry and
> will save (Isa. 46: 4).

That is a particular favourite when facing great difficulty. "I will carry you," says the Lord. Instead of battling through the situation in your own way, you can learn to let your loving Father 'carry you'.

His Guidance:

> I am the Lord your God, who teaches you to profit,
> who leads you in the way you should go (Isa. 48: 17).

His Promise for my children:

> I will pour my Spirit upon your descendants, and my
> blessing on your offspring (Isa. 44: 3).

His Promise for living in obedience to His Word:

> The word is very near you; it is in your mouth and in your heart, so that you can do it (Deut. 30: 14).

His Promise when I feel that I have failed the Lord completely:

> I have sworn that I will not be angry with you and will not rebuke you (Isa. 54: 9).

The Faith that His faithfulness inspires in my heart:

> The Lord is my shepherd, I shall not want (Ps. 23: 1).

And many, many, more. It builds my faith just to write them down again, even though they are so familiar.

The God who says all these things is my God, my FATHER. I am His child. And He loves me. So He will never deceive me. He will never speak false words or fail to honour them. He is faithful.

> I the Lord speak the truth, I declare what is right (Isa. 45: 19).

Whenever I put my trust in Him and believe the words He speaks, I see these promises being fulfilled in my life. That is what God wants; to see His promises being worked out in the lives of all His children, including YOU!

As you read the Old Testament you will find many, many more. They build your faith, because they enlarge your vision of how great your God is, and how wonderful His love for you, His beloved child.

Spend time 'receiving' them, as outlined in the previous chapter, so that they will become personal to *you*.

Your words of faith: Any of the verses listed above, particularly: "YOU ARE PRECIOUS IN MY EYES, AND HONOURED, AND I LOVE YOU."

13

A New Promise

YOU ARE A child of God, a citizen of His kingdom. He wants to see the words and works of His kingdom in your life. That will happen as you learn to pray with the faith that Jesus speaks of, believing the promises that He gives.

So it is with the prayer promises of Jesus that we will be principally concerned.

Asking Prayer

Asking is only a part of praying, but an important part because every day of our lives we have needs. Every day there are others for whom we want to pray, asking God to bless, guide or heal them.

Jesus died on the Cross to make it possible to know God as our Father. That privilege is not to be wasted. Because He loves His children, He wants to meet their needs; He longs for them to come to Him with faith, believing that He will give.

It is in asking that our faith is really tested, for Jesus tells us that His Father wants to give us *anything* we ask.

> If you abide in me, and my words abide in you, ask whatever you will, and it shall be done for you (John 15: 7).

The promise is clear; ask whatever (anything) you will (you want) and it shall be done for you. Not it may be, or could be, or might be, or can be. IT SHALL BE DONE FOR YOU.

It seems, however, that Jesus is making a condition: "If you abide in me, and my words abide in you."

In the Vine

It is the night of Jesus' arrest. Within twenty-four hours He will have been crucified and His body laid in the tomb. This is the last occasion before the Cross, when He can sit down with His disciples to teach them. He has already told them not to grieve over the events that are to take place, and has given the promise that the Holy Spirit will come to live in them.

He turns to the imagery of the vine and its branches to describe the relationship they are to continue to have with Him. "I am the true vine", He says, "my Father is the vine-dresser", and you, He tells the disciples, "are the branches". They are parts of Him; they live in Him and cannot exist without Him. "Apart from me you can do nothing."

The purpose of every branch in a vine is to bear fruit. In the True Vine, it is only possible to be fruitful by 'abiding' in Jesus:

> As the branch cannot bear fruit by itself, unless it abides in the vine, neither can you, unless you abide in me (John 15: 4).

'Abide' meas 'rest', 'remain', 'stay', 'continually live'. When Jesus says: "Abide in me, and I in you", He means:

> Remain in me, and I in you.
> Continually live in me, and I in you.

If you do so, you will be fruitful. "He who abides in me, and I in him, he it is that bears much fruit" (John 15: 5).

You are in Jesus

You are already 'in Jesus'. You are already a branch of the True Vine – if you have acknowledged that your life belongs to God, if you have 'given' yourself to Him (see chapter 8). When you came to the Cross, you acknowledged that you were 'in Christ'. That is where God put you. You were 'in Jesus' when He was crucified, so that you might die with Him, and be raised with Him to a new and better life. You could not get into Jesus by your own efforts. You could not work your way there. You were put there by God Himself, so that you might live your whole life 'in Christ Jesus'.

So when Jesus says "if you abide in me", He doesn't mean "if you can manage to work your way to that very privileged position of living in the Son of God". Rather, He is saying, "If you go on living in the place where my Father *has already put you*, in Jesus, in the True Vine, in His Son."

His Words in You

Not only do you live 'in Jesus'; He lives *in you*. "Abide in me, AND I IN YOU." He lives in you by the power of His Holy Spirit. His Spirit will declare His words to your heart, so that you can believe them and live them out in your life.

Like a branch you are in Jesus all the time. You are part of Him, of His Body here on earth. You are 'in Him' like a page in a book. Without you the book is incomplete; yet a page without the rest of the book is virtually meaningless.

Stay in the book and believe the words that the Spirit prints upon your page, and the promise of Jesus is that you can "ask whatever you will, and it shall be done for you".

Don't look back on the failure of the past; look ahead with the eyes of faith and see what your life can become as you continue to live in Jesus and allow His words to live in you: a fruitful life, that will cause your Father to rejoice.

Hear His words:
Believe them;
Act upon them!

Much Fruit

Your heavenly Father wants to see 'much fruit' in your
life. Jesus says that the Father 'prunes' disciples that they
"may bear more fruit". He will cut out of your life the sin,
disobedience and unbelief that hinder the fulfilment of His
promises in you. And you will be happier without those
negative, destructive things eating away at your faith.

Praying with faith, believing that God will do for you
whatever you ask, is the kind of fruitfulness that God wants
to produce in you. And remember, a branch cannot produce
fruit by itself; it is the result of the flow of the life-giving sap
within it. God has put His life-giving Spirit in you to make
you fruitful.

**Your words of faith: "IF YOU ABIDE IN ME, AND MY
WORDS ABIDE IN YOU, ASK WHATEVER YOU
WILL AND IT SHALL BE DONE FOR YOU."**

14

Chosen and Appointed

HAVE YOU EVER wondered why God has chosen you out of the vast sea of humanity, to be His child; to love you and care for you in a personal way? It is a great mystery, isn't it? I never cease to wonder at it myself. What a mighty privilege to be chosen by God to belong to Him!

> You did not choose me, but I chose you and appointed you that you should go and bear fruit and that your fruit should abide; so that WHATEVER YOU ASK THE FATHER IN MY NAME, HE MAY GIVE IT TO YOU (John 15: 16).

There are four important points to notice from what Jesus says here:

First, a disciple does not choose to be part of the Vine; Jesus chooses those who will live in Him. He has chosen you.

Second, disciples are appointed to a task. They are not living in Jesus for a purposeless existence, nor to fulfil their own ends. God has not only chosen you; He 'appoints' you to fulfil a particular purpose.

Third, the task to which disciples are appointed is that of bearing fruit; God has chosen and appointed you to "go and bear fruit and that your fruit should abide".

Fourth, Jesus immediately links this fruitfulness with answered prayer: "so that whatever you ask the Father in my name, he may give it to you." This is the climax of the whole process. A disciple is chosen, appointed to a fruitful life in which God will give Him whatever He asks. This is the life for which God has chosen and appointed *you*.

A Fruitful Life

Imagine how fruitful your life would be if every time you asked God to do something He did it! And every time you asked Him to give you something He gave it!

Think how many people would be healed through YOUR prayers.

Think how many needs could be met through YOUR prayers.

Try to imagine the miracles that God would do in your life, and in others, through your prayers.

Consider how much you would be able to give to others if you received from God all that you asked for in *your* prayers. And that is precisely what Jesus has in mind! That you should have the fruitful kind of life in which your prayers are answered.

That when *you* ask, God does!

That when *you* ask, God gives!

Not so that you may be selfish and self-indulgent, but that your heavenly Father may be glorified.

> By this my Father is glorified, that you bear much fruit, and so prove to be my disciples (John 15: 8).

That is the ultimate aim of the Christian life: to glorify the Father. Jesus glorified Him by speaking His words and doing His works. All those who live in Jesus, will glorify Him by believing those words and seeing Him perform those same works in their lives.

Your Father doesn't want to answer only the occasional prayer, so that you are surprised when anything happens in response to your asking. He wants you to KNOW that when you ask, He WILL do, He WILL give.

The world around us will recognise us as disciples of Jesus when they see our prayers being answered. People don't

want to hear our claims about a God of love; they want to
see a demonstration of that love in the way He meets our
needs. And God wants us to prove His faithfulness to the
world, that He is the covenant God who keeps His promises
because we, His children, believe them.

God Wants to Answer

God is love, He *wants* to give to His children. He *wants* to
meet their needs, He *wants* to heal their bodies and minds.
He *wants* to answer their prayers.

If you are a parent, and you love your children, you don't
need any encouragement to help them when they are sick or
have any need. Your desire is to give yourself in any way
you can to help your child. Young children are sometimes
easier to help than older ones, who want to assert their independence, to be self-sufficient and so may reject your desire
to help. Sometimes you have to wait until they are prepared
to come to you and ask.

When your child does come, are you going to reject him?
Human parents may on occasions, but the Heavenly Father
never will, because His love is perfect. He has given His
Word that can never be broken; He will give to His new
covenant children. He has sealed that promise with the
blood of His Son, Jesus. And He will never deny that blood.

You are chosen and appointed to be fruitful. Your Father
wants you to be, and He will give you every encouragement
so that you can pray believing He will answer. He sent His
Son to teach you how to pray with faith.

**Your words of faith: "YOU DID NOT CHOOSE ME,
BUT I CHOSE YOU AND APPOINTED YOU THAT
YOU SHOULD GO AND BEAR FRUIT AND THAT
YOUR FRUIT SHOULD ABIDE; SO THAT WHAT-
EVER YOU ASK THE FATHER IN MY NAME, HE
MAY GIVE IT TO YOU."**

15

Have Faith

HAVE FAITH IN God. Truly, I say to you, whoever says to this mountain, "Be taken up and cast into the sea," and does not doubt in his heart, but believes that what he says will come to pass, it will be done for him (Mark 11: 22–23).

Have faith in God

You already have faith. The question is: in whom do you put your faith? A Christian does not necessarily put His faith in the Lord.

Your faith can be in yourself

There may be occasions when you do not consult the Lord about things you have to do, or problems you have to face. You may even feel good about battling through a situation on your own, without any help from anyone. A sad example of pride. You may not truly expect God to help, if you did ask Him.

Many ask God for help, particularly in difficult circumstances, when they realise that their own human resources are insufficient. But the substance of the prayer is often, "Help *me* do it."

Jesus emphasises the fact that God wants to work *for* His children; "it will be done *for him*." Jesus wants you to ask God to do things FOR you, to work *for you* in your needs. He wants you to know that He is so utterly faithful and trustworthy that He will not fail you if your confidence is in Him.

Your faith can be in other people

It is a temptation to trust people instead of the Lord Himself. You can look to some particular minister or servant of the Lord, believing that he will give you the answer to your needs. This is a particular temptation when healing is needed: "If I go to so-and-so, he will heal me." And if he doesn't work, then try someone else!

When a person has a desperate need, it is understandable that he will turn anywhere, to anyone for help. Understandable, but not necessarily the answer to the problem. Jesus says: "Have faith in *God*": know in your heart that He has not lost control of the situation, that He is more than equal to the need. That nothing is impossible for *Him*!

Your faith can be in God

The one person in whom you must have faith is your heavenly Father. He may use a human instrument to give you help, to meet a need, to be a vehicle of His healing power. But that human instrument is His answer to your faith in Him. He has chosen to answer your faith through that particular channel. "Have faith in God", Jesus says, not in the human instrument.

To have faith in God, is to have faith in His Son Jesus, who is God's Word. To believe Jesus, is to believe the Father who sent Him. Likewise, to believe His words is to believe the Father; they are His words that Jesus speaks.

In many situations, God is the only answer; a miracle is needed if the problem is to be met. You may think the word 'miracle' is beyond you; in which case you need "a mighty answer to prayer"! Your God is Almighty and promises that He will do anything you ask.

Faith and Experience

"But it doesn't work! There have been occasions when I have prayed and God hasn't done what I have asked. And I do have faith in God."

There is no point in having our heads in a cloud of spiritual unreality. If the words that Jesus speaks are true, then they can be tested by experience and found to be true! The difficulty is that often there seems to be a confrontation between the words of Jesus and our experience. When that happens, which is true?

The problem is not so clear-cut as that. The confrontation is not really between what Jesus says and our experience. It is between 'faith' and our experience. God's promises will *never* fail, when they are believed. Believing His words means expecting those promises to be fulfilled.

There are many occasions when we honestly think that we are believing and expecting God to do what Jesus means by this word 'faith'. There can be a great difference between our ideas of 'faith' and His teaching about it. It isn't that we need to have *more* faith, but the right kind.

The Disciples' Failure

When Jesus came down from the Mount of Transfiguration with Peter, James, and John, He was confronted with the failure of the other disciples to cure an epileptic boy. After Jesus had healed him, the disciples asked, "Why could we not cast it out?" He said to them,

Because of your little faith. For truly, I say to you, if you have faith as a grain of mustard seed, you will say to this mountain, Move from here to there, and it will move; and nothing will be impossible for you (Matt. 17: 20–21).

Their failure was due to their little faith. And yet Jesus goes on to tell them that they only needed as much faith as a tiny seed and they would not only have been able to move this mountain, but that "nothing will be impossible" for them. Obviously the kind of faith Jesus was referring to, was different from the faith that the disciples were exercising when they were praying with the boy.

Mark records Jesus' answer to the disciples' question as being: "This kind cannot be driven out by anything but prayer" (Mark 9: 29).

Is Jesus saying something different here? No, in trying to heal the boy the disciples would have prayed, but their prayer had been ineffective because their faith was ineffective. It was not the 'mustard seed' type of faith that Jesus referred to. If it had been, the mountain would have moved when they prayed.

"Because of your little faith" and "this kind cannot be driven out by anything but prayer", amount to the same thing.

We may speak many prayers to God and ask Him to do many things. Do we pray with Jesus' kind of faith? That is the burning question. You can look at your experience for the answer. Where that kind of faith is being expressed in your praying, "nothing will be impossible for you." You may want to cry out with the father of that epileptic boy: "I believe; help my unbelief."

Jesus wants to answer that prayer, and teach you to pray with His kind of faith. "Have faith in God" can be literally translated: "Have the faith of God." The Lord not only wants our trust to be in Him; He wants His own faith to be in us.

Your words of faith: "HAVE FAITH IN GOD."

16

Moving Mountains

JESUS SAYS:

> Whoever says to this mountain, "Be taken up and cast into the sea," and does not doubt in his heart, but believes that what he says will come to pass, it will be done for him (Mark 11: 23).

'Whoever' means 'anyone'. That includes YOU. Jesus wants that faith in YOUR life, so that you can look at the mountain before you and tell it to move – and it will! The mountain is that need, that problem that has to be met.

No doubt, we would all like to demonstrate such faith and exercise such authority. Are we wishing for the moon? Not according to Jesus.

Obviously it isn't a question of what words we use. There is no prayer formula to learn that will solve all our needs. Jesus warns about the meaningless repetition of words.

God is not impressed by the words that come from our lips. He is concerned about the faith with which we speak, with what is going on in our hearts. And so when Jesus tells us how the mountains in our lives are to be moved, He used the phrase "and does not doubt in His heart". It is not what you say to the mountain that matters, so much as what you believe in your heart when you say it.

Speak to the Problem

Many people pray about their problems; but not everyone talks to them! And yet that is what Jesus tells us to do. Speak to the mountain and tell it to move.

When I feel the early symptoms of an attack of 'flu or a cold, I talk to the problem: "Cold germs, I utterly reject you in the name of Jesus Christ. My body is a temple of the Holy Spirit and you don't belong here."

Then I speak to God in whom I put my faith, for He is the answer to the problem, and I praise Him for His victory over the infection. Sometimes the symptoms disappear very quickly. More often, there are a few hours of conflict but they do not develop as I keep trusting in the victory of the Lord.

Resisting cold and 'flu may seem only a small matter, but the principle is the same for bigger things in our lives. You will not have the confidence, the faith and authority to address mountains if you have not learned how to deal with foothills! As you see the victory in small matters, your faith is enlarged to trust God for bigger things. Why should our lives be disrupted even by colds and 'flu? We cannot prevent those infections being around us, but we can "fight the good fight of faith" against them.

Jesus tells us that, as we speak to the mountain, we must not doubt in our hearts that it will move. Once again, it is not a question of what you say, but of what you believe.

Dealing with Doubts

You cannot prevent yourself from being assailed by doubts. Sometimes they seem to come at you from all sides. In fact there are three main sources of doubt and you will need to know how to deal with each of them.

1. *Doubts come from others around us*: You live in a doubting, unbelieving world and many people around you will be full of negative talk and ideas, always grumbling and complaining. They do not have a positive faith that God will act in the circumstances of their lives; all they do is moan about them. Their ideas, attitudes and words can be contagious, and if you listen to those negative views instead of

the positive promises of God's Word, faith will very easily be eroded. You certainly don't want what faith you have to be disrupted by the negative attitudes of others.

2. *Doubts come from your own unbelief*: The more you look at the mountain, the higher it seems, and the more impossible to move. You can try to think of a way round it but you cannot move it. And you are not sure that God will either.

Many Christians are negatively-minded people. To 'think faith' requires a renewal of our minds and the whole of our attitude to life. That doesn't happen overnight. It takes time, and God allows problems in our lives to confront us with the doubting, negative attitudes and unbelief that we still have within us. It is important that as you become aware of them you bring your doubts to the Lord honestly and ask Him to forgive you and to inspire His kind of faith within you, by the power of His Holy Spirit.

3. *Doubts come from Satan*: He will try to sow seeds of doubt whenever possible, for he loves to destroy faith in God if he can. In scripture he is described as "the deceiver" and "the father of all lies".

The kind of thoughts that he directs at us are: "You don't really believe, do you?" "You don't have enough faith, do you?" "You aren't worthy enough for God to do such a great thing in your life, are you?" Satan is "the accuser of the brethren". No accusing thoughts come from the Holy Spirit, but from the one who wants to destroy faith.

Paul says that we are to take "the shield of faith, with which you can quench all the flaming darts of the evil one" (Eph. 6: 16), all those lying, deceiving, accusations. James says: "Resist the devil and he will flee from you" (James 4.7).

Hold on to the promises that your Father gives to you as His new covenant child and refuse to accept any of the enemy's lies.

So the attacks on our faith are threefold:

From the negative attitudes around us.

From our own doubting.

From the one who loves to destroy faith.

In other words, the world, the flesh and the devil.

Instead of this doubt, Jesus says that the man who speaks to the mountain with faith "believes that what he says will come to pass". He is not speaking and *hoping* that the problem will go away. He *knows* that it will! He appreciates that God does not want that mountain there, any more than he does.

God Wants the Mountains Moved

Now this is where we come up against a major problem. Many Christians are brought up to believe that God wants them to have mountains, insurmountable problems and difficulties. Jesus would hardly teach us to exercise faith to remove them if all the time God wanted us to be stuck with them!

It is easy to give in to a situation, if you know in your heart that you do not have the faith to see the mountain moved. You are tempted to look for an excuse for it to stay. You may start using such phrases as:

"God is teaching me something through it."

"It is the cross I have to carry!"

"There are others worse off than me."

It is true that God teaches us through all the circumstances of our lives, and that the mountains would not be there unless He allowed them. But His purpose is to give life, not destroy it or make it almost unbearable for His people. He wants to see the faith in His children that will believe the mountains to move, not be left there.

If you think that your problems are your cross, then you are carrying the wrong one. Jesus died on His Cross to save you from all that is negative – sin, disease, fear and death. The cross that Jesus tells us to carry is the one that we willingly take up for ourselves – not problems that we don't want. It is the cross of self-denial in order that we might live for the glory of the Father and the good of His kingdom. "If any man would come after me, let him deny himself and take up his cross and follow me" (Matt. 16: 24).

There may be many others who are worse off than yourself. That does not alter the fact that God wants to meet every need in your life. St. Paul was not afraid to say to the Philippians:

> My God will supply every need of yours according to his riches in glory in Christ Jesus (Phil. 4: 19).

He is your God too and these words are addressed to you. The fact that God meets every need in your life will not take away from His giving to others. God is prepared to meet every need, not out of limited human resources, but "according to his riches in glory in Christ Jesus". And those riches are inexhaustible! You will never come to the end of what God is prepared to give you through His Son.

No Excuses

Perhaps the most common excuses are: "I am not worthy", and "Your will, not mine be done, O Lord".

Of ourselves, none of us is worthy to receive anything from God. But through the Cross of Jesus we are made worthy. So you can say: "Of myself I am unworthy, but God has made me worthy to receive His riches through the blood of His Son, Jesus. God loves me; He has accepted me; and He wants to give to me. He wants to meet '*every need*' of mine 'according to his riches in glory in Christ Jesus'. I am one of His new covenant children."

Jesus' prayer: "nevertheless not my will, but thine, be done," is so often misused by Christians when they pray. It is the prayer of submission that Jesus prayed in the Garden of Gethsemane immediately before His arrest, prior to the crucifixion.

Jesus already knew the will of His Father when He prayed it. He knew that He had come to Jerusalem and there would "suffer many things from the elders and chief priests and scribes, and be killed and on the third day be raised" (Matt. 16: 21). He had repeatedly warned the disciples of these things. He wanted His father's purpose to be worked out in some other way, if at all possible. But He was not prepared to allow His will to come into conflict with His Father's plan. So He submitted to what He knew His Father was asking of Him. He was denying Himself for the sake of God's kingdom.

His prayer is only appropriate for you when you need to submit to something that God is asking of you that you do not want for yourself. They are not appropriate words to tack on to the end of every prayer in which you ask God to do something. When used in such a way they often indicate that you don't really believe that God will do what you ask. If the prayer is not answered in the way you want, then you can say: "It obviously wasn't the Lord's will." Then you won't have to face uncomfortable questions, such as:

"Did I really believe when I prayed?"

"Did I expect God to do it?"

"Did I persist in my prayer?"

There are many situations when we pray, but don't see the desired result, not because God did not want to answer, but because we did not pray with faith and persistence – as Jesus tells us to!

There is so much in scripture that shows us that God does want to heal us and meet our needs, He wants the mountains moved. We don't need to pray "if it be thy will" in such situations. Instead we need the faith to make God's will effective.

God loves you as one of His new covenant children and He wants that mountain moved. In fact, He will be blessed when it is moved and so will you. So Jesus wants you to speak to your mountains and believe that what you say will come to pass. And what is His promise if you do? "It will be done *for you.*"

He does not say that you have to move the mountain. You have to speak to it, believe that it will move, and it will be done for you. God is the One who will move it – not you.

You speak,
You believe,
God moves the mountain for you.

Your words of faith: "NOTHING WILL BE IMPOSSIBLE FOR YOU."

17

The Prayer of Faith

How ARE WE to ask? Jesus says:

> Therefore I tell you, whatever you ask in prayer, believe that you have received it, and it will be yours (Mark 11: 24).

You not only speak to the mountain, believing it will move. You also speak to God, believing that you have received what you ask. And Jesus says: "it will be yours." You speak to the God of promise, who always keeps His word.

'Whatever' here, literally means, 'all things'. All the things that you ask God in prayer to give you 'will be yours'. When you ask, you are to believe that you have already received the answer to your prayer. You can only believe like that, if you know that God wants to give you that particular thing for which you ask, if the spirit witnesses that truth to your heart.

That is why it has been so important to dig a 'firm foundation', before looking at these prayer promises. You will not find it easy to believe that you have already received it unless you know the utter faithfulness of God in keeping all the words of the covenant that He has established with His children.

Of His own choice, God has put Himself in the position of binding Himself by His Word. He has sealed the covenant with the blood of His Son, Jesus. He *must* do what He has promised. That is no problem for Him, because He wants to keep His promises. He would not have made them otherwise.

They are applicable to all the new covenant children of God. He has made you His child because He loves you; He wants to bless you and pour His riches into your life. He has accepted you through the blood of His Son, Jesus. The Cross removes any hindrance there may be to receiving what God has to give you and also provides the victory over every manifestation of evil. He wants to answer your prayers.

God has given you the power of the Holy Spirit to inspire faith in you, the faith that Jesus talks about, and to reveal His Word to you so that you can act upon it.

God will Answer

We have already discovered twenty good reasons why God wants to answer your prayers.

1. God is faithful.
2. He makes an everlasting covenant with His children.
3. He keeps all the promises of that covenant.
4. He seals the covenant with the blood of Jesus; His words cannot be broken.
5. He loves you.
6. He has accepted *you* as His child of the new covenant.
7. He is your Father. *You* belong to Him.
8. He gives *you* promises as your inheritance as His child.
9. He wants to bless *you*.
10. He wants to give to *you*.
11. He wants to meet *every need* in your life.
12. He wants to move the mountains.
13. He wants to heal *you* in body, soul and spirit.
14. He has given *you* His Holy Spirit to live in you.
15. He wants to inspire faith in *you* by His Spirit.
16. He wants *you* to ask and pray.
17. He wants to answer your prayers.
18. He wants to be glorified in giving to *you*.

19. He wants your joy to be full as you receive.
20. He wants others to see that you are His disciples, because much fruit is produced from your prayers.

These are twenty good reasons for praying. Twenty good reasons for asking. Twenty good reasons for believing that when you ask, God will answer: "If you ask anything in my name, I will do it."

When these truths begin to take hold of your heart, you will realise that you can dare to EXPECT answers to your prayer. Not to some of them; to *all* of them.

We often say God is 'almighty' and so He is! That means that He is all-powerful. Nothing is too great or too hard for Him. Jesus teaches us that anything is possible for someone who has faith; that 'mountain-moving' faith of which He speaks.

St. Paul talks of "the immeasurable greatness of his power in us who believe, according to the working of his great might" (Eph. 1: 19): a power so great that it cannot be measured. In us who *believe*.

He is ALMIGHTY. That is reason No. 21 for asking! Nothing is beyond Him. And yet so often we come to Him full of fears and doubts.

"Will He do it?"

"Does He really want to?"

"Does He love me enough?"

Ask With Confidence

Jesus wants you to approach your Father with confidence; not expecting *any* answer, but believing that He will do what you ask.

Where in His teaching does Jesus tell us to expect the answer: 'No'?

Nowhere!

As we approach the Lord in prayer, it is natural that we

should want to stand before Him with heads bowed, because we have sinned and we need to be forgiven. When we have confessed and received His forgiveness, He doesn't want us to continue to stand 'afar off' looking crestfallen.

We are forgiven!

So we can look up, as Jesus did when He prayed expectantly to His Father. He knew that He would always honour His prayer, because He is faithful. "And Jesus lifted up his eyes and said, 'Father, I thank thee that thou hast heard me. I know that thou hearest me always' " (John 11: 41–42). He said those words before He commanded Lazarus to come out of the tomb, where he had been buried for four days. Jesus obviously believed that He had received the answer to His prayer, even before He asked.

When He ministered to those who came with their needs, we see Him talking to the mountains, knowing that His Father's works would be accomplished.

That is how God wants us to approach life, full of expectancy that God is going to be at work in every situation as we release our faith in Him. With a God like ours, with a Father like our heavenly Father, we can dare to believe that we have already received it when we ask, because He will be faithful in giving to us. "It will be yours", says Jesus.

When 'Faith' is Not Faith

"Father, we bring before you our dear sister, Agatha, who has been given only a few weeks to live by her doctor. We praise you that you love her and that you are the Lord our Healer. We ask you now, in the name of Jesus, to lay your hand upon her and heal her. We thank you for your promise; and we claim that promise now. We thank you that it is done for your glory. Thank you, Father."

And everybody says: "Amen".

It sounds impressive! It seems that the person praying really believes that the Lord's healing gift for Agatha has

already been received. However, after the meeting the same
voice which uttered this 'prayer of faith' is overheard saying
to a friend: "Poor old Agatha. Her husband, Bert, will be
very lonely without her!"

What does that person really believe: the impressive
words of that prayer or the remarks made afterwards? The
two are inconsistent. The people saying 'Amen' may have
'believed' many different things.

"I was hoping the Lord would take the pain away."

"I was praying that she would have a quick and peaceful
death."

"I was thinking of poor Bert. He won't know how to
cope on his own!"

"I was thinking of dear Amy who died of the same disease only last month."

"I was trying to believe."

"I was imagining her getting out of bed, healed by God."

"I could see Jesus standing by her and comforting her."

A variety of attitudes, some displaying a measure of faith;
yet many negative and certainly not the prayer of faith.

Your faith, what you really believe, is seen as much
in your conversation with other people, as in your
conversation with God. You believe what you say to
others, no matter what words you speak during your
time of prayer.

How Would God Answer?

Put yourself in God's position, wanting to heal Agatha
and waiting to see the faith that will release your healing
into her life. How would you answer this situation? Remember that under the terms of the covenant you will keep your
promises but your children are expected to believe them, to
believe that they have already received what they ask.

Would you not want to show your children that they are
not truly believing you? They are saying the right words, but

by no means all of them have faith-full, expectant attitudes. Most would be more than a little surprised if Agatha were healed.

> Let him ask in faith, with no doubting, for he who doubts is like a wave of the sea that is driven and tossed by the wind. For that person must not suppose that a double-minded man, unstable in all his ways, will receive anything from the Lord (James 1: 6–8).

Know What You Believe

Before I ask God to do or give something, I ask myself a question: "Colin, what are you expecting the Lord to do as a result of this prayer?" I have be be honest with myself. It is not a question of how I would like Him to answer, or what I hope He will do; but what I *believe* that He will certainly do. What I KNOW IN MY HEART HE WILL DO.

Sometimes I am well aware that I do not really believe God for the answer that will meet the need. I want to, but I don't. I have to confess my doubt and ask the Lord to inspire, by His Spirit, the faith that is lacking.

God has promised to do what we believe. In His generosity, He is likely to do much more, but He has pledged Himself, as our covenant God, to do whatever we believe He will do.

Be Specific

If you are praying with faith, expecting God to answer you, then you will be specific in what you ask. Vague prayers are the expression of vague faith Those who pray vague prayers are not sure what they believe.

How can you "believe that you have received it", if you are not sure what you are asking God to do? Before you can be specific with God, you need to be clear in your own mind as to what you are believing.

Those who pray vaguely are pleased with any answer they receive. "That must have been the Lord's will", they say. Those who pray with faith are only satisfied when they have received the answer they expect, that they want. And they will keep on praying and believing until that specific prayer receives its specific answer. Nothing less will do.

That does not mean that we can dictate to God *how* He is to answer, or even *when* the answer is to come. It does mean that, as His new covenant children, we can afford to be specific and clear about what we ask, believing that we have already received the answer, knowing our Father *will* do it for us as He has promised. How He does it and when is up to Him. The promise Jesus gives is: "It will be yours."

The Way to Ask

Here is a simple way to pray the prayer of faith, as Jesus teaches in Mark 11: 22–24.

1. *Set* your mind on God. Remember His love for you; that you are His child. Spend some time in praise – giving yourself to Him in worship.

2. *Ask* yourself the question: "What do I believe God will do in answer to my prayer?"

3. *If* you have any doubts that He will meet the need, confess them and ask Him to give you the faith of Jesus, the tiny seed that when planted will surely bring the harvest.

4. *Bring* to the Lord anything else that needs to be put right with Him, especially any sin that needs to be forgiven.

5. *Forgive* anybody who has wronged or hurt you.

6. *Thank* the Lord for His forgiveness.

7. *Look* at your mountain – the problem or need that is before you. Don't spend time anxiously thinking about it; rather—

8. *Tell* it to move! It often helps to picture in your mind

the problem being resolved. See it happening with the eyes of faith.

9. *Look* again to the Lord and thank Him that what you are seeing with the eyes of faith, He will do. He will move the mountain.

10. *Praise* Him for His faithfulness, in fulfilling His promise.

11. *Maintain* that attitude of praise and thanksgiving every day until you see the answer to your prayer. Take the shield of faith to parry all the negative thoughts, words and attitudes, and the lying accusations of Satan. (Following chapters will help to show you how to do this.)

12. Continue to give to the Lord and know that He will give to you.

The above is only a guide – not a formula. The only way to learn to pray with faith is by doing it.

Your words of faith: "WHATEVER YOU ASK IN PRAYER, BELIEVE THAT YOU HAVE RECEIVED IT, AND IT WILL BE YOURS."

18

It Will be Yours

THEREFORE I TELL you, whatever you ask in prayer, believe that you have received it, *and it will be yours* (Mark 11: 24).

Jesus does not say that if you 'feel' anything it will be yours. He doesn't say, if you 'experience' anything it will be yours. He doesn't say, if your healing happens *instantly* it will be yours.

He says: "Believe that you have received it, and IT WILL BE YOURS."

Often the testing time for your faith will not be the time of prayer, the moment you ask, but your attitude afterwards.

Praying with faith is knowing that God is your faithful loving Father, who has bound Himself to you under the covenant, to keep all His words of promise. Therefore whatever you ask in the name of Jesus, He will do for you. You continue to pray believing that you have received it, knowing that "it will be yours." You cannot dictate to God how He will do it or when He will do it. But YOU KNOW THAT HE WILL DO IT.

'Rockets' and 'Tortoises'

When talking with our children about God answering prayers, we talk about 'rockets' and 'tortoises'. Some answers come zooming home fast like a rocket, right on targe'. We like those answers; fast, immediate. If we had our way, every prayer would have a 'rocket' answer!

In practice, other answers seem to come so slowly, creeping towards us like tortoises, plodding along step by step. But the answer is coming, It is on its way. It will arrive in due course, in God's time. So we keep believing. We continue to pray with thanksgiving that the answer *is* on the way, the healing, the guidance, or whatever it may be.

"It will be yours"; "it will be given you"; "it will be done for you"; these are the words of Jesus.

> No distrust made him (Abraham) waver concerning the promise of God, but he grew strong in his faith as he gave glory to God, fully convinced that God was able to do what he had promised (Rom. 4: 20–21).

But it is so easy to give up before the 'tortoise' arrives. And when you stop believing, the tortoise stops moving towards you. Its head shoots back into its shell! There the answer to your prayer remains, suspended somewhere between heaven and you. And when it doesn't arrive, it is so easy to blame God for not answering. "Why, Lord, why?"

> Therefore, do not throw away your confidence, which has a great reward. For you have need of endurance, so that you may do the will of God and receive what is promised (Heb. 10: 35–36).

God wants you not only to ask with faith, believing that you have received it, but also to patiently endure until you see the fulfilment of the promise, until the answer arrives.

> Let us draw near with a true heart in full assurance of faith ... let us hold fast the confession of our hope without wavering, for he who promised is faithful (Heb. 10: 22–23).

Don't Believe the Doubts

While waiting for the arrival of the answer, there will be many temptations to doubt. There have been occasions when I have started to believe God, but at some time during the waiting period I have begun to believe the doubts instead. The tortoise goes into its shell! It stops moving until I begin to believe again!

It is easier to believe the circumstances before your eyes, rather than the promise that God gives you, to meet the need and remedy the problem. Things may appear to get very much worse, before they get better. That is a real test of faith whether to believe the words of God, or one's own experience. The confrontation between 'faith' and experience.

When people give up and stop looking to God for the answer to the problem, it is often an indication that they did not truly believe in the first place. They did not believe that they had received it. God wants to use the time of waiting to build our trust and confidence in His faithfulness. All too often He has to show us that we do not have the faith that He wants to see in us.

Persist in Prayer

Some people interpret the phrase "believe that you have received it", by saying that you should only pray for a situation once, believe it is done and then forget it. If healing is being sought, you should only ask for ministry once. The repetition of the prayer or request for the laying on of hands, is an indication of a lack of faith, that the individual does not really believe. "If you believe that you have received it," some people argue, "how can you ask again? How can you ask to receive what you believe you have already received?"

It is certainly true that much repetitive prayer demonstrates a lack of faith. For example if I need healing I could say: "Lord, please heal me." Tomorrow I could repeat the same prayer, and the day after, and the day after that. In a month's time I could still be praying the same prayer: "Lord, please heal me."

I am obviously persisting in prayer, but I am not persisting in praying with faith. In which case I could still be praying the same words in a year's time and wondering why God wasn't answering!

If I had faith for my healing, my prayer would be different: "Lord, please heal me, according to the promise of your Word and I thank you for your faithful answer." After that it would be a question of continuing in thanksgiving: "Thank you, Lord, for my healing." And I would need to persist in that faithful attitude until the healing was manifested in my life. That would mean continuing in thanksgiving through all the times when assailed by doubts, when the circumstances seemed unchanged or when it appeared that the prayer had made no difference. Persevering in thanksgiving because my Lord said: "Believe that you have received it, and *it will be yours.*"

This is not, of course, a matter of words, but of believing in your heart, the words that you speak.

The same principle applies to seeking ministry for a specific need. I have known many people to have been healed over a prolonged period of time, having received the laying on of hands on several occasions. But the ministry needs to be in a spirit of thanksgiving that the original request for healing is being answered, and the healing received. It is happening!

Perhaps on the first occasion, the person did not have much confidence that God would heal. But as the healing begins, so the faith and expectancy grows. Subsequent times of ministry can therefore be more fruitful.

To suggest that we should pray only once and then forget the matter, closes the possibility for such answers and is not consistent with Jesus' teaching on persisting in prayer.

"And he told them a parable to the effect that they ought always to pray and not lose heart" (Luke 18: 1).

Jesus' words: "Ask, and it will be given you", can be literally translated, "keep on asking and it will be given you." And in the next verse, "everyone who keeps on asking receives."

So we are told to persist in our praying, which is another way of saying that we are to persist in our believing, until the answer arrives. We do not lose heart if the outward circumstances do not change immediately. Paul says:

> Have no anxiety about anything, but in everything by prayer and supplication with thanksgiving let your requests be made known to God (Phil. 4: 6).

Mistaken Attitude

Some people have been hurt by a mistaken interpretation of Jesus's words: "believe that you have received it, and it will be yours" – particularly in the realm of healing. There are those who assert: "As soon as you have prayed, you are healed! Ignore all the symptoms and pain, and exercise your faith!"

Sometimes people are advised to discharge themselves from hospital, to stop all medical treatment, get out of their sick-beds and behave as if they were healed. It is not difficult to imagine the disastrous consequences that can result from such advice.

The promise is: "it WILL be yours". Jesus does not say that it will be yours *immediately*. He does not tell us to perform acts of foolhardy bravado to try to prove that we believe and that we are trusting Him. In fact, if anything, such acts indicate a lack of faith. It seems that people who adopt such an approach are not prepared to trust God to honour His promise in the way that He decides, at the time that He knows is best.

Beware of those who encourage such acts of so-called

'faith'! The problem is accentuated by the authority that they claim. "The Lord says you are to do this," they say. "God is telling me that you are to discharge yourself from hospital."

And if the sick person refuses, or obeys but has to take to his bed again, he is merely told: "You don't have the faith, brother!"

As Christians, we are to forgive such unloving spiritual blundering. It is not easy always to do so. It doesn't seem to occur to such people that, if they are involved in the situation, their own faith is just as much at stake. A pertinent question can be asked of them: "Do you have the faith and authority to address the mountain and see it moved?"

No Spiritual Blackmail

Praying with faith is not dictating to God; it is trusting Him to keep His word, knowing in your heart that He will. Dispensing with medical attention does not impress God. Often that is the channel that He will use to bring healing into a person's life.

A young woman wanted her eyes to be healed. She prayed, and then as an 'act of faith' she broke her glasses and threw them away. She spent several weeks with impaired eyesight before having to obtain a new pair of spectacles.

The breaking of the glasses proved nothing. If you believe the promise, you know God is going to heal regardless of how many pairs you have! In this particular case it was the action of a new Christian; so it is easy to understand her making such a mistake. The time to throw away your glasses or your crutches is when the Lord has healed you, and your body manifests the evidence of that healing. God is not honoured by a well-meaning Christian hobbling into his doctor's surgery, saying, "The Lord has healed my foot. By faith I believe it."

Our faith needs to be in His words of promise, not in gestures of spiritual bravado. Before Peter climbed out of the boat, when Jesus was standing on the water, he waited until he heard for himself the command: "Come". His faith was in response to the words of Jesus.

Anyone who jumps out of the boat before he personally hears the Lord telling him to, can expect to sink.

It is fine to say, "By faith I believe it." Keep on saying it. But wait until you have seen the evidence of the answer in your body before you testify about your healing.

"All Prayer is with Faith"

On the other hand, there is much teaching on prayer and healing that assures people that whatever they do is an expression of faith. The very fact that people pray it is claimed, demonstrates 'faith'. There is some truth in this; but because a person prays does not mean he has the 'mustard seed' faith that Jesus speaks of, knowing that the prayer seed will certainly produce the required harvest.

It is easier to pray than to believe! It is possible to ask, but without the faith that Jesus speaks of.

"I Really Believe"

Many people come for prayer, the laying on of hands or anointing and really 'believe' that God is going to heal them. But they go away disappointed because they feel that "nothing has happened". It is then assumed that God must have some other purpose, that perhaps it is not His will to heal in that situation. Yet that would be a denial of Jesus' prayer promises: "*whatever* you ask . . ."

We are confronted again, with two different interpretations of 'faith': what Christians usually mean by this word, and what Jesus means by it.

The person coming for a time of ministry is not going to leave disappointed if He believes that He has already received. He will go away rejoicing knowing the faithfulness of God and that it will be done. He has asked in faith and God will answer that faith. Even if at the time there is no outward evidence of healing.

The problem for him may be that the healing hasn't happened instantly. Jesus does not promise that it will. He says that the answer to the prayer 'will be yours'.

Faith says: "I BELIEVE."

Doubt, expressed in disappointment says: "I BELIEVED!"

Faith is a continuous attitude of believing until the answer is seen.

In recent years I have prayed with countless people to be healed. Many, at the time of prayer, would have said that they did not experience or feel anything happening. And yet within a few days they are testifying to their healing. Only this week I received a letter telling of two people with whom I prayed recently, both with back troubles. I had been teaching about the prayer of faith, and the need to go on believing until the answer was received.

Apparently when we prayed on the Sunday evening, neither person noticed any significant change in their physical condition. By the following Wednesday, both had received their healing. On the Sunday, they could have said that the prayer hadn't worked, although they had believed. They could have given in to their disappointment and adopted the attitude: "We'll try another time, somewhere else."

Instead, they had heard the promises of Jesus and they held on to them until the healing was received. Two or three days does not seem very long to wait for the answer to arrive – unless you are the one who has the bad back! There can be a lot of temptation to doubt in three days, many opportunities to give up believing and give way to disappointment.

But if you believe that you have received it your only

disappointment will be that the healing did not come like a 'rocket'. You will still be rejoicing and praising God because you know it will be yours.

Not 'Feelings'

Some people don't get as far as the time of waiting. They only believe in 'rockets'. This can be a danger, particularly when seeking ministry for healing. If, when they pray, they do not 'feel' or 'experience' anything, they often doubt whether God is honouring His promise. In reality, their trust can be in the 'feeling' or the 'experience' rather than in the words of God: "it will be yours". In which case their faith is built on sand, and they are destined for many disappointments until they build on rock.

During times of ministry, the Lord sends many 'rocket' answers. We have to learn to be just as thankful for the 'tortoises'. God's wisdom is infinitely greater than ours; He knows best, when and how we are to receive the answer. And His Spirit, alive within us, will lead us faithfully to that point of receiving as we continue to believe the words of Jesus that He declares to us.

Failure is Forgiven

I have had to look back over my Christian life and ask God to forgive all the times when I gave in to the doubts and believed them over and above His promises. How wonderful it is that every time we confess our failure, God wipes the slate clean! He forgives completely. He gives a new start. He doesn't condemn us for the past, but gives us a new opportunity to believe for the future.

He does not want *you* to feel condemned either. He does not want you to be constantly living under the cloud of your past failures. If He has shown you that there were times when you didn't really believe Him for the answer to a problem, perhaps an important need, bring the failure to Him straight away, and receive His forgiveness. If you began to believe for an answer, but gave up after a while because you believed the circumstances, rather than the promise, ask the Lord to forgive your lack of perseverance. If you have only looked for 'rockets' in the past, pray the prayer of faith now and believe that "it will be yours".

Know that God is concerned about the future; that you can have a new, positive, faith-full attitude towards asking in prayer. As you learn to pray the prayer of faith, you will believe Him and hang on to His promises, even if it is only by your finger-nails – as it will be sometimes!

Your words of faith: "IT WILL BE YOURS." "IT WILL BE GIVEN YOU." "IT WILL BE DONE FOR YOU."

19

In My Name

IF YOU ASK anything IN MY NAME, I will do it (John 14: 14).

By now these words will be familiar to you. In the previous verse Jesus says:

Whatever you ask IN MY NAME, I will do it, that the Father may be glorified in the Son (John 14: 13).

In both, Jesus speaks of asking "in my name", and later He talks of receiving "in my name".

Truly, truly, I say to you, if you ask anything of the Father, he will give it to you IN MY NAME (John 16: 23).

The name of Jesus is more than a title; it implies His whole Person. It is "in the name" of Jesus that the disciples are given power to heal the sick and cast out demons. They are given the authority to do the same works as Jesus did, as if it was He Himself doing them.

"Where two or three are gathered IN MY NAME, there am I in the midst of them" (Matt. 18: 20). The Person of Jesus is present because they come together "in His name".

"Whoever receives one such child IN MY NAME receives ME" (Matt. 18: 5). To receive anyone "in His name" is to receive the Lord Himself, the Person of Jesus.

To pray in the name of Jesus is to bring His Person into the prayer. It is as if Jesus Himself was praying that prayer to His Father. Jesus tells us to "ask in my name". That is the way He wants us to pray.

To bring the person of Jesus into the prayer is to pray with His love, His purpose and His *faith*. If that seems impossible for you, remember that God has given you His Holy Spirit, so that you can be filled with His love, know His purpose and be inspired with His faith!

As you face a situation that requires prayer, you can ask yourself these questions:

1. How would Jesus *love* in this situation?
That is the way I want to love.

2. What would Jesus *do* in this situation?
That is what I want to do.

3. What would Jesus *believe* in this situation?
That is how I want to believe.

As you learn to pray in the name of Jesus, you learn to put yourself in His shoes, so that you approach the problem as He would, knowing that all the resources of heaven are at your disposal. Your Father does not want you to be full of doubt, insecurity and despair. He wants you to pray with the confidence of Jesus, knowing that you are God's child.

Jesus in the Prayer

To pray "in the name of Jesus" means that you bring Him into the prayer. He prays along with you. He approaches the problem with you. You face it together, in His power, with His faith, that mustard-seed faith that moves mountains; with His love. "Abide in me, and I in you." When you pray, you live in Jesus, and he lives in you. Your prayer is a combined operation!

So if you pray "in the name of Jesus", your prayers can have the effectiveness of those of Jesus Himself. We cannot conceive of the Father ignoring any prayer of His own Son. Neither will He ignore any of the prayers of His children who pray in His name, within the covenant relationship that He has given them.

Not a Formula

Unfortunately, "in the name of Jesus" has become a formula that is tacked on to the end of most prayers, to give them an air of authenticity and so that others present know when it is time to say, 'Amen'! Prayer does not achieve significant results when it is reduced to a series of formulae. It is not the words spoken that are significant, but what is going on in the heart of the one praying. Is he praying along with Jesus? Is his prayer expressing the love and concern of Jesus? Is he believing God to work, as Jesus believes His Father to work in every situation?

When Jesus prayed, He looked up to heaven expectantly. He didn't look at the mountain and think it immovable! He knew the resources that were available to Him and those same resources are available to *you*. You don't have to feel defeated before you begin. You have been given the privilege of praying in Jesus' name, of having Him in your prayer. Use that great privilege.

Remember that He promises you that, "if you ask anything in my name, I will do it"!

If Jesus is in the prayer with you, He will make sure that the promises are fulfilled, that "it will be yours". Together you will look to the Father so that, "if you ask anything of the Father, he will give it to you in my name." The Father will give to you, as He gives to Jesus, because you are at one with Him in your prayer.

What possibilities lie before you, as you pray "in the name of Jesus", realising that He is praying with you!

Your words of faith: "WHATEVER YOU ASK IN MY NAME, I WILL DO IT."

20

Anything You Want

TRULY, TRULY, I say to you, if you ask *anything* of the Father, he will give it to you in my name. Hitherto you have asked nothing in my name; ask, and you will receive, that your joy may be full (John 16: 23–24).

ANYTHING! "Truly, truly, I say to you ..." means, "I say this with great emphasis". The disciples were to take particular note of what Jesus was to say.

During the course of His ministry, they had become used to His physical presence with them, speaking His Father's words and doing His works. They would have prayed to God as 'Father', as Jesus had taught them. But they had never asked God to do anything as if it was Jesus Himself asking. They had never prayed "in the name of Jesus".

With the crucifixion imminent, He had given them the promise that the Holy Spirit would soon come to live in them: "your hearts will rejoice, and no one will take your joy from you" (John 16: 22). Jesus will then be alive in them to pray in them, and to perform His Father's works through them:

Truly, truly, I say to you, he who believes in me will also do the works that I do; and greater works than these will he do, because I go to the Father (John 14: 12).

That is a promise for "he who believes in me"; any one who puts his faith in Jesus. For those who truly pray "in the name of Jesus" pray with Him, with the limitless resources

of His power. During the days of His earthly ministry, Jesus
was limited like all humans, by time and space. Now that He
reigns in glory with the Father, He has to suffer no such
limitations. He is in us and with us as we pray in His name,
and yet Presence and power can be directed anywhere at
any time, through believing prayer. That is one of the
reasons why Jesus did not want the disciples to be sad about
His imminent death; it would open up untold possibilities
for the future.

Jesus told them to pray "in my name", so that as His
continuing Body here on earth, the Father could go on
giving to them as He had been giving to Him during the days
of His humanity.

Father or Son

You can pray to either the Father or the Son. Jesus said:
"I and the Father are one" (John 10: 30).

> Whatever you ask in my name, *I will do it.*
> If you ask anything in my name, *I will do it.*

Jesus is making it clear that He wants to *do* things *for* His
followers, even after the crucifixion and resurrection. At the
same time, He tells them to pray to His Father:

> Whatever you ask the Father in my name, *he may give*
> *it to you.*
> If you ask anything of the Father, *he will give it to you*
> in my name.

The Father wants to give to His children, as He has given
to His Son, during the days of His humanity.

Whether you pray to the Father or the Son, what matters
is that you pray in the name of Jesus, with His faith, knowing the willingness of your covenant God to give to you and

to work for you; that your prayer is filled with the presence of Jesus, with His love, life and power.

Two Motives

Jesus says that He will do anything we ask Him "in His name", "that the Father may be glorified in the Son". That is His purpose; to glorify His Father. That is also our purpose as Christians, to bear fruit for His glory.

He says that the Father will give us anything we ask in Jesus' name, "that your joy may be full". A loving Father is blessed by giving to His children, and seeing their joy in receiving.

To say that God wants to bless His children, is to realise that He wants them to be happy, for their "joy to be full".

He wants to give to *you*.

Whatever You Want

Jesus is not afraid to tell us to pray for "whatever you will", anything you want, because He knows that the Holy Spirit is going to stir right desires in the new hearts that God has given His new covenant children. If you or someone else is sick or in some other need, it is instinctive for you, as a Christian, to pray for that person. The Spirit within you urges you to pray.

Your mind may tell you something else. You may think, "It is useless. It is pointless. No good will come of my prayer." But the Spirit will say "Pray!" And Jesus living within you will want you to pray, with His faith, in His name, believing that you have received it.

Believing God to meet needs is one thing, but does He really mean we can ask for *anything* that we want? Yes, He does.

It has often delighted me that God has answered prayers

for unnecessary, even trivial things that could hardly be described as necessities. But then any loving Father wants to provide His children with more than the bare necessities of life. And our heavenly Father loves supremely, more abundantly than any human father. He is concerned about every area of our lives, even the seemingly insignificant ones. He will not allow us to abuse His generosity; but He doesn't want us to waste it either!

James says: "You do not have, because you do not ask" (James 4: 2). God wants to teach you to trust Him in all the small details, as well as the great needs. To be looking to Him to "do for you" and to "give to you", anything that you ask in the name of Jesus.

And remember that not only is He glorified in giving to His new covenant children, but that He also wants "your joy to be full". He delights in giving, He delights in seeing the faith that believers give to Him, and He delights in the joy of His children as they receive.

Asking Amiss

"How can I be sure that what I am praying for is right in the eyes of God?" To pray according to God's will is rightly a great concern for Christians. Some are quick to quote James's words:

> You ask and do not receive, because you ask wrongly, to spend it on your passions. Unfaithful creatures! (James 4: 3–4).

Jesus did not pray to indulge His passions! You will not be able to pray "in the name of Jesus" to indulge yours either. You cannot pray with Jesus, or be confident that He is praying with you, for anything that you know is contrary to His purpose. It is possible to pray for wrong things with selfish motives. But you cannot pray such things with the faith of Jesus. The Holy Spirit within you will not inspire such faith to pray for anything opposed to the Father's will. Neither is Jesus going to be praying with you in that prayer. And you can be sure that the Father is not likely to give you what is opposed to His loving purpose for you.

There are many things that your 'flesh' may tell you that you would like to have right now. You do not pray the prayer of faith for them because you know all too well that you would only be indulging your passions, and not praying as Jesus would.

However, most of your asking prayer will be for genuine needs, in your own life and in the lives of others. You need not hesitate in approaching those needs as Jesus would, with love and compassion, with power and with faith. You need not be tentative in your thinking or in your praying. Jesus never was.

Confront that need before you now. Tell the mountain to move and ask Jesus to work for you in that situation; ask the Father to give whatever is necessary. And remember:

God *wants* you to ask.

He *wants* you to believe that you have it.

He *wants* you to pray "in the name of Jesus".

He *wants* to be glorified in giving to you.

He *wants* your joy to be full.

He *wants* you to have a fruitful prayer life.

Your words of faith: "ASK, AND YOU WILL RECEIVE, THAT YOUR JOY MAY BE FULL."

21
Every Need

FEAR IS THE opposite of faith. When you are afraid, you are not trusting God.

We all experience fear and anxiety during the course of our daily lives; fears about work, children, finance, the future and so on.

God gives us a very simple command: "Fear not" – a command that is repeated hundreds of times in the Bible. This was a phrase often on the lips of Jesus. He assured his hearers that His Father knew their needs, and wanted to meet them. So there was no necessity to be fearful or anxious.

> In praying do not heap up empty phrases as the Gentiles do; for they think they will be heard for their many words. Do not be like them, for *your Father knows what you need before you ask him* (Matt. 6: 7–8).

God is looking for the faith in your asking that will release the answers to those needs into your life.

> Therefore I tell you, do not be anxious about your life, what you shall eat or what you shall drink, nor about your body, what you shall put on (Matt 6: 25).

"Your heavenly Father feeds the birds", Jesus goes on to say. Trust Him to feed you, to meet your needs. Besides, "Which of you by being anxious can add one cubit to his span of life?" (v. 27). What good will all your worrying do you? None. Instead, have faith in the promises of your Father.

If God so clothes the grass of the field, which today is alive and tomorrow is thrown into the oven, will he not much more clothe you, O men of little faith? Therefore DO NOT BE ANXIOUS, saying, What shall we eat? or What shall we drink? or What shall we wear? For the Gentiles seek all these things; and your heavenly Father knows that you need them all (vv. 30–32).

The 'Gentiles' here are the faithless ones, those who were outside the covenant relationship between God and Israel. You are within the new covenant and so need have no anxiety about anything.

God is YOUR Father. You are His child, a child of the new covenant. All His promises are for *you*. He loves *you*. He cares for *you*. He wants to meet *all your* needs. And He knows about them, even before you ask Him,

The Kingdom First

When you pray, you are not asking God to do something that He doesn't want to do. You are blessing Him by allowing Him to honour your faith and give to you. And so Jesus tells us:

But seek first his kingdom and his righteousness, and all these things shall be yours as well (Matt. 6: 33).

Another great promise, following an important command. Every need in your life will be met if you seek first the kingdom of God and are in a right relationship with Him. This is why you need to give yourself whole-heartedly to the Lord, so that you might be made righteous through the blood of Jesus, brought into a right relationship with Him, knowing Him as 'Father' and being filled with his Holy Spirit. Submitting everything to Him that He might be 'Lord' and 'King' in your life. That He might reign supreme in you. That you might live, not for your own selfish ends, but for Him. To honour Him. To give Him glory.

The Lord's Prayer

If you live for Him, God promises that "all these things will be yours as well". Jesus tells us to pray to:

"Our Father who art in heaven": That is the wonderful privilege of His children; not only to know Him as 'Father', to be in that kind of a relationship with God, but to call upon Him to use all His heavenly resources to meet our needs according to His promises. Remembering, of course, that we are not to demand from God. If we believe His promises, He will give.

That word 'Father' is most precious to a Christian. It speaks of His love, care, concern, of His willingness to give.

"Hallowed be thy name": If you 'know' God, the greatest desire of your heart is to praise Him for all that He is: the great, almighty, holy God, who is *your* Father. There is no greater joy than that of praise, of being lifted before the throne of God in worship and adoration.

All your asking needs to be set within the context of praise. For it is then that your eyes will be fixed, not on the problem, but on the One who is the answer to it. And the more you praise, the greater your awareness of the immensity of God, and the wonder of His love for you.

To praise the name of your God, is to praise Him 'in Person'. That is *your* privilege.

"Thy kingdom come, thy will be done, on earth as it is in heaven": You can only pray these words "from the heart" if you relate them to your own life. You cannot meaningfully pray God's will to be done on earth unless you are prepared to do His will yourself. So you are saying to your Father: "I want you to reign in my life and in the lives of all your

people. I want your will to be done in me and in everybody else."

Jesus wants you to live 'kingdom life' here on earth. That means that you do not approach every situation from a purely human point of view, but realise that all the resources of heaven are available to you. As you pray, believing the promises of your Father, those resources are brought to earth.

It is not only the faith of Jesus that the Father wants to see in His children. He is looking for His love in them, to see His life being lived out in them, expressed in their care for one another and their desire to reach out with their heavenly resources to meet the needs of others.

"Give us this day our daily bread": Again Jesus impresses upon us His wish that we ask our Father to *give* to us. "Daily bread" means that we ask Him for everything that we need to enable us to do His will and to live that kingdom life here on earth.

And Jesus tells us to pray: "Give us *this day*." Our prayers are not to be those of vague hope that one day in the future we might receive something from God. Rather, our expectancy is to be that God will meet our needs *today*; He will provide for us *today*.

"And forgive us our debts, as we also have forgiven our debtors": Unforgiven sin can so easily prevent us from receiving what our Father wants to give to us. He is always prepared to forgive His children and to restore them to that union with Himself that He enjoys with them.

So often His way is that He will give to us, only when we have given first. This is particularly true of forgiveness. Notice the words Jesus uses: ". . . as we also have forgiven."

You forgive those who wrong you, and God will forgive you for the ways in which you have wronged Him.

At the end of the Lord's prayer, Jesus underlines this point emphatically by saying: "For if you forgive men their trespasses, your heavenly Father also will forgive you; but if you do not forgive men their trespasses, neither will your Father forgive your trespasses" (Matt 6: 14–15).

"*And lead us not into temptation*": God does not want us to disobey His will, to deny His reign in our lives, or to disbelieve His words. Throughout all the times when we are tempted to doubt His promise or give up trusting Him for the answer to our prayers, He is with us. He never gives up on us; He never deserts us: "I will be with you; I will not fail you or forsake you."

Against every temptation to doubt, He wants us to take the shield of faith, and hold on to His words, that our trust and confidence will always be in Him.

"*But deliver us from evil*": It is God's purpose to save us from every manifestation of evil: bodily sickness, mental fear and a doubting spirit. He sent His Son to die on the Cross to make that possible. And He wants the victory of Calvary to be brought in every situation of need in our lives, by believing prayer.

Good Things

> Ask and it shall be given you; seek, and you will find; knock and it will be opened to you. For EVERYONE WHO ASKS RECEIVES, and he who seeks finds, and to him who knocks it will be opened (Matt. 7: 7–8).

It will be . . . It will be . . . It will be . . . It will be . . .
That is the emphatic promise of Jesus.

"Everyone who asks receives." EVERYONE – that includes YOU.

Everyone who asks from the heart, believing the promise that God gives through His Son. And when you ask, remember what kind of a Father you have in heaven:

> Or what man of you, if his son asks him for bread, will give him a stone? Or if he asks for a fish, will give him a

serpent? If you then, who are evil, know how to give good gifts to your children, HOW MUCH MORE WILL YOUR FATHER WHO IS IN HEAVEN GIVE GOOD THINGS TO THOSE WHO ASK HIM! (Matt. 7: 9–11).

That is your Father's good pleasure: to give you good things. He sent His Son to deliver you from all that is evil so that in His Fatherly love He may give you that abundance of life, prosperity and healing, which is His purpose for you.

The thief comes only to steal and kill and destroy; I came that they may have life, and have it abundantly (John 10: 10)

Satan is 'the thief', He sets out to steal from you. He wants to take away your joy and fill your life with worry and anxiety. He wants to take the love for others out of your life and fill you with fear and suspicion and even hate. He wants to destroy your faith in God and fill you with unbelief. He is dedicated to destroying your health of body, mind and spirit. He wants to disturb your peace, give sickness and pain to your body.

And God does not want you to bow before any of these works of Satan and submit to them. If he is given the opportunity the enemy will kill you physically and he will destroy your faith. His ultimate joy would be to kill you spiritually, so that you do not enjoy that eternal life with your Father, that is your inheritance as His child.

Victory

But Jesus came to bring life, not death; to bring victory, not defeat; to bring healing, not sickness; to do you good, not evil. It is His Father's will and purpose to "give good things to those who ask him".

He sent His Son to die on the Cross to make the defeat of Satan and all His works absolute, total. The victory is there waiting for you to enter into through faith.

You do not have to ask if God wants any of these evil things in your life. Imperfect human fathers know how to give good gifts to their children. How much more will your Father, who is perfect love and perfect goodness, want to do good things in your life and set you free from every manifestation of evil. It cost Him the life of His dear Son to make that possible. And he doesn't want that cost wasted.

And He doesn't want you to believe in anything less than God's perfect wholeness for you; health of body, soul and spirit. He wants to meet every need of whatever nature.

> Beloved, I pray that you may prosper in every way and that you may be in health; I know that it is well with your soul (3 John 2).

Your words of faith: "YOUR FATHER KNOWS WHAT YOU NEED BEFORE YOU ASK HIM."

22

The Healing Lord

JESUS WAS NOT one to preach one thing and practise another. In the previous chapter we looked at some of the things He said during the Sermon on the Mount.

> "Your Father knows what you need before you ask him."
> "Do not be anxious about your life . . ."
> "Seek first his kingdom and his righteousness, and all these things will be yours as well."
> "Give us this day our daily bread."
> "Ask and it will be given you."
> "Everyone who asks receives."

How did Jesus put these words into operation in His own ministry? We will follow the events recorded in Matthew's Gospel, after the Sermon on the Mount. Chapter eight opens with the healing of a leper.

A Leper

"Lord, if you will, you can make me clean" (Matt. 8: 2), the leper says to Jesus. Many people approach healing today with a similar diffidence. They ask to be healed, but add "if it be your will" at the end of their prayer. The 'if' must go. Jesus answered the leper simply "I want to" (or "I am willing to" or "I will"). It is His purpose to give abundant life, not see us die from crippling and evil diseases.

You cannot pray the prayer of faith, looking to God with

confidence and expectancy, when there is an 'if' to your prayer. Ask "in my name," said Jesus, "as if I was praying the prayer myself, with my faith, my expectancy, with my life and power and Presence." Jesus never turned anyone away who came to Him. And He did not use any 'ifs' when He prayed for people to be healed.

> And he stretched out his hand and touched him, saying "I will; be clean." And immediately his leprosy was cleansed (v. 3).

Jesus heals the leper with a touch and a word of authority: "Be clean". Here we see the Son speaking the words His Father gives Him to speak, and doing the works He saw His Father doing. Loving, Caring. Healing. Restoring. Meeting with the leper at his point of need. Jesus didn't preach Him a sermon. He healed him!

You need not doubt that God, your loving Father, desires to heal you. Either you have to say: "God wants me to have this sickness", or you have to believe "God does not want me to have this sickness". If you think He wants you to have it then you have no right to go to a doctor, or try to lessen the pain, or even to pray about it. To do any of these things would be to go against what you say is God's will for you.

This seems clearly ridiculous! He is certainly not a loving Father who wants to "give good things" to His children, if you think His best purpose for you is sickness and pain.

So what is the alternative? He wants to heal! In which case you have every right to pray; to ask, believing His promise; to seek the good offices of the medical profession. To believe God, not only to alleviate the pain, but remove the disease, whether it is physical, mental or emotional; and to give you the healing you seek in the way He chooses.

The Centurion

As Jesus entered Capernaum, He was approached by a Roman centurion, who said "Lord, my servant is lying paralysed at home, in terrible distress" (Matt. 8: 6). Did Jesus say: "Well leave him alone; it is my Father's will that he is sick and is suffering so terribly?" Of course not! Jesus said: "I will come and heal him" (v. 7).

Both the leper and the centurion CAME to Jesus with their need. It is made clear in the gospels that Jesus met the needs of ALL who CAME to Him. He did not go to every sick person in every city, town and village that He visited in order to heal them.

Occasionally Jesus took the initiative, as, for example, with the man by the pool of Bethesda. But the general principle is that all who came, or were brought, were healed.

If you need healing, it is for you to 'come' to Jesus, rather than sit back and wait for Him to come to you. To come to Him with faith, believing "that you have received it" and being sure of His promise to you: "and it will be yours".

The centurion came on behalf of His servant; then Jesus offers to come and heal the man. This is the Lord's way: "You come to me FIRST and then I will come to you."

The Roman soldier surprises Jesus by saying to Him:

> "Lord, I am not worthy to have you come under my roof, but only say the word and my servant will be healed. For I am a man under authority, with soldiers under me and I say to one, 'Go', and he goes, and to another 'Come', and he comes, and to my slave. 'Do this', and he does it." When Jesus heard him, he marvelled ... (Matt. 8–10).

Men often marvelled at the things Jesus said; here Jesus marvels at the words the centurion speaks. "Truly, I say to you, not even in Israel have I found such FAITH" (v. 10).

This Gentile, this Roman soldier of the occupation forces, comes to Him calling Him 'Lord'. And when Jesus offers to come and heal his servant, the man says: "That won't be necessary; you only have to give the order and it will be done. I know that because I have to obey orders, and give them. And when I give an order I expect instant obedience."

Jesus says that the centurion's words and attitude demonstrated more FAITH than He had found in Israel – even among His own disciples! What is so remarkable about the centurion? He understood the authority of Jesus.

Jesus is the Son of God; nothing is impossible for Him. He only has to speak the word, or give the order, and it is done. When Jesus speaks, Almighty God speaks. When Jesus acts, His heavenly Father is at work.

Do you understand the authority and power of the One whom you call: 'Lord'? If so, you know that He only has to speak His word to your heart and you will be healed. The Holy Spirit only has to take the words of Jesus and declare them to you, and the promise will be fulfilled.

Faith, as Jesus understands it, is believing "that you have received it". And He saw that quality of faith in the Roman soldier. Jesus links directly this faith with the healing that follows. He speaks the word of authority. He gives His order. "Go; be it done for you *as you have believed*" (Matt. 8: 13). Ask with faith – and it WILL be done.

Peter's Mother-in-law

Next, Jesus entered Peter's house, where the disciple's mother-in-law was "lying sick with a fever. He touched her hand, and the fever left her, and she rose and served him". What better motive could there be for receiving healing from Jesus, than rising to serve the Lord?

Jesus healed the centurion's servant with a word: Peter's mother-in-law with a touch; the leper with a word and a touch.

Touch can be so important in ministering to those who need healing. To sit and hold the hand of a sick person can be a great comfort to them, even if no words are spoken. The physical contact can convey love and concern.

The Laying on of Hands

When we minister to others "in the name of Jesus", it is as if the Lord Himself is making the physical contact. When we lay hands on one another, He is using a pair of ordinary human hands, but it can be His touch, if that is what we believe. So we should expect much more than human love and concern to be expressed in a deliberate laying on of hands in the name of Jesus. We can expect nothing less than the healing power of the Lord to be conveyed to the one who is receiving ministry.

That faith and expectation ideally needs to be in both the patient and those ministering to him. All concerned should have adequate preparation before such a time of ministry. Jesus heals those who 'come' to Him and so, when possible, the one seeking healing should be encouraged to come, offering his life afresh and whole-heartedly to God (see Chapter 8). And those who are ministering should be similarly prepared.

Laying hands on people without any result is not glorifying to the Lord, or helpful to the sick person. Whenever a person comes GIVING himself, the Lord responds by GIVING Himself. When people are only interested in receiving from Him, then the results can be disappointing. When they come without faith, they are unpredictable.

So during the time of preparation before personal ministry it is good for both patient and those praying with him, to 'receive' the promises that God gives in His word concerning answered prayer and healing. (See Chapter 11).

Not Always Instant

We pray according to the promises of Jesus. He does *not* promise instant answers to all our prayers. He does say: "it will be done for you." "It will be given you." "It will be yours." *It will be.*

Sometimes there will be instant healing; at other times a measure of improvement will be seen immediately in the patient. In some, there will be no discernible improvement in the condition, at the time. This is when it is so easy to believe your doubts, rather than the promises of Jesus. "Nothing has happened." "It hasn't worked." "God doesn't want to heal me."

"Believe that you have received it, and it will be yours," Jesus says. Go on believing until you see the answer, the promise fulfilled. Don't give up! Or be tempted to believe your doubts. Don't be concerned if you have not experienced or felt anything.

Why was nearly everyone who came to Jesus healed instantly, and yet that is obviously not the case at healing services today?

At healing services Jesus is ministering His healing power, but imperfect channels, with imperfect faith exercise less than the total authority of Jesus. Obviously, there are some who come looking to the man ministering and not to the Lord: so that can lead to disappointment. There will be others who are hoping for the best, and who do not believe that they have received what they asked for. There are others who come wanting only to receive and not to give to the Lord; they are not seeking first the kingdom of God.

There can be many imponderables; but the promises of Jesus are clear, that, if we believe (in the way that He teaches) then *whatever* we ask will be given to us. In His way. And in His time.

Much distress can be caused when people are taught that the healing must happen instantly, or it will not happen at all. That is not a statement of faith. It is believing our experiences (or lack of them) rather than the promises of Jesus.

When you come to the Lord, either in prayer or in prayer coupled with the laying on of hands, you can come with faith, believing that God is going to heal, and after the prayer, believing that He has. And you need to maintain that faith until the evidence of that healing is plain, rather than be disappointed because God has not acted in the *way* you wanted, *when* you wanted.

"It will be", Jesus promises.

Praise God for the 'rocket' answers! Praise Him for the 'tortoises'; Praise Him for the faith to believe the promises!

Your words of faith: "GO; BE IT DONE FOR YOU AS YOU HAVE BELIEVED."

23

The Healing Cross

THAT EVENING THEY brought to him many who were possessed with demons; and he cast out the spirits with a word, and *healed all who were sick* (Matt. 8: 16).

This is one of the many statements that occur throughout the gospel accounts which show us the outworking of Jesus' promise: "For every one who asks receives." He "casts out" the evil spirits "with a word" of command and authority; and He healed all who were sick, all who were "brought to him".

The following verse is of paramount importance in understanding why healing played such a significant part in Jesus' ministry, why He healed all who came or were brought to Him, and why He will still heal today when we come to Him.

This was to fulfil what was spoken by the prophet Isaiah, "HE TOOK OUR INFIRMITIES AND BORE OUR DISEASES" (Matt. 8: 17).

To understand the healing of Jesus we have to come back to the Cross. In that remarkable prophecy of the Crucifixion in Isaiah, Chapter 53, we read:

Surely he has borne our griefs (sicknesses)
and carried our sorrows (pains);
yet we esteemed him stricken,
smitten by God, and afflicted.
But he was wounded for our transgressions,
he was bruised for our iniquities;
upon him was the chastisement

that made us whole,
and with his stripes we are healed (Isa. 53: 4–5).

These words were written hundreds of years before the Cross. We look at them hundreds of years after the crucifixion. When they were first spoken they looked forward to what would happen; as we read them, we look back at what has already taken place.

Griefs and Sorrows

Jesus *has borne our griefs and carried our sorrows*. He has taken them to the Cross and crucified them with Him so that all who come to Him can be set free from them.

Many people hold on to their grief, particularly when a very close relative has died. It is natural to grieve; but grief is negative and even self-destructive. It is really a form of self-pity. As Christians, we believe that God's children are liberated at the time of physical death, to enjoy His eternal glory. Resurrection is a time for rejoicing, not mourning. Of course, it is natural for those who loved that person to feel the loss deeply. However, God does not want that loss to cloud the rest of their lives and destroy them with self-pity.

At a meeting in New Zealand, I had been talking about God purchasing us for Himself with the blood of the Cross. Everything that we are and have is His.

In the congregation was a woman whose young grandson had been tragically killed about six weeks previously. This boy was the "apple of her eye". She doted on him and so felt the loss greatly. She was a Christian, but no longer knew what to believe. Grief can so easily shatter faith.

As she listened that day, she realised that she had been holding on to that boy, believing him to be her own. She knew that she had to give him to God, to acknowledge that he was His child. And when it came to the time of ministry, she came forward bringing her grief to the Cross.

On the following day she gave a brief, but deeply moving testimony. She said that previously she was unable to mention the boy's name without breaking down in tears. Yet now as she spoke she looked radiant. She knew that the boy was with the Lord, but more than that, Jesus had "borne her grief" on the Cross and had filled her anew with the joy of His Spirit.

That is our God, the God of love, meeting His children right in the middle of their needs.

Our Sicknesses and Pains

Jesus has borne our sicknesses and carried our pains to the Cross. The Hebrew words used can be translated either 'grief' or 'sickness', and 'sorrow' or 'pain'. Grief and sorrow are mental anguish; sickness and pain are physical suffering. The truth is that Jesus has taken upon Himself both the mental and physical suffering of men, so that, through the Cross, they may be healed of both.

Many people look upon the Cross as a time of victory for the enemies of Jesus. They think of the pitiful sight of the Son of God being crucified: "yet we esteemed him stricken, smitten by God, afflicted." There is no question that His Father led Him deliberately to the Cross, because He was prepared to pay the price with His precious life for our full healing, wholeness and salvation; the healing that He wants in our bodies, minds, spirits, emotions, relationships, problems, and needs.

Jesus was "smitten by God" that we might be healed. That healing is already accomplished! Matthew renders Isaiah 53 verse 4: "He took our infirmities and bore our diseases." As He hung on the Cross Jesus said: "It is accomplished", or "It is finished". It is done. All that is needed for the healing of God's people. Every manifestation of evil was defeated and Jesus' victory made available to

God's children. The resurrection of Jesus is the evidence of that victory. Even death has been defeated.

Our Sin

He was wounded for our transgressions, he was bruised for our iniquities. It is more commonly understood that the sins of men are forgiven because of the finished, accomplished work of the crucifixion. When we enter into fellowship with our heavenly Father, we do so through the Cross; we come to the Lord, confessing our sins and knowing that He is faithful and just to forgive us.

Because of the sacrifice of Jesus, God's forgiveness awaits those who come to Him. When a sinner turns to God, Jesus does not have to die all over again so that he might be accepted and forgiven. His salvation has already been accomplished and awaits that act of turning, or repentance.

So it is with all our other healing needs, which are all part of the salvation that God makes available to us. We come to the Cross, to the place where our grief and sorrow, our sickness and pain, as well as our sins, have been defeated by Jesus.

Those who proclaim forgiveness without preaching healing, are only teaching a partial Cross, an incomplete Gospel. There would be much more evidence of healing in the lives of God's children if they were to BELIEVE as readily in healing through the Cross, as they do in forgiveness. The Lord's forgiveness is taught from infancy in most Christian homes; His healing is sometimes never taught at all!

There are some who claim that the forgiveness is for now, and the healing is in resurrection, in life after death. That plainly will not do. If the forgiveness of the Cross is for NOW, then so is the healing of grief, sorrow, pain, sickness, infirmities and diseases! The rest of verse 5 is the very confirmation of this.

Being Made Whole

> Upon him was the chastisement that made us whole,
> and with his stripes we are healed (Isa. 53: 5).

The chastisement of Jesus "MADE US WHOLE". Not,
"will make us whole after death": but "MADE us whole".
'Whole' means being complete and made perfect in every
way, as whole people: healing of body, of the soul, of the
mind, of fear and anxiety and doubt; healing of relationships and marriages, of attitudes and problems. Everything.
A healing already accomplished and waiting for those who
come to Jesus, giving themselves to Him and believing Him.

For "with His stripes WE ARE HEALED". Not, "we
will be after death"; "WE ARE HEALED." God gives His
Son to the world to heal the world, to heal even the nations.

During this life on earth, we will only appropriate partially this fullness of life that is ours. That is why we do not
need to fear physical death. For the Christian, that is a release into the total healing of Jesus.

In the diagram opposite, the oval shape represents the
life of a child of God and the solid line, the ideal time for
physical death. God's perfect purpose is for us to manifest
now the wholeness of body, soul and spirit that is available
through the Cross of Christ.

However, none of us does manifest the life of Jesus perfectly. Physical death occurs before that, represented by the
dotted line. Obviously the Lord wants that dotted line to
occur near the solid line, so that as much as possible of the
wholeness He desires for us, is manifested during this life on
earth. It is right, therefore, to come to the Lord with our
healing needs and believe Him to restore us in body, soul
and spirit.

Physical death, for the Christian, is the gateway to resurrection, to the attaining of that full life that is his; the inheritance he has as a child of God. Death becomes the

release into the total healing of Jesus, that he has only appropriated partially in this life.

So the Christian has the best of both worlds! He knows that God has done all that is necessary for his wholeness on the Cross, and desires him to appropriate that healing as

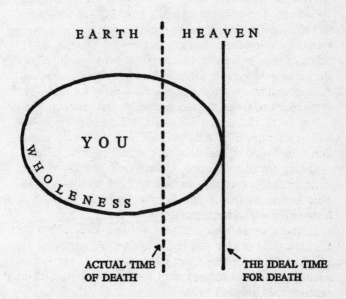

EARTH   HEAVEN

YOU

WHOLENESS

ACTUAL TIME
OF DEATH

THE IDEAL TIME
FOR DEATH

much as possible now. But death is not failure and defeat; rather the means through which he receives what he has not fully appropriated on earth.

That is not an excuse for complacency. This wholeness is available now, because the Cross is an accomplished fact and "with His stripes *we are healed*."

God loves you and wants you to glorify Him by revealing His life, His healing, His wholeness, as fully as possible. He wants you to understand that Jesus took your infirmities and bore your diseases. That you can pray with faith about those healing needs in your life, knowing that the Spirit is leading you towards that perfection that God has planned for you.

Your words of faith: "HE TOOK OUR INFIRMITIES AND BORE OUR DISEASES."

24

Setting Free

From Fear

"A GREAT STORM arose on the sea" as Jesus crossed with His disciples (Matt. 8: 24). In their fear and consternation, they awaken Jesus:

> "Save, Lord; we are perishing." And he said to them, "Why are you afraid, O men of little faith?" (Matt. 8: 25–26).

Faith, as Jesus uses that word, is not only what you believe when you pray. It is an attitude to the whole of your life, to all the problems and difficulties that arise. We all know that there will be plenty of them. Jesus does not promise that our lives will be free of problems; but He promises that as we pray with faith, we will see God overcoming them for us.

Faith reduces the size of the mountains. The bigger God is in our hearts, the smaller the mountain will seem.

The fear of the disciples would have been understandable, but for the fact that Jesus was with them. That same Presence who was with them is IN US, who are filled with the Holy Spirit. So Jesus might well say to us: "Why are you afraid, O men of little faith?"

It is so easy to give in to fears, to believe the situation and momentarily forget the Lord; to forget His Presence, and His words of promise. When we remember that He is with us, we ask Him to forgive our faithlessness. He forgives, and we can begin to face the mountain with a new confidence.

The trouble is that some of the difficulties happen suddenly, unexpectedly, like this great storm. Before you know where you are, they are upon you. It is the storms that show each of us clearly how solidly (or not) our lives are built on Jesus. How much (or little) our faith and trust is in Him. Whether we believe our feelings above His Word, or His Word above our feelings of fear, despair, defeat and failure.

God allows the storms to strengthen the foundation of our lives, to build us in faith – not destroy us. He wants us to believe Him to act in the middle of the storms, as the disciples did. Yet even when our prayer is one of desperation: "Save, Lord, we are perishing!", He will hear us. It is a cry that comes from the heart, and God answers the prayers of His children's hearts. "Then he rose and rebuked the winds and the sea; and there was a great calm" (Matt. 8: 26).

Sometimes you will reckon that you have failed the test when your faith is tried. You can take comfort that Jesus often referred to His disciples as "men of little faith" and yet God used them to perform miracles and to be the foundation of His Church after His Ascension.

On other occasions you will rejoice at the outcome of your faith. Remember, God forgives the failures and deserves the credit for the successes. That faith is the result of the Holy Spirit's work within you. And there will be other trials ahead, when once again your faith can be strengthened because you will need to trust Jesus more completely.

From Bondage

There follows the healing of two demoniacs. The demons are commanded to depart with a simple word of authority: "Go".

> So they came out and went into the swine; and behold, the whole herd rushed down the steep bank into the sea, and perished in the waters (Matt. 8: 32).

This shows the destructive power of these evil forces that afflict the lives of some people. It also shows that God's purpose is to set them free. This is another aspect of the total victory that Jesus has over the powers of the enemy; the victory that is made available to us through the Cross.

To see the almighty power of God at work can be an awesome sight: "When they saw him, they begged him to leave their neighbourhood" (v. 34). But how tragic that fear should prevent so many today from ministering the victory of Jesus to those who are bound and need to be set free.

Praise God for the completed and perfect work of the Cross and for every demonstration of His victorious and liberating power.

From Sin and Sickness

Matthew, chapter 9, opens with the account of the paralytic who is brought to Jesus, "lying on his bed".

And when Jesus SAW THEIR FAITH he said to the paralytic, "Take heart, my son, your sins are forgiven" (v. 2).

Faith is completed only when it results in positive action. That may mean, to pray the prayer of faith, believing God, and waiting faithfully for the fulfilment of the promise. It may mean seeking a time of personal ministry as an occasion when you believe you will receive the answer from Jesus. It may mean some action that God asks of you, a visible evidence of the faith that is within.

It was apparent to Jesus that those who brought the paralytic believed that if they did so, he would be healed. God answers such faith. The men 'knew' that their friend would be healed; that is what Jesus perceived. They were not coming in hope, but with faith.

Jesus tells the man his sins are forgiven. That is the most

crucial and far-reaching act of healing in our lives, restoring us to fellowship with the Father. This underlines the importance of coming to Jesus and giving ourselves wholeheartedly in the healing of our need.

> "But that you may know that the Son of man has authority on earth to forgive sins – he then said to the paralytic – "Rise, take up your bed and go home" 9: 6).

Those watching were questioning Jesus' authority. So Jesus speaks again and heals the man of paralysis. The second word of authority is the evidence of the authenticity of the first. It is one aspect of the healing of the Cross, following upon another. Not forgiveness or healing. Forgiveness AND healing.

> When the crowds saw the man get up and go home, they were afraid, and they glorified God, who had given such authority to men" (Matt. 9: 8).

And this was an authority that Jesus was to give to His followers.

Jesus Answers Faith

In Matthew 9 verse 18, a ruler *comes* to Jesus, saying:

> My daughter has just died; but come and lay your hand on her, and she will live.

That is a statement of faith. A beautiful example of what Jesus teaches about asking: "believe that you have received it, and it will be yours". The child is dead, but the ruler has the faith that if Jesus comes into the situation there is no doubt about the outcome: "she will live"!

Jesus answers the faith that is presented to Him. The centurion believed that Jesus did not even have to come to his house. He only had to speak the word of authority and his servant would be healed. So when He spoke that word, "the servant was healed at that very moment" (Matt. 8: 13).

The ruler's expectation is different: "Come and lay your hand on her, and she will live." That is the faith that is presented to Him, and so that is the faith that Jesus answers. "Jesus rose and followed him, with his disciples" (Matt. 9: 19).

To put it crudely: You get what you expect! That is still true for us today. If we only expect a little, we have no right to be disappointed if we only receive a little. Often we do not aim high enough in our praying, which is an indication that we do not believe 'high enough'.

As Jesus made His way to the ruler's house "a woman who had suffered from a haemorrhage for twelve years came up behind him and touched the fringe of his garment; for she said to herself: If I only touch his garment, I shall be made well" (Matt. 9: 21).

That was the woman's expectancy. That was the faith that she presented to the Lord. There was no 'maybe' about it. "I SHALL BE MADE WELL."

The centurion believed that his faith would be answered by a word of authority from Jesus.

The ruler believed that his faith would be answered by the touch of Jesus' hand.

This woman believed her faith would be answered by touching the clothing of Jesus.

Jesus answers all three methods. Why? Because He is not interested in the method, but answering the faith of each one.

That is God's way with you. He will answer what you believe – always.

Jesus turns to the woman and says to her: "Take heart, daughter, your faith has made you well. Instantly the woman was made well" (Matt. 9: 22).

"Your faith has made you well." That is the power of faith. We are not to have faith in our faith! Our trust is to be in Jesus. The woman had faith, not in herself, not in her own faith, but *in Jesus* to heal her. He is saying to her: "Your faith in me to heal you has made you well."

When Jesus arrives at the ruler's house, He dismisses the mourners and then: "He took her by the hand, and the girl arose" (v. 25). Jesus has answered the faith of the ruler. He has come. He has touched her with His hand. She lives.

It is impossible to have the kind of faith demonstrated by those who came to Jesus, unless you really believe that God wants to heal you, or the one for whom you pray. If there is any doubt about God's will to heal, you cannot pray the prayer of faith. That is why it is so important to understand healing in relation to all that Jesus has already accomplished on the Cross.

Do not be afraid to bring your need to Jesus. Your prayer may be a cry from the heart, a cry of desperation. He will hear you and will answer.

Your coming may be more calculated like that of the centurion, the ruler, or the woman. Jesus will reward your faith and give you what you believe.

He *wants* you to come. He *wants* you to ask. He *wants* to answer. He *wants* to give.

Your words of faith: "TAKE HEART, MY SON; YOUR SINS ARE FORGIVEN." "TAKE HEART, MY DAUGHTER, YOUR FAITH HAS MADE YOU WELL."

25

Do You Believe?

AND AS JESUS passed on from there, two blind men followed him, crying aloud, "Have mercy on us, Son of David" (Matt.9: 27).

The way to approach Jesus is to say: "Have mercy on us". We need to hear His words of forgiveness, before any other word of healing.

We can never come to Jesus deserving to be healed, as if it is our right. True, we come as the new covenant children, knowing the love and faithfulness of our Father. True, we come knowing that every promise of Jesus will be fulfilled, when we believe Him. That still does not mean that we *deserve* to be healed or forgiven. We don't deserve to receive anything from God.

It is only out of His abounding graciousness that He desires to give to His children.

I regularly receive letters from people asking me to pray for their Christian friends or relatives. Many of these letters list the loving qualities of the sick person and hint at the seeming injustice that they should be ill at all, because they are such good people. It is suggested that the Lord surely wants to heal such loving and saintly children.

It is certainly true that God wants to heal His children. But His healing does not come as a reward for our goodness, or love, or saintliness. It comes out of His loving and generous heart and is given to those who *deserve nothing*. Children of God we are, but we still sin. We still disobey. We still grieve our heavenly Father. We still need His forgiveness and His mercy. That is why whenever we are seeking healing for ourselves or others, we do so through the Cross.

The two blind men came to Him and Jesus puts a test question to them: "Do you believe that I am able to do this?" (Matt. 9: 28).

Do you BELIEVE? Jesus is not asking a theoretical or academic question. He is not saying, "Do you believe that it is within my powers to heal you one day?" He does not mean, "Do you believe I can do such things?"

He is saying: "Do you believe me TO DO IT?"

The blind men give a simple answer of faith, "Yes, Lord."

Is it really that simple? Yes, it is – when there is the kind of faith that Jesus talks about.

Testing Questions

Several years ago, when I first began to minister the healing of Jesus to those who came, I learned to ask simple test questions, to draw out people's faith. I might say casually: "It's going to happen, isn't it?" Or, "Jesus is going to heal you, isn't He?"

Usually the answer would be the simple statement of faith; "Yes, He is," or "I believe He is." There would be a calmness and a quiet assurance in the answer. A 'knowing'. The time of preparation (coming to the Cross and 'receiving' the promises) was important to bring people to that point of simple expectancy.

However, on some occasions, instead of a simple statement of faith, there would be a telling pause, followed by such a phrase as: "Well, I hope so!"

Hope is not faith. In such situations faith needs to be ministered to that person, before healing. There is no point in rushing into prayer and "hoping for the best". It is better to encourage the person to face honestly their doubts and bring them to the Cross; to point them to the promises of the Lord and His faithfulness. Some people are healed gradually, and receive ministry on a number of occasions, because God is having to build faith and expectancy all the time.

On a few occasions, in answer to the test question, people have gone into a tirade: "Oh, I believe He is. He really is. Oh, He's given me so much assurance. I have such faith that He is going to do it ..." The longer they go on, the more obvious it becomes that they do not really believe that God is going to heal them. They are trying to encourage faith within themselves. If they believed in the way they professed, the healing would have happened already.

These are usually the most difficult situations to deal with, because the person thinks he believes, when it is apparent that he doesn't. Again, there is no point in rushing into the laying on of hands. Real faith has to be ministered first.

According to Your Faith

The two blind men have that simple, quiet 'knowing' that it will be done. And Jesus "touched their eyes, saying, 'According to your FAITH be it done to you' " (Matt. 9: 29).

According to your FAITH ... He keeps saying the same thing in different ways!

To the Roman centurion Jesus says: "Go; be it done for you, AS YOU HAVE BELIEVED" (Matt. 8: 13).

To the woman with the haemorrhage, Jesus says: "Take heart, daughter; your faith has made you well" (Matt. 9: 22).

To the two blind men, Jesus says: "According to your faith be it done to you" (Matt. 9: 29).

To the Canaanite woman, Jesus says: "O woman great is your faith! Be it done for you as you desire" (Matt. 15: 28).

To blind Bartimaeus, Jesus says: "Go your way, your faith has made you well" (Mark 10: 52).

To the leper who returned to give thanks Jesus says: "Rise and go your way; your faith has made you well" (Luke 17: 19).

Authority

After the incident with the two blind men, a dumb demoniac was *brought* to him. And when the demon had been cast out, the dumb man spoke; and the crowd marvelled, saying, "Never was anything like this seen in Israel" (Matt. 9: 32–33).

When the problem was one of demon possession, Jesus does not elicit faith from the person; He uses His own faith and authority to deal with the matter.

"But the Pharisees said, He casts out demons by the prince of demons" (v. 34). Of course, if you don't want to believe, you won't. Any excuse will do as a justification for unbelief.

Every Disease

And Jesus went about all the cities and villages, teaching in their synagogues and preaching the gospel of the kingdom, and healing every disease and every infirmity (Matt. 9: 35).

"EVERY disease and EVERY infirmity", because he took *all* our infirmities and bore *all* our diseases. Yet Jesus does not separate the healing from His preaching of the kingdom of God. "Seek first his kingdom and his righteousness, and all these things shall be yours as well" (Matt. 6: 33).

If our concern is to seek His Father's kingdom first in our lives and to be in a right relationship with Him, Jesus promises our needs *will* be met. We will not need to be anxious about anything.

Jesus passed on to the disciples not only His commission to preach the Gospel, but also the same authority and power.

And he called to him twelve disciples and gave them authority over unclean spirits, to cast them out, and to heal every disease and every infirmity (Matt. 10: 1).

"EVERY disease and EVERY infirmity!" The authority of this commission to His followers was not for the time of the ministry of Jesus alone, but extended through the apostolic church and the centuries of Christendom until the present day. It extends into the future until Jesus returns, according to His promise, when all the healing of God in the lives of His children will be completed.

Now many signs and wonders were done among the people by the hands of the apostles ... they even carried the sick out into the streets, and laid them on beds and pallets, that as Peter came by at least his shadow might fall on some of them. The people also gathered from the towns around Jerusalem, bringing the sick and those afflicted with unclean spirits and they were healed (Acts 5: 12, 15–16).

Those were days of expectant faith. And whenever among God's people today that same expectant faith re-emerges, the healing power of God is seen at work again. What we are witnessing of the renewing power of God at work within His Church at present is only a beginning compared with what needs to be seen, with what God, our Father, wants for us.

Your Healing

Jesus asks you the same question as He asked the two blind men: "Do you believe I am able to do this?" Answer Him honestly. Where you know there is doubt, be open with God about it. Ask the Holy Spirit to witness the prayer and healing promises of the Lord to your heart. When you *know*

He wants to heal you, pray the prayer of faith and hold on to your Father's promises until your answer has arrived.

Your words of faith: "DO YOU BELIEVE I AM ABLE TO DO THIS?"

26

Hearing With Faith

ST. PAUL ASKS: "Did you receive the Spirit by works of the law, or by hearing with faith?" (Gal. 3: 2). By "hearing with faith", of course!

"Does he who supplies the Spirit to you and works miracles among you do so by works of the law, or by hearing with faith?" (Gal. 3: 5). By "hearing with faith", of course.

It makes no sense to say that the Holy Spirit was only poured out in power upon the Church in the time of the apostles, and that miracles belong only to that period of the Church's history. Paul makes it clear that both were the result of "hearing with faith". An absence of either the Spirit's power or the mighty works of God anywhere in the Church, is evidence, not that God is withholding His Spirit and His works, but that there is no longer "hearing with faith".

With the coming of Jesus Christ and the establishing of the new covenant came the age of the Spirit, the era of faith. *Through faith*, the Galatians received the inheritance of Abraham and could enter into all the old covenant promises. *Through faith* in Jesus Christ they had received the precious gift of the Holy Spirit. *Through faith* they saw God working miracles among them.

And yet Paul cries: "O foolish Galatians! Who has bewitched you?" For having tasted the freedom of the Holy Spirit and His mighty power at work amongst them, they were already returning to their conventional religious attitudes. Paul knew that there could be no more serious deviation from the truth of the Gospel. As soon as the working of Jesus Christ by the power of His Spirit becomes limited by Christian legalism, faith immediately dwindles, and the receiving of all that God wants to give His children, diminishes.

Christian 'Law'

Many church-going people have been brought up with a very legalistic view of Christianity. Traditions are exalted above the Word of God and create the attitude of 'no change' within the life of the Church. The future is to be bound by the law of "what we have done in the past". The mind is exalted above waiting upon the Spirit for His direction concerning the life and affairs of the congregation. It becomes more important to have the right doctrine, than the right life. The Bible is treated as God's Law book.

Many congregations settle into a routine way of life, where the system is perpetuated week by week, month by month, year by year – just as for centuries Israel observed her feasts and did the works of the law.

Where is the vibrant faith of the new covenant? Where are the promises of God being fulfilled among His people? Where does the Holy Spirit have His rightful place of leadership within the Church?

The Spirit is the mighty wind of God that needs to blow freely through the life of His Church and the individual lives of His children. The Spirit is the One who will inspire faith. And yet so often the mind is allowed to stifle the working of the Spirit. That is what happens when people hold on to their conventional, legalistic attitudes, and think more highly of their 'party' attitudes than the Word of God.

Either the Spirit will be allowed to inform the mind; or the mind will stifle the Spirit.

A New Approach

Jesus taught His disciples to approach problems, not with an intellectual appraisal of the situation, but with a spiritual attitude. In other words, not by saying "What can we do here?" but rather, "What can God do?" The feeding of the multitude is a good example.

A great crowd of people had been following Jesus "because they saw the signs which he did on those who were diseased" (John 6: 2). He puts a test question to Philip:

> "How are we to buy bread, so that these people may eat?" This he said to test him, for he himself knew what he would do (John 6: 5–6).

Jesus begins at Philip's level. He knows that the disciple will approach the situation with his mind, rather than with the eyes of faith. It is his faith that is being tested! "Philip answered him, Two hundred denarii would not buy enough bread for each of them to get a little" (v. 7).

That is the answer of the mind; a good, sound, logical appraisal of the situation. Andrew's attitude is similar: "Andrew, Simon Peter's brother, said to him, 'There is a lad here who has five barley loaves and two fish, but what are they among so many?' " (vv. 8–9).

True. But neither statement takes into account that Jesus is at hand!

> Jesus then took the loaves, and when he had given thanks, he distributed them to those who were seated; so also the fish as MUCH AS THEY WANTED (v. 11).

He is the One who can take a paltry, insignificant offering and multiply it, so that it meets not only the *needs* of people but satisfies all they *want*. He told the disciples to gather up all the fragments left over and they filled twelve baskets; one for each of them. No doubt that rubbed the lesson home! From being defeated by the enormity of the task when they approached it with their minds, they now feast on the abundance of what Jesus has provided by the Spirit.

Every Problem is a Spiritual Problem

Jesus approached every situation from a spiritual angle. We often limit the working of God because we consider the problem with our minds, instead of "hearing with faith" what our Father is able to accomplish, through the promises of His Word.

If your Christian life depends upon your rational thinking, then you will limit God to the level of your mind. You make Him smaller than yourself. In truth, He is infinitely greater, and His power is beyond your understanding, beyond anything that your mind can conceive.

You will need to learn to approach each situation, not with the limitation of your mind, but seeing the potential of the Spirit. Often the mind will encourage a negative, defeatist attitude. "This situation is hopeless. So many people to feed. A vast sum of money would be needed – if we had it! All we have is a small boy's picnic. What good is that for all these people?"

The Spirit will encourage faith, believing God to turn the problem into an opportunity to witness His hand at work; to see His glory revealed among His people. The Spirit will declare God's word to you.

No amount of intellectualising will produce a miracle or an answer to prayer.

What is to be the relationship between the mind and Spirit then? *The mind is to be submitted to the Spirit, for the Spirit will enlarge your mind and expand your thinking to include the 'impossible' things of God.*

The Conflict

Paul speaks of the conflict between the Spirit and the 'flesh'. We have been baptised into the death of Jesus; he has taken us to the Cross and we have been crucified with Him, so that we might no longer live as the people we once were, believing our lives to be our own, bound by fear, and sin, full of doubt, unbelief and ignorance of God's love for us and the promises that He wants to fulfil in our lives.

> We know that our old self was crucified with him so that the sinful body might be destroyed, and we might no longer be enslaved to sin (Rom. 6: 6).

That 'old self', the 'flesh', the person you were before you met personally with Jesus Christ, is dead and buried. You are now a new creature, a child of God. Instead of being 'enslaved to sin', you now have Jesus living in you. He is the centre of your new being, of your new life.

The apostle gives three clear directions, to enable people to live freely in the power of the Spirit, to believe and to see the promises of God fulfilled in their lives.

First Direction: "Consider yourselves dead"

> You also must consider yourselves dead to sin and alive to God in Christ Jesus (Rom. 6: 11).

You MUST consider yourselves DEAD to that old life where sin dominated, and ALIVE TO GOD IN CHRIST JESUS. You live in Jesus, because that is where the Father has placed you. In His beloved Son. In the Vine. You are a child of God no longer alienated from Him by your sin, but called, accepted, washed clean by the blood of the Cross. You are a child of the new covenant and all God's promises are your inheritance.

Let not sin therefore reign in your mortal bodies, to make you obey their passions. Do not yield your members to sin as instruments of wickedness, but YIELD YOURSELVES TO GOD as men who have been brought from death to life, and your members to God as instruments of righteousness (Rom. 6: 12–13).

Second Direction: "Yield yourselves to God"

It is not enough to have acknowledged at some point in the past that your life belongs to God. You need to live as someone whose life is 'yielded' to God. This means:
You want His will above your own.
You want to give him glory in every aspect of your life.
You are living to give yourself to Him in praise and worship, and in loving service of others.
You are living to be like him, a 'giving' person.

As you continue to yield yourself to God, to give yourself to Him so you will be able to receive what He desires to give to you. Paul warns: "you are slaves of the one whom you obey, either of sin, which leads to death, or of obedience, which leads to righteousness" (Rom 6: 16).

So don't obey your own selfish desires, your sinful passions. Don't obey your doubts, your fears and feelings of inadequacy. Obey the Spirit, for He speaks faith to you.

But thanks be to God, that you who were once slaves of sin have become obedient from the heart to the standard of teaching to which you were committed (v. 17).

Don't reduce God in size and say: "He can do only what I experience Him doing." He wants your experience raised to the "standard of teaching to which you were committed", to the teaching of His Word by the Holy Spirit, that you might "hear with faith".

"Obedient from the heart" because under the terms of the

new convenant, you now have a 'new heart' with the law of God written upon it. You have a new spirit, with God's Spirit living within you, to cause you to walk in obedience to him.

Third Direction: "Set Your Mind on the Things of the Spirit"

> Those who live according to the flesh set their minds on the things of the flesh, but those who live according to the Spirit set their minds on the things of the Spirit. To set the mind on the flesh is death, but to set the mind on the Spirit is life and peace. For the mind that is set on the flesh is hostile to God; it does not submit to God's law, indeed it cannot; and those who are in the flesh cannot please God (Rom 8: 5–8).

Although you have the Spirit of Jesus living in you, there will be many temptations to return to a life "in the flesh", putting yourself first, believing your fears, doubts and feelings of failure, having a negative attitude to your problems. But Paul reminds you:

> You are not in the flesh, you are in the Spirit, if in fact the Spirit of God dwells in you (Rom. 8: 9).

As you set your mind on the things of the Spirit, your attitude to life will become more positive, because you will learn to look at every situation with the eyes of Jesus, knowing that your Father is prepared to give to you. Your mind will be enlarged by the Spirit to include the impossible!

> For all who are led by the Spirit of God are sons of God. For you did not receive the spirit of slavery to fall back into fear, but you have received the spirit of sonship. When we cry, "Abba! Father!" it is the Spirit himself bearing witness with our spirit that we are

children of God, and if children, then heirs, heirs of God and fellow heirs with Christ, provided we suffer with him in order that we may also be glorified with him (8: 14–17).

To follow the leading of the Spirit is to live as a son of God, His new covenant child. In every situation you can cry 'Father' and know that He hears you; He cares, He loves and He will answer you.

To set your mind on the 'flesh' is to take your eyes off 'Father', the source of life and love, the only one who can meet your needs.

God does not want you to be a 'mindless' Christian, with a non-intellectual approach to your faith in Him. Rather, He wants to fill your mind with His thoughts and rejoice that your intellect has been offered to Him to become a consecrated intellect, understanding more fully the ways of your heavenly Father.

Your words of faith: "THROUGH GOD YOU ARE NO LONGER A SLAVE BUT A SON, AND IF A SON THEN AN HEIR" (Gal. 4: 4–6).

27

In Giving You Receive

"THE MEASURE YOU give will be the measure you get," says Jesus (Matt. 7: 2). That is true of your dealings with God, it is true also of your relationships with other people. "Whatever you wish that men would do to you, do so to them" Matt. 7: 12).

Jesus demonstrated a life of giving; He came to show His Father's desire to give out of His great love for His creation:

> For God so LOVED the world that he GAVE his only Son, that whoever believes in him should not perish but have eternal life (John 3: 16).

Jesus has made you acceptable to the Father, and has filled you with the Holy Spirit. Before you could receive this rich inheritance, you had to come to the Cross and *give* yourself to the Lord. Many people do not have the relationship with God that they desire, because they have not given themselves to God, for that fellowship to be established.

When we give, it is God's way to give back.

> Give and it will be given to you; good measure, pressed down, shaken together, running over, will be put into your lap. For the measure you give will be the measure you get back (Luke 6: 38).

We give God our lives; He gives back His life.
We give God our sin and failure; He gives back forgiveness and peace.

We give God our bodies; He gives back His Holy Spirit and makes those bodies His temples.

That is God's way. Give and He will give.

Jesus teaches that it is important to give to others, if you expect to receive from God. For example, you are to forgive others in order to receive the forgiveness that God wants to give you. "Forgive, and you will be forgiven" (Luke 6: 37). Forgive others FIRST, and then God will forgive you.

We do not mind giving away sin if we obtain forgiveness from God. We do not object to giving Him our fears and anxieties, if He is going to take them away from us. We do not mind being rid of our dirt, if we are going to be made clean as a result. It is one thing to give away what we do not want. It is another to give what is precious or valuable to us. Our minds immediately caution us against giving away what is of value, because to give implies that we are going to lose something.

We want to lose sin and failure; we want to lose fear and anxiety; we want to lose pain and sickness.

We don't want to lose money or property; we don't want to lose time or control of our lives; we don't want to lose our independence.

Jesus teaches us that it is only in losing that we shall gain. That offends our thinking. By choice it would not be our way. *It is God's Way.*

> Whoever would save his life will lose it, and whoever loses his life for my sake will find it. For what will it profit a man, if he gains the whole world and forfeits his life? Or what shall a man give in return for his life?' (Matt. 16: 25–26).

This is God's way – no matter what we think about it. He is saying to us that it is only in giving away that we are going to receive.

Faith is like a two-sided coin. 'Believe' is on one side; 'give' on the other. Put the two together and you have the way open for successful prayer. For time and time again, your faith will be tested by God asking you to give before you receive. Are you prepared to trust Him to fulfil His Word so that you do not end up the loser, but the one who has gained because you have approached the problem, not with your mind controlling events, but according to God's way?

Your mind will tell you that you will lose, that you do not need to give. God tells you that you will receive and that you do need to give. Who are you going to believe?

Sowing and Reaping

The imagery of the sower and the seed is used extensively in the New Testament to teach the importance of giving before expecting to receive. St. Paul says:

> The point is this; he who sows sparingly will also reap sparingly, and he who sows bountifully will also reap bountifully (2 Cor. 9: 6).

A farmer knows that he has to sow seeds before there will be a harvest. He has to give to the soil before he can expect to receive back from it. If he only sows sparsely, he will receive a poor crop. If he sows plenty of seed there will be a much better harvest.

The quality of the seed is also important. If he sows poor quality seed, he will receive a poor quality harvest. If he sows the best, he will receive a harvest rich in quality.

So a farmer will sow plenty of seed of the best quality, and then *expect* his harvest to be good.

God wants each of us to be 'good farmers'. He wants to teach us to give plentifully – of our best. Because this is God's way of working. He kept to it Himself when He sent His Son. He gave of His very best. He gave Himself. He wanted a rich harvest. He gave the best Seed. And Jesus Himself said:

> Truly, truly, I say to you, unless a grain of wheat falls
> into the earth and dies, it remains alone; but if it dies, it
> bears much fruit (John 12: 24).

The Father not only gave the best Seed; that Seed had to
die in order to be fruitful to restore men to God's kingdom.

Only by 'dying' to self will we be able to live for God
and be fruitful in the way that He desires. Only by losing our
lives, do we gain His life and the rich inheritance that He has
for us as His children. The best seed is costly. To sow plentifully is costly. And so our minds say: "Don't do it. You
will lose!"

The Spirit urges us: "Do it. You will gain!" That is why
so many people have a time of great tension and turmoil
before their conversion, or before seeking the release of the
Holy Spirit in their lives.

> Each one must do as he has made up his mind, not
> reluctantly or under compulsion, for God loves a cheer-
> ful giver (2 Cor. 9: 7).

An Abundant Harvest

You have to make up your mind whether you are going to
trust God or your own human thinking. And God does not
want you to give to Him begrudgingly, but out of a heart that
overflows with love for Him and for others. God does not
give begrudgingly to you; He gives out of His love and concern for you. He gives because He wants to provide for you.

> And God is able to provide you with every blessing in
> abundance, so that you may always have enough of
> everything and may provide in abundance for every
> good work (2 Cor. 9: 8).

That is God's way. He wants to provide for YOU in

ABUNDANCE. Not meagrely, not miserly. In ABUN-
DANCE.

Your mind will often tell you that God does not want
to give you, that you are unworthy. If He does give, it will
only be the bare minimum to meet your greatest needs,
to "see you through". God says that He wants to provide
for YOU in ABUNDANCE. Not a little bit of blessing
here and there, occasionally. His Word says: "EVERY
BLESSING – so that YOU may ALWAYS have enough of
everything."

ALWAYS!

ENOUGH OF EVERYTHING!

Somehow we Christians have exalted poverty and depri-
vation. And all the time our God is the God of love, the
ABUNDANT GIVER of EVERY BLESSING, so that we
ALWAYS have enough of EVERYTHING.

Why don't we manifest this abundance? Because it only
happens when we learn to *give* first and *believe* God for the
abundance that He promises.

Not that God wants to provide for self-indulgence. He
will "provide in abundance *for every good work*". He gives
freely and in abundance to us, in order that we may give
freely and in abundance to others.

God's Way

How difficult it is to understand the ways of God with the
mind! The committees of so many churches demonstrate
their lack of faith by approaching their finances like any
worldly organisation. They do not believe God's way; that
you give first, even out of your poverty, and then expect
God to give of His abundance. They think so poorly of such
an idea that many have never done it. They have not walked
by faith. It is unreasonable. Others have, and have witnessed
the faithfulness of God.

> He who supplies seed to the sower and bread for food
> will supply and multiply your resources and increase
> the harvest of your righteousness (2 Cor. 9: 10).

Do you believe this? And believing means that you will
not only hear it, and agree with it, but that *you will act upon
it*.

Paul says that God "will supply and multiply your resources". But first the seed has to be sown, to be given to the
ground. Every seed produces a whole ear of corn, containing
many seeds. That is God's way of taking what is given and
multiplying it back. But not for our own self-indulgence!

> You will be enriched in every way for great generosity,
> which through us will produce great thanksgiving to
> God (v. 11).

The more that God supplies to His children, the more
they have to give to others. And God is prepared to give
EVERY BLESSING IN ABUNDANCE.

He will give His love, that we might overflow with love
and service to others. He will give His power that we might
be instruments through which His power can be ministered
to others. He will even give to us financially so that we will
have plenty to give.

The richer the harvest, the more seed there is to put back
into the ground: to give to God. And He will multiply that
back in even greater abundance, that not only we, but all
who receive through us, will rejoice and be thankful to Him.

> For the rendering of this service not only supplies the
> wants of the saints but also overflows in many thanks-
> givings to God (v. 12).

God will provide many opportunities for you to give,
whether directly to Him, or to others. In giving to others,
you will be giving to Him.

There will be opportunities to love and serve; to give yourself to God in praise; to pray believing prayers for the needs of others; to give to the work of the Gospel; to give to others.

How we respond to such opportunities will be a real test of our faith, especially when we have little time, or ability, or money to offer for the situation placed before us. Paul is writing to the Corinthians about one such situation where they needed to give financially. The principle is the same in every area of our Christian lives; it is in giving that we receive.

> Under the test of this service, you will glorify God of your obedience in acknowledging the gospel of Christ, and by the *generosity* of your contribution for them and for all others (v. 13).

When the angel of the Lord spoke to Cornelius, he said: "Your prayers and your alms have ascended as a memorial before God" (Acts 10: 4). And what harvest did the Lord give back to Cornelius? He sent Peter to his house and the Holy Spirit fell upon all who heard him speak, including Cornelius.

This is not to imply that we can buy blessing from God! As he had been faithful in praying and giving to God, so God was faithful in answering his prayers and giving to him.

The spiritual poverty of many people is shown by a marked unwillingness to give:

Of themselves; "I don't want to get involved."

Of their time; "I'm so busy"

Of their abilities; "I couldn't."

Of their money; "It's all I can afford."

Of their prayer; "I don't seem to get any answers."

Of their worship; "It better be finished within the hour."

People want to receive. Their minds tell them that they ought to receive, that they have the right to receive. And so often they are left wondering why they don't receive.

Like the farmer, when you plant seed you have to wait for the harvest. The crop is not available immediately. And many of the problems are in the time of waiting. It is so easy to give up.

The farmer is expectant. He is always looking for the signs of the coming harvest. As you pray, believing the promises of God, have the same expectancy. Give to the One who will supply all your needs, in the way that you believe He is asking of you. And expect the harvest; keep looking for the signs that the seeds of giving you have planted are being multiplied back to you by your loving Father who teaches you ...

Your words of faith: "GIVE AND IT SHALL BE GIVEN TO YOU; GOOD MEASURE, PRESSED DOWN, SHAKEN TOGETHER, RUNNING OVER, WILL BE PUT INTO YOUR LAP. FOR THE MEASURE YOU GIVE WILL BE THE MEASURE YOU GET BACK."

28

Believing Ground

THE FARMER IS concerned with the quality of the ground as well as the seed he puts into it.

God gives His Word to us as a seed. He wants that Word to produce a rich harvest of His giving to us. The 'soil' quality of our lives will determine how fruitful that Word is.

> A sower went out to sow his seed; and as he sowed, some fell along the path, and was trodden underfoot, and the birds of the air devoured it (Luke 8: 5).

In the interpretation of the parable, Jesus said:

> The ones along the path are those who have heard; then the devil comes and takes away the word from their hearts, that they may not believe and be saved (Luke 8: 12).

Satan is the thief who wants to steal, destroy and kill. He delights in encouraging us to disbelieve the Word. "The ones along the path" are those who do not even begin to believe that God will give to them.

> And some fell on the rocks; and as it grew up, it withered away, because it had no moisture (Luke 8: 6).
> And the ones on the rock are those who, when they hear the word, receive it with joy; but these have no root, they believe for a while and in time of temptation fall away (Luke 8: 13).

There is no depth to their faith. They believe at first, but when the going gets tough they easily give up. They believe their doubts and fears.

Whenever you are believing God for an answer to prayer, the tempter will encourage you to doubt. You will have to use the "shield of faith, with which you can quench all the flaming darts of the evil one" (Eph. 6: 16).

> And some fell among thorns; and the thorns grew with it and choked it (Luke 8: 7).
> And as for what fell among the thorns, they are those who hear, but as they go on their way they are choked by the cares and riches and pleasures of life, and their fruit does not mature (Luke 8: 14).

You cannot isolate your prayers from the rest of your life. Their fruitfulness will depend largely upon the kind of life you are living; whether you live to give to God, or whether you are still living for yourself, "choked by cares and riches and pleasures of life." Whether you only want to receive, or become a generous giver.

It is not only worldliness that 'chokes' the seed; Jesus says it is also choked by 'cares'. By problems, worries, anxiety, fear. All these things are the opposite of faith.

> And some fell into good soil and grew, and yielded a hundredfold (Luke 8: 8).
> And as for that in the good soil, they are those who, hearing the word, hold it fast in an honest and good heart, and bring forth fruit with patience (Luke 8: 15).

The fruitful hearers are the believers. They not only hear the word; they *hold it fast*, no matter what the situation, no matter how many doubts are pushed in their direction. They hold on to the promise of God. They believe Him.

Their believing comes from the heart. And they *bring forth fruit with patience*. They wait for the fulfilment of the promises of God, knowing that He will be faithful.

Differences

There is an interesting difference in the version of the parable given in St. Luke's Gospel, from that in Matthew and Mark. Matthew reads:

> As for what was sown on good soil, this is he who hears the word and understands it; he indeed bears fruit, and yields, in one case a hundredfold, in another sixty, and in another thirty (Matt. 13: 23).

The productivity varies for he who "hears the word *and understands it*". And apparently diminishes. Mark reads:

> But those that were sown upon the good soil are the ones who hear the word and accept it and bear fruit, thirtyfold and sixtyfold and a hundredfold (Mark 4: 20).

The productivity varies for "those who hear the word *and accept it*". And apparently increases. As their acceptance grows, so does the level of fruitfulness in their lives.

In Luke's account those in the good soil are those who "hearing the word, hold it fast in an honest and good heart, and bring forth fruit with patience".

And the only level of productivity mentioned in Luke is "a hundredfold". Those who "hold fast" the word are consistent in their yield, and it is the highest yield. No wonder Jesus said:

> Take heed how you hear; for to him who has will more be given, and from him who has not, even what he thinks that he has will be taken away (Luke 8: 18).

Take heed HOW you hear. Hold the promises fast with an

honest and good heart, before God and man. And see the Lord's harvest in your life.

> You did not choose me, but I chose you and appointed you that you should go and bear fruit and that your fruit should abide; so that WHATEVER you ask the Father in my name, he may give it to you (John 15: 16).

Your words of faith: "HEARING THE WORD, HOLD IT FAST IN AN HONEST AND GOOD HEART, AND BRING FORTH FRUIT WITH PATIENCE."

29

The Heart of the Matter

THE 'GOOD SOIL' in which God plants His seed, consists of those who "hearing the word, hold it fast in an honest and good *heart*, and bring forth fruit with patience". There is much in the teaching of Jesus about 'the heart', which has an important bearing on the fruitfulness of our prayers. He said:

> No good tree bears bad fruit, nor again does a bad tree bear good fruit; for each tree is known by its own fruit (Luke 6: 43–44).

If you want to see good fruit, you need to be concerned with the health of the tree. It is no use looking for the best quality fruit on a tree that is bad. The tree, Jesus says, is the heart.

> The good man *out of the good treasure of his heart* produces good, and the evil man out of his evil treasure produces evil; for out of the abundance of the heart his mouth speaks (v. 45).

Our Father wants us to have loving, obedient hearts. Jesus continued: 'Why do you call me Lord, Lord, and not do what I tell you?" (v. 46).

Love Involves Obedience

> If I have all faith, so as to remove mountains, but have not love, I am nothing. If I give away all that I have . . . but have not love, I gain nothing (1 Cor. 13: 2–3).

Without love, our believing and giving will come to nothing. Paul is not putting alternatives before us: either you love, or you believe and give. We are to love and believe and give. Believing and giving that is without love will 'gain nothing', it will not result in receiving.

"If you love me", Jesus said, "you will keep my commandments" (John 14: 15); you will be obedient to me.

> If you keep my commandments, you will abide in my love, just as I have kept my Father's commandments and abide in His love (John 15: 10).

Jesus prayed within a relationship of loving obedience to His Father, knowing that His Father would hear and answer Him. That love was manifested in the way in which He gave Himself to others. So John says:

> Beloved, let us love one another; for love is of God, and he who loves is born of God and knows God. He who does not love does not know God, for God is love. (I John 4: 7–8).
> If we love one another, God abides in us and his love is perfected in us (4: 12).

God has put His resources of love within us, by the power of His Holy Spirit. It is no use having His love, unless we allow it to be released in our lives; unless we give it to others.

Living Water

> Jesus stood up and proclaimed, "If any one thirst, let him come to me and drink. He who believes in me, as the scripture has said, 'Out of his heart shall flow rivers of living water.' " Now this he said about the Spirit, which those who believe in him were to receive (John 7: 37–39).

God wants the river of His love to flow out from our hearts, from the depths within us, expressed in our giving to one another.

God wants the river of praise and worship to flow from deep within us. That may be a quietly flowing river; it may be a noisy, rushing river. But God wants it to be a *full* river, expressing our love for Him.

God wants the river of joy to flow from within us, even in the most trying circumstances, because we know the love, the care and the faithfulness of our Father.

God wants the river of peace to flow from deep within us, so that we do not become anxious and fearful, but trust Him and rest in Him.

God wants the river of power to flow from within us, into every situation; so that we are not overcome and defeated but learn to use His resources.

God wants the river of faith to flow from our hearts, believing Him to act generously in His love.

God wants the river of healing to flow from the depths of our being, making us whole in body, mind and spirit.

God wants all these rivers of life to flow from within us, out of us and all around us, so that others become influenced by:

> the love of God within us;
> the praise of God on our lips;
> the joy of God in our hearts;
> the peace of God in our souls;
> the power of God in our praying;
> the faith of God in our attitudes;
> the healing of God as we forgive and reach out to others with His love.

These "rivers of living water" are the Spirit at work within us. They flow from the heart. God is not concerned about our doctrines of the Holy Spirit; He wants to see the reality of those "rivers of living water" in our loving, our praise and worship, our joyful hearts, our peace, our powerful praying, our faithful attitudes, our whole and healthy lives and our generous giving. God does not want us to 'possess' those rivers. He wants them continually flowing out from within us. He wants to see the love flowing by our obedience to Him and our service to others. He wants to see the faith causing us to "hold fast" to the words and promises of God "in an honest and good heart".

Faith with love!

Love with faith!

Selfishness can stop the flowing out of love to others. Resentment, bitterness, pride, jealousy all have the same effect. And when one river becomes blocked, the flow of the others can easily be disrupted. That is why Jesus said:

> And whenever you stand praying, forgive, if you have anything against anyone; so that your Father also who is in heaven may forgive you your trespasses (Mark 11: 25).

Our ability to pray with faith and see God answering is hampered by wrong relationships with others.

> If you are offering your gift at the altar, and there remember that your brother has something against you, leave your gift there before the altar and go; first be reconciled to your brother, and then come and offer your gift (Matt. 5: 23–24).

It is not easy to feel full of faith:

> if you know that you are being unloving to someone.
> if there is little praise in your heart for God;
> if there is little joy within you;
> if there is anxiety instead of peace;
> if there is doubt instead of trust in God's power.

You do not pray in a vacuum. That prayer comes out of

the person you are and the relationships you have with God and with others. That does not mean that you should stop praying because you feel empty or inadequate. When you know faith is lacking, ask God to show you what is blocking the flow of the "rivers of living water" from out of your heart.

He may point to any one of many reasons; a bad relationship, unloving attitudes, selfishness, lack of praise, anxiety, lack of giving or one of many others. It is things like these that the Lord often sorts out during the time of 'waiting' for a prayer promise to be fulfilled.

Like me, you would probably like 'rockets' every time you prayed. Often the 'tortoises' are far more valuable, not only because God builds faith in us as we continue to trust Him, but also because He uses the opportunity to sort out many things in our lives.

People are complex, and one problem can easily affect so many others in our lives. It is generally accepted that a high proportion of physical disorders are caused by mental stress of one kind or another. It is certainly true that spiritual sickness can prevent our receiving physical and emotional healing. That is why every time we come to the Lord wanting to receive, we need to be prepared to give first. Give the sin, the failure, the doubt, the emptiness, the tension, the anxiety, the troubled relationships, as well as the positive offering of ourselves.

God does not demand that we reach a stage of spiritual perfection before He gives to us; He does require us to be open and honest with Him, letting Him forgive and put right what is wrong. He accepts us as we are and changes us into what He wants us to be.

Unbelief is the cause of many prayers seeming to be powerless and unfruitful. Lack of love for God or others has a similar effect. God always wants to get to the heart of the matter. And that often means our own hearts.

What comes out of a man is what defiles a man. For

from within, *out of the heart of man*, come evil thoughts, fornication, theft, murder, adultery, coveting, wickedness, deceit, licentiousness, envy, slander, pride, foolishness. All these evil things come from within, and they defile a man (Mark 7: 20–23).

That list contains things that are obviously evil and others that are socially more acceptable, but still 'defile' us and therefore the power of our believing and praying.

Compare that list with what Paul calls the fruit of the Spirit: "love, joy, peace, patience, kindness, goodness, faithfulness, gentleness, self-control." These are the qualities that God wants to produce in our lives, that He wants to see flowing out of our hearts. Fruit grows, and this particular fruit only grows through the work of the Holy Spirit within God's children.

Keep your new covenant heart pure before God, so that the flow of the rivers of living water remain unhindered. Then God will produce in you the fruit He desires to see, above all the love and faith that are outworking of His Spirit within you. Come back to the Cross again and again, tasting the love, mercy and forgiveness of your gracious Father. Know that it is He who will supply you with the grace to reach out to others in love, service, compassion, giving yourself willingly and joyfully for the delight of pleasing Him and furthering the work of His kingdom here on earth.

Your words of faith: "IF WE LOVE ONE ANOTHER, GOD ABIDES IN US AND HIS LOVE IS PERFECTED IN US."

30
Praise

TO BE FILLED with the Spirit is to be filled with praise for God. For praise is one of those "rivers of living water" that flows out of your heart.

David

Asking with faith will take place within the context of praise. David says:

> Bless the Lord, O my soul; and all that is within me, bless his holy name! Bless the Lord, O my soul, and forget not all his benefits, who forgives all your iniquity, who heals all your diseases, who redeems your life from the Pit, who crowns you with steadfast love and mercy, who satisfies you with good as long as you live (Ps. 103: 1–5).

David knew that the Lord whom he was blessing, or praising, was the God who was active in his life. He was not worshipping a remote being unidentified with his needs. Everything within him cried out in praise to the living God, because he knew the Lord's forgiveness and healing; His love, mercy and redemption; and His eternal goodness towards His children.

David knew, not only God's love for him, but for all His people. He tells *you* to praise God and be mindful of all His blessings, because:

> He forgives all *your* iniquity;

He heals all *your* diseases;
He redeems *your* life from the Pit, from the deepest darkness;
He crowns *you* with His perfect love and mercy;
He satisfies *you* with good as long as you live!

David didn't speak such words lightly. He knew what it was to be afflicted, persecuted, oppressed, hemmed in on all sides by his enemies; to feel separated from God, as if His prayers were not being answered. And what is his response in such circumstances? To PRAISE God.

I will bless the Lord at all times; his praise shall continually be in my mouth. My soul makes its boast in the Lord; let the afflicted hear and be glad. O magnify the Lord with me, and let us exalt his name together (Ps. 34: 1–3).

Again, he does not speak only of his own practice. From his experience of how God works he calls upon the 'afflicted', those in trouble, to join with him in praise: "O magnify the Lord with me, and let us exalt his name together." For he knows that God answers prayer; he sets His people free from fear and saves them from all trouble.

I sought the Lord, and he answered me, and delivered me from all my fears. Look to him, and be radiant; so your faces shall never be ashamed The poor man cried, and the Lord heard him, and saved him out of all his troubles (Ps. 34: 4–6).

David knew what 'affliction' was all about; his life was full of it. He also knew the faithfulness of his God: "Many are the afflictions of the righteous; but the Lord delivers him out of them all" (v. 19).

This is a statement of faith, based upon his own experience of clinging to the Word of his God, even when all the circumstances around him seemed to point to disaster. Psalm 71 will serve as a good example:

> In thee, O Lord, do I take refuge; let me never be put to shame!
> In thy righteousness deliver me and rescue me; incline thy ear to me, and save me!
> Be thou to me a rock of refuge, a strong fortress, to save me, for thou art my rock and my fortress.
> Rescue me, O my God, from the hand of the wicked, from the grasp of the unjust and cruel man.
> For thou, O Lord, art my hope, my trust, O Lord, from my youth.
> Upon thee I have leaned from birth; thou art he who took me from my mother's womb.
> My praise is continually of thee (Ps. 71: 1–6).

Asking and praising go together for David. He is not afraid to lean on God, to come to Him and declare openly and honestly his need. He does not look at the situation as hopeless, because he knows the power and faithfulness of God. He does not listen to the doubts that are fired at him, but knows the Lord to be his trust.

> My enemies speak concerning me, those who watch for my life consult together and say, "God has forsaken him; pursue and seize him, for there is none to deliver him" (vv. 10–11).

David's answer is: "But I will hope continually, and will praise thee yet more and more" (v. 14). God has not lost control of his life. David belongs to Him. "Thou who hast made me see many sore troubles wilt revive me again" (v. 20). And the Psalm ends on a note of triumph:

> I will also praise thee with the harp for thy faithfulness, O my God;

I will sing praises to thee with the lyre, O Holy One of
Israel.
My lips will shout for joy, when I sing praises to thee;
my soul also which thou hast rescued.
And my tongue will talk of thy righteous help all the
day long, for they have been put to shame and disgrace
who sought to do me hurt (vv. 22–24).

Those are words of faith, for they show that David believed the victory that had not yet happened! He was praying, believing that he had received it and knowing that it
would be his. So praise fills his heart, for he knows that God
will act to save him from his enemies.

The Psalms are rich in inspiration for faith. They do not
hide us from the deep yearnings of the heart, or the most
impossible of situations; and yet they are shot through with
praise for the faithful God of steadfast love.

David faithfully prays in the way that Jesus was to instruct his disciples centuries later. He addresses the 'mountains':

Depart from me, all you workers of evil; for the Lord
has heard the sound of my weeping. The Lord has
heard my supplication; the Lord accepts my prayer. All
my enemies shall be ashamed and sorely troubled; they
shall turn back, and be put to shame in a moment
(Ps. 6: 8–10).

Why could David be so certain, when circumstances
seemed to contradict such optimistic faith? Because GOD
HAD MADE A COVENANT with him.

The steadfast love of the Lord is from everlasting to
everlasting upon those who fear him, and his righteousness to children's children, to those who keep his covenant and remember to do his commandments (Ps.
103: 17–18).

He is mindful of his covenant for ever, of the word that he commanded, for a thousand generations (Ps. 105: 8).

And David remembered the covenant promises that he had been given by God. The Lord said:

I will not remove from him my steadfast love, or be false to my faithfulness. I will not violate my covenant or alter the word that went forth from my lips (Ps. 89: 33–34).

We are the new covenant children of God. He will be faithful to every promise that He has given us by Jesus. He will not violate the covenant that is in His blood. He will not alter one word spoken by His Son. So we can have boldness and confidence when we approach our Father, knowing that it is His purpose to answer us, to heal us and deliver us, to honour the word of Jesus: "If you ask anything in my name, I will do it."

We can come with praise for God, knowing that He will be faithful and true to His Word, that His love for us will never fail.

The Early Church

The church in Jerusalem, newly filled with the Holy Spirit, came together daily "praising God and having favour with all the people". It was at that time that "many wonders and signs were done through the apostles" (See Acts 2: 43–47). Faith led to the release of God's power among them.

And his name, by faith in his name, has made this man strong whom you see and know; and the faith which is through Jesus has given the man this perfect health in the presence of you all (Acts 3: 16).

Even in prison Paul and Silas "were praying and singing hymns to God". And what was the outcome of the combination of prayer and praise?

> And suddenly there was a great earthquake, so that the foundations of the prison were shaken; and immediately all the doors were open and everyone's fetters were unfastened (Acts 16: 26).

When you pray, ask with praise and thanksgiving because all your needs have already been met in Jesus. Paul begins his great passage in Ephesians, chapter 1, with the words:

> Blessed be the God and Father of our Lord Jesus Christ, who has blessed us in Christ with every spiritual blessing in the heavenly places (v. 3).

He *has* blessed us. As we come to our Father in faith, so we appropriate what He has already made available to us through His precious Son, who "by the power at work within us is able to do far more abundantly than all that we ask or think" (Eph. 3: 20).

Many Christians have discovered that praising God is not simply singing hymns or psalms with the mouth. That is an activity that goes on in many church buildings, without ever reaching the heights of real praise.

Praise starts deep within us. When filled with the Holy Spirit, people experience the praise that flows from the heart and lifts them into the company of the heavenly host that surrounds the throne of God with ceaseless praise.

> Through him (Jesus) then let us continually offer up a sacrifice of praise to God, that is, the fruit of those who acknowledge his name (Heb. 13: 15).

No matter what the situation, the flow of praise in our lives needs to be continuous, because God is always worthy of praise. When we come to Him to ask anything, we come to the one who deserves to be praised, worshipped and adored. And if we love Him that will be our joy.

Some people say that they feel hypocritical if they praise or worship God, without "feeling like it". This is to suggest that He should only be praised when we have the right feelings. That is obviously not right, for although feelings can easily change from one moment to the next, God does not change. Jesus is the same "yesterday, today and forever".

God the Father and God the Son are always worthy of praise in the power of God, the Holy Spirit.

The Value of Tongues

It is the Holy Spirit that comes to your aid when you feel unable to praise. You can use the prayer language, or tongue, that the Spirit gives you. As you allow the Spirit to pray in you and through you in this way, He will turn your attention to the Lord. When you begin to pray you may feel sorry for yourself, but in a few minutes you will be filled with the awe and wonder of knowing that you are before the throne of God in praise.

It is the language of praise because it is the language of the Spirit. Because you do understand the words you speak "in a tongue" it is easy to belittle this gift.

No gift of God should be under-rated. Paul valued it greatly. "I want you all to speak in tongues", he tells the Corinthians (I Cor. 14: 5); "I thank God that I speak in tongues more than you all" (v. 18). However, he was con-ᴄerned to teach them the proper use of this gift, *in public*, "So, my brethren, earnestly desire to prophesy, and do not forbid speaking in tongues" (v. 39). During the course of public worship, prophesy is the better gift to use because that is God speaking to His people in their native language that can readily be understood by all.

However, Paul does not denigrate the gift of tongues. Far

from it; he values it highly and obviously used it extensively in his personal prayer and praise. "I will pray with the spirit and I will pray with the mind also; I will sing with the spirit and I will sing with the mind also" (vv. 13–15).

Give Yourself in Praise

We cannot talk of praying with faith without seeing all that God has made available to us for this purpose. We can praise Him with both mind and spirit. And praise builds faith because it directs our attention away from the 'mountains' and on to the One who has the power to move them. It releases His power into the situation, where before there may only have been fear or despair.

Many people who seek healing, go from one healing service to another hoping to receive their answer. Their need can easily claim their whole attention. Whenever they pray, much of the time is spent dwelling upon their own problem.

I have known many people to receive their healing, when they least expect it. While attending an act of worship where the people have been free to express their praise for God "in the Spirit", they have been caught up in the praise and have forgotten all about their needs. They have simply given themselves in worship to the Lord, whose Presence is so real. Then they discover that the healing has taken place, without anyone praying for them or ministering to them.

"It is more blessed to give than to receive," Jesus said. In giving you receive. Praise is giving to God the love and adoration of our hearts, no matter what our feelings or the circumstances in which we find ourselves. And He gives His Presence to us. "Pray at all times in the Spirit, with all prayer and supplication" (Eph. 6: 18).

Paul spoke of the importance of rejoicing, praising and thanking the Lord, no matter what the circumstances. "Rejoice always, pray constantly, give thanks in all circumstances; for this is the will of God in Christ Jesus for you"

(1 Thess. 5: 16–18). "Rejoice in the Lord always; again I will say, Rejoice" (Phil. 4: 4).

There will be many occasions when you won't feel like rejoicing. The last thing in the world you will want to do is praise the Lord. Those are occasions when you need to praise Him. That may require a big effort; you really have to make yourself sometimes. But it will never cease to amaze me how praise transforms a situation. The mountains look smaller! And God seems so much bigger!

Jude sums up much of what we have discovered about praying the prayer of faith:

> You beloved, build yourselves up on your most holy faith; pray in the Holy Spirit; keep yourselves in the love of God; wait for the mercy of our Lord Jesus Christ unto eternal life (Jude 20–21).

These verses bring together the words 'faith', 'pray', 'Holy Spirit', 'love', 'wait', and 'mercy'.

By His Holy Spirit, God wants to encourage faith within you. He wants to teach you to pray with faith, believing His promises. He wants that faith and prayer to come from a heart that is full of love and praise for Him. He wants you to learn to wait patiently until you see the fulfilment of the promise, that God has indeed had mercy upon you as the child He loves.

Your words of faith: "BLESS THE LORD, O MY SOUL AND ALL THAT IS WITHIN ME BLESS HIS HOLY NAME."

31

In Great Adversity

COUNT IT ALL joy, my brethren, when you meet various trials, for you know that the testing of your faith produces steadfastness. And let steadfastness have its full effect, that you may be perfect and complete, lacking in nothing (James 1: 2–4).

It is not easy to greet trials and difficulties with a sense of joy. You are more likely to feel angry, bitter and resentful, even towards God for allowing such trials in your life. Yet James knows that God lets these things happen so that our faith may be built up and made steadfast, dependable – like the love God has for us. Discovering that love in the midst of adversity is one of the greatest of human needs. The prophet, Habakkuk, demonstrates his faith in the face of great adversity:

Though the fig tree do not blossom, nor fruit be on the vines, the produce of the olive fail and the fields yield no food, the flock be cut off from the fold and there be no herd in the stalls, yet I will rejoice in the Lord, I will joy in the God of my salvation. God, the Lord, is my strength; he makes my feet like hinds' feet, he makes me tread upon my high places (Hab. 3: 17–19).

God is *your* Father, no matter how bad things are.

Jesus is *your* Saviour, no matter how desperate they appear.

The Holy Spirit fills *your* life and you can never be separated from the presence of God *within* you, even in the most dire situation.

As a new covenant child of God, He is your Father, your Saviour, your Counsellor and your Lord.

> The steadfast love of the Lord never ceases, his mercies never come to an end; they are new every morning; great is thy faithfulness. "The Lord is my portion," says my soul, "therefore I will hope in him." The Lord is good to those who wait for him, to the soul that seeks him (Lam. 3: 22–25).

Job

Satan was given leave by God to test the faith of Job, who is described as "a blameless and upright man, who fears God and turns away from evil" (1: 8). He lost his cattle, sheep, camels, servants and even his children. Yet "in all this Job did not sin or charge God with wrong" (1: 22).

Then Job was subjected to intense physical suffering, but still he "did not sin with his lips" (2: 10). Three friends came to "comfort" him. "They sat with him on the ground seven days and seven nights, and no one spoke a word to him, for they saw that his suffering was very great" (2: 13). They then proceeded to give him chapter after chapter of good advice.

This servant of God was on the receiving end of a three-fold battering.

1. He suffered because of what Satan did to him, his possessions and loved ones.

2. He suffered the criticism of his friends, who told him that he must be to blame for all that had befallen him.

3. He suffered as a result of his own fear: "For the thing that I fear comes upon me, and what I dread befalls me." He had been expecting trouble and he got it!

God does not promise us a life free from affliction and trial; but in Jesus, He has given us the victory over all the works of Satan. The Lord will never forsake the man whose trust is in Him.

Job was no longer able to trust in his wealth, the love of his children or the useless advice of his friends. His faith had to be in God alone. He said to the Lord: "I know that thou canst do all things, and that no purpose of thine can be thwarted" (44: 2).

And God proved faithful to His Servant. "And the Lord restored the fortunes of Job, when he had prayed for his friends; and the Lord gave Job twice as much as he had before,' (42: 10).

Even in his deprivation and loss, Job gave first by praying for his friends, useless though they had been with all their advice. And then God gave to him, "twice as much as he had before."

During a time of intense difficulty and stress it is not easy to hang on in faith. It seems that one's cries of desperation go unheard by God. There are friends with advice, but with no power to change the circumstances. And yet our covenant God is not deaf or blind to our needs.

Joseph

Joseph had two dreams, which clearly indicated that he would "have dominion over" his eleven brothers, all older than himself. Everything that happened to Joseph from that moment seemed to indicate the opposite. The older brothers decided first to kill him and then to sell him. Hardly a fulfilment of the promise given to Joseph in his dream!

He is taken to far away Egypt where he is sold as a servant, and thrown into prison on a false charge laid against him by his master's wife. Is that the fulfilment of the promise? It seems that the God of justice has deserted him, has forgotten him altogether. Is he to believe the circumstances, or the dream he has been given?

How do you hold on with faith, when you feel as if you

have been thrown into a deep pit, or treated unjustly by people, when you feel imprisoned by your situation? Joseph had to battle through all the adverse circumstances before he saw the promise fulfilled.

The Spirit's Prayer

When the going is tough and we find it really difficult to see how God is going to break through the problem, "the Spirit helps us in our weakness; for we do not know how to pray as we ought" (Rom. 8: 26).

The Spirit wants the Father's victory in every situation. There are times when we do not know what to pray with the mind. We will need to pray "with the Spirit", using the tongue, or language that God makes available to us. Through this gift the Spirit inspires the right words for the occasion, even though you cannot understand them. The answer to the need is beyond your understanding. No problem, however, is beyond the comprehension of the Holy Spirit, and He will pray the right words through you. Having prayed in tongues, you then pray again in your native language, asking God for the interpretation to the prayer that the Spirit has given you. In this way your mind is informed by the Spirit and becomes 'fruitful'. You know what to pray for more clearly; you understand the situation better.

If you have been filled with the Holy Spirit, the gift of 'tongues' is one of the resources that God has made available to you. Don't waste it, for every gift of the Holy Spirit is precious.

Even when you think your mind fully understands the situation, it is good to use the Spirit's language also. For God's wisdom is infinitely greater than yours; the Spirit always knows what to pray. Paul says:

I will pray with the spirit and I will pray with the mind

also; I will sing with the spirit and I will sing with the mind also (1 Cor. 14: 15).

Not the spirit *or* the mind; the spirit *and* the mind. "Pray at all times in the Spirit, with all prayer and supplication" (Eph. 6: 18).

Groans

There are occasions when "the Spirit himself intercedes for us with sighs too deep for words". In the depths of our despair He prays for us, not only from heaven, but in us. The Holy Spirit wants to direct us to the Father, to His love, to his promises and to inspire faith within us that, no matter how black the situation, God will honour His Word as we put our trust and confidence in Him.

> We know that in everything God works for good with those who love him, who are called according to his purpose (Rom. 8: 28).

There will be many situations in which you cannot understand the purpose of God; you cannot see why He should have allowed that particular problem to arise.

As you continue to look to Him, to set your mind on the things of the Spirit, to allow the Spirit to pray in you and through you and for you, to hold on to promises of your faithful Father, you will see His hand at work resolving the needs and giving understanding of His purpose.

> He who did not spare his own Son but gave him up for us all, will he not also give us all things with him? (Rom. 8: 32).

It does not matter what the situation.

In all these things we are more than conquerors

through him who loved us. For I am sure that neither death, nor life, nor angels, nor principalities, nor things present, nor things to come ... will be able to separate us from the love of God in Christ Jesus our Lord (Rom. 8: 37–39).

And that love is the Love that gives, the Love that cares, the Love that heals, the Love that will meet us where it hurts, where the need is.

Whenever the going is tough, it is hard to believe, to hold on to the promises. Remember, nothing can separate YOU from the love of God in Christ Jesus your Lord. NOTHING! "Nor things present, nor things to come." NOTHING!

When God speaks He does not fail to keep His Word. Joseph was vindicated, rose in the nation to be second only to the Pharaoh himself, and during the time of famine received his brothers, who bowed before him and begged to be allowed to buy food. As with Job, the Lord turned His adversity to great blessings and riches.

God is going to take you through your problem, to His rich purpose beyond.

Your words of faith: "THE STEADFAST LOVE OF THE LORD NEVER CEASES, HIS MERCIES NEVER COME TO AN END."

32

The Household of Faith

GOD INTENDS HIS children to be one. Loving one another. Encouraging one another. Bearing one another's burdens. Rejoicing together. Weeping together. Jesus prayed for all those who would come to believe in Him, "that they may become perfectly one, so that the world may know that thou hast sent me and hast loved them, even as thou hast loved me" (John 17: 23).

The very evidence of that love, will not be in our sermons or doctrines, but in the quality of our life together that is demonstrated to the world, in two ways in particular; the way we love one another, and the way that we believe together for God to answer our prayers.

The evidence of the Father's love for Jesus was seen in their loving relationship and in the way that the Father honoured the words and prayers of His Son, performing His works through Him. No one man will reflect the perfect love and power of Jesus. Those who believe in Him are incorporated in the Body of Christ. It is through that Body that the love, life and power of the Lord are to be ministered to the world.

The unity of life among Christians is stressed time and again in scripture. As members of the Body of Christ we are "members one of another". We "belong to each other". We are "one person in Christ Jesus". We are "branches" of the Vine, so that the sap of God's Spirit can flow from branch to branch and cause us to be fruitful.

Believing Together

It is not surprising, therefore that Jesus spoke about praying together in faith:

> Again I say to you, if two of you agree on earth about ANYTHING they ask, it WILL BE DONE FOR THEM by my Father in heaven (Matt. 18: 19).

There is that word again: 'ANYTHING'! Not 'some things' or a 'few things' or even 'many things', ANYTHING!

Jesus does not mean if any two of you agree the same verbal prayer, or form of words. It is not the words that matter, but the belief in the hearts of those who are praying.

He does not mean someone praying and everybody else saying 'Amen' at the end. There may be no 'agreeing' or unity of faith on occasions.

Jesus does mean that if any two of you agree to pray "in my name"; that you agree to pray as if Jesus Himself is asking, with His faith and His expectancy, believing that you have received it. Then "it will be done for them by my Father in heaven".

There can be great value in praying the prayer of faith with others who will believe with you until you see the promise fulfilled. Together you can reject the doubts when they assail you, and refuse to believe the circumstances against the promises of your loving and faithful Father. Believing together.

"For where two or three gathered in my name, there am I in the midst of them" (Matt 18: 20). If you are gathered "in my name", Jesus is present to pray along with you, and you with Him. His Presence can inspire faith and expectancy in your hearts, as you look together with Him to your Father. You are agreeing with Jesus in this prayer. AND HE IS AGREEING WITH YOU.

Talk Together

Again it needs to be emphasised how important it can be for Christians, whether praying in two's and three's or in larger groups, to talk together first before they pray; talk about what they believe God will do in answer to their prayer. Discover what their faith and expectancy is, or needs to be.

Perhaps this will mean that the members of the group will need to minister to one another. Perhaps some will have to confess doubt and bring that to the Lord. He does not condemn us for our doubts. What matters to Him above all else, is that we are prepared to be open and honest with Him.

Obviously within the context of a large number of people praying (a whole congregation, for example) it is not always possible to do this before praying. But faith of the kind that Jesus talks about, should never be assumed by those who are responsible for the leading of worship or the conducting of large prayer meetings. A very short time of teaching should be possible on some occasions, reminding people that they are children of the new covenant, looking to their Father to honour His promises. And a short time can be spent in which those present can silently bring their fears, anxieties and doubts to the Lord before the prayer of faith is prayed together.

Some will need to be assured that any doubts that may be afflicting them will not 'spoil' the prayer. Jesus says: 'if TWO of you agree . . .", not a whole congregation! The more positive the faith, the greater the power there will be in the praying capacity of that body of people.

Learning to pray with faith can best be done in small groups, meeting in the informality of a home. It is there that you will feel more relaxed and able to share your fears and doubts, your problems and needs. It is within such groups that you can best learn to 'receive' the promises (see chapter 10). It is there that you can best learn to pray the prayer of faith with one another and for one another, as well as for others outside the group. Instead of praying and "hoping for the best", you can begin to believe together and be an encouragement to one answer during the time of 'waiting' for the 'tortoise' answers.

Answers

Whether in the congregation or prayer group, large or small, formal or informal, encourage one another by sharing week by week the answers received through prayer. As the faith of the congregation or group grows, so there will be more and greater answers to give thanks for. That faith will depend upon the openness of the congregation or group to the faith-inspiring work of the Holy Spirit, for it is His ministry to witness the words and promises of Jesus to our hearts.

But answered prayer also encourages faith. As we see God is faithful in honouring even our 'little faith', we learn to trust Him for bigger and greater things. You even learn to trust Him for your own needs. These answers to prayer are also a witness to others. They testify to the fact that God really does love His people and care about them by meeting their needs.

When there is 'Jesus faith' in a congregation, it will not be possible to announce the answer to every prayer. A selection will need to be made, not only of great miracles, but also of the answers to everyday needs. These will be an encouragement to those starting out on the way of faith. They will understand that God is concerned about everyday problems and situations; He does not only deal in mighty miracles! Extravagant claims on the one hand, and pettiness on the other should be avoided.

There does not need to be a prolonged time of personal testimony. The leader can simply give thanks to God for the answers received, giving only brief details, when that is more appropriate. And remember 'tortoise' answers are just as important as 'rockets' and will be an encouragement to others who are waiting.

The Ministering Body

> Is any one among you suffering? Let him pray.
> Is any cheerful? Let him sing praises.
> Is any among you sick? Let him call for the elders of the church, and let them pray over him anointing him with oil in the name of the Lord; and the PRAYER OF FAITH WILL SAVE THE SICK MAN, and the Lord will raise him up; and if he has committed sins, he will be forgiven.
> Therefore confess your sins to one another, and pray for one another, that you may be healed.
> The prayer of a righteous man has great power in its effects (James 5: 13–16).

Those who suffer are to pray – with faith, of course, as Jesus teaches. Those who are cheerful are to sing praises.

The sick are to ask for ministry that they may be healed – not given piles of good advice and loads of sympathy. The prayer of faith will save the sick man from the disease that afflicts him. The Lord will raise him from his bed of sickness.

James gives us a good picture of the "household of faith" in action, praying with one another, ministering in faith to each other. A praising people. Openly and honestly confessing their faults to one another, and knowing the forgiveness of God.

No wonder we find the going tough if we try to "go it alone". God has provided for us a fellowship of believers, that together we may come to the Lord and see the fulfilment of His Promises. The sad thing is that this picture of the praying, believing, ministering church is so different from what is often found today.

Congregations often pray for the sick, but do not necessarily understand what it is to pray the prayer of faith that will heal the sick man. Some are not aware of the resources of the Holy Spirit that are available to them, to enable them to pray effectively.

Sick people often battle alone and do not call for the elders. Perhaps they do not believe anything would happen if they did. Perhaps the elders would not know what to do if they were called.

We need not despair! God has not given up on His Church, and He never will. If there is not 'faith-full' fellowship to support you in your local congregation, hold on to the last part of this passage: "The prayer of a righteous man has great power in its effects."

The Healing Sacrament

Why should there be so much sickness among Christian people? Paul gives the Corinthians an answer: because they do not believe the power of Jesus in the healing sacrament of His Body and Blood, the 'Holy Communion' or 'Eucharist' (the 'Thanksgiving').

> For anyone who eats and drinks without discerning the body eats and drinks judgment upon himself. That is why many of you are weak and ill, and some have died (1 Cor. 11: 29–30).

They were not believing the words: "This is my body which is given for you." "This cup is the new covenant in my blood."

If they had believed them, they would have come properly prepared and not with the casual approach they obviously had. So Paul warns them:

Whoever therefore, eats the bread or drinks the cup of the Lord in an unworthy manner will be guilty of profaning the body of the Lord. Let a man examine himself, and so eat of the bread and drink of the cup (1 Cor. 11: 27–28).

The sacrament was not a piece of magic that would automatically solve their problems and meet their needs. It was to be approached with faith.

In the sacrament of Holy Communion we have the opportunity of 'discern' the body and blood of the Lord. If it is regarded simply as a memorial of a past event, it will seem lifeless and powerless. If people believe that in some mystical way Jesus is conveying His Presence to His children, then it is the opportunity for them to believe that they will receive the healing and life that they need in response to their prayers of faith.

The Eucharist can be for you a meeting with the Lord. It is the opportunity for you to offer yourself to Him afresh. (The Offertory always precedes the sharing of the bread and wine; the giving before the receiving!) It is the ideal time to pray your prayer of faith, and let it be sealed with the "new covenant in my blood."

It is the occasion when you not only come to Jesus, but He comes and gives Himself afresh to you, in the way you need to receive Him, to bring His life into your need.

In times of sickness, when it is extremely difficult to pray, the sacramental acts of the laying on of hands, of anointing, and of the Holy Communion are God's provision, through the ministry of His Body, for your needs. Make full use of them, for God has much to give you through them.

Your words of faith: "IF TWO OF YOU AGREE ON EARTH ABOUT ANYTHING THEY ASK, IT WILL BE DONE FOR THEM BY MY FATHER IN HEAVEN."

33

Exciting Future

ALL OF US have to face the future; it is better to do so with trust in Jesus' words, than be the victim of your own fears and doubts. Faith is believing a Lord that you do not see, trusting Him to accomplish things that are as yet unseen.

> Now faith is the assurance of things hoped for, the conviction of things not seen (Heb. 11: 1).

The 'assurance' of things hoped for. When you pray, you want God to do what you ask. That is your hope. Hope becomes faith when you have that assurance in your heart that God will do it. Because:

You are His new covenant child;

He loves you and wants to give to you;

He will keep His promises;

He will be glorified in answering your prayers;

He wants your "joy to be full".

Faith is "the conviction of things not seen", the certainty in your heart that, although at the time of praying you cannot see the answer, yet with the eyes of faith you do see it. It will happen. God will do it.

Jesus said to Thomas:

> Have you believed because you have seen me? Blessed are those who have not seen and yet believe (John 20: 29).

I have not pretended that it is always easy to walk by faith; but it is exciting.

Often you will feel that God is asking you to step out of the boat on to the water. As you keep your trust in Him, it will be as rock beneath your feet. James says: "Faith by itself, if it has no works, is dead." Those are the works of faith that he is speaking of.

Like Noah, Abraham, Moses and all the men of faith in the Bible, the Lord will ask you to do things that will test, stretch and strengthen your faith. As a new covenant child, you are pledged to obedience to the Lord. It will not only be your faith that is tested, but your obedience too. And that means God is seeing whether you really love him.

The flood only came after Noah had built the ark in faith.

Abraham did not receive his inheritance until he had obeyed God and left his homeland.

Naaman, the commander of the Syrian army, was not healed of his leprosy until he had obediently washed seven times in the river Jordan.

Elijah challenged the prophets of Baal to the contest on Mount Carmel because he trusted the Lord's word to him that He would send rain.

Shadrach, Meshach and Abednego asserted positively, "our God is able to deliver us from the burning fiery furnace" before Nebuchadnezzar had them thrown into the flames.

Jesus told the ten lepers to go and show themselves to the priests; and they were healed as they obeyed His instruction.

The blind man in John, Chapter 9, did not receive his sight until he had gone and washed in the pool of Siloam, in obedience to Jesus.

And so on. The examples of faith are innumerable in the Bible. But there are these common features; the men of faith listened to the words of God and of His Son and obeyed them. They put their trust and confidence in Him rather than believe the circumstances, which were often desperate.

It is that walk of faith to which Jesus calls you. He will not test you beyond your capacity to believe. Yet He wants to show you how much more you can see of Him at work in your life when you exercise fully that faith He has already given you.

Often you will want to sit back and suggest to the Lord that He works the whole situation out for you. And just as often He will show you that the problems will only be resolved when you step out in faith first, obeying what He says and proving what you are truly believing Him to do.

Ahead of You

Yes, many exciting times lay ahead of you as you pray the prayer of faith. Many testing times. Many wonderful times, as you see the faithfulness of your Father.

There will be some failures – whenever you fail to trust and believe; whenever you stop giving and lapse back into only wanting to receive; whenever you allow sin and disobedience to spoil your relationship with God; whenever you fail to forgive others.

God will even use those failures. I thank Him that He allows me to fail whenever I put my trust in myself, rather than in Him. My failures indicate my need to be more generous and full of faith in my giving. I thank Him because he can use the opportunity to point out some area of disobedience in my life, or something that is not completely yielded to Him; or that there is something that needs to be put right with someone.

God does not answer the prayers only of the spiritual giants, but of ordinary folk like us. Those who are prepared to give themselves to Him and live for Him.

If you have not yet done the exercise outlined in Chapter 8, turn back and read it again. Give everything to God and you can then be confident and expectant that He will give everything to you.

Faith in the person of Jesus to heal and meet needs was high during His lifetime. It would be easy for us to say that the level of faith is not so high today, and that is why we do not see so many instantaneous miracles. There is truth in this, borne out by the number of people that are instantly healed at services where their faith in Jesus to act immediately, has been quickened.

I could have included many accounts of actual healings and answers to prayer, many of them instantaneous. I have not done so for two reasons. First, not everybody receives instant answers and the 'tortoises' are as important as the 'rockets'. Secondly, the illustrations of the teaching in this book need to come from your own life. They need to be the answers God gives *you* to *your* prayers.

Write and tell me about them; they will encourage me. Answers always do.

What I have written here I try to live out myself, and could tell you of many wonderful gifts received from my Father, some big things, many smaller ones. But I won't.

What I will share with you is the agony that I sometimes experience, holding on to the promises when nothing appears to be happening, when everything appears to be going wrong. Its an agony you often can't share with others; but it goes on deep inside you.

Yet there is always the thrill of the Spirit of God declaring those words of Jesus to my heart, in the face of all the difficulties. We'll share them together once more:

> Whatever you ask in my name, I WILL DO IT, that the Father may be glorified in the Son (John 14: 13).
> If you ask anything in my name, I WILL DO IT (John 14: 14).
> If you abide in me, and my words abide in you, ask whatever you will, and IT SHALL BE DONE FOR YOU (John 15: 7).
> Truly, truly, I say to you, if you ask anything of the Father, HE WILL GIVE IT TO YOU in my name (John 16: 23).
> Ask, and YOU WILL RECEIVE, that your joy may be full (John 16: 24).

Whatever you ask in prayer, believe that you have received it, and IT WILL BE YOURS (Mark 11: 24).

Ask, and IT WILL BE GIVEN YOU (Matt. 7: 7).

Again I say to you, if two of you agree on earth about anything they ask, IT WILL BE DONE for them by my Father in heaven (Matt. 18: 19).

Whatever you ask in prayer, YOU WILL RECEIVE, if you have faith (Matt. 21: 22).

There can be no doubt that it is God's purpose to give you whatever you ask in faith. IT WILL BE DONE. IT WILL BE GIVEN. Over and over again Jesus repeats the same promise.

Praise God for all the instantaneous answers to prayer. Praise Him for all those that involve faithful, patient enduring until the promise is received.

And once again we need to affirm positively that Jesus is talking about 'anything' or 'whatever' we ask:

WHATEVER you ask in my name . . . (John 14: 13).

If you ask ANYTHING . . . (John 14: 14).

. . . ask WHATEVER YOU WILL . . . (John 15: 7).

. . . if you ask anything of the Father . . . (John 16: 23).

WHATEVER you ask in prayer . . . (Mark 11: 24).

. . . if two of you agree on earth about ANYTHING they ask . . . (Matt. 18: 19).

WHATEVER you ask in prayer . . . (Matt. 21: 22).

Jesus promises the answer to ALL your prayers of faith. Every one!

I said just now that the answers to prayer encourage me, and so they do. But I have to honestly say that the promises of Jesus encourage me more. For there is always more to receive from our Father. And that means more opportunities to give first and have my faith deepened, stretched, extended. To see those promises more completely fulfilled in my life.

Use This Book

Now that you have read this book, go back over it again and again. Spend time on each chapter absorbing the teaching and receiving the words of faith so that they become part of you. And put those words to work in your asking prayer.

If you have found it helpful, give this book to others. There are many people around you who need God to answer them; other Christian friends, those you meet at church, your neighbours, at work and at home.

That word 'give' will be very important to you as you learn to pray with faith. Use every opportunity to give and expect God to give back to you "good measure, pressed down, shaken together, running over".

Seek first his kingdom and his righteousness, and all these things will be yours as well (Matt. 6: 33).

It's staggering, but its true. God loves you and wants to give you His best. "If YOU ask anything in my name, I will do it" (John 14: 14).

Yes, YOU!

Your words of faith: "SEEK FIRST HIS KINGDOM AND HIS RIGHTEOUSNESS. AND ALL THESE THINGS SHALL BE YOURS AS WELL."

Appendix: Your Words of Faith

1. "If you ask anything in my name, I will do it."
2. "He did all that the Lord commanded him."
3. "Is anything too hard for the Lord?"
4. "I will be your God and you shall be my people."
5. "You are a God ready to forgive, gracious and merciful, slow to anger and abounding in steadfast love."
6. "A new heart I will give you and a new Spirit I will put within you."
7. "I have been crucified with Christ."
8. "It is no longer I who live, but Christ who lives in me."
9. "I will put my Spirit within you, and you shall live."
10. "Heaven and earth will pass away, but my words will not pass away."
11. "My words . . . are life to he who finds them and healing to all his flesh."
12. "You are precious in my eyes, and honoured, and I love you."
13. "If you abide in me, and my words abide in you, ask whatever you will and it shall be done for you."
14. "You did not choose me, but I chose you and appointed you that you should go and bear fruit and that your fruit should abide; so that whatever you ask the Father in my name he may give it to you."
15. "Have faith in God."
16. "Nothing will be impossible for you."
17. "Whatever you ask in prayer, believe that you have received it, and it will be yours."
18. "It will be yours." "It will be given you." "It will be done for you."
19. "Whatever you ask in my name, I will do it."
20. "Ask, and you will receive, that your joy may be full."
21. "Your Father knows what you need before you ask him."
22. "Go; be it done for you as you have believed."
23. "He took our infirmities and bore our diseases."

24. "Take heart, my son; your sins are forgiven you." "Take heart, daughter; your faith has made you well."
25. "Do you believe I am able to do this?"
26. "Through God you are no longer a slave but a son, and if a son then an heir."
27. "Give and it shall be given to you; good measure, pressed down, shaken together, running over, will be put into your lap. For the measure you give will be the measure you get back."
28. "Hearing the word, hold it fast in an honest and good heart, and bring forth fruit with patience."
29. "If we love one another, God abides in us and his love is perfected in us."
30. "Bless the Lord, O my soul, and all that is within me bless his holy name."
31. "The steadfast love of the Lord never ceases, his mercies never come to an end."
32. "If two of you agree on earth about anything they ask, it will be done for them by my Father in heaven."
33. "Seek first his kingdom and his righteousness, and all these things shall be yours as well."

THE POSITIVE KINGDOM

The Positive Kingdom

Colin Urquhart

HODDER AND STOUGHTON
LONDON SYDNEY AUCKLAND

The Positive Kingdom

Copyright © 1985 by Colin Urquhart

First published as a single volume 1985 by Hodder and Stoughton.

The right of Colin Urquart to be identified as the author of this
work has been asserted by him in accordance with the Copyright,
Designs and Patents Act 1988.

For all those who feel they
have little or no hope; that
they may come to know the
power of the Positive
Kingdom in their lives.

Acknowledgments

My thanks to all those who have helped with the preparation of this book – those with whom I share in the life of the Positive Kingdom. Principally that means my wife, Caroline, who is such an encouragement to me in my ministry; and my children, Claire, Clive and Andrea, who are greatly used by the Lord to remind me that Kingdom living has to be an earthly business! My thanks to all the members of my household and of the Bethany Fellowship, especially to Annette, for all her typing, and to Barbara.

Contents

Chapter 1

OUR POSITIVE GOD

Jesus came to give you a Kingdom! A Kingdom with resources far beyond those of any earthly kingdom. An eternal Kingdom. If you receive the gift of this Kingdom now, you can reign with Him for all eternity.

Great claims! But then Jesus makes staggering promises to those who believe in Him. It is God's intention for you to possess the Kingdom of heaven now. Yet many Christians have gained the impression, or have even been taught, that this Kingdom can be entered only beyond death, and that there is always an element of uncertainty as to whether they will actually be accepted by God.

Our Heavenly Father intends us to know we have received the Kingdom as a gift from Him, not because we deserve such generosity, or are able to make ourselves worthy of such a gift, but because He is the God of grace; He gives His everything although we deserve nothing.

The phrases 'Kingdom of heaven' and 'Kingdom of God' are used interchangeably in the New Testament. The Kingdom of God is the Kingdom of heaven; the Kingdom of heaven is the Kingdom of God.

He wants you to know you have received His gift and He wants to teach you how to live in the power of His Kingdom; to be a Kingdom child living His Kingdom life, filled with His Kingdom power, using His Kingdom authority, drawing constantly on His Kingdom resources by exercising Kingdom faith.

How can these things be a practical reality for you? First, realise that the Kingdom reflects the nature of the King.

There is a principle that runs through several areas of our experience. The life of a nation reflects the nature of the government of that nation. It may have a democratically elected government or be a totalitarian state. In either case the policies and decisions of government will be worked out in the life of the nation.

The same principle applies in business. The policy decisions of management are worked out on the shop-floor and in the marketing of the product. In a school, the nature of the headship will determine the whole ethos of the institution, its discipline, priorities and objectives. In the home the leadership of the parents, and particularly the father, will be reflected in the whole family. The children are the product of the kind of headship that is exercised over them.

Any congregation or fellowship reflects the nature of the spiritual and pastoral leadership given by those in authority. You may find individual believers blessed or anointed by God beyond anything experienced by their leaders. Nevertheless, the congregation as a whole cannot grow beyond the example given by those in leadership; the people can only go where they are led.

The principle, then, is clear. Those in authority have a profound effect on those over whom they have authority.

This is supremely true of God's Kingdom: *the Kingdom of heaven reflects the nature of the King of heaven*. So if we want to know what kind of a Kingdom God offers us, we need to see what kind of a God He is.

THE KING

Everything about God is positive. There are no negatives in Him.

God is holy. He is whole, complete and perfect in Himself. He is above and beyond all He has made. Something of His beauty and majesty can be seen in His creation and yet He is far greater than creation, remembering that this planet is only a minute part of all He has made.

God is righteous. He is right in all He does. It is His nature to be right and He cannot deny Himself. He is the absolute standard by which everything and everyone is judged. Whatever He does is right by definition. Whatever opposes Him or His ways is unrighteous.

God is just. Again it is by His standards that true justice is to be assessed. He has never acted unjustly towards anyone. It is in His justice that He declares that sinners are worthy of death, eternal condemnation and separation from Him – a godless eternity. That is not what He wants for His people, but it is what they deserve, because the unholy and the unrighteous cannot be made one with the Holy and Righteous, unless they are first cleansed of their ungodliness. Equally, it is in justice that He declares sinners 'not guilty' when they ask for His forgiveness. Jesus carried their guilt to the cross, and paid the price for their sins with His own death.

God is love. In His love He sends His Son to live a godly life among men, and to offer His sinless life as a sacrifice on behalf of all sinners. God's love does not change with emotion like human love; it is steadfast, sure and dependable. It is a love that must be given, shared and communicated to those He loves. It is a love that knows no limits.

God is gracious. If He dealt with people as they deserved, He would wipe them off the face of the earth. Instead He offers them His Kingdom. In His grace He is willing to give His riches to those who deserve nothing.

God is almighty. He has demonstrated His almightiness in creation. Nothing is impossible for Him. Through Jesus, He has shown He has the power over sin, sickness and even death. He is the God who raises up nations and has the power to cause them to fall. He is working His purpose out and there is nothing able to prevent the fulfilment of His plans.

God is life. He alone could give life to man at a natural level.

He alone can impart His own supernatural life, the gift of eternal life. He sent His Son that men might receive that life in all its fullness.

God is joy. When the Father speaks of His own Son, He declares: 'God, your God, has set you above your companions by anointing you with the oil of joy.' (Heb. 1: 9) He causes heaven to rejoice over all sinners who repent. The words Jesus gives His disciples makes their joy full and complete, and God's purpose for us is to rejoice in Him always.

God is peace. Jesus gave His peace to His disciples before His crucifixion, and greeted them with His peace when He appeared to them in His risen body. His peace is a positive gift such as the world is unable to give, a peace that is beyond understanding or description. The peace of God is not simply the absence of war, noise or anxiety. It comes from having a sense of well-being with God, even in the midst of turmoil and difficulties.

God is the provider. Again and again He assures His people of His willingness to meet their every need, if they remain faithful and obedient to Him. Jesus gives a series of startling prayer promises, indicating it is His Father's purpose to give His people anything they ask in His name. In His love He *wants* to give to His children and provide for them.

God is the healer. Throughout His earthly ministry Jesus demonstrated His Father's desire to heal. He had not come to do His own thing, but to perform the will of His Father who sent Him. He said He could do nothing Himself; He did only what He saw His Father doing. Clearly then it is God's desire to bring healing, in the fullest sense of that word, into the lives of His people.

God is truth. There is nothing false about God. The words He speaks both through the prophets in the Old Testament and His Son in the New, prove to be true because they have their source in the one who will not deceive. Jesus proclaims that He is the truth and His Spirit, given to those who believe in Him, will guide them into all truth.

God is faithful. He is always reliable and dependable, and so are His words. He abides by the promises He gives. Even when His children prove unfaithful to Him, He remains faithful to them.

This is only a partial list of God's attributes, but enough to show that everything about Him is positive. He is holy, righteous, just, loving, gracious, almighty, life-giving, joyful, peace, the Provider, the Healer, the truth, the faithful one.

Above all *God is our Father.* He reveals Himself to His people as having personality, and demonstrates that He wants them to have a personal relationship with Him. He sends His Son to die on the cross to make such a relationship possible.

We are not to judge the fatherhood of God by our experience of human fathers. Even the best human father would only be a poor reflection of God as Father. All human fatherhood is to be seen in relationship to Him, not the other way round. He is the perfect Father and the Scriptures reveal Him as the holy Father, the righteous Father and the loving Father who is not afraid to discipline His children.

God is our Saviour. Without His atoning work on the cross it would not be possible for sinful men to be reconciled with the sinless God. Because He is the Saviour He sends His Son to perform that work of salvation whereby we may be justified, or made acceptable to God, and able to receive the gift of His Kingdom.

Everything He is and everything He does is positive. Even the wrath of God is positive: God dealing positively with those who positively need to be dealt with! He is the Judge whose judgments are always just.

Because it reflects the nature of the King, the Kingdom is holy, righteous and just; a Kingdom of love and power. Those who belong to it experience not only these qualities of God's life, but also His grace, joy and peace. They can receive His promises and healing and know their lives are led by the God who is both truthful and faithful. He is their Father, who by

His own initiative has given them salvation and the gift of eternal life.

Everything about the King is positive; therefore everything about His Kingdom is positive.

Chapter 2

THE NEGATIVE WORLD

It is immediately obvious that we live in a world in which we encounter many negatives. We can see why Jesus said: 'My kingdom is not of this world.' (John 18: 36) He came from the Father to bring His positive Kingdom into this negative world. This at once raises the question which has plagued mankind: 'Why does the negative exist if God is positive and His Kingdom positive?'

We must understand that there are two spiritual kingdoms – not one. There is the Kingdom of God or the Kingdom of heaven, which is the Kingdom of light. There is also the dominion of Satan, the kingdom of darkness, where everything is negative.

Just as the Kingdom of God reflects the nature of the one who rules over it, so does the dominion of darkness.

Satan was once the archangel Lucifer enjoying the glory of God's heavenly Kingdom. He became discontent leading others to worship God and decided it was time he was worshipped himself. He wanted to be as God instead of honouring Him.

His rebellion against the Lord led to his immediate dismissal from heaven, along with the angels who followed him. Jesus said: 'I saw Satan fall like lightning from heaven.' (Luke 10: 18) He no longer has access to heaven; but ever since his fall has done all he can to incite others to rebel against God.

Jesus describes him as the thief who comes only to steal, kill and destroy. He is a liar from the beginning, the father of all lies, the deceiver. He is the tempter who even tried to tempt Jesus in the wilderness. He is God's enemy, and ours too! What a contrast to the Positive God!

Everything about Satan is negative and he wants to create the negative in people's lives.

He was once holy and righteous, but now constantly tempts people to be unholy and unrighteous. He loves to cause injustice, hatred, sickness and poverty. His tactics vary. He encourages some to believe they are in his power; he persuades others not to believe in him at all. Supremely, he wants to encourage people to worship him by practising black magic and witchcraft.

When we are born into this world we belong to the kingdom of this world. Because of our fallen nature, we belong to the kingdom of darkness, not the Kingdom of light. Like Satan, we instinctively want our own way. Through our sin and disobedience we rebel against God. We are full of unbelief and are often the victims of fear and sickness. Many are soon caught, even at an early age, in a web of lies, intrigue and deception.

The majority of people do not know God in a loving, personal relationship, and many even deny His existence. Relatively few truly desire His will for their lives.

It is Satan's ultimate deception to encourage people to believe that everyone will go to heaven in the end, regardless of their religious beliefs or practices. If they doubt the reality of his existence, they will question the existence of hell or the possibility of a Godless eternity.

The evidence of the negative in the world around us is too obvious to need much comment. But does God intend people to live their lives dominated by negative spiritual forces and experiences?

GOD'S ANSWER

The gospel of Jesus Christ is good news. It is obvious from His teaching that God desires to free people from the negative. He came and 'rescued us from the dominion of darkness and brought us into the kingdom of the Son he loves'. (Col. 1: 13)

For God to free His people from rebellion, sin and disobedience, a rescue act was needed. He wanted to free them from fear and want, from sickness and poverty. He wanted to give them life – His life in all its fullness, positive life. Instead of deception He wanted to see the hearts and lives of His people full of truth and love. He wanted a people who knew His love, experienced His joy, enjoyed His peace and depended on His faithfulness.

God sent Jesus to save His people: save them from the dominion of darkness; save them from sin, fear and unbelief; save them from condemnation to a Godless eternity, the judgment hanging over all who do not belong to the Kingdom of heaven. To save them, then, from hell and restore to them the gift of eternal life.

Anyone is lost until he sees the need of a Saviour, someone to rescue him from himself and to give him a Kingdom, not only as a future hope, but as a present reality.

The opening words of Jesus's ministry were a brief command and mighty promise from God: 'Repent, for the kingdom of heaven is near.' (Matt. 4: 17)

With the coming of the Son of God from heaven the Kingdom of heaven was now brought within the reach of men; it was 'at hand'. Until then it could only have been a future hope, a possibility. Now it became actual in the lives of those who repented, who turned their lives over to Jesus, recognising His sovereign reign and rule in their lives.

That act of repentance had to be coupled with faith in Him: 'The kingdom of God is near. Repent and believe the good news!' (Mark 1: 15) Men's lives need no longer be dominated by the negative. Satan need no longer be their master. The prince of this world may have dominated their lives in the past, but having submitted their lives to the King of heaven they can know and experience the glorious liberty of the sons of God. The prince of this world stands condemned. He can no longer usurp the rightful place of God in the life of anyone who submits to Jesus, the King of heaven and earth.

Later Jesus was to unfold a simple but astonishing truth to the disciples: 'Do not be afraid, little flock, for your Father has been pleased to give you the kingdom.' (Luke 12: 32)

That is the truth, amazing as it may seem. The Father sent His Son so that all who received Him and believed in Him would be given the Kingdom of God. Jesus came so believers could receive the Kingdom now and thereby receive all that is positive. He made it possible for their negative lives to be transformed into positive ones.

There was no way that they, or anybody else, could deserve to receive such a gift from God, no way in which they could earn entrance into His Kingdom. It is only by the grace and mercy of the God of love that a person can be given such an inheritance.

If we try to see the situation from God's perspective we shall gain some insight into His purpose. He had created man in His own image, to be like Him. The human race was to reflect His nature, character and personality. In the story of Adam and Eve we see what God wanted: men and women living in close union and fellowship with Him and with one another; sinless, innocent, with provision made for all their needs.

Everything in their lives was positive. But along comes Satan with his negative temptation. First Eve, and then Adam, are tempted to disobey God, to deny the word He had spoken to them. When they lose their innocence by yielding to temptation, they want to hide from God and from one another. The beauty of their fellowship is shattered. Now they are sinners, have to work to survive and are excluded from the garden paradise.

Sin has entered their lives. The negative has infected what before was completely positive. Now the image of God in them is marred.

None of this caught the Lord by surprise. He knew it would happen, would even be inevitable, if He was to create a creature with free-will, the freedom to love or hate, obey or disobey. Now He sees His people pursuing their own ways instead of His, intent on fulfilling their own lusts and desires, infected through and through with the rebellion of Satan. Their lives become confused by the introduction of so many negative elements. Now they curse and blaspheme; they are full of selfishness and pride. They create their own false gods to worship and their hatred leads them to destroy one another.

GOD'S OWN PEOPLE
Among all this confusion God is determined to have a people for Himself, a holy people who will reflect His own holiness, who will love Him and worship only Him, who will be loyal and obedient to Him, fulfilling the commandments He gives them. He chooses the Israelites to be such a people. He reveals His almightiness and love by delivering them from the oppression of their Egyptian overlords. Through Moses He gives them the commandments they are to obey and the promises He will fulfil whenever they prove obedient.

Again and again, He sees His people turning away from Him whenever they prosper, and seeking Him only when their plight is desperate. He has those who remain faithful, the prophets who address the mass of the people, calling them to repentance and warning them of the consequences if they fail to do so. Time and again His spokesmen are ignored and the people persist in their rebellion and disobedience.

Before the creation of the world, God had determined what He would do. There was no alternative but to become man Himself. He would take human flesh as Jesus Christ, the Son of God. The Word that had been spoken for centuries from heaven would now dwell among men, so that all could hear His voice clearly.

God the Father sends His Son to rescue His people from all the effects of the negative, from sin, fear, unbelief and sickness. He sees that many refuse to hear Him, especially the religious ones – those intent on serving God by obeying their traditions, those with the outward form of religion but lacking the inner reality of a living relationship with God. He sees their opposition, fear and determination to do away with His Son.

On the other hand, God sees many recognising their need of a saviour and turning to Him for forgiveness, deliverance and healing. He watches over His Son as He proclaims the good news that He has been sent by His Father with the gift of God's Kingdom. He sees some believing, while others use their free-will to pursue their own ways.

The Father sees His Son gather around Him a group of disciples, who can be taught the principles of the Kingdom and how to live as those who receive divine authority from heaven. His Son performs the works of the Kingdom among the people, healing the sick, raising the dead, cleansing lepers, casting out demons and performing many miraculous signs.

However, Jesus has to do more than speak about the Kingdom and demonstrate its imminence with His presence in the world; He has to do what is necessary to make it possible for sinners to be received into the Kingdom. His mission would have been a failure if He had demonstrated an unattainable Kingdom to the people. They had to understand that God was prepared to forgive them for all the ways in which they had been negative, under the dominance of the prince of this world, and that He was willing to pour His own positive life into them. They needed a Saviour!

Chapter 3

THE CROSS

The cross was a necessity to enable sinners to enter and possess the Kingdom of God. There Jesus offered to the Father His holy life on behalf of all those tainted by unholiness, His righteous life for all who had lived in unrighteousness or self-righteousness, believing they could make themselves acceptable to God. It was on the cross that Jesus gave His perfect life for the imperfect, His sinless life for sinners. He gave to the Father the one, complete sacrifice that was necessary to satisfy the just demands of the Holy, Righteous and Loving Judge. The Sinless One had to die for sinners. His life-blood had to be poured out in sacrifice that they might be able to receive God's life.

The Father led His own Son to that cross because of His love for the world. He watches over the agony of decision in the Garden of Gethsemane, over the harsh and rude repudiation of His divinity in His rejection, beatings and mock crowning. He sees the desolation of the cross when His Son hangs in pain, so totally identified with the depravity of sinful humanity that He cries out, 'My God, my God, why have you forsaken me?' (Mark 15: 34)

When Jesus went to the cross, He took all the negatives that men experience so that they may be delivered from them. He took all their sins; He carried their sicknesses, spiritual, emotional and physical. He took their conflicts and all that make them lose peace with God, with one another and with themselves. He suffered rejection from the religious authorities, from the state, from the people and even His own disciples, so that we might be freed from every experience of rejection.

'Surely he took up our infirmities and carried our sorrows, yet we considered him stricken by God, smitten by him, and afflicted. But he was pierced for our transgressions, he was crushed for our iniquities; the punishment that brought us peace was upon him, and by his wounds we are healed.' (Isa. 53: 4–5) He even suffered the punishment that we deserve so that we do not have to suffer it.

What a God of love, mercy and grace! He deals with all the negatives to make us able to receive His positive life.

He raises His Son, demonstrating that His Kingdom is eternal and victorious over death. During the forty days of His resurrection appearances to His disciples, He continues to teach them about the Kingdom. Then the Father receives Him back into the glory of that Kingdom so that, as the sacrificial Lamb slain for His people, He could reign with Him for all eternity. 'Worthy is the Lamb, who was slain, to receive power and wealth and wisdom and strength and honour and glory and praise!' (Rev. 5: 12)

This is victory indeed. Now to every man there is a sacrifice available, able to cleanse him from his sins and make him acceptable to God. Now there can be freedom from the negative for all who come to the cross and put their faith in Jesus and what He has accomplished for them. Now the way is cleared for people to receive the gift of the positive Kingdom that Jesus makes available.

NEW BIRTH

It is inconceivable to some that God should simply *give* them an eternal Kingdom. If God is so great, so much higher and more holy than men, then surely they should work hard with every part of their being to make themselves acceptable to Him? Surely they have to earn the right to participate in God's Kingdom? Does not Jesus teach that a man will be judged by the works he has done?

Such attitudes are the result of pride, not of humility. What can anyone do to atone for his own sins? How can a sinner make himself acceptable in the sight of the holy God, no matter how many good deeds he claims?

Certainly church membership does not make a man acceptable to God; neither can his religious opinions, attitudes or works justify him. It is only the work of Jesus Himself, the Saviour, that can undo his sinfulness and make the repentant sinner a saint – someone whose life is made holy in God's sight, someone set apart for His glory, someone who becomes a child of God's Kingdom.

It was to Nicodemus, a Pharisee, a man brought up in strict religious traditions, to whom Jesus said: 'I tell you the truth, unless a man is born again, he cannot see the kingdom of God.' (John 3: 3)

He uses the phrase 'I tell you the truth' when He knows that what He is about to say will be met with unbelief; it will be hard to hear and receive such revelation. To be part of this Kingdom a man *must* be born again. There can be no compromise on that statement of truth. To Jesus it is a fact and the matter is not open to debate.

The only people (whether they go to church or not) who do not like talk of being born again are those who have never experienced a second birth. It is only the unconverted man who feels resentful when challenged as to whether he has been converted or born again!

Jesus explains: 'Flesh gives birth to flesh, but the Spirit gives birth to spirit.' (John 3: 6) When each of us is born into the world, we are born in flesh. Our birth is the result of a physical relationship between a man and woman. We are born with a fallen sinful nature, will inevitably sin, displease God and need a Saviour.

When we are cleansed from our sins through that perfect, sinless sacrifice of Jesus on the cross then, and only then, can we be 'born from above' and experience a personal relationship with God whereby we know Him intimately as

'Father'.

This second birth is the result of the activity of God's own Holy Spirit bringing to life the human spirit of the repentant sinner. He is then born of the Spirit. Jesus emphasises the point: 'I tell you the truth, unless a man is born of water and the Spirit, he cannot enter the kingdom of God.' (John 3: 5)

Baptism in water signifies that a man has come to personal repentance, acknowledging Jesus as his Saviour, and a personal faith in Him, submitting to Him as the Lord of his life. Baptism is not a magical formula that brings a person into the Kingdom of God apart from repentance and faith. Rather, it signifies that the sinner has taken off his old life of opposition to the purposes of God, and has put on the new life of Jesus, made possible only through His redeeming love, mercy and grace. He recognises that Jesus purchased him for heaven; He paid the price that no other could ever pay. The cost was the shedding of His own blood.

Once the sinner identifies with the work of Jesus on the cross by repentance and faith, then he is set free from his past with all its rebellion, fear, doubt and sin. He is born again, is given a new beginning to his life; he has become a new creation. 'The old has gone, the new has come!' (2 Cor. 5: 17)

There can be no avoiding this fundamental truth of the gospel of Jesus Christ: a man *must* be born again to be part of God's Kingdom. Once he has experienced that new birth, the glorious possibilities of what it means to be part of that Kingdom begin to unfold before him.

It is possible to attend church services for years, even as ministers and leaders, yet without a saving experience of new birth, or a heart revelation of being God's Kingdom children. When churchmen are born again, their lives, ministries and preaching are transformed. Nicodemus and Saul of Tarsus were very religious men, devoted to serving God and pleasing Him; yet Jesus had to teach both their need of new birth if they were to be men of the Kingdom. And what a glorious transformation came about in the life of the one who had persecuted the early Christians, when he experienced new birth: he became the apostle to the Gentiles.

I constantly meet faithful church members, who have only recently experienced new birth in Jesus and the power of the Holy Spirit in their lives. I am frequently asked such questions as: 'Why did nobody tell us such things were possible before? Why did we have to wait all these years?' Why indeed!

INCLUSIVE OR EXCLUSIVE?

Some object that this teaching is exclusive; it excludes the vast majority from entering God's Kingdom. They want an inclusive gospel, a universal one through which all men will enter God's Kingdom. They point out that it was for His love of the whole world that God sent His Son, and He died on the cross for all mankind. 'Everyone will be all right in the end' is a popular notion, but totally contradicting New Testament teaching.

The truth is that the gospel is both inclusive and exclusive. It is true that Christ came to die for all sinners, and that through His sacrifice salvation becomes a possibility for all men. However it is also true that only those who come to personal repentance and faith receive the benefit of His cross. It is only they who experience new life, because they have been cleansed from their sins and made acceptable to God. It is only they who are able to receive the gift of His Kingdom.

Jesus took all men to the cross, but it is only those who repent and believe in Him who are raised to new life. The cross is inclusive, making salvation possible for all men; the Kingdom is exclusive, and is for those whose lives are submitted to the sovereignty of the heavenly King, by their personal repentance and faith.

AS LITTLE CHILDREN

Jesus said: 'Therefore I tell you that the kingdom of God will be taken away from you and given to a people who will produce its fruit.' (Matt. 21: 43) As in the time of Jesus, so today. He warns that there will be some who imagine they will be accepted into the Kingdom, but who have never produced the fruit seen in those who are already children of the Kingdom.

God is not the harsh judge who desires to exclude people. Quite the opposite: He teaches His disciples to gather people into the Kingdom and He dies to make it possible for all who repent and believe to receive that rich inheritance.

The plain fact is that many refuse to repent; some see no reason why they should, perhaps because they have never heard the gospel truly proclaimed.

'Let the little children come to me, and do not hinder them, for the kingdom of heaven belongs to such as these.' (Matt. 19: 14) This is not a sentimental picture of Jesus blessing children, to be framed and hung on walls at Sunday Schools, but a profound statement of truth about the nature of the Kingdom of God.

Jesus does not say the Kingdom belongs to little children but to 'such as these' – those who come humbly and trustingly to Him; those who don't argue against, or question, His authority. Little children or grown adults can enter the Kingdom and know Jesus as their Lord; but only as they submit their lives to the authority of the King.

This is the beginning of a continual process of submission. At several stages of their development children will need to submit their lives afresh to Jesus. *They are to grow up in Him, not away from Him.*

TRUE RIGHTEOUSNESS

So He makes it clear that 'unless your righteousness surpasses that of the Pharisees and the teachers of the law, you will certainly not enter the kingdom of heaven.' (Matt. 5: 20) For all their religious fervour they were not part of the Kingdom; nor would they ever be unless they were born again.

Neither an appearance of godliness nor an external moral fervour would satisfy Jesus. He saw straight to men's hearts where good or bad fruit originate. The righteousness that concerned Him began with the heart, a man being in right relationship and right standing with God.

Later Jesus was to describe the teachers of the law and the Pharisees as hypocrites. They were concerned about petty details but neglected such essentials as justice, mercy and faithfulness. They were concerned about outward appearances, but inwardly were full of greed and self-indulgence, of dead men's bones and everything unclean; they were full of hypocrisy and wickedness. Their hearts were negative.

The righteousness Jesus gives is of a totally different order. Through the shedding of His own blood, those who believe in Him have all their sin and guilt washed away and are given new hearts. Christians are put right with God through the blood of the cross, and enabled to live righteous lives through the power of the Holy Spirit, who is God coming to live in His people.

Such righteousness exceeds that of the scribes and Pharisees and is only possible through Jesus. They chose to hang on to their superficial self-righteousness (which is as filthy rags to God), instead of recognising their need of a change of heart. They felt threatened by Jesus's teaching and actions and wanted to destroy Him, rather than repent and submit to His authority.

There is no righteousness acceptable to God except that obtainable through Jesus Christ. Without His righteousness 'you will certainly not enter the kingdom of heaven'.

Chapter 4

RECEIVING THE KINGDOM

For three years Jesus taught about the positive Kingdom and performed the supernatural works that demonstrated the nature of this Kingdom. 'Jesus went throughout Galilee, teaching in their synagogues, preaching the good news of the kingdom, and healing every disease and sickness among the people.' (Matt. 4: 23) He refused to remain too long in one place, saying: 'I must preach the good news of the kingdom of God to the other towns also, because that is why I was sent.' (Luke 4: 43) He 'travelled about from one town and village to another, proclaiming the good news of the kingdom of God.' (Luke 8: 1)

GOOD NEWS

The revelation of the Kingdom is good news! It is good news that men can be delivered from the kingdom of darkness and brought into the Kingdom of light. It is good news that they can be released from any bondage to Satan and be brought into the freedom of God's reign. It is good news that God is a loving Father, who sacrifices His own Son on the cross to enable many sons to be born into His Kingdom. It is good news that He is a God of such infinite grace and mercy, that He is willing to forgive the sins of those who repent and promises His Kingdom life and power to those who believe.

Having received the revelation that God offers a Kingdom to those who believe in Him, how could anyone be so foolish as to refuse such a wonderful offer?

Paul says: 'The kingdom of God is not a matter of talk but of power.' (1 Cor. 4: 20) Jesus demonstrated this truth in His own ministry. Along with the spoken revelation of the Kingdom went the visible manifestations of the power of that Kingdom. He did not expect people to believe a gospel of words without giving evidence of the truth of what He said. From the very beginning His gospel was confirmed with signs following, which demonstrated the imminence of the Kingdom He came to make available. He welcomed the crowds and 'spoke to them about the kingdom of God, and healed those who needed healing.' (Luke 9: 11)

He did not want their concentration to be on the signs but on the revelation of the Kingdom. But wherever His words were met with faith, the positive power of God's Kingdom overcame the negative problems in people's lives. By that power Jesus healed the sick, raised the dead and delivered people from bondage to evil spirits.

When the gospel of the Kingdom takes effect in people's lives there are powerful consequences.

Everything Jesus said relates in one way or another to the Kingdom. At the beginning of the Sermon on the Mount He says: 'Blessed are the poor in spirit, for theirs is the kingdom of heaven.' (Matt. 5: 3) The poor in spirit are those who recognise their spiritual poverty without Jesus. They know their need of God and are prepared to turn to Him in repentance, putting their faith in His grace and mercy. Their salvation depends on God alone and the mighty love He has poured out for them.

Such people are blessed, which the Amplified Bible describes as 'happy, to be envied and spiritually prosperous (that is, with life-joy and satisfaction in God's favour and salvation, regardless of their outward conditions).' (Matt. 5: 3)

The poor in spirit recognise their nothingness before the Almighty and Holy God. And yet because the Son of God became poor, they are made rich! They already possess the Kingdom.

REPENTANCE

What does repentance involve? Literally, a change of mind, a turning to God.

Paul points out that: 'The god of this age has blinded the minds of unbelievers, so that they cannot see the light of the gospel of the glory of Christ, who is the image of God.' (2 Cor. 4: 4) When a man receives revelation, light begins to penetrate his spiritual darkness. He sees that he is a sinner needing God's salvation, and senses Jesus calling him to the cross that he may be cleansed and born again.

That does not necessarily mean he will respond to God's call. Because of his love of sin, or desire to live independently of God's authority, he may choose to remain in his sins, alienated and cut off from the Lord. He will not know peace until he has a change of mind and is prepared to submit to the Lordship of Jesus Christ.

Revelation that God wants to give him His Kingdom will encourage the sinner to 'turn around', to turn his life over to God. Until he repents, he will remain outside that Kingdom; when he does submit his life to God, he becomes a child of that Kingdom, with all its attendant privileges and responsibilities.

When he is prepared to respond to God's initiative in offering him His Kingdom, he will confess he is a sinner in need of a Saviour. He will ask Jesus to forgive everything in his life that has been opposed to God's purposes. There will be specific things about which he feels particularly convicted and guilty, which will need to be brought to Jesus for His forgiveness.

The sinner not only recognises he has done wrong; he *is* wrong and needs to be put right with God. He has lived in unbelief, or with only a token recognition of God in his life.

He needs to be cleansed, made acceptable to God, to be born again, and made a new person. And so he gives his life to Jesus. He wants Him to be his Lord and King, to rule and reign in every area of his life, for his body to become a temple of the Holy Spirit. He is prepared to submit his future to God, to be led and guided by Him; to use his time as He determines. He wants the Lord to reign in his relationships, family, work, the use of his money and property. He realises that God cannot be a side interest in his life; He has to become the centre around whom everything revolves.

This is indeed a change of mind. From leaving God out he now invites Him into everything.

Together with this repentance he expresses a personal faith in Jesus to forgive him, cleanse him, accept him and make him new; faith that He will love him and care for him, lead and guide him and bring him into His Kingdom for all eternity.

For some, the initial act of repentance is a very simple act of heart submission to God that leads to this thorough cleansing and change of life. For others, a yielding of themselves in detail is necessary. In either case, the newly-converted person needs to know that God will no longer hold against him the sins He has forgiven. He is completely free of the guilt and punishment that his sins deserved, for even his punishment was suffered by Jesus on his behalf.

The Spirit of God, now living in him, will enable him to follow obediently in the way that Jesus leads him, to live as a child of His Kingdom. He is highly valued by God and greatly privileged to have received every spiritual gift that God has in heavenly places.

GOD'S SUPERNATURAL LIFE
Some people attend church services for years without ever being challenged with their need to repent, or to express personal faith in Jesus and His Word. You cannot separate God from His Word. To have a relationship with Him, once

you are born again, means that the Holy Spirit will want to lead you into the truth of God's Word.

Some pride themselves on their power of rational thinking, saying that God has given them the ability to reason for themselves. They think nothing of picking and choosing from the Scriptures the things that accord with their own thinking, denying what offends them as unreasonable.

As a result there are many congregations where there is a great fear of the supernatural. God is supernatural and the Kingdom He gives is supernatural. To remove the supernatural from the Bible leaves you only the cover! It is the revelation of the supernatural God working supernaturally in the lives of His people.

Jesus tells Nicodemus that a man must experience a supernatural birth if he is to enter God's supernatural Kingdom. This does not mean that God wants us to be mindless. But no man has ever thought his way into God's Kingdom. A learned theologian may be very knowledgeable about the Scriptures, church history or Christian doctrine and yet not know the reality of the Kingdom in his life. For receiving the gift of the Kingdom does not depend upon his knowledge, but on repentance and faith, leading to new birth.

To have faith in Jesus is actually to have our thinking enlarged, not diminished. Our minds need to be submitted to God's authority along with every other area of our lives, so that He can expand our thinking to embrace His supernatural thoughts. God is not irrational or unreasonable; He is simply beyond reason. Our rational thoughts cannot contain Him. That is why the Scriptures are a constant challenge to our faith; some of the things God says seem outrageously impossible. Yet we discover that when we apply faith to the Word, what He says proves true and what He promises comes to pass.

The Kingdom Jesus offers is a supernatural Kingdom. When arrested, Jesus made it clear; 'My kingdom is not of this world.' (John 18: 36) It comes from another place beyond the natural world. But He teaches us to pray: 'Your kingdom come, your will be done on earth as it is in heaven.' (Matt. 6: 10)

It is God's purpose that His supernatural Kingdom be spread in this natural world. Wherever Jesus is allowed to reign in the hearts and lives of His people, there His Kingdom is established and His will can be performed. It is there that His supernatural working will be in evidence. And that supernatural activity begins in the act of new birth, but is manifested in many other ways as Jesus demonstrates in His earthly ministry. The life of the believer is to be filled with God's supernatural activity and the Christian has available to him the infinite resources of God's power.

THE KINGDOM FIRST

Jesus goes on to teach His listeners not to be worried about their lives, their needs or the details of their circumstances. Rather 'seek first his kingdom and his righteousness, and all these things will be given to you as well.' (Matt. 6: 33)

The Kingdom is to be your priority. To seek first the Kingdom means that the heavenly King has pre-eminence in your life. You are no longer in bondage to your past, neither do you have to allow your life to be dominated by adverse circumstances. Your heavenly Father sees you living in His Son. He does not regard you, or deal with you, as if you are separate from Him. You are a child of His Kingdom; you belong to Him and He lives in you.

Every need will be met for those who put God's Kingdom and righteousness first – that is what Jesus promises. They do not have to be anxious about tomorrow. They do not need to be concerned about whether they will have enough to eat or wear. The Christian is to live as a child of the King, with the purposes of His Kingdom the priority in his life. He is to live in a position of righteousness before God, and is therefore to live in righteous ways each day of his life. When he falls into sin, the believer needs to be cleansed afresh by his Lord.

If the Christian entrusts himself to the King, desiring His purposes first, then the King will care for him in every detail. He can be confident that: 'In all things God works for the good of those who love him, who have been called according to his purpose.' (Rom. 8: 28) Christ will lead him in His triumphal procession, teaching him that mountains of need are to be moved and tossed in the sea; that nothing is impossible for the one who has faith in Jesus. Such victory is implied in living as a child of the Kingdom of God. For wherever the truth, the power and authority of His Kingdom is brought to bear, deception, need and rebellion are overcome.

So Jesus's simple, direct promise to those who believe in Him is: 'Ask and it will be given to you; seek and you will find; knock and the door will be opened to you. For everyone who asks receives; he who seeks finds; and to him who knocks, the door will be opened.' (Matt. 7: 7–8)

However, Jesus also makes it clear: 'Not everyone who says to me, "Lord, Lord," will enter the kingdom of heaven, but only he who does the will of my Father who is in heaven.' (Matt. 7: 21) Acknowledgment that Jesus is Lord is not the same as submission to Him as Lord in your life. It is the latter which concerns Jesus. Mighty things could be accomplished in the name of Jesus, for that name is greater than any other name and has power over all things. But Jesus will only recognise those who personally submit to His rule and reign in their lives; those who live as the children of the Kingdom. 'Many will say to me on that day, "Lord, Lord, did we not prophesy in your name, and in your name drive out demons and perform many miracles?" Then I will tell them plainly, "I never knew you. Away from me, you evildoers!"' (Matt. 7: 22–3)

To live as a child of the Kingdom is to do the will of the heavenly Father and that means putting God's Word into practice. The house built on sand could not withstand the storm. Jesus describes the man who built there as foolish. 'Everyone who hears these words of mine and does not put them into practice is like a foolish man who built his house on sand.' (Matt. 7: 26)

By contrast the wise man builds his house on rock; he hears the words of Jesus and puts them into practice. No matter how great the difficulties he encounters, his house proves to be unshakeable.

Those who have received the Kingdom have received a Kingdom that cannot be shaken. As the believer lives in the power of that positive Kingdom, he will not be shaken neither will he fall. The children of His Kingdom do not need to fear the power of the negative kingdom of darkness, for He who lives in them is greater than he who lives in the world. As their light shines before men, so the light of Christ can penetrate spiritual darkness and others can be brought into the glorious liberty of the sons of God.

Chapter 5

ETERNAL LIFE

In his account of the gospel, John rarely uses the phrase 'Kingdom of God'. Instead he speaks of the gift of eternal life, God's gift to those who believe, who are the children of God's Kingdom. He sent His Son that men might receive this gift: 'For God so loved the world that he gave his one and only Son, that whoever believes in him shall not perish but have eternal life.' (John 3: 16)

Those who reject Him 'perish', condemned by their own unbelief: 'Whoever believes in him is not condemned, but whoever does not believe stands condemned already because he has not believed in the name of God's one and only Son.' (v. 18)

'Whoever believes in the Son has eternal life, but whoever rejects the Son will not see life, for God's wrath remains on him.' (John 3: 36) Jesus speaks of eternal life as a present reality rather than a future hope – for the believer. Those who are thirsty for the reality of God in their lives will come to Him and find that He alone can give the water that will satisfy their thirst. 'Whoever drinks the water I give him will never thirst. Indeed, the water I give him will become in him a spring of water welling up to eternal life.' (John 4: 14) 'He who comes to me will never go hungry, and he who believes in me will never be thirsty.' (John 6: 35)

The one who hears the words of Jesus and believes His Father 'has eternal life and will not be condemned; he has crossed over from death to life.' (John 5: 24)

Knowing the Scriptures is not sufficient to give anyone this life. That was the mistake the Pharisees made. Jesus told them: 'You diligently study the Scriptures because you think that by them you possess eternal life. These are the Scriptures that testify about me, yet you refuse to come to me to have life.' (vv. 39–40)

In the same way, knowing the words and parables of the Kingdom does not make anyone a child of the Kingdom, or enable him to live in the power and authority of that Kingdom. He has to believe the Word and surrender his life to the King, before the Kingdom can be a reality in his experience.

Jesus told the people: 'Do not work for food that spoils, but for food that endures to eternal life, which the Son of Man will give you.' (John 6: 27) In other words, seek first the Kingdom of God and His righteousness and all that you need will be given you by Him. 'The work of God is this: to believe in the one he has sent.' (v. 29)

EVERLASTING KINGDOM

To those who receive God's gift of eternal life now, there is the promise of resurrection: 'For my Father's will is that everyone who looks to the Son and believes in him shall have eternal life, and I will raise him up at the last day.' (John 6: 40) The Kingdom Jesus came to give is eternal. In the prophecy of Daniel, we read: 'His kingdom is an eternal kingdom; his dominion endures from generation to generation.' (Dan. 4: 3) 'His kingdom will not be destroyed, his dominion will never end.' (Dan. 6: 26) And there is the glorious promise: 'The saints of the Most High will receive the kingdom and will possess it for ever – yes, for ever and ever.' (Dan. 7: 18)

The saints, those who have been redeemed by Jesus, can look forward to the final manifestation of the Kingdom in its fullness: 'Then the sovereignty, power and greatness of the kingdoms under the whole heaven will be handed over to the saints, the people of the Most High. His kingdom will be an everlasting kingdom, and all rulers will worship and obey him.' (Dan. 7: 27)

Over and over again Jesus impresses on His hearers the truth: 'He who believes has everlasting life.' (John 6: 47) 'Whoever eats my flesh and drinks my blood has eternal life, and I will raise him up at the last day.' (v. 54)

The disciples recognised that He had the words of eternal life. Those who kept His words would never see death. (John 8: 51) Jesus said that He came to give men life in all its fullness – not human life, for they already have that; but God's divine life, eternal life. Paul says: 'You have been given fullness in Christ.' (Col. 2: 10)

When speaking of Himself as the Good Shepherd, Jesus says: 'My sheep listen to my voice; I know them, and they follow me. I give them eternal life, and they shall never perish; no-one can snatch them out of my hand.' (John 10: 27-8) Again we notice the present reality of the gift of eternal life and also the fact that those who receive the gift are prepared to follow Him. 'His command leads to eternal life.' (John 12: 50) God does not give Himself to His children so that they may continue to pursue their own ways, but to follow Him along His way.

When praying before His arrest, Jesus said: 'Now this is eternal life: that they may know you, the only true God, and Jesus Christ, whom you have sent.' (John 17: 3) There is no other way to the Kingdom, to receiving the gift of eternal life, than through Him.

From this scriptural evidence we can see clearly that those who receive the gift of eternal life can expect to experience resurrection and the glory of God's Kingdom eternally. Paul speaks of what this means in 1 Corinthians 15.

RESURRECTION

The natural body is perishable, but there is also a spiritual body which is imperishable. The natural came first, then the spiritual. Adam signifies natural man, while Christ is the man of the Spirit. Natural men follow after Adam, while 'those who are of heaven' are as 'the man from heaven'. Those who have faith in Jesus 'bear the likeness of the man from heaven'.

Paul makes it clear that 'flesh and blood cannot inherit the kingdom of God, nor does the perishable inherit the imperishable.' (v. 50) Natural man cannot inherit the Kingdom; he must experience a supernatural, spiritual rebirth. He must become spiritual in order to enter the spiritual Kingdom of God.

God is in the business of transforming us into His likeness. But there will come the moment of complete change: 'Listen, I tell you a mystery: We will not all sleep but we will all be changed – in a flash, in the twinkling of an eye, at the last trumpet. For the trumpet will sound, the dead will be raised imperishable, and we will be changed.' (vv. 51-2) The perishable will then be clothed with the imperishable, and what is mortal with immortality. Death itself will have been defeated for the children of the Kingdom. 'But thanks be to God! He gives us the victory through our Lord Jesus Christ.' (v. 57)

And so Paul advises the Corinthians to stand firm and let nothing move them from their faith in Jesus and obedience to Him. They are always to give themselves to the Lord's work, confident that their labour in the Lord is not in vain. It will reap an everlasting reward. Jesus will reign until He has put all His enemies under His feet. Then He will hand over the Kingdom to His Father. Every negative dominion, authority and power will then have been destroyed.

In Revelation we read of those who have been purchased for God by the blood of Jesus: 'You have made them to be a kingdom and priests to serve our God, and they will reign on the earth.' (Rev. 5: 10) They will share in His exalted reign. Then the vision John had will be fulfilled: 'The kingdom of the world has become the kingdom of our Lord and of his

Christ, and he will reign for ever and ever.' (Rev. 11: 15)

When writing his first Epistle, John said: 'God has given us eternal life, and this life is in his Son. He who has the Son has life; he who does not have the Son of God does not have life.' (1 John 5: 11–12) And Paul urges Timothy to 'take hold of the eternal life to which you were called'. (1 Tim. 6: 12)

By the atoning work of Jesus we have been set free from sin and have become 'slaves to God', Paul tells the Romans. (6: 22) The benefit you reap, he says, leads to holiness, and the result is eternal life.

As those who inherit the Kingdom, we need to live as the children of the King *now*. As those who inherit eternal life, we need to live His life *now*. He gives us the Holy Spirit to enable us to do that. As we seek to follow His leading lovingly and obediently, we can live in the peace of God, confident of our heavenly destiny.

In the New Testament these two aspects of the Kingdom and God's gift of eternal life are held together. Both are a present reality for believers and, at the same time, a future hope, when they will know fully what is only experienced partially at present.

'The wages of sin is death, but the gift of God is eternal life in Christ Jesus our Lord.' (Rom. 6: 23) That gift is received by grace, by God's free gift; and it is by the continuing work of grace in the Christian's life that he lives in union with the will and purpose of Jesus. 'The one who sows to please the Spirit, from the Spirit will reap eternal life.' (Gal. 6: 8)

Chapter 6

THE SEED OF THE KINGDOM

SECRETS REVEALED

Jesus never taught without using parables. These parables of the Kingdom could be understood by some but not by others, which prompted the disciples to ask Jesus: 'Why do you speak to the people in parables?' (Matt. 13: 10)

Perhaps they were politely suggesting that Jesus should improve His teaching methods; after all, a good teacher can surely be understood by those he is teaching! Certainly they were genuinely perplexed themselves, making it necessary for Jesus to explain the parables to them.

His answer to their question is highly significant: 'The knowledge of the secrets of the kingdom of heaven has been given to you, but not to them.' (Matt. 13: 11) It seems that Jesus did not intend that everyone should understand His teaching on the Kingdom.

REVELATION

The secrets of the Kingdom of heaven can only be made known through revelation. They cannot be understood by reason alone. Not everybody is able to receive such revelation. To understand he is a child of the Kingdom, with all the resources of heaven available to him, places within a man's reach such infinite power and riches that can only be entrusted to those who are prepared to submit their lives to the King. Such resources cannot be made available to those who would abuse such gifts.

The presence of God's Kingdom on earth is a complete mystery to the vast majority of the population. There are many Christians even, who have never received the revelation in their hearts that they are children of the Kingdom, with God's infinite resources available to them.

Revelation of the Kingdom comes to a man in proportion to his willingness to submit to the authority of the King. The more submitted a man, the more Kingdom power and authority can radiate from his life. God's intention is that there should be progressive revelation of the truth of the Kingdom in a Christian's life that will lead to a progressive increase in spiritual power and authority, in faith and the manifestation of Jesus in his life.

It is for this reason that Jesus continues His answer to the disciples' question about why He uses parables, by saying: 'Whoever has will be given more, and he will have an abundance. Whoever does not have, even what he has will be taken from him.' (Matt. 13: 12)

At first this might seem unjust. But it is God's purpose that each of His children should experience His abundance in their lives. That means that they receive from God all they need and more. They have more than enough of His resources for themselves spiritually and materially, and are enabled to express His generosity by the way in which they give to others.

Whoever has the Kingdom as a gift from God will experience the Lord pouring His riches abundantly into his life, as he continues to seek first the Kingdom of God and His righteousness. Whoever does not have the Kingdom as a gift will ultimately experience what he has being taken from him.

This is a hard truth to face. Jesus made it clear to the Jews that, although as God's chosen people they should have been the ones to inherit the Kingdom, many Gentiles would be preferred before them. Those who by virtue of their birth should be the children of the Kingdom will instead be thrown out because of their rejection of the King, their Messiah: 'I say to you that many will come from the east and the west, and will take their places at the feast with Abraham, Isaac and Jacob in the kingdom of heaven. But the subjects of the kingdom will be thrown outside, into the darkness, where there will be weeping and gnashing of teeth.' (Matt. 8: 11–12)

Jesus is the only Saviour; He is the Way, the Truth and the Life, and no-one will come into the Kingdom of His Father except through Him.

Evangelism is always the priority of the Church, and that often needs to begin with those already sitting in the pews on Sundays. Judgment begins with the household of God. He expects great things of those who claim to be His people and gives mighty promises to those who genuinely are His children. It is not a question of calling Him 'Lord' but of doing His will, of living lives submitted to Him as King.

Those who do not belong to His Kingdom see and yet do not see; they hear but do not understand the revelation of the Kingdom. But to the believing disciples Jesus says: 'But blessed are your eyes because they see, and your ears because they hear. For I tell you the truth, many prophets and righteous men longed to see what you see but did not see it, and to hear what you hear but did not hear it.' (Matt. 13: 16–17)

Even the men of God who preceded Jesus were not able to receive the gift that is offered through Jesus. This is true even of John the Baptist who was sent to prepare the way for the ministry of Jesus, with his call to repentance and righteousness. Jesus said: 'I tell you the truth: Among those born of women there has not risen anyone greater than John the Baptist; yet he who is least in the Kingdom of heaven is greater than he.' (Matt. 11: 11)

What a privilege to be a child of the Kingdom! To belong to the Kingdom of God raises a person above his natural heritage. For the Kingdom of God is supernatural and when a person is born again, God's supernatural activity gives him supernatural life; he possesses eternal life. Those from former generations found righteous by God will enjoy His heavenly inheritance. But none of them, neither the prophets nor John the Baptist, could experience the Kingdom of God NOW, could enter that Kingdom NOW, receive the benefits of that Kingdom NOW. That only became possible when Jesus, the King of heaven, came to dwell among men with His sovereign call: 'Repent, for the kingdom of heaven is near.' (Matt. 4: 17)

John the Baptist had spoken these same words (Matt. 3: 2). On his lips they were pregnant with significance, for they proclaimed that the King was about to come. On the lips of Jesus they are even more significant. The King has come and now the Kingdom is made available to those who believe in Him. The Baptist willingly makes way for the Messiah.

THE SOWER

In His parables of the Kingdom Jesus often used examples of growth. No parable is better known than that of the Sower. The farmer sows seed which falls on four different types of ground. Some falls on the path, where it is eaten by birds. Some falls on rocky places where the plants wither when the sun scorches them, because they have no depth to their roots. Other seed falls among thorns which choke the plants; but other falls on good soil producing a crop – a hundred, sixty or thirty times what was sown.

It was after hearing this that the disciples put their question to Jesus about why He should speak in parables. He explained that the seed represents the Word or gospel of the Kingdom. There is nothing wrong with the seed; it is the same wherever it falls. It is the quality of the ground that is different.

THE PATH

The path, Jesus says, represents the one who 'hears the message about the kingdom and does not understand it'. He does not receive the revelation that is given to him. So 'the evil one comes and snatches away what was sown in his heart.' (Matt. 13: 19) Satan is represented in the parable by the birds that eat the seed.

Those represented by the path do actually hear the message of the Kingdom; God sows the Word in their hearts. They are given revelation but they reject it. 'Satan comes and takes away the word that was sown in them.' (Mark 4: 15). 'The devil comes and takes away the word from their hearts, so that they cannot believe and be saved.' (Luke 8: 12)

Satan obviously is concerned that people should not receive the message of the Kingdom. This is hardly surprising. Until a man believes and is saved he belongs to Satan's domain, the kingdom of darkness; he is still spiritually blinded by the god of this age. The enemy wants to hold on to those he controls, whether they recognise the reality of that control or not. He knows that as soon as a man responds with repentance and faith to the revelation that God is offering to give him the Kingdom of Light, he will lose control over that individual. Until his conversion, Satan is able to manipulate that person.

When a man responds to the gospel, he becomes part of that Kingdom from which Satan has been dismissed. This fact not only fills the enemy with envy but also with fear. Jesus explains why. To those who are part of the Kingdom He has given 'authority to trample on snakes and scorpions, and to overcome all the power of the enemy'. (Luke 10: 19) Nothing will harm them.

We can see why Satan has such a vested interest in trying to prevent people from receiving the revelation of the Kingdom. Whereas formerly he was able to control and manipulate the unbeliever, encouraging him to deny the lordship of Jesus in his life and urging him to live by his own natural powers and resources, now the roles are reversed. The believer is not only delivered from the domain of darkness and Satan's control; he is given power and authority to overcome all the power of the enemy. Whereas before Satan could constantly defeat him, even without him being aware of his influence, now the Christian can inflict one defeat after another on Satan.

Jesus explains to the disciples why this is: 'Your names are written in heaven.' In other words, they belong to the Kingdom of which Satan is no longer a part. Instead of fearing his influence, they can now rise up in victory over him. For wherever Light shines, the darkness has to disappear. They should rejoice, not so much in the victories themselves, as in the reason for them: 'Your names are written in heaven.' (Luke 10: 20) Not will be written, but already are written! The authority of heaven is already available to those who believe and are part of God's Kingdom.

So if the enemy can prevent someone from responding to the initial revelation of the Kingdom, he will most certainly do so. He does not like to lose control of people's lives and suffer defeat.

THE ROCKY SOIL

The rocky places represent 'the man who hears the word and at once receives it with joy. But since he has no root, he lasts only a short time. When trouble or persecution comes because of the word, he quickly falls away.' (Matt.13: 20-1)

This man receives the revelation of the Kingdom with joy. How wonderful that God, the Almighty Creator, should love him, be prepared to forgive him all his sins and make him an inheritor of the Kingdom of heaven. He responds positively to the revelation, but his life is not deeply rooted in the Word of God. He is the one who clamours for experiences of the Lord, but does not know how to live as a child of the Kingdom. He does not know the rights God gives him, or the power and authority that are vested in him.

Because he is not a man of the Word, when he is in the middle of adverse circumstances he does not know how to cope. He believes his feelings and fears, rather than the truth of God's Word. 'In the time of testing they fall away.' (Luke 8: 13)

It is not enough to receive the gift of the Kingdom. Every child of God needs to learn how to live Kingdom life, exercise Kingdom authority, have Kingdom faith and enjoy Kingdom victories. But he will only be able to do all this if his life is deeply rooted in Kingdom words; if he believes the gospel of the Kingdom and puts those words into practice. Then his house will be built on rock, not sand, and will withstand any storm.

THE THORNY SOIL

The thorns represent those who hear the Word, which begins to be rooted in their lives and to grow in them, but who allow other things to choke their spiritual growth, making them unfruitful. They do not mature as Christians.

Fruitfulness and maturity are God's purpose for all His children. To receive the gift of the Kingdom is only the beginning of His purpose for the believer. 'You did not choose me, but I chose you to go and bear fruit – fruit that will last', Jesus tells His disciples. (John 15: 16) He calls us not only to enjoy the benefits of the Kingdom but to bear fruit for His glory: 'This is to my Father's glory, that you bear much fruit, showing yourselves to be my disciples.' (John 15: 8)

Paul urges his readers to 'become mature'. Spiritual maturity is dependent on the Christian allowing the Word of God to be increasingly expressed in his life through the enabling of the Holy Spirit.

Jesus says there are three things in particular that prevent fruitfulness and the believer becoming mature.

1. The worries of this life. Nothing hinders faith more than

anxiety. Worry demonstrates that the person is failing to trust God in those particular circumstances. He believes the problems rather than the Lord. In effect his attitude is: 'God can't handle the situation, so I shall worry about it!'

Jesus clearly says that if the Kingdom is first in your life and you are seeking to live in righteousness, then you need have no worries or be anxious about anything. Even if your immediate reaction to a difficult situation is to be fearful, you can confess the sin of that negative reaction and entrust the whole matter to the Lord. He is able to cope with every circumstance and promises to give you everything you need.

Worry, fear and anxiety are all negative and do not, therefore, belong to the positive Kingdom of God. They emanate from the negative domain of darkness and are encouraged by the prince of this world. During our years of unbelief many of us become accustomed to being worriers, meeting every difficulty with anxiety. This is not Kingdom living. We cannot live in victory over our circumstances if we constantly worry about them.

2. 'The deceitfulness of wealth' is another thorn that chokes the life of the Kingdom in a believer.

Jesus was to tell His disciples: 'I tell you the truth, it is hard for a rich man to enter the kingdom of heaven. Again I tell you, it is easier for a camel to go through the eye of a needle than for a rich man to enter the kingdom of God.' (Matt. 19: 23–4)

Jesus is talking here of *entering* the Kingdom. It is hard for rich people to *enter* the Kingdom. Those who have no material need are usually in love with the things of this world, and have no time or place for God. Certainly most wealthy people do not want to submit themselves to the authority of Another, albeit the Son of God. Each wants to reign in his own little kingdom.

That is true for many who would not be described as 'wealthy', but who are by no means impoverished. Pride encourages any person stubbornly to refuse to submit to the authority of Jesus. Wealth easily enhances such pride.

It is hard for a rich man to enter the Kingdom because he is unlikely to see the need to do so. He has all he wants to fulfil his ambition and probably does not want the course of his life to be changed by anyone, even God.

Jesus does not preach against wealth as such; neither does He say it is impossible for rich people to become part of His Kingdom. He is simply stating that much is stacked against them, for the flesh is opposed to the Spirit and it is so easy to indulge the flesh when wealthy.

There are many fine Christians who are wealthy people. Their lives have been submitted to the King and Jesus is therefore allowed to rule over their finances. He teaches: 'Give, and it will be given to you. A good measure, pressed down, shaken together and running over, will be poured into your lap. For with the measure you use, it will be measured to you.' (Luke 6: 38)

This is a spiritual principle that relates to many areas of our lives, irrespective of our material resources. It is true of forgiveness, for example. If we forgive others their sins, God will be willing to forgive us. If we do not judge we shall not be judged. If we do not condemn, we shall not be condemned.

The same principle applies to money. If we honour God in our giving (no matter the level of our wealth), He will cause us to prosper materially. He is no man's debtor and will always measure back to us more than is freely, willingly and joyfully given to Him.

Jesus says that it is the *deceitfulness* of wealth that will choke the life of the Kingdom in a believer. Money encourages deceit. Many (not only the wealthy) desire to hide the amount they possess from tax officers, neighbours and fellow Christians. It is considered a very private area of our lives.

As Christians we should have nothing to hide. We should not be ashamed of others knowing what we possess, or what we give for the work of the Kingdom, although Jesus warns us not to parade our giving before others.

The devil is the deceiver. Deceit does not belong in the lives of the children of light. Wealth itself is not necessarily evil; it is the love of money that is the root of all evil. It is the misuse of our wealth, using it for our own ends rather than to serve God, that chokes Kingdom growth in our lives.

We are to honour God in our giving. The tithe is rightfully His; that is, the first tenth of all we have or earn. It is His by right and is to be given to Him for the use of His Kingdom. Over and above that we make our free-will offerings.

The first tenth is a minimum, for the Christian acknowledges that all he is and has rightly belongs to the Lord. Giving the tithe faithfully is a necessary indication that we are truly submitted to the authority of God in our lives. We are ready to give generously to the One who has given His everything for us and to us.

Our money is Kingdom money, and we are not to try and hide it deceitfully from the Lord. When you desire to serve the King with your finances, He knows He can cause you to prosper so that more resources can be released through you for the work of the Kingdom.

It matters, therefore, where you give as well as what you give. Because your money is Kingdom money, what is given away needs to be used for the work and extension of the Kingdom. Paul teaches that the man who sows sparingly will reap sparingly, and the one who sows plentifully will reap plentifully. The nature of the soil into which the seed is sown is also of vital importance. There is no point in sowing good seed in a spiritual desert, on a path, rocky soil or among thorns. Sow it in good soil where you know it will be productive.

3. 'Desires for other things' also choke the life of the Kingdom. Wealth can encourage such desires; but those who are without can be full of envy and greed also.

The Kingdom must remain first in the Christian's life. That will only be a reality if he places the King Himself at the centre of his life.

Some claim to have a close and loving relationship with the Lord but care little for His Kingdom. They are deceived. To care for the King is to care for what He counts dear. He wants to see His Kingdom come and His will done on earth as in heaven. 'If you love me, you will obey what I command', Jesus said. (John 14: 15) Obedience is submission to the will and authority of God out of love for Him. If the motive is love, it will not be a begrudging obedience or submission, but a joyful one.

Nothing, or nobody, comes before the Lord in our lives. Putting anything or anyone before Him stifles the growth of Kingdom life within us. We cannot be seeking first the Kingdom and putting other desires first at the same time.

The Christian, therefore, yields his independence to the Lord. He no longer wants his life ruled by selfish ambition, but by the Word and Spirit of God. He cannot seek his own ends and God's purposes at the same time. All that matters to him, if he is to be increasingly fruitful, is that God should be glorified in his life by His purpose being fulfilled in him.

THE GOOD SOIL

The good soil represents those who hear the Word of the Kingdom with an honest and good heart, and retain it. They hold fast to that Word; they keep it; they live it. Because they live as Kingdom children they are fruitful, 'yielding a hundred, sixty or thirty times what was sown.' (Matt. 13: 23)

The capacity for each may differ, but God's purpose is that each of His children should increase in fruitfulness. 'Every branch that does bear fruit he trims clean so that it will be even more fruitful.' (John 15: 2) The Father cuts out of our lives the things that are negative, so that more of the positive life of His Kingdom may be manifested in us.

If God chooses to give us His Kingdom, which is positive, how is it that so many negative things can persist in our lives? These negatives obviously hinder fruitfulness.

Many of these parables of the Kingdom are parables of growth. We cannot grow to the point where we receive the Kingdom; that is God's gift to those who repent and believe. But this gift of the Kingdom is like a seed that God plants in the heart and life of that believer.

Like all natural seeds, the seed of the Kingdom contains all the life that will potentially develop out of it. The seed needs the right soil in order to grow to maturity and fruitfulness; it also needs to be watered spiritually.

Jesus describes the Holy Spirit as 'living water'. The seed of the Kingdom planted in the life of the believer is watered by the Holy Spirit. Having given the gift of the Kingdom, God does not tell the new Christian to try his hardest to live as a child of the Kingdom. His own natural resources are inadequate to enable him to do so.

God gives you His Holy Spirit to enable you to live the life of His Kingdom here on earth. He asks nothing of you without supplying all the grace and resources to fulfil His purposes. The living water of the Holy Spirit waters the seed of the Kingdom within you, enabling its life to grow within you.

This is a progressive work and as you continue to allow the Holy Spirit to water the seed it will become a shoot, then a plant that will mature and become fruitful. And a fruitful plant reproduces a number of identical seeds to that from which it came. Fruitfulness produces 'a crop, yielding a hundred, sixty or thirty times *what was sown.*'

'What was sown' was the seed of the Kingdom; it produces Kingdom seeds. In other words the presence of the Kingdom within you will influence others to seek first the Kingdom of God and His righteousness. Every Christian should have a great desire to see the life of the Kingdom reproduced in others. God gives His Holy Spirit that you will have the power to be a witness of the Kingdom in the world.

It is for this reason that, in His great prayer recorded in John 17, Jesus says: 'As you sent me into the world, I have sent them into the world.' (John 17: 18) You are a witness of the presence of God's Kingdom in the world. Your citizenship is now in heaven and there will come the time when you will be able to enjoy His heavenly glory without the temptations of the world, the flesh and the devil. Until then you resist these temptations and become increasingly fruitful by living Kingdom life in the world, with a heart full of enthusiasm and zeal that God will use you to spread the influence of His Kingdom.

Chapter 7

KINGDOM GROWTH

WEEDS

Another Kingdom parable of growth is that of the Weeds. A man sowed good seed in his field. 'But while everyone was sleeping, his enemy came and sowed weeds among the wheat, and went away.' (Matt. 13: 25) Both the wheat and weeds grew together.

The man's servant suggested that the weeds be pulled up. But the master said 'No' to this suggestion 'because while you are pulling the weeds, you may root up the wheat with them.' (v. 29) Both were to be allowed to grow together until harvest time. The harvesters will be told: 'First collect the weeds and tie them in bundles to be burned, then gather the wheat and bring it into my barn.' (v. 30)

Like that of the Sower, this parable also had to be explained privately by Jesus to the disciples. The one who sowed the good seed is the Son of Man, Jesus Himself. The field is the world and the good seed are the sons of the Kingdom. Jesus has sown the seed of the Kingdom in the world and those who have responded to His gospel grow like the wheat towards fruitfulness.

But the devil has also sown his negative seeds, and Jesus describes the weeds as 'the sons of the evil one'.

The servant wants to do away with the evil ones so that the good seed will be unhindered in its growth. This, however, is not God's way. The servant may uproot good seed in his zeal to do away with all those who are evil. New birth turns what was formerly a weed into a stalk of wheat! God alone knows the heart of each individual and the time will come when the fruitfulness (either positive or negative) of each person's life will be obvious.

The harvest time, Jesus says, is the end of the age, when He will send out the harvesters who are His angels. We should note carefully the sequence of events as Jesus explains them.

First the angels 'will weed out of his kingdom everything that causes sin and all who do evil. They will throw them into the fiery furnace, where there will be weeping and gnashing of teeth.' (vv. 41–2)

It seems, at first sight, that those who cause sin and do evil are actually part of the Kingdom. But this is not the case. At the end of the age, the sovereignty of Jesus will suddenly be established everywhere. Every knee will have to bow before Jesus and every tongue will have to confess that He is Lord.

But those who have resisted His gospel and have remained in their sins will not be able to stand this day of His coming. For them, this is the time of judgment and the angels of God will swiftly root them out of the Kingdom. They will be condemned to a Christless eternity, separated from God. Hell is described as the 'fiery furnace, where there will be weeping and gnashing of teeth.'

By contrast Jesus teaches: 'I tell you the truth, whoever hears my word and believes him who sent me has eternal life and will not be condemned; he has crossed over from death to life.' (John 5: 24)

What a contrast! There is no condemnation for those who are in Christ Jesus. By their faith in Him crucified, they have already been raised to new life, have received the gift of eternal life and are children of God's Kingdom.

As Jesus concludes this parable He says that 'the righteous will shine like the sun in the kingdom of their Father.' (Matt. 13: 43) Is it not worth seeking first His Kingdom and righteousness?

MADE PERFECT

As you remain faithful to the end, you will be numbered among those made righteous through the blood of Jesus. You will be so radiant with the reflected glory of God that no human eye could look at you. You will shine like the sun in the Kingdom of your Father, in that Kingdom of which you are already a part, but which has only been imperfectly manifested in you and around you.

'But when perfection comes, the imperfect disappears.' (1 Cor. 13: 10) Not only will unforgiven sinners be rooted out and condemned to hell, the final refining of the saints of God will take place in the twinkling of an eye.

> So will it be with the resurrection of the dead. The body that is sown is perishable, it is raised imperishable; it is sown in dishonour, it is raised in glory; it is sown in weakness, it is raised in power; it is sown a natural body, it is raised a spiritual body ... as is the man from heaven, so also are those who are of heaven. And just as we have borne the likeness of the earthly man, so shall we bear the likeness of the man from heaven. I declare to you, brothers, that flesh and blood cannot inherit the kingdom of God, nor does the perishable inherit the imperishable. Listen, I tell you a mystery: We will not all sleep, but we will all be changed – in a flash, in the twinkling of an eye, at the last trumpet. For the trumpet will sound, the dead will be raised imperishable, and we will be changed ... But thanks be to God! He gives us the victory through our Lord Jesus Christ. (1 Cor. 15: 42-4, 48-52, 57)

Paul is addressing Christians when writing these words. Although they have entered into their inheritance of God's Kingdom because of His precious and gracious gift to them, they can long for the full manifestation of that Kingdom when Christ returns, not as a humble servant, but as the reigning King.

Then all who have denied His sovereignty will pass away, but those who have acknowledged His lordship and lived under His reign will know this glorious transformation. Death has lost its sting and they are given the victory over it through Jesus.

The glorious promise that we have as the King's children is that, when we see Him face to face, we shall be like Him. God's purpose for us will be fulfilled. He gives us the gift of His *Holy* Spirit to make us holy, like Him, and to bring us to that perfection which is His plan for us.

THE MUSTARD SEED AND THE YEAST

Both these short parables of the Kingdom speak to us of growth. 'The kingdom of heaven is like a mustard seed, which a man took and planted in his field. Though it is the smallest of all your seeds, yet when it grows, it is the largest of the garden plants and becomes a tree, so that the birds of the air come and perch in its branches.' (Matt. 13: 31-2)

There is both an individual and a corporate sense in which we can understand this parable. At the personal level, God has planted the seed of His Kingdom in the lives of those who believe in Him. As that seed is watered by the Holy Spirit, so it will grow to maturity and become fruitful. What started as a tiny seed in the new-born Christian becomes a 'tree' that can minister to others in the world.

Corporately, the Kingdom of God on earth seems tiny and perhaps insignificant to the great majority of people. Nevertheless, throughout the world that Kingdom is being extended every day and in due course its power and influence will overshadow everything else. There will be times of great spiritual conflict on earth before Christ finally returns in glory. But God's Kingdom will prevail; it is the unshakeable Kingdom.

Meanwhile the children of the Kingdom are like yeast: 'The kingdom of heaven is like yeast that a woman took and mixed into a large amount of flour until it worked all through the dough.' (Matt. 13: 33)

God's Kingdom people seem a tiny minority of the world's population. Yet amid all the religions, philosophies and ideologies that exist, it is those Kingdom children who will finally prevail. Their lives are to be like yeast working through this large amount of flour, tiny and seemingly insignificant, yet powerful with the ability to change the world in which they live.

Individually, the message is consistent with the other Kingdom parables. Just as the seed is planted in the heart of the believer, so the life of the Kingdom within him is like the yeast that will spread its influence through every area of his being, so that every part of his life will be brought under the sovereignty of Jesus. His reign already established in him will progressively take a more complete hold on his life.

THE HIDDEN TREASURE AND THE PEARL

These two short parables speak of the inexpressible value of the Kingdom. 'The kingdom of heaven is like treasure hidden in a field. When a man found it, he hid it again, and then in his joy went and sold all he had and bought that field.' (Matt. 13: 44)

Jesus says the Kingdom is the treasure – not Himself. We cannot possess the Kingdom without submitting to the King. But God does not desire people to submit to Jesus without realising that they have been given a Kingdom to possess. Possessing that Kingdom is the treasure.

Again Jesus speaks here of the hidden nature of the Kingdom. It is present among men and yet unnoticed by most people. It requires revelation to understand that God is offering this Kingdom to those who repent and believe. Once a man sees what God is offering, it becomes supremely important to him that he obtains that Kingdom. All his worldly possessions are insignificant by comparison.

Of course the Kingdom cannot be purchased, and Jesus does not mean to imply that it can. He simply makes clear that, once a man has received revelation of the Kingdom, his overwhelming desire will be to possess that Kingdom.

It is possible for someone to be a Christian for some time before receiving this heart-revelation. Jesus does not intend any believer to acknowledge Him as King without entering into this inheritance of the Kingdom. Even to the believer, it is like discovering treasure to realise suddenly that God has chosen to give him the Kingdom, that He has given him in Christ every spiritual blessing in heavenly places.

'Again, the kingdom of heaven is like a merchant looking for fine pearls. When he found one of great value, he went away and sold everything he had and bought it.' (Matt. 13: 45–6)

The message of this parable is similar. Like the merchant many today are searching. They see there must be a meaning and purpose to life, and feel a sense of emptiness and frustration because they have not found it.

Most try to create purpose for themselves, endeavouring to find happiness and fulfilment in a variety of ways. They may try the route of self-indulgence, seeking many fleshly pleasures for themselves. They may be so disillusioned with the world that they try to escape from reality through drugs or drink. They may try to find fulfilment through their work, devoting themselves to advancing in their chosen career, often regardless of other considerations.

They may even devote themselves to the welfare of others through various social activities. Yet none of these things can bring spiritual fulfilment or satisfaction. None can produce that peace which is beyond all understanding.

Like the merchant, a person's search for meaning and purpose only ends when he discovers the reality of the Kingdom of God. Then he knows he must become part of the Kingdom. Then he discovers that fleshly pleasures are illusory; ultimately they create more pain than pleasure. He no longer needs to try and escape from his circumstances through drugs or drink, for now he has within him the resources, not only to cope, but to be part of God's mission to extend His Kingdom in the world. From a position of passive defeat, he can move to one of active victory.

He will not try to lose himself in his career, for he desires only to please God by fulfilling the ministry and purpose to which He calls him. More than ever before, he will share God's love for people and will be concerned about their welfare. He will not only want to see the hungry fed and the homeless housed, he will be concerned for their spiritual welfare. He will want them, and indeed all men, to know the joy of discovering the Kingdom of heaven as a present reality.

Chapter 8

MANY CALLED, FEW CHOSEN

THE NET

A net was let down into the lake and caught all kinds of fish. When full, the fishermen hauled it to the shore, sat down and collected the good fish into baskets, but threw the bad away.

As with the parable of the Weeds, Jesus relates this to the end of the age. 'The angels will come and separate the wicked from the righteous and throw them into the fiery furnace, where there will be weeping and gnashing of teeth.' (Matt. 13: 49–50)

On this occasion Jesus asks His listeners if they have understood, and they reply affirmatively. It is not fashionable to talk or preach about hell today. When teaching about the Kingdom, Jesus did not want people to be under any illusion that 'everyone will be all right in the end'. There will be a judgment when the wicked will be consigned to hell. The righteous, those cleansed by the blood of Jesus and made righteous in God's sight, need not fear this judgment, for they have already passed from death to life.

To those who reject Jesus, as much by their apathy and indecision as by their down-right opposition, this judgment and its inevitable consequences will be an awful reality. 'He who is not with me is against me,' said Jesus. (Matt. 12: 30)

Every believer will have to give an account of his stewardship, of how he has used the Kingdom resources made available to him. This we shall see clearly in Kingdom parables Jesus taught later in His ministry. But the man who is assured of his salvation does not have to fear being condemned to hell.

Some question how a God of love could allow people to endure such an eternity. In His love He sent His Son to save men from such punishment, which they deserve because of their sin and rebellion against Him. In His love and mercy He has opened the way of salvation to them – not only by making provision to deliver them from all the negatives of sin, fear, unbelief and ultimate death, but also by offering them the positive gift of His Kingdom and pouring His own positive life into them through the Holy Spirit.

If some choose to reject what God offers, it is not He who condemns them; they condemn themselves. Jesus warns them that there will be inevitable consequences to their rejection of Him.

Whoever believes in him is not condemned, but whoever does not believe stands condemned already because he has not believed in the name of God's one and only Son. This is the verdict: Light has come into the world, but men loved darkness instead of light because their deeds were evil. Everyone who does evil hates the light, and will not come into the light for fear that his deeds will be exposed. But whoever lives by the truth comes into the light, so that it may be seen plainly that what he has done has been done through God. (John 3: 18–21)

These words speak for themselves. But Jesus precedes these with the statement: 'God did not send his Son into the world to condemn the world, but to save the world through him.' (v. 17) That demonstrates the Father's heart and desire. The salvation He wants for the world is available '*through Him*', through Jesus. To reject Jesus is to reject the only way of salvation. 'For my Father's will is that everyone who looks to the Son and believes in him shall have eternal life, and I will raise him up at the last day.' (John 6: 40)

A man's eternal destiny is dependent on whether he accepts or rejects Jesus; on whether he accepts God's offer of His Kingdom now or throws it back in His face. To reject the Kingdom in this life will lead to eternal exclusion from it.

Every Christian needs to sense the urgency of sharing his faith with non-believers. God calls him to do that, no matter what reaction he receives from others. It is not for us to judge the eternal destiny of any individual; only to make others aware of the gospel. God alone is the Judge.

Jesus will not come again until the nations have heard the gospel. But what of all those deceived by the world's false religions, or those who have never heard of Jesus? There are not many ways to the one God. The other major religions (Judaism apart) worship false gods and demonic spirits. Their adherents are tragically deceived. They live in the kingdom of darkness, for Christ alone can rescue men and transfer them to the Kingdom of Light.

UNDER JUDGMENT

For the ungodly, the consequences seem inevitable. Paul says: 'The wrath of God is being revealed from heaven against all the godlessness and wickedness of men who suppress the truth by their wickedness, since what may be known about God is plain to them, because God has made it plain to them.' (Rom. 1: 18–19)

There is ample evidence for the existence of God and He will be found by all who seek Him. There can be no excuse for unbelief in God; no excuse for not seeking Him. 'For since the creation of the world God's invisible qualities – his eternal power and divine nature – have been clearly seen, being understood from what has been made, so that men are without any excuse.' (Rom. 1: 20)

To know or believe there is a God does not mean that people will care about Him, seek His will, worship Him or acknowledge Him in any other way. To believe in the existence of God does not give anybody a ticket to heaven. All have sinned and fallen short of God's glory, and will not be restored to that glory without a Saviour.

When people chose to please themselves rather than obey God, He 'gave them over in the sinful desires of their hearts to sexual impurity for the degrading of their bodies with one another. They exchanged the truth of God for a lie, and worshipped and served created things rather than the Creator.' (Rom. 1: 24–5) That is the sorry truth for many brought up as children to believe in God, but who have chosen to live in their own way instead of His.

> Furthermore, since they did not think it worth while to retain the knowledge of God, he gave them over to a depraved mind, to do what ought not to be done. They have become filled with every kind of wickedness, evil, greed and depravity. They are full of envy, murder, strife, deceit and malice. They are gossips, slanderers, God-haters, insolent, arrogant and boastful; they invent ways of doing evil; they disobey their parents; they are senseless, faithless, heartless, ruthless. Although they know God's righteous decree that those who do such things deserve death, they not only continue to do these very things but also approve of those who practise them. (Rom. 1: 28–32)

That is a very apt description of modern Western society. If men choose to go their own way instead of His, He allows them to do so. He will force nobody to obey Him. He desires our love. He will not make us as robots programmed to do His will, or puppets dancing because He pulls the string.

Paul continues: 'we know that God's judgment against those who do such things is based on truth.' (Rom. 2: 2) Because of the riches of His kindness, tolerance, patience and love He leads men to repentance so that they might know the joy of His Kingdom.

What of those who refuse to be so led, who seem to care nothing for the purposes of God? 'Because of your stubbornness and your unrepentant heart, you are storing up wrath against yourself for the day of God's wrath, when his righteous judgment will be revealed.' (Rom. 2: 5)

He will certainly deal justly with every man. 'God "will give to each person according to what he has done." To those who by persistence in doing good seek glory, honour and immortality, he will give eternal life. But for those who are self-seeking and who reject the truth and follow evil, there will be wrath and anger.' (Rom. 2: 6–8)

These are the two options open to every person. But Paul does make it clear that God will judge each according to the revelation he has received. 'All who sin apart from the law will also perish apart from the law, and all who sin under the law will be judged by the law. For it is not those who hear the law who are righteous in God's sight, but it is those who obey the law who will be declared righteous.' (Rom. 2: 12–13)

UNDER LAW

This, of course, refers to the Jewish law given by God through Moses. But what of those who come neither from a Jewish nor Christian background and who are ignorant of the real God? Paul says that even though they do not have God's law, some do by nature what the law requires. 'They are a law for themselves,' he says. 'They show that the requirements of the law are written on their hearts, their consciences also bearing witness, and their thoughts now accusing, now even defending them.' (vv. 14–15)

People will not be judged by the amount of revelation they have received, but by whether they have lived according to that revelation. This however falls far short of the glory God holds out to us through Jesus Christ. Through Him we can know forgiveness of sins, have peace with Him, assurance of our salvation and receive the gift of His Kingdom. God Himself comes to live in us by the power of the Holy Spirit that we might know the glorious liberty of the sons of God NOW.

This revelation is far superior to any other, even that given by God to Moses. But if the revelation is greater, so is the responsibility to live in righteousness, loving and obeying our heavenly Father. The Christian is not, therefore, in the position of a judge of the eternal destiny of particular individuals. It is for him to ensure that he is being faithful, so that he may be most effective in his witness to those who do not know the truth.

Jesus says: 'every teacher of the law who has been instructed about the kingdom of heaven is like the owner of a house who brings out of his storeroom new treasures as well as old.' (Matt. 13: 52) Jesus came to fulfil the law, which reveals what God requires of His people. They are unable to fulfil His demands by their own efforts, or work their way to heaven by trying to be righteous. The Jews, like everyone else, needed the revelation of the Kingdom. Receiving the life and resources of that Kingdom makes obedience possible; God's purposes can then be fulfilled.

If he is wise, the Jew who has sought to keep the law of God will embrace what is newly revealed to him. The heavenly Father has supplied a Saviour, who has made it possible for him to be delivered from his sins, and receive the gift of His Kingdom. Now the Father wants to live in him by the Holy Spirit.

Then the believer can fulfil the law because he has already been made acceptable to God. He can worship and pray, not according to prescribed rites and ceremonies, but in the power of the Holy Spirit. He no longer has to strive to be worthy of entering the Kingdom of heaven. It is already his by God's gracious gift.

Chapter 9

GOD'S OPEN INVITATION

Jesus made it clear that it was never too late in this life to receive the Kingdom from God. However, the sooner a person inherits this glorious gift, the sooner he can live in the good of it. He will have the joy of serving the King in this life as well as reigning with Him eternally.

WORKERS IN THE VINEYARD

Jesus likened the Kingdom of heaven to a landowner who went out early in the morning to hire men to work in his vineyard. He agreed to pay them a denarius for their day's work. He went out again at the third hour to hire others promising, 'I will pay you whatever is right.' He did the same again at the sixth, ninth and even the eleventh hour.

When he paid their wages at the end of the day all received the same amount, whether they had been hired early or towards the end of the day. Some 'began to grumble against the landowner. "These men who were hired last worked only one hour," they said, "and you have made them equal to us who have borne the burden of the work and the heat of the day."' (Matt. 20: 11–12)

The landowner said he was not being unfair. They had agreed to work for a denarius and had received what was promised them. 'I want to give the man who was hired last the same as I gave you. Don't I have the right to do what I want with my own money? Or are you envious because I am generous?' (vv. 14–15)

Jesus is here revealing more of the nature of the King and, therefore, of His Kingdom. The Lord, represented by the landowner, is the one who calls people into His Kingdom at various stages of their lives. Some live a lifetime of devotion to the King, giving themselves wholeheartedly to the work of the Kingdom. Others repent and acknowledge His Lordship only late in their lives. Yet to all there is the same reward: they inherit the Kingdom of heaven. There can be no greater reward, neither can there be anything less because God has made His Kingdom available to all who repent and believe.

He does not make part of His Kingdom available to some and less of His Kingdom to others. His Kingdom is present where He rules and reigns, and the full privileges and resources of the Kingdom are made available to all Christians. The whole 'seed' is planted in every believer's life.

Those 'who have borne the burden of the work and the heat of the day' have the additional privilege of having spent a greater part of their lives in serving the King and have been able to enjoy the privileges of the Kingdom longer than those who come to faith in Jesus later in life. They should rejoice that others have come to the same inheritance because of the Lord's gracious and merciful generosity, not be full of negative grumbling.

Those who live as Kingdom children should submit to God's purposes rather than grumble against His mercy and righteousness. None received more nor less than what was promised them.

Anyone coming to a personal knowledge of Jesus and into the revelation of His Kingdom regrets what seem to be the wasted years before that great life-transforming event. The Lord promises to redeem 'the years the locust has eaten', and all who are part of the Kingdom, young or old, can serve the purposes of the King. He certainly rejoices over every sinner who repents and causes all heaven to rejoice with Him.

The cost of serving the King will be greater for some than others. 'From everyone who has been given much, much will be demanded; and from the one who has been entrusted with much, much more will be asked.' (Luke 12: 48)

Some 'have renounced marriage because of the Kingdom of heaven', (Matt. 19: 12) although that is not God's calling for every Christian. Some are told to sell everything they have, because their worldly riches stand in the way of their submission to God and dependence on Him. But that is not a universal law for all believers.

God does not ask for legalistic obedience, but for obedience which flows from a sincere love for the King and a desire to be faithful to His Kingdom purposes. It is not a matter of good intentions, but of actually doing His will.

THE TWO SONS

Jesus told another parable to illustrate this point. A man had two sons. He told the first to go and work in his vineyard and received the answer, 'I will not.' But 'later he changed his mind and went.' (Matt. 21: 29)

The father then told his second son to go and work in the vineyard. 'He answered, "I will, sir," but he did not go.' (v. 30)

Jesus simply asked the question: 'Which of the two did what his father wanted?' His listeners had no difficulty in answering correctly.

This is a telling little illustration. It is easy to be full of good intentions, saying what we should to the Lord, without our hearts being in what we are saying.

Time and again God's Kingdom purposes are going to conflict with our own plans and desires. Then our initial reactions tend to be like that of the second son; but if our hearts truly belong to the Lord, it is not long before we have repented of our selfishness, thought better of disobeying our Lord, and have done what He asked of us.

Jesus used this parable in a powerful way to warn the religious leaders and those who opposed Him. 'I tell you the truth, the tax collectors and the prostitutes are entering the Kingdom of God ahead of you. For John came to you to show you the way of righteousness, and you did not believe him, but the tax collectors and the prostitutes did. And even after you saw this, you did not repent and believe him.' (v. 31-2)

Religious pedigree will not ensure any person a place in the Kingdom; faith in Jesus will. Human goodness cannot earn such an inheritance; it does not matter how many and great a man's sins, God's forgiveness following repentance washes them all away. The way of self-righteousness is no substitute for true righteousness which can only be given through Jesus.

The life-style of the swindling tax collectors and immoral prostitutes demonstrated their rejection of the Kingdom, until such time as they repented and received that glorious inheritance. The religious are full of the right-sounding phrases and responses, but without actually repenting, submitting their lives to the heavenly King's authority. Those who repent, regardless of the nature of their former life, enter the Kingdom ahead of those who refuse to repent.

THE WEDDING BANQUET

Jesus told the parable of the Wedding Banquet to illustrate the fact that many who hear the gospel of the Kingdom refuse to respond. He said that the Kingdom of heaven is like a king who prepared a wedding banquet for his son. His servants carried the invitations to the guests, but they refused to come. He sent more servants to urge them to come as everything was prepared for them. 'But they paid no attention and went off – one to his field, another to his business. The rest seized his servants, ill-treated them and killed them.' (Matt. 22: 5-6) The king sent his army to destroy the murderers and to burn their city.

He was determined to have the banquet filled with guests.

So he told his servants: 'Go to the street corners and invite to the banquet anyone you find.' (v. 9) They did as they were told and found both good and bad. The banquet was filled; but those originally invited did not deserve the feast.

When the king came in to see the guests, one had no wedding clothes. 'How did you get in here without wedding clothes?' the king asked him. The man was speechless.

'Tie him hand and foot, and throw him outside, into the darkness, where there will be weeping and gnashing of teeth.' (v. 13) The parable concludes with the truth that 'many are invited, but few are chosen.' (v. 14)

Again it is impossible to avoid the obvious conclusion that many who had heard the gospel of the Kingdom would be passed over because they had never responded, and so had not been able to bear the fruit of the Kingdom in their lives. Hearing it again and again is no virtue if there is no heart response. Agreeing with the gospel is not the same as submitting one's life to the authority of the King.

Many are invited but few chosen, and those who are will have wedding garments. They will be clothed with the righteousness of Jesus so they can stand before their heavenly Father without fear of rejection or condemnation. They do not come in their own name, but in the name of Jesus who is the Way, and who shed His blood to make them acceptable in God's sight and able to inherit His eternal Kingdom.

He is not content with bringing the gospel of the Kingdom to those who are nominally His people; He sends His disciples out to all who will hear and respond. There can be no such person as a 'nominal Christian'. He is no Christian at all who is not part of the Kingdom of heaven. And all who are His children are sent out to witness, regardless of the rejection they suffer from those who oppose the gospel.

The Pharisees were always looking for an occasion to trap Jesus by what He said, much as those who fail to respond to the gospel today try to find some intellectual flaw in the argument of the Scriptures to excuse their unbelief. Even to

Nicodemus, who was an honest enquirer, Jesus said: 'I have spoken to you of earthly things and you do not believe; how then will you believe if I speak of heavenly things?' (John 3: 12)

MODERN 'PHARISEES'

There is no excuse for unbelief: 'Woe to you, teachers of the law and Pharisees, you hypocrites! You shut the kingdom of heaven in men's faces. You yourselves do not enter, nor will you let those enter who are trying to.' (Matt. 23: 13) Tragically even this Scripture has its parallel today.

Many who have been brought up in religious formalism in the churches are hungry for spiritual reality. They want to know the Lord and to experience His power in their lives. Increasingly, they hear of the movement of the Holy Spirit that is gathering momentum in this generation. However, many are held back by their clergy or leaders, for whom the Kingdom may not be a reality. They scoff at the idea of conversion, dismissing genuine experiences of God as 'mere emotionalism'. They claim there is no need to seek Him personally, only to be true to the traditions of the denominational church. To be faithful has been reduced, for some, to the level of attending a service weekly.

Such men are deeply offended at the suggestion that people need to repent and to submit their lives personally to the Lordship of Jesus. It is widely assumed that He is a God of universal love and everyone will be received into the Kingdom of God finally anyway.

This is not only to be deceived, but to lead others into deception.

Even when some of their people have genuine new birth experiences and know the power of the Holy Spirit in their lives, they are told that such things are of no consequence: 'You will soon get over it!' Often they are deliberately prevented from sharing their new-found faith with others in the congregation.

When they ask for instruction in the Scriptures, they are met with embarrassment. When they want to have a prayer meeting, permission is refused. They are reduced to frustration by the lack of leadership given to them.

Is it not true today of some: 'You yourselves do not enter, nor will you let them enter who are trying to'? How this must grieve Jesus.

Do those who scorn new birth experiences and the empowering of the Holy Spirit manifest the life and power of the Kingdom themselves? Is their preaching accompanied by signs following? Do they give the example of faith to their congregations? Are they men consumed with zeal to reach the lost with the good news of the Kingdom? Or are they men afraid to face their spiritual inadequacy, too proud to repent and cry out to God for His enabling?

TRANSFORMED MINISTRIES

Praise God that many clergy in recent years have experienced great changes in their ministries because they have sought God and met with Him. 'He who seeks finds; and to him who knocks, the door will be opened.' (Matt. 7: 8) I have lost count of the number of men, ordained for many years, who have testified to becoming Christians only recently. Their ministries have been transformed as a result. Instead of teaching religious observance and urging their congregations into church activity, they have been able to lead people into the Kingdom, see them filled with the Holy Spirit and have been able to encourage their growth in ministry. They have become teachers of the Word instead of critics of it, and have known dimensions of true praise and worship formerly beyond their experience.

The Church is not the Kingdom; neither is the Kingdom the Church. However a congregation of church people are properly those who are children of the Kingdom because all have come to true repentance and faith in Jesus. They share together the life of the Kingdom, pray together with the authority of the Kingdom and reach out into the world with the truth and power of the Kingdom. They are a people with a sense of mission and with zeal for God's purposes. Their personal devotion for Jesus is seen not only in their worship, but in their relationships also. They love one another and count the unity the Holy Spirit creates among them as precious.

When a church is a Kingdom-conscious people, Jesus causes it to grow both in depth and size. He tells His people to proclaim the Kingdom in word and deed and promises that He will build the Church.

Chapter 10

EACH ONE PRECIOUS

THE SHEEP AND COINS

Jesus told several parables expressing His desire to reach the lost with the good news of the Kingdom. If someone owning a hundred sheep loses one, what does he do? 'Does he not leave the ninety-nine in the open country and go after the lost sheep until he finds it?' (Luke 15:4) Having found it, he is so full of joy he gathers his friends and neighbours saying: 'Rejoice with me; I have found my lost sheep.' (v. 6)

What lessons does Jesus draw from this? 'I tell you that in the same way there is more rejoicing in heaven over one sinner who repents than over ninety-nine righteous persons who do not need to repent.' (v. 7)

Heaven rejoices with the Lord in seeing His reign extended, in seeing a lost soul under condemnation coming to repentance, new life and the inheritance of the Kingdom.

Jesus tells another similar parable of a woman with ten coins who loses one. She searches diligently and finds it. She too gathers her friends and neighbours to share her joy that what was lost has been found. 'In the same way, I tell you, there is rejoicing in the presence of the angels of God over one sinner who repents.' (Luke 15: 10)

How precious each soul is to the Lord! They are so precious that He sent His Son to die and thus save them from condemnation, death and hell. How it must grieve Him to see people turn away from Him and deny Him.

THE LOVING FATHER

The parable of the Loving Father (often known as the Prodigal Son, or the Two Sons) must be one of the best-known and most commonly quoted passages of teaching from the New Testament.

A man had two sons. The younger asked his father for his share of the inheritance, which he squandered on wild living in a distant country. When he had spent everything, there was a severe famine. In great need, he was hired to feed pigs and longed to eat their food; 'but no-one gave him anything.'

The son 'came to his senses' and decided to return home. His father saw him coming and ran to meet him, throwing his arms around him and kissing him. 'Father,' the son said, 'I have sinned against heaven and against you. I am no longer worthy to be called your son.' (Luke 15: 21)

The father ordered his servants to put the best robe on him, a ring on his finger and sandals on his feet. The fattened calf was to be killed so they could have a feast in celebration: 'For this son of mine was dead and is alive again; he was lost and is found.'

The older brother was angry when he came home from the fields to discover the feast was in honour of his brother. He refused to go in. His father came out and pleaded with him; but he only complained that he had never been given a feast to celebrate with his friends even though he had remained diligent and obedient – unlike his wasteful younger brother.

'My son,' the father said, 'you are always with me, and everything I have is yours. But we had to celebrate and be glad, because this brother of yours was dead and is alive again; he was lost and is found.' (vv. 31–2)

What a wealth of meaning is woven into each of Jesus's parables!

First we need to notice that both those brothers were sons of the father and therefore had an inheritance to come from him. When the younger son asked for his inheritance his father gave it to him, although he must have realised it would be wasted. There are many who ask for Kingdom inheritance, but because their lives are not truly submitted to the authority of God and they do not have genuine love for Him, they squander that inheritance. They are more intent on doing what they please and the Father knows He cannot force their love for Him.

However, He is always ready to extend His mercy and grace, His love and forgiveness to any who return to Him in repentance. Once that breaking and humbling has taken place, the son is able to enter into his father's joy. He experiences the father lavishing gifts on him that he certainly does not deserve. There is even a feast to celebrate his home-coming. The father is overjoyed that his son returned. Now he can allow himself to be loved by his father in a way he would not allow before.

The sin of the elder son was two-fold. First, he refused to forgive his brother, even though the father had forgiven him. But secondly he too had failed to live in the power of his inheritance. In that sense he was as bad as his brother.

'You are always with me,' the father tells the elder son, 'and everything I have is yours.' There are many today who have Kingdom inheritance and Kingdom resources available to them. But they are so busy, diligently serving with their human resources, they fail to take account of the divine, supernatural resources that are theirs through Jesus.

The parable teaches the folly of failing to live in the power of the Kingdom, and both brothers were guilty of that. Above all we see the amazing love and wisdom of the father in watching his younger son leave, knowing that he would have to wait until, willingly and humbly, he was prepared to accept his love.

What a picture of our heavenly Father's patience, refusing to force any of His children into love or obedience! Respecting their freedom of choice, He waits for their willing response to submit to His reign and rejoices in them when they do. He not only waits for the sinner, He pleads with the self-righteous to enter the joy of true inheritance.

THE SHREWD MANAGER

There was a rich man whose manager was accused of wasting his possessions. He was called to account and told he was dismissed.

At first the manager was perplexed as to what to do. He decided to summon his master's creditors and enquired how much each owed. The manager asked for immediate payment, but reduced the amounts due. His master commended him for acting so shrewdly. 'For the people of this world are more shrewd in dealing with their own kind than are the people of the light.' (Luke 16: 8)

Jesus then tells His listeners to 'use worldly wealth to gain friends for yourselves, so when it is gone, you will be welcomed into eternal dwellings.' (v. 9) This suggestion does not need to cause us problems; worldly wealth is to be used with wisdom and astuteness. There is no point in hoarding it, or 'storing it up in barns'. We certainly cannot take it into eternity with us. All financial resources and worldly wealth are given us to use.

Such generosity as the shrewd manager showed would seem out of place in the world's business standards and yet accomplishes far more than the cut-throat tactics of many traders. Jesus points out: 'Whoever can be trusted with very little can also be trusted with much, and whoever is dishonest with very little will also be dishonest with much. So if you have not been trustworthy in handling worldly wealth, who will trust you with true riches? And if you have not been trustworthy with someone else's property, who will give you property of your own?' (vv. 10–12)

A person's attitude towards money reveals so much about their spiritual attitudes. Do not store up for yourselves treasure on earth, Jesus said, 'But store up for yourselves treasures in heaven, where moth and rust do not destroy, and where thieves do not break in and steal.' (Matt. 6: 20) It is the rich resources of the Kingdom that have permanent value.

God knows our hearts. 'For where your treasure is, there your heart will be also.' (Matt. 6: 21) If a person lives for worldly wealth and advancement, that is where his heart is set – on things that pass away. If his heart is set on heavenly things, he has an eternal Kingdom as his inheritance and he will handle wisely, honestly and well the worldly resources put at his disposal.

'No servant can serve two masters. Either he will hate the one and love the other, or he will be devoted to the one and despise the other. You cannot serve both God and Money.' (Luke 16: 13) Whatever you serve becomes your master!

The Pharisees, who loved money, sneered at this teaching of Jesus. To them He said: 'You are the ones who justify yourselves in the eyes of men, but God knows your hearts. What is highly valued among men is detestable in God's sight.' (Luke 16: 15)

Jesus has received considerable criticism for commending the shrewdness of the manager. His purpose is to direct us to the things that truly matter. We are not created to serve money; money is there to serve us. As the children of the Kingdom we can afford to be generous, to forgive debts altogether, and God sometimes requires us to do that. 'But love your enemies, do good to them, and lend to them without expecting to get anything back.' (Luke 6: 35)

Such attitudes do not belong to the world; but they are of the Kingdom. Jesus continues: 'Then your reward will be great, and you will be sons of the Most High, because he is kind to the ungrateful and wicked. Be merciful, just as your Father is merciful.' (vv. 35–6)

THE RICH AND THE POOR

Jesus told the parable of the rich man and Lazarus. The one lived in luxury, the other was a beggar at his gate. Both died.

The beggar was carried by the angels 'to Abraham's side.' The rich man went to hell where he was tormented and cried out: 'Father Abraham, have pity on me and send Lazarus to dip the tip of his finger in water and cool my tongue, because I am in agony in this fire.' (Luke 16: 24)

Abraham replied: 'Son, remember that in your lifetime you received your good things, while Lazarus received bad things, but now he is comforted here and you are in agony. And besides all this, between us and you a great chasm has been fixed, so that those who want to go from here to you cannot, nor can anyone cross over from there to us.' (vv. 25–6) Our eternal destiny is determined by our actions in this life!

The rich man asked for someone to be sent to warn his brothers, who were no doubt also wealthy, disobedient unbelievers. He wanted them to be spared the torment he was experiencing. But he was told they had Moses and the Prophets to warn them.

The rich man persisted. Surely if someone from the dead went to them, they would repent! Jesus knew such an argument to be false: 'If they do not listen to Moses and the Prophets, they will not be convinced even if someone rises from the dead.' (Luke 16: 31).

Sadly, this has proved prophetically true. Even though Jesus conquered death and rose again, the fact of His resurrection does not convince all. Faith comes from hearing the Word of God. Salvation comes from responding to that Word. Then a man believes whole-heartedly in the resurrection, because he has experienced the risen Christ for himself.

If we are living as the children of the Kingdom we know that all our worldly wealth is under the sovereignty of Jesus. He is ruler even in our financial affairs. Our substance is made available to Him for the extension of His Kingdom. Even with our money we put the Kingdom first.

Like so much of what Jesus says, this parable makes it abundantly clear that a man's eternal destiny is determined by his response to the gospel of the Kingdom during his life on earth. If he chooses to go his own way instead of following Jesus, he will discover he is lost for eternity. A great gulf will separate him from God and His glory. To reject the way of glory now will result in being excluded from it beyond death.

The wonder is that God makes His eternal glory available to sinners who are prepared to come to the cross in repentance and faith. He is willing to cancel all the sins, fears and doubts that have separated him from God and make all the riches of His Kingdom available to him.

THE KINGDOM WITHIN YOU

Jesus said: 'The kingdom of God does not come visibly, nor will people say, "Here it is," ... because the kingdom of God is within you.' (Luke 17: 20–1) The Greek word translated 'within' can also mean 'among'. Although 'within' is the better rendering, both are true: the Kingdom is both within and among. It is not a visible Kingdom, a piece of territory; it is present wherever Jesus reigns in His sovereign power. It is present within those who live the life of the Kingdom, albeit imperfectly. God has planted the seed of the Kingdom within them, with all its potential. They are to demonstrate its presence, its power and reality in the world.

Wherever the King is, there the Kingdom is present. He is among those who gather in His name. So whenever Christians gather for fellowship or worship, the resources of the King and His Kingdom are present and available to them.

This means that worship should be dynamic. A conventional service, predictable in its lifelessness, is hardly an expression of Kingdom worship! The book of Revelation gives us a pictorial glimpse into the courts of heaven. There the heavenly host worship the Lord, continually aware that He reigns as the Holy King in majesty and glory.

Those who worship Him on earth are given access to His heavenly throne by Jesus: 'Therefore, brothers, since we have confidence to enter the Most Holy Place by the blood of Jesus, by a new and living way opened for us through the curtain, that is, his body, and since we have a great priest over the house of God, let us draw near to God with a sincere heart in full assurance of faith, having our hearts sprinkled to cleanse us from a guilty conscience and having our bodies washed with pure water.' (Heb. 10: 19–22)

The way into the holy Presence of the Lord is open to Christians. They can enjoy that privilege in this life and can be assured of enjoying that heavenly Kingdom eternally. Those who, like the rich man, fail to come to that living way and walk with Jesus, will find themselves separated from Him eternally – and will be unable to warn their loved ones of the dire consequences of their unbelief and disobedience. Those who recognise their need of forgiveness and salvation will come to Him and will discover His love, forgiveness and acceptance now, and the eternal reward of rejoicing with Him.

What a choice! And what does the cost of discipleship matter when so much is at stake? 'I tell you the truth,' Jesus said to them, 'no-one who has left home or wife or brothers or parents or children for the sake of the kingdom of God will fail to receive many times as much in this age and, in the age to come, eternal life.' (Luke 18: 29–30)

Chapter 11

FREE TO BE POSITIVE

SET FREE

'It is for freedom that Christ has set us free,' says Paul. (Gal. 5: 1) It is always important to notice the tenses of the verbs used in Scripture. Here the apostle points his readers to the fact of what God has already done for them in Christ: they *have been* set free.

Free from what? Free from bondage to the law, from trying to please God and win His favour through obedience to a code of legalistic practice, knowing that they will inevitably fail to do so. Free from relating to God by religious observance instead of through a loving personal relationship in which He is known as 'Father'.

Free from bondage to the flesh, so that human passions and desires no longer rule them. Their minds, wills and emotions can be brought under the sovereignty of the Holy Spirit. It is no longer the law of sin and death that operates within them, but the law of the Spirit of life.

Free from the devil's dominion. They have been rescued by Jesus from the dominion of darkness and brought into the Kingdom of God. Satan no longer need have any control over them. The only activity he is allowed in their lives is that which they willingly choose to give him through their disobedience.

Free from the demands of worldliness. They no longer have to live as the world lives, no longer conformed to the pattern of this world, but transformed through the renewing of their minds. Their values have been completely changed by their seeking first the Kingdom and allowing Jesus to reign over their lives.

All this is accomplished because of what Jesus did on the cross. There sin was dealt with, the power of negative bondage was broken. There sinners were crucified with Christ, so that they may be dead to the old life lived without Him and alive with new life lived in Him.

The believer is freed from the power of the negative kingdom and is given the gift of the positive Kingdom.

Paul contrasts these two for the Galatians. 'The sinful nature desires what is contrary to the Spirit, and the Spirit what is contrary to the sinful nature. They are in conflict with each other, so that you do not do what you want.' (Gal. 5: 17)

The sinful nature is negative by nature, which is why we live in such a negative world. It is therefore utterly opposed to the working of God's Spirit, who is positive by nature. 'The acts of the sinful nature are obvious:' says Paul, 'sexual immorality, impurity and debauchery; idolatry and witchcraft; hatred, discord, jealousy, fits of rage, selfish ambition, dissensions, factions and envy; drunkenness, orgies, and the like.' (Gal. 5: 19–21) Such things are obviously not the working of God's Spirit. As far as He is concerned, they are all negative and stand opposed to His positive Kingdom.

So Paul warns: 'I warn you, as I did before, that those who live like this will not inherit the kingdom of God.' (Gal. 5: 21) How can anyone inherit the Kingdom when he lives a life opposed to the very nature of this spiritual Kingdom? That is like suggesting a man should be honoured by one nation, while being a traitor who has spied for another.

God is not to be mocked and will not be fooled. It is not those who call Him 'Lord' who will be part of that Kingdom, but those who do His will.

When a man accepts the power of the cross in his life, he is freed from all the sin and bondage of the past. He does not have to look back or imagine that he is held back by spectres of his past. Faith in the atoning work of Jesus sets him free from the past. He is now a new creation with a new heart.

Jesus said: 'Every good tree bears good fruit, but a bad tree bears bad fruit. A good tree cannot bear bad fruit.' (Matt. 7: 17–18) Then he warns: 'Every tree that does not bear good fruit is cut down and thrown into the fire.' (v. 19) It is good for nothing else.

CALLED TO BE FRUITFUL
At the Last Supper, He made it clear that God expects fruitfulness in the lives of His children because He wants to be glorified in their lives: 'This is to my Father's glory, that you bear much fruit, showing yourselves to be my disciples.' (John 15: 8)

Fruitfulness can only be through the activity of the Holy Spirit within the believer. So, having warned the Galatians of the negative things of darkness that prevent a person from inheriting the Kingdom of God, he then goes on to speak of the fruit of the Spirit.

'But the fruit of the Spirit is love, joy, peace, patience, kindness, goodness, faithfulness, gentleness and self-control.' (Gal. 5: 22–3) All these are definitely positive by nature and in their effect on the believer and those around him. They are in striking contrast to the negative works of the flesh.

The Christian may want more of the positive fruit of the Spirit in his life, but he is often painfully aware of the pull towards the negative things of the flesh. All too often he has to confess he has sinned by doing the very thing that stands opposed to the working of God's Kingdom in his life.

Does this mean he stands condemned before God, or is not truly a part of His Kingdom, or stands in danger of losing his inheritance?

He cannot be in condemnation if he knows God's forgiveness, which blots out his transgressions as if they never happened. The page is wiped clean and He does not keep on record the sins that have been forgiven. There is no condemnation for those who are in Christ Jesus. How could there be condemnation in the Son of God or in His Kingdom? The believer has been brought out of the kingdom of darkness, where all are under condemnation, and has been brought into the Kingdom of light, where there is no condemnation.

The Lord has planted the seed of the positive Kingdom in a life that has been conditioned to be negative. Although the cross has dealt with all those negatives, the individual Christian has to learn how to apply the victory of the cross to the circumstances of his life so that he may live in freedom. He has to allow the water of the Holy Spirit to nurture that seed towards maturity and greater fruitfulness in his life.

A LIFE OF CHOICES

The fact that he still thinks, reacts and behaves in negative ways should not be surprising. *He no longer needs to do so* and the Lord will continue to teach him not to do so. God's refining in his life will result in change so that he chooses increasingly to live Kingdom life, rather than react or indulge himself in a fleshly way. As he matures in the life of the Spirit, he will choose to live according to his rich Kingdom inheritance, rather than choose the alternative of fleshly disobedience.

Of course if a man chooses to walk his own way, deliberately denying his inheritance, then the life of the positive Kingdom will be choked, as Jesus makes clear in the parable of the Sower.

Although Kingdom life can only be lived through the grace and power of the Holy Spirit within the believer, God does require his co-operation with the Spirit. He will never interfere with the Christian's free-will, for He desires a loving response to His purposes.

STAND FIRM

Paul gives sensible, practical advice to his readers: 'Stand firm, then, and do not let yourselves be burdened again by a yoke of slavery.' (Gal. 5: 1) Stand firm against all the pressures to live negatively. Stand firm against the temptations to allow your faith to be reduced again to the level of religious observance. Stand firm against the devil tempting you to indulge yourself and express the old nature; stand firm against him and he will flee from you. Stand firm against the pressures of worldliness and the desires to be accepted by those who live worldly lives, by allowing your standards to be reduced to theirs. Stand firm against the desires you know to be alien to God's purposes for you. Stand firm against the temptation to contradict God's Word, to believe you know better than the truth He reveals. Stand firm against the desire to compromise His Word in your life. Stand firm against the temptation to neglect what is necessary for your spiritual health and what the flesh dislikes: prayer, study of the Scriptures, praise and worship, sharing your faith with others. How the flesh dislikes such things!

'The only thing that counts is faith expressing itself through love.' (v. 6) To live by faith is to depend on what God has accomplished already for you through Christ. You will walk in liberty as you trust in the victory He has already won over all the negative forces of evil. You do not have to fight a battle He has already fought and won; you only have to trust in His victory. Fighting the good fight of faith is applying that victory to the circumstances of your life.

The positive Kingdom of God can only be manifested when people live by faith, faith that is expressed in love. For this is a Kingdom of both faith and love. In no way are these two contradictory; they are complementary.

Faith is a way of life; it cannot suddenly be switched on in a time of need. Love is another aspect of the same way of life. It is to be expressed by the Christian at all times in all situations, not only when he chooses to do so.

'A little yeast works through the whole batch of dough,' Paul warns. (v. 9) Satan encourages Christians to be negative. The mind is his first line of attack. He feeds to the believer a negative thought that will stimulate fleshly desire, or a doubt that will undermine faith, or an unloving thought that will inspire criticism, judgment, fear or even hatred. If the first negative is received he is quick to follow it with another and then another. It is not long before the Christian finds himself in a totally negative frame of mind, at which point he is easy prey for the enemy to begin accusing him. He will suggest that his fleshly desires demonstrate how unacceptable he is to God; his doubts are an indication of how weak and feeble his faith is; his critical, judgmental attitudes show how unlike Jesus he is and totally unworthy of His Kingdom.

If the negative thoughts and the accusations are believed, the Christian feels utterly condemned. But if he had stood firm against the first negative the whole process could not have developed.

Satan is the father of all lies; he is to be resisted. He wants to sow seeds of negativity within us so that we do not act positively with faith and love as the children of the Kingdom of God.

'A little yeast works through the whole batch of dough.' One negative can easily lead to a completely negative, unbelieving attitude. But in the same way, the seed of the positive Kingdom can cause positive life to flow through the believer. As Satan sows the negative seed from without, so the Holy Spirit sows the positive seed from within.

He is the voice of God within you, and constantly draws you to God's words and gives you the witness as to what is, and is not, right in His sight. To believe the word He speaks is to encourage faith; to act on that word is always to act in love.

Negative attitudes and actions have a repercussive effect on others around. One person expressing negative criticism can easily affect others, so that they too become critical. They may have no knowledge of the particular matter, but if they receive the criticism the spirit of criticism will influence them to pass on judgmental attitudes to others.

Many ungodly situations arise among Christians (as well as others) in this way. There can even be pleasure in criticising others – the result of pride and a lack of self-assurance.

Similarly, Christians can, and should be, an influence in spreading the attitudes of the positive Kingdom. In this way they are to be leaven in the lump, light for the world and the salt of the earth. Their difficulty is to spread the positive in the midst of so much negativity. They will be ineffective in doing this unless they stand firm against the temptation to be negative in their own lives.

Our mouths so often give us away. Jesus says it is from the overflow of the heart that the mouth speaks. If we say negative, unbelieving, critical things, that is only an indication of what is going on in our hearts. The new heart given at new birth becomes tainted by sin and needs to be purified. We need to ask God, not only to forgive the negative things that persist in our experience, but to purify our hearts. With David each of us can pray: 'Create in me a pure heart, O God, and renew a steadfast spirit within me.' (Ps. 51: 10)

Again and again we shall have to reckon ourselves dead to sin. We do not need to live in it any longer. If you imagine that you are still in bondage to it, you will simply resign yourself to a life of constant spiritual failure, which is totally the opposite to the Kingdom life God intends for you. Jesus does not reign in failure! 'You, my brothers, were called to be free.' (Gal. 5: 13) So live in the glorious liberty of the sons of God. You do not have to live as if still a child of the devil, resigned to serving him. You do not have to give him any pleasure or satisfaction by responding to his temptations to make you negative again.

Even when you do, for none of us is without sin, you do not have to give him further satisfaction by allowing him to accuse you. He cannot accuse you in heaven; he has been expelled. You, however, are a child of the Kingdom and reign in Christ Jesus. The Lord sees you sitting in heavenly places where Satan does not belong. You do not have to allow him to kick you around like a spiritual football. You have the power to stand firm against him and see him flee, and the authority to dismiss him from the circumstances of your life in the name of Jesus.

He always seems to know where to attack as he probes for our weaknesses. We give him a foothold in our lives by our love of sin and desire to please ourselves, rather than our heavenly Father. When we set our hearts on living in righteousness we resist the enemy and find that he is ineffective in luring us with temptations that previously seemed too alluring to resist.

LIBERTY, NOT LICENCE

As Christians, we are free from the bondage to law. We can serve God by following the leading of the Holy Spirit. But Paul warns of a subtle temptation: 'Do not use your freedom to indulge the sinful nature.' (Gal. 5: 13)

Freedom in Christ is not freedom to do what we like. It is being free to love Him and therefore to love others. And so Paul continues in the same verse: 'rather, serve one another in love. The entire law is summed up in a single command, "Love your neighbour as yourself." If you keep on biting and devouring each other, watch out or you will be destroyed by each other.' (Gal. 5: 13–15)

It is freedom to walk away from the negative and live in the positive power of God. To sin deliberately is an act of rebellion against God, and He does not reign in rebellion. We deny our position as Kingdom children by such actions. That undermines the power of God in our lives, and prevents Him from working through us in the way He desires.

The secret is not to have our hearts and minds set on ourselves and our own desires, but on Him and our wish to please Him. 'So I say, live by the Spirit, and you will not gratify the desires of the sinful nature.' (Gal. 5: 16)

The best way to counteract the negative is to concentrate on the positive, to seek first the Kingdom and to fix your eyes on the King: 'Therefore, holy brothers, who share in the heavenly calling, fix your thoughts on Jesus, the apostle and high priest whom we confess.' (Heb. 3: 1)

Concentrate on the negative and you will become pre-occupied with it, and will spend your Christian life fighting all the ungodly desires you have. Concentrate on Jesus and you concentrate on the positive King who has overcome the negative. Draw near to Him and come near to the One who is altogether positive.

Speak as He speaks, and you speak positively. Think with the mind of Christ, and you think positively. Act in obedience to the leading of His Spirit, and you act positively. 'Since we live by the Spirit, let us keep in step with the Spirit.' (Gal. 5: 25)

For the Christian life is a walk with Jesus. It is not a static life, holding on to what you hold dear, resisting change, doubting your prayers will be answered. It is moving on with Jesus in the way He leads, taking His positive life into the negative world. Where there is doubt, we can bring faith. Where there is bitterness and resentment, we can bring forgiveness. Where there is sorrow, we can bring joy. Where there is hopelessness and despair, we can bring God's hope. Where there is sickness, we can bring His healing. Where there is bondage to evil spirits, we can bring deliverance in the name of Jesus. Where there is need, we can bring the Lord's provision. Where there is fear and anxiety, we can speak the words of His peace. Where there is futility, we can bring His purpose. Where there is weakness, we can bring His power and strength.

Wherever there is the negative we can bring the power of His positive Kingdom to bear. We are commissioned by Him personally to do just that. And wherever the positive meets the negative the positive prevails, as when light meets darkness the light prevails.

There has to be a constant determination to think, speak

and act according to the principles of the positive Kingdom to which you belong. There needs to be an equally constant determination to resist every impulse to think, speak and act negatively – the way of the world, the flesh and the devil. In both, the Holy Spirit will be your helper if you are prepared to call on Him.

Chapter 12

RIGHTEOUSNESS, PEACE AND JOY

'The kingdom of God is not a matter of eating and drinking, but of righteousness, peace and joy in the Holy Spirit, because anyone who serves Christ in this way is pleasing to God and approved by men.' (Rom. 14: 17–18)

Paul is referring to religious rules about food and drink. No observance of religious rules will enable a person to enter the Kingdom, or empower him to live as a child of the Kingdom. It is only by the working of the Spirit within him that the Christian can express the life of the Kingdom in righteousness, peace and joy. Only by the Spirit is he able to please God and to live the godly life approved by men.

To live as a child of the Kingdom is to live in righteousness, in right standing with God, in right relationship with Him, walking with Him in righteous ways. The Spirit will cleanse and purge out of your life all that is unrighteous. He will convict you of the sin of deceit and untruthfulness, whether in your personal relationships or business practices. He will convict you of unbelief and your failure to trust the Lord. He will teach you to believe His promises and expect His positive answers to prayer. He will show you where you fail to love and are filled instead with self-love, selfishness and self-pity.

To live as a child of the Kingdom is to know that you are at peace with God because, having been convicted, you have repented and turned away from your sins. You have been forgiven because of the grace, mercy and love of your heavenly Father. You know you are forgiven and that nothing interferes with your unity with God; you have received peace beyond understanding and have a sense of total well-being before God.

Furthermore, this peace leads to joy. As a child of the Kingdom, you know that no man or situation can steal your joy from you. No one can snatch you from the hand of your heavenly Father, whom you delight to serve. Everything is working together for good because of your love for God, and because you are called according to His purpose. Even in the midst of adversity you rejoice in Him. You learn that you are able to rejoice in the Lord always, for at no time are you deprived of Him or of the treasure of His Kingdom.

THE FRUIT OF RIGHTEOUSNESS

Because the Kingdom is a matter of righteousness, peace and joy in the Holy Spirit, we should expect to see the power of the Kingdom evidenced in miracles and signs of His Kingly power and authority among us. Paul certainly did. In fact, he did not consider that he had fully preached the gospel of the Kingdom unless he could demonstrate its presence with works of power: 'I will not venture to speak of anything except what Christ has accomplished through me in leading the Gentiles to obey God by what I have said and done – by the power of signs and miracles, through the power of the Spirit. So from Jerusalem all the way around to Illyricum, I have fully proclaimed the gospel of Christ.' (Rom. 15: 18–19)

These words should encourage all preachers of the gospel. Whenever and wherever that same gospel of the Kingdom is proclaimed today, in the power of the same Holy Spirit, the signs and miracles can be seen. God is as powerful today as ever, His words as efficacious and His Spirit as freely given. Only unbelief in the preacher or people can hinder the demonstrations of Kingdom power. 'Our gospel came to you not simply with words, but also with power, with the Holy Spirit and with deep conviction.' (1 Thess. 1: 5)

Certainly the power and evidence of the Kingdom will not be seen where there is unrighteousness. 'Do you not know that the wicked will not inherit the kingdom of God? Do not be deceived: Neither the sexually immoral nor idolaters nor adulterers nor male prostitutes nor homosexual offenders nor thieves nor the greedy nor drunkards nor slanderers nor swindlers will inherit the kingdom of God.' (1 Cor. 6: 9–10)

It is not unknown to have people from some, or all, of these categories claming to be Christians, while persisting in their sinful ways. Paul continues: 'But you were washed, you were sanctified, you were justified in the name of the Lord Jesus Christ and by the Spirit of our God.' (v. 11)

The Christian is expected to manifest a transformed life, because he is intent on living as a child of the Kingdom rather than persisting in his old ways.

If we have new life, we are to live new lives. If we are to inherit the Kingdom, we are to live Kingdom lives. We are cleansed from the old, made acceptable to God and filled with His Spirit to make this possible. It is He 'who has qualified you to share in the inheritance of the saints in the kingdom of light.' (Col. 1: 12) So why continue to walk in darkness?

Paul is confident: 'The Lord will rescue me from every evil attack and will bring me safely to his heavenly kingdom.' (2 Tim. 4: 18) All those who seek first the Kingdom of God in their lives can dare to have a similar confidence.

Of His Son, God says: 'Your throne, O God, will last for ever and ever, and righteousness will be the sceptre of your kingdom. You have loved righteousness and hated wickedness; therefore God, your God, has set you above your companions by anointing you with the oil of joy.' (Heb. 1: 8–9) He desires all His children to love righteousness, and it is only by living in light that Christians will be able to bring effectively the gospel of light into the darkness of the world.

Our God is the consuming fire, who purges and cleanses

the lives of believers and who stands in judgment on all unrighteousness.

James asks: 'Has not God chosen those who are poor in the eyes of the world to be rich in faith and to inherit the kingdom he promised those who love him?' (James 2: 5) Like Paul, he emphasises the twin pillars of faith and love. The children of the Kingdom will be men and women of faith and love. They are to be rich in faith. God delights to see His children laying hold of eternal life, applying the victory of the cross to their circumstances and availing themselves of the heavenly resources at their disposal. They are not to be negative, denying their inheritance, saying they are weak in faith, without blessing or resources. Faith enables them to enter more and more fully into all that is already theirs in Christ.

Our love for the Lord is always the motivation for obedience to His purposes. Disobedience points to a crisis of love.

Peter bids us make our calling and election sure by making every effort to add to our faith goodness, knowledge, self-control, perseverance, godliness, brotherly kindness and love. These things will keep us from being ineffective and unproductive. Without these qualities Christians are 'near-sighted and blind' and have forgotten the significance of being cleansed from past sins.

With these qualities believers will never fall and 'will receive a rich welcome into the eternal kingdom of our Lord and Saviour Jesus Christ.' (2 Peter 1: 11)

God requires your performance to be the evidence of your position before Him. It is no use claiming to have relationship with Jesus, if your life does not demonstrate evidence of that; or saying that you are a child of the Kingdom if you do not live accordingly. He knows we do not become perfect in our performance overnight; but He does expect progress and perseverance so that with John you can say: 'To him who loves us and has freed us from our sins by his blood, and has made us to be a kingdom and priests to serve his God and Father –

to him be glory and power for ever and ever! Amen.' (Rev. 1: 5–6)

Chapter 13

KINGDOM FAITH

Jesus devoted Himself to prayer during His earthly ministry. If it wasn't possible to be alone with His Father because of the pressures of ministry and the demands of the people, He prayed through the night. Nothing must stand in the way of maintaining fellowship with His Father in prayer.

'Then Jesus told his disciples a parable to show them that they should always pray and not give up.' (Luke 18: 1) In this story there was a judge 'who neither feared God nor cared about men.' (v. 2) A widow kept coming to him pleading for justice against her adversary. Although for some time he refused, he finally gave her justice to stop her from persistently bothering him.

'And will not God bring about justice for his chosen ones, who cry out to him day and night? Will he keep putting them off? I tell you, he will see that they get justice, and quickly. However, when the Son of Man comes, will he find faith on the earth?' (vv. 7–8)

Jesus does not separate prayer from faith. The woman believed in her cause and so was prepared to be persistent. Jesus says His chosen ones are prepared to call out to Him day and night and will receive justice *quickly*.

Often Christians pray in a tentative and half-hearted manner, as if hardly daring to believe their heavenly Father would answer their cause. There is little virtue in prayer itself; Jesus warns that we shall not be heard for our many words. But prayer that is a true expression of positive faith will receive positive answers from God. The promises Jesus gives us overwhelmingly point to this truth. 'I will do whatever you ask in my name, so that the Son may bring glory to the Father. You may ask me for anything in my name, and I will do it.' (John 14: 13–14)

The all-embracing nature of this promise seems startling and almost unbelievable, especially to those who have prayed, but with little consideration of the faith God looks for in our praying.

To pray in the name of Jesus is to pray in the person of Jesus, to pray as He would. He always prayed with faith, with the expectation that He would receive from His loving Father what He asked for. It is inconceivable to think that He would have prayed without faith, for all that is not of faith is sin; and Jesus certainly never sinned.

To pray with faith, so that God answers our prayers, will bring glory to the Father and is the evidence of fruitful Kingdom living. 'You did not choose me, but I chose you to go and bear fruit – fruit that will last. Then the Father will give you whatever you ask in my name.' (John 15: 16) Again the promise is both emphatic and far-reaching: 'whatever you ask'. 'I tell you the truth, my Father will give you whatever you ask in my name.' (John 16: 23)

If we allow Him, the Holy Spirit will guide us in our praying. We are to pray at all times 'in the Spirit'. He will not only show us what to pray but will inspire the faith with which to pray.

FAITH OR HOPE?

Sometimes we have to acknowledge that we lack the faith necessary for a situation. As an extension of our Kingdom Faith ministry, God impressed on the elders of the Bethany Fellowship the need to open a college where people could be trained for ministries that would be effective in the life and power of the Kingdom.

Within a few days we heard of a college in the near vicinity that was for sale. When we viewed this, it was ideal for our needs. When we prayed, it seemed right to offer £570,000 plus £10,000 for the contents – in cash. We are a faith ministry looking to the Lord for His provision. We do not raise money, nor do we ask others for it. If we have need, we pray to our Father in heaven.

We did not have the money when making the offer, but we were confident that this was the property God was wanting us to use for the college. Later we heard that our offer was accepted (although there had been higher ones) because we were the only ones to be offering cash! You need to be sure of your guidance from God before taking such a step of faith.

This happened just prior to my departure to the Far East for a time of ministry. While there I had to face a personal dilemma. Although I had often been in similar positions of faith, never had the sum involved been so great. I had to face the fact that I was not in a position of faith for nearly £600,000.

I believed God wanted us to have the college and I knew that He *could* supply the money. But that is not faith. I believed that He *would* supply the money; but that is not faith either. It is hope to believe that something will happen in the future. Faith says it has already happened, even if you have no visible evidence to substantiate your confidence.

When Jesus taught His disciples to pray with faith, He told them: 'Therefore I tell you, whatever you ask for in prayer, believe that you have received it, and it will be yours.' (Mark 11: 24)

Believe that you have received it. I believed my heavenly Father could supply the necessary money, that He would do so; but I did not believe I had received it.

When you are not in a position of faith you can either shrug your shoulders and say that this cannot be the will of God, or you can seek Him for the faith you need. The former course is actually unbelief. I had to begin my seeking by confessing my unbelief and asking for God's forgiveness.

He usually uses our times of seeking Him to sort out several issues in our lives, and I experienced a prolonged time of repentance lasting about two hours. This was followed by a timely encounter with the Lord in which I also received healing from Him. The details are unimportant for our purposes here.

He then said to me: 'Colin, I give you a million dollars.' Now faith comes from hearing God. Immediately I knew God had given the faith I needed. I was up from my knees and dancing around my hotel room with joy, praising God for His generosity.

I could not see the money, but it was as if it had already dropped on to the bed. I could go back to England and tell the others in the fellowship, 'The Lord has given me a million dollars.' That encouraged others in their faith. In Scripture, leaders are to give an example of faith for others to follow.

In the following months the Lord supplied about £280,000, but that was barely half way to the amount needed. There was only one week to go before the money was due to be paid when I left for an extensive time of ministry in Australia. There had been moments of doubt since my encounter with the Lord; but I had always had to repent of them and praise the Lord for the million dollars.

On the day before the money was due I telephoned home, but was told the money had not arrived. However, everyone was at peace, confident the Lord had the whole matter in hand. I also was given peace by the Lord, although I felt a tremendous sense of responsibility. It seemed we had laid our whole ministry on the line.

The other elders had to tell the vendors we did not have all the money, but were praying for it! They did not share our faith in prayer, but we had good relationships with them during the negotiations over the property, and they offered to delay completion for a further month. That had to be the final dead-line.

Every time I 'phoned home I was told that no further gifts of a substantial nature had been received. On my way to England from Australia I stopped for twenty-four hours in the city where I had received the promise from God of the million dollars. I was due to speak at two services there.

Some friends had invited my companions and me to dinner before driving us to the airport. At the end of the meal, my friend asked me how the college project was going. I said we were really on the faith rack, needing £300,000 by the following Friday. To my astonishment he said that his bank would wire the money to our bank so that we would have the money in time to complete the purchase.

Three hundred thousand pounds is one million dollars of the currency of that nation!

On the plane I discovered that a Jumbo jet is not the ideal place to dance in the Spirit! It was not the money itself that was the cause of joy. Being given such a sum seemed unreal, and I never saw the money. It simply passed from one bank to another. It was the faithfulness of God that was overwhelming. He had spoken, He had promised and He had provided.

Needless to say, I was deeply grateful also for my friend who had been the loving, responsive channel of His giving. The purchase was duly completed and the college was full for its first term, without any need to advertise for students!

Hope says it will happen; faith believes it has! 'If you believe, you will receive whatever you ask for in prayer,' says Jesus. (Matt. 21: 22)

AGREEING TOGETHER

The power of agreeing together in faith is immense. During the whole episode of the college, my great friend and fellow-elder Bob Gordon was at the heart of things. He is now director of the college and was utterly convinced of God's purpose in supplying the money. When others questioned whether our guidance was right, or doubted that the Lord would provide, Bob would direct them to both the written word of Scripture and the many spoken words of prophecy God had given us.

It encouraged him no end when I returned from the Far East with the promise God had spoken to my heart, and there were several times when we were reminded of the Scripture: 'Again, I tell you that if two of you on earth agree about anything you ask for, it will be done for you by my Father in heaven. For where two or three come together in my name, there am I with them.' (Matt. 18: 19–20)

Again we are faced with the tremendous resources God makes available to those who agree in faith. God is always willing to supply whatever resources are necessary for the work of His Kingdom. James points out that some do not receive because they do not have the faith even to ask: 'You do not have, because you do not ask God.' (James 4: 2) And he also warns about asking out of wrong, selfish motives. 'When you ask, you do not receive, because you ask with wrong motives, that you may spend what you get on your pleasures.' (James 4: 3)

CONFIDENCE BEFORE GOD

John, like James, heard Jesus make all His prayer promises. Writing his first Epistle some fifty years later, he could look back over a long time of ministry and see that the promises held good: 'Dear friends, if our hearts do not condemn us, we have confidence before God and receive from him anything we ask, because we obey his commands and do what pleases him.' (1 John 3: 21–2)

We do receive anything we ask from God, but we need confidence before Him. That confidence comes out of knowing you are in a right relationship with Him, cleansed of your sins by the blood of Jesus and that you are listening to His Word. Furthermore that word needs to be obeyed because your heart desire is to please Him. In other words, these prayer promises are set within the context of living in the power of the Kingdom.

We ask in the name of Jesus as we seek to follow Him, our lives submitted to His authority. Just as effective prayer cannot be separated from faith, so it cannot be separated from the lives we live. Prayer cannot be seen as an activity separated from the rest of life. We pray as the people we are, out of the relationship with God that we have.

'This is the assurance we have in approaching God: that if we ask anything according to his will, he hears us. And if we know that he hears us – whatever we ask – we know that we have what we asked of him.' (1 John 5: 14–15)

Here again in John's words is that same confidence and the all-embracing scope of the word 'whatever'. If we pray in the name of Jesus, we pray in the will of God, led and inspired by His Spirit. He has given us His Spirit to water the seed of the Kingdom planted within us as believers in Jesus Christ. Part of the fruit that is borne out of that seed is the confidence to ask in prayer, believing it is God's purpose to give us whatever we ask in Jesus's name. 'Ask and it will be given to you... For everyone who asks receives... how much more will your Father in heaven give good gifts to those who ask him!' (Matt. 7: 7, 8, 11)

God does not want you to feel condemned because of what appears to you as previous failure in prayer. If you think that in some situations you have been guilty of praying without faith, then confess that sin immediately and know the forgiveness of God. Do not allow the enemy to have any victory over you.

Often groups of Christians have prayed for a sick person and believed confidently that God would heal him. Their faith is shattered if the person dies. 'We really felt God was going to heal him,' they will say.

It is not always easy to point out lovingly that faith does not say God will do something, but believes He already has done it. Even if a promise is given, it has to be appropriated with that same mustard-seed faith. It is such a tiny thing but makes all the difference. It brings about the transformation needed in the situation.

In prayer we are to come with confidence, but not pride. Jesus told the parable of the Pharisee and the tax collector to illustrate this: 'To some who were confident of their own righteousness and looked down on everybody else, Jesus told this parable'. (Luke 18: 9) Two men, a Pharisee and a tax collector, went to the Temple to pray. The Pharisee prayed about himself: 'God, I thank you that I am not like all other men – robbers, evildoers, adulterers – or even like this tax collector. I fast twice a week and give a tenth of all I get.' (v. 11–12)

The tax collector would not even look up to heaven but beat his breast and said: 'God, have mercy on me, a sinner.' (v. 13) Jesus said that he went home justified, acceptable in God's sight, not the Pharisee. 'For everyone who exalts himself will be humbled, and he who humbles himself will be exalted.' (v. 14)

If that is what Jesus says, it will surely happen. What God requires of us more than anything else is that we come humbly and honestly before Him, prepared to confess our sins and whatever unbelief is in our hearts. There is no point in trying to make God think we believe and trust Him when we don't. He is willing to give us faith when we admit our need of it.

In my hotel room in the Far East two hours of heart-searching under the convicting power of the Holy Spirit, a time of further breaking in my life, preceded the word of faith I needed to receive from the Lord. May He forgive us for all the perfunctory and superficial prayers we pray. And may He draw us before His throne of grace, humble in the knowledge of what we are in ourselves, yet overwhelmingly grateful for His forgiveness and love. May He speak words of faith to our hearts as we wait on Him, for He is the rewarder of those who diligently seek Him.

Chapter 14

KINGDOM POWER AND AUTHORITY

In the life of every Christian there are moments of crisis or decision which will have far-reaching impact on his life. The events at Caesarea Philippi were particularly significant for 'esus's disciples.

They had heard His teaching about the Kingdom, including many of the parables. They could see the Kingdom as a present reality, not only by the things Jesus said, but also by what He did. The Kingdom had not come theoretically; it had come in power. 'Jesus went through all the towns and villages, teaching in their synagogues, preaching the good news of the kingdom and healing every disease and sickness.' (Matt. 9: 35)

The presence of the Kingdom was manifested in the way Jesus ministered to the needs of the people. He brought the positive power of God to bear on their negative situations. Nothing could be more negative than to be in spiritual bondage to Satan.

DEMONS ROUTED

Many today who do not have experience of ministering in the power of the Kingdom doubt the existence of demons. In some cultures their presence is more obvious than others, as they are openly worshipped and invoked by prayer or to bring curses on others. But the occult is present everywhere with all its demonic activity. People consult spiritualists and mediums, ignorant perhaps of the direct commands of Scripture not to do so; many certainly ignorant that they consult demonic forces, not the living God.

Others are involved in freemasonry and other societies, whose beliefs are contrary to the gospel of the Kingdom (even though Scriptures may be read at their meetings) and whose practices are demonically inspired.

The devil certainly does not want people to believe in demons. He is the deceiver who encourages the things of secretive darkness. The children of light have nothing to hide. It is folly for anybody to close his eyes to the nature of what he is involved in, because of personal gain and influence or because he enjoys the camaraderie.

Jesus certainly believed in demons, evil spirits that are messengers or servants of the devil. They could possess people causing them great torment (as with 'Legion', the man possessed by many demons); they could cause sickness and disease, and they could oppress people spiritually.

Some try to explain away these manifestations of evil spirits by saying that Jesus used the thought-forms and beliefs of His time. This will not do. It is heresy to suggest that Jesus, the Truth, should lie or deceive the people by supporting beliefs He knew to be untrue. That is completely contradictory to His purpose and ministry. He corrects error and falsehood, and teaches His disciples to do the same. He was in constant confrontation with the Pharisees because of their hypocrisy: they said one thing and inwardly believed something totally different. It is unthinkable that Jesus could be open to the same charge.

He knew the reality of the demonic spirits, and the gospel accounts are full of references to His power and authority over these. This is hardly surprising. We have noted already how Satan and the angels who followed him in rebellion were immediately thrown out of heaven. Jesus is the King of heaven and wherever His sovereign power is brought to bear those demonic forces have to give way to His authority.

'People brought to him all who were ill with various diseases, those suffering severe pain, the demon-possessed, the epileptics and the paralytics, and he healed them.' (Matt. 4: 24) Those with need were attracted to Jesus because they saw He had the power and resources to meet those needs, including the ability to free them from demonic forces. 'When evening came, many who were demon-possessed were brought to him, and he drove out the spirits with a word and healed all the sick.' (Matt. 8: 16)

The way Jesus dealt with demons was by ordering them out of people's lives with authoritative commands; 'he drove out the spirits with a word'. For example, to Legion He said: 'Come out of this man, you evil spirit!'

Demons could talk through the one they possessed, although nowhere does Jesus become involved in lengthy conversations with them. In fact He would not let them speak because they knew His identity. On this occasion, He gave permission for the evil spirits to enter two thousand pigs who immediately 'rushed down the steep bank into the lake and were drowned.' (Mark 5: 13)

This may seem to be a senseless waste; but Jesus was allowing a demonstration of the destructive power and intention of these demonic forces.

A demon-possessed man who could not talk was brought to Jesus. 'And when the demon was driven out, the man who had been dumb spoke. The crowd was amazed and said, "Nothing like this has ever been seen in Israel."' (Matt. 9: 33)

'Then they brought him a demon-possessed man who was blind and dumb, and Jesus healed him, so that he could both talk and see. All the people were astonished and said, "Could this be the Son of David?"' (Matt. 12: 22–3)

His power over demons not only amazed the people, but encouraged this searching question as to whether He was their long-expected Messiah, their King from heaven. The Pharisees accused Him of casting the demons out by

Beelzebub, the prince of demons. They could not face the implications of this being the hand of God at work.

Jesus made it clear that this was indeed the work of God and the very evidence that, with His coming, the Kingdom had come. 'But if I drive out demons by the Spirit of God, then the kingdom of God has come upon you.' (Matt. 12: 28)

He made it clear to those who opposed Him: 'I tell you the truth, the Son can do nothing by himself; he can do only what he sees his Father doing, because whatever the Father does the Son also does.' (John 5: 19) Jesus came to perform the works of His Father. When we see the Son at work, we see the Father at work. He desires to see His people free from demonic bondage and from sickness; and He sends His Son to demonstrate that the power of His Kingdom is greater than all the powers of darkness.

The demonic causes of sickness are not always evident. The other disciples were unable to heal the epileptic boy while Jesus was on the Mount of Transfiguration with Peter, James and John. When they descended, Jesus upbraided them for their unbelief. Then 'Jesus rebuked the demon, and it came out of the boy, and he was healed from that moment.' (Matt. 17: 18)

This is not to suggest that all sickness is due to demon-possession. There are numerous occasions when Jesus healed people without there being any references to demons. Certainly all sickness is negative and cannot be a manifestation of the positive Kingdom of God.

The Lord, however, is able to redeem every evil situation. He can use negative experiences to bring people through to a closer walk with Himself, or to a true appreciation of the power and reality of His Kingdom. This is not to imply that sickness is His best purpose for His children. He allows the negative to bring us to deeper repentance, to sharpen our faith and trust in Him.

Matthew certainly sees both deliverance from evil spirits and healing of every infirmity and disease by Jesus as a fulfilment of Isaiah's prophecy: 'He took up our infirmities and carried our diseases.' (Isa. 53: 4 – quoted in Matt. 8: 17) They were evidence that He was the Messiah, the Man sent from heaven with the message and gift of the Kingdom. They were signs that accompanied the proclamation of the gospel.

THE CRUCIAL QUESTION

The dialogue between Jesus and His disciples at Caesarea Philippi was a crunch point because it was then that Jesus said to them: 'But what about you? Who do you say I am?'

In the light of the evidence of all they had heard Him say and seen Him do, who did they think He was? No doubt for some time this question had occupied much of their thinking and discussion. None of them had dared to speak out that He was the Messiah, even if they had thought Him to be. To Jews such a suggestion, if untrue, was blasphemous.

On this occasion however, Peter blurts out the glorious revelation: 'You are the Christ, the Son of the living God.' (Matt. 16: 16) Jesus immediately commends him, telling him he has received revelation from His heavenly Father. He then speaks of the building of His Church which hell cannot overcome and says: 'I will give you the keys of the kingdom of heaven; whatever you bind on earth will be bound in heaven, and whatever you loose on earth will be loosed in heaven.' (Matt. 16: 19)

The precise translation of the original Greek is important here. The translation above suggests that if something is bound by Peter it will then be bound in heaven, or if loosed by him it will be loosed in heaven. Jesus actually told Peter that what he binds on earth is *already* bound in heaven; what he looses on earth is *already* loosed in heaven.

The apostle binds on earth what is already bound in heaven; he is given the authority to do that because by proclaiming Jesus to be the Christ, the Messiah, the King sent from heaven, he receives the authority of the Kingdom.

Similarly, he is given authority to loose what is loosed in heaven.

That same authority is given to all who submit their lives to the authority of Jesus and so become part of His Kingdom. They do not need to allow any of the powers of darkness to bind them or keep them in oppressive bondage.

Jesus sends His disciples out with the Kingdom authority to speak the words of the Kingdom and to perform its acts of power. As soon as Peter proclaims Jesus to be the Christ, He warns them that He must be rejected and killed, although on the third day He will be raised to life.

This same Peter immediately wants to argue: 'Never, Lord!' he said, 'This shall never happen to you.'

Earlier he was the mouthpiece of the heavenly Father; now he speaks for the enemy! 'Jesus turned and said to Peter, "Out of my sight, Satan! You are a stumbling block to me; you do not have in mind the things of God, but the things of men."' (Matt. 16: 23)

Jesus directs the rebuke to Satan. He constantly tries to direct people away from God's purposes and encourages them to view every situation rationally, with the limited perspective of human understanding. Revelation expands the mind rather than diminishing our thinking capacity.

The revelation that He is King expands the thinking of the disciples towards Jesus. Satan immediately tries to counteract that. But Jesus is alert to his devices. He uses His Kingdom authority to dismiss Satan from the situation. He will go forward in the way the Father sets before Him and will allow nothing to divert Him from that.

MOVING ON WITH JESUS

And then He points out to His disciples the cost of following Him. They are to exercise Kingdom authority and power in their lives. If they do, they will have to face opposition and cost: 'If anyone would come after me, he must deny himself and take up his cross and follow me. For whoever wants to save his life will lose it, but whoever loses his life for me will find it.' (Matt. 16: 24-5)

No man will be able to serve his own ends and those of the Kingdom at the same time. No man will be able to submit his life to Jesus as King and still reign himself, ruling his own life with stubborn independence. Acknowledging the kingship and lordship of Jesus means that the 'self' in his life has to be dethroned.

The greater the submission to the authority of Jesus in his life, the greater the authority of Jesus can be exercised in a Christian's life. The Lord gives Kingdom authority to every believer; his capacity to exercise that authority is determined by his submission to God's authority in his life.

Peter would have to learn to submit to His plans and purposes, not argue with the Lord, if he was to exercise properly the Kingdom authority Jesus was giving him.

Jesus goes on to speak of His return in glory with His angels, when the full authority of His sovereignty will be established on earth. Each man will then receive his due reward, and Jesus adds: 'I tell you the truth, some who are standing here will not taste death before they see the Son of Man coming in his kingdom.' (Matt. 16: 28)

This does not imply that Jesus thought His Second Coming would take place during the disciples' lifetimes. Elsewhere He makes it clear that the Father alone knows the timing of that event. However, it does imply that some of those disciples, like Peter, were going to experience the reality, the authority and power of His Kingdom. Mighty things are to happen to him and through him in others' lives.

Later Jesus addresses these same words to the disciples generally: 'I tell you the truth, whatever you bind on earth will be bound in heaven, and whatever you loose on earth will be loosed in heaven.' (Matt. 18: 18) Again we are faced with the tremendous authority and power available to the children of the Kingdom, a power that is to be manifested also in prayer. Christians are called to live in Christ's victorious power.

Jesus does not separate prayer from faith. All the prayer promises He gives presuppose that we pray in faith expecting the answer we need from God. He does not anticipate receiving the answer 'No'! So in the very next verse, after telling the disciples of their Kingdom authority to bind and loose, He says: 'Again, I tell you that if two of you on earth agree about anything you ask for, it will be done for you by my Father in heaven.' (Matt. 18: 19)

This is not agreement in a form of words, but agreement in faith, being in full accord and harmony. Such unity is a basic principle of Kingdom living. The promises Jesus gives show the tremendous resources available to the children of the Kingdom.

Nothing will upset the flow of authority and power in Christians' lives quicker than pride and its consequent disunity. On one occasion the disciples argued among themselves as to who was the greatest – while walking along with the Son of God! On another occasion they asked who was the greatest in the Kingdom of heaven.

Jesus answered by standing a child in their midst and saying: 'I tell you the truth, unless you change and become like little children, you will never enter the kingdom of heaven. Therefore, whoever humbles himself like this child is the greatest in the kingdom of heaven.' (Matt. 18: 3–4) The principles of God's Kingdom are the opposite of worldliness. Jesus Himself came as the humble servant and yet was the Man of authority and power.

As we have seen, a man has to humble himself under the authority of Jesus if he is to enter the Kingdom; he needs to stay in a place of humble submission to Him if he is to exercise Kingdom authority and power effectively. The proud cannot enter the Kingdom, and authority will not be given to those who want to exalt themselves rather than Jesus. Simon the sorcerer offered Peter and John money, hoping to buy the ability to lay hands on others to receive the Holy Spirit. He was rebuked strongly, told to repent and get his heart right before God.

To His Kingdom children God gives His commission. His gifts cannot be earned or bought; they are freely given to equip them for witness and ministry. Jesus made so much spiritual power available to the disciples; and yet faith and obedience had to be exercised or they would not be able to avail themselves of the authority at their disposal. Put very. simply, because they were children of the Kingdom Jesus was teaching them a simple truth: whatever I can do you also can do.

We can sympathise with the disciples in finding it difficult to grasp such a truth, for the same principle holds good to this day. The Lord wants to see His authority and power exercised in the lives of believers, so they can proclaim and demonstrate that the Kingdom of God is among us *today*!

Chapter 15

SENT OUT

It was not long before Jesus sent His disciples to share the message of the Kingdom and demonstrate its power: 'As you go, preach this message: "The kingdom of heaven is near." Heal the sick, raise the dead, cleanse those who have leprosy, drive out demons. Freely you have received, freely give.' (Matt. 10: 7–8)

Jesus's own proclamation had been that the Kingdom was near; so this was to be their message. Whatever He had said, they were to say. He had healed the sick, so they too were to heal. He had cast out demons in their presence; now they were to take authority over them and cast them out in His name. They were even to raise the dead!

No doubt they found it easier to identify with His words; 'I am sending you out like sheep among wolves.' But He also promised that when they were under pressure and persecution they need not worry what to say; 'At that time you will be given what to say, for it will not be you speaking, but the Spirit of your Father speaking through you.' (vv. 19–20)

This is an important principle of ministry. It is not God's purpose that we should work for Him, but that He should work through us. Only then will we be able to do the things He does: 'I tell you the truth, anyone who has faith in me will do what I have been doing. He will do even greater things than these, because I am going to the Father.' (John 14: 12)

When He returned to the Father, He prayed for the Holy Spirit to be given. Only by His Spirit working in us can we speak from God and work signs and wonders in His name.

It was not only to the original twelve that Jesus gave such commands, with the expectation they would use their Kingdom faith and authority to execute them. He sent out seventy-two other disciples with a similar charge; and when He gave His great commission to the Church in His risen body, He said: 'All authority in heaven and on earth has been given to me. Therefore go and make disciples of all nations, baptizing them in the name of the Father and of the Son and of the Holy Spirit...' (Matt. 28: 18-19)

That much is commonly quoted, but the sentence continues: *'and teaching them to obey everything I have commanded you.'* (v. 20) As the nations came to faith in Jesus, they too would see the same authority and power being manifested in Jesus Himself as in the lives of those first Christians.

'Anyone who has faith', Jesus says, *'will do what I have been doing.'* Such statements as this have always challenged the faith of Christians, both individually and corporately. It is much easier to opt for the notion that such power and authority was only for the apostolic age, although there is nothing in Scripture to warrant such a position. Quite the opposite. The life and power of the Kingdom have not diminished at all since the time of Jesus.

SIGNS FOLLOWING

Those first disciples saw the power of God at work as they went out to proclaim the gospel of the Kingdom. They did not go out as healers, miracle-workers or as those seeking signs as ends in themselves. They were sent out with the Kingdom message, but expected their words to be confirmed by God with demonstrations of Kingdom power. They expected to see signs following the preaching of the Word.

Signs will not accompany preaching that is only a pale imitation of the gospel, or a partial gospel that has selected certain moral or pastoral elements of what Jesus said. The gospel of the Kingdom embraces the whole counsel of God.

Signs are the evidence that Kingdom power and authority is still given to men. The first disciples did not manifest such gifts as perfectly as Jesus. Their perception, faith and authority fell far short of His. There was nothing imperfect in Jesus to hinder His unity with His Father. The works of heaven could be seen supremely in Him.

Nevertheless, the disciples did see God working powerfully through them. The seventy-two were overjoyed that 'even the demons submit to us in your name.' (Luke 10: 17)

The disciples were sent out in Jesus's name and all the works they performed were in His name – on His behalf, with His power and authority.

Similarly today, believers are not only to speak in His name but work in His name, on His behalf, with His power and authority. Anyone who has faith in Jesus will do what He did – and even greater things still.

IN THE POWER OF THE SPIRIT

The fulfilment of this promise began on the day of Pentecost. The Holy Spirit came on the disciples gathered in Jerusalem. When they preached the gospel, three thousand became Christians and the Spirit came upon them also. Nothing like that had happened during the earthly ministry of Jesus, because the Spirit had not then been poured out.

Once they were filled with the Spirit, those diffident men became men of power and authority. Instead of God being with them in His Son, He was now in them by His Spirit. This was the greater event that would cause their joy to be full, as Jesus had promised at the Last Supper.

With the coming of the Spirit, the disciples had received the power Jesus promised when appearing to them in His risen body. The opening chapter of Acts tells us that, 'He appeared to them over a period of forty days and spoke about the kingdom of God.' (Acts 1: 3) He told them not to leave Jerusalem but to wait for 'the gift my Father promised'. (v. 4)

'In a few days you will be baptised with the Holy Spirit,' He said, (v. 5) and then explained the implications of that: 'You will receive power when the Holy Spirit comes on you; and you will be my witnesses in Jerusalem, and in all Judea and Samaria, and to the ends of the earth.' (v. 8)

After these promises had been fulfilled at Pentecost, the transformation in these men immediately became apparent. First they were filled with such praise for God, He needed to give them languages they had never learned to enable them to express the joy in their hearts. The crowd that gathered heard them declaring the wonders of God in these other languages.

During the days that followed many believers were added to their number. 'Every one was filled with awe, and many wonders and miraculous signs were done by the apostles.' (Acts 2: 43) Notable among these was the healing of the crippled beggar at the Temple gate.

They also proclaimed the gospel of the Kingdom with increased boldness. When arrested and brought before the Jewish Council, they were forbidden to speak in Jesus's name again. They counted it more important to obey God than men, and so returned to their preaching. But not before holding a prayer meeting.

The content of their prayer is significant. With the hardening of opposition, they realised their need to see God act more powerfully in their ministries. No longer were they the fearful men meeting secretly for fear of the Jews. Now they are men of the Spirit, given by God to water the seed of the Kingdom planted in them. So they pray: 'Enable your servants to speak your word with great boldness. Stretch out your hand to heal and perform miraculous signs and wonders through the name of your holy servant Jesus.' (Acts 4: 29-30)

They had been before the council for their boldness; they recognised their need for greater boldness. They had seen great healings, still they prayed for God to stretch out His hand to heal. They were moving in the dimension of the miraculous; they asked for more in the name of Jesus.

And how does God answer such prayer? 'After they prayed, the place where they were meeting was shaken. And they were all filled with the Holy Spirit and spoke the word of God boldly.' (Acts 4: 31) They had another Pentecost. God knew their need was to be filled with the Holy Spirit again. That was not to deny the value or validity of their former experience. They were learning that as Kingdom men with the commission to extend the Kingdom of God on earth, they were going to need constant empowering by the Holy Spirit.

Even though they did not ask for another infilling of the Holy Spirit on this occasion, God knew that to be their need. This was His answer to their prayer which expressed their heart-cry. And He shook the building to demonstrate that the wind of the Spirit was blowing on them afresh – why else do such a thing? He was not simply revitalising the gift within them; He was coming upon them in the person of the Holy Spirit with a fresh anointing.

If those first disciples were intent on preaching the gospel of the Kingdom, and seeing the signs and wonders that evidenced the presence of that Kingdom, they were also concerned to see that the church in Jerusalem established a corporate life consistent with the principles of the Kingdom: 'They devoted themselves to the apostles' teaching and to the fellowship, to the breaking of bread and to prayer.' (Acts 2: 42)

FELLOWSHIP

Kingdom people are men and women of the Word, with their lives deeply rooted in the gospel of the Kingdom. To have fellowship is to share life together. Those early believers were learning that to belong to God's Kingdom involves sharing your life with other Kingdom children. 'They broke bread in their homes and ate together with glad and sincere hearts.' (v. 46)

The all-embracing nature of their fellowship has been a

challenge to the Church ever since. 'All the believers were together and had everything in common.' (v. 44) 'No-one claimed that any of his possessions was his own, but they shared everything they had.' (Acts 4: 32)

Just as some have wanted to believe that the authority and power those early Christians enjoyed passed away with the apostolic age, so there have been those who say that such fellowship is an impossible ideal today. It is a temptation to reduce Scripture to the level of our experience, instead of seeing our experience raised to the level of Scripture.

There is nothing in the teaching of Jesus to support the idea that our commitment to Him and to one another is to be less today than in Biblical times, or that His power among believers will not be as great now as then. These are attractive ideas if we want to diminish the meaning and significance of Christian discipleship; but that is certainly not God's purpose.

Even in the history of the Church there have always been those who have experienced the signs and wonders (many are recognised as particular saints by some churches), just as there have been expressions of corporate fellowship similar to that described in Acts.

These cannot be imitations of the Biblical precedent. Both the signs and fellowship were the work of the Holy Spirit then and will be today, wherever He is allowed liberty in the lives of contemporary Christians.

Kingdom life and Kingdom power are inseparable. They are perfectly united in Jesus. As the early Christians lived the teaching He had given, so they saw God's powerful acts which demonstrated His Kingly presence among them.

Every expression of Kingdom life mirrors something of the nature of the King Himself. Forgiveness is a good example.

THE UNMERCIFUL SERVANT

Jesus told the parable of the Unmerciful Servant when Peter asked how often he was supposed to forgive his brother. The

Kingdom of heaven is like a king who wanted to settle accounts with his servants. A man who owed him millions was unable to pay; so the master ordered that he and his family be sold. The servant begged for patience and promised to repay the debt. The master took pity on him, cancelled the debt and ordered his release. Such is God's forgiveness for each of us!

The master was angry when he discovered that same man had demanded repayment of a paltry debt owed him by a fellow servant, only to have him thrown into prison when unable to pay. 'You wicked servant,' the master said. 'I cancelled all that debt of yours because you begged me to. Shouldn't you have had mercy on your fellow servant just as I had on you?' (Matt. 18: 32–3) In anger the master had him thrown in jail until he could pay back all he owed.

Jesus ends the parable by saying: 'This is how my heavenly Father will treat each of you unless you forgive your brother from your heart.' (v. 35)

In one parable Jesus embraces several principles of what it means to live as Christians, as children of His Kingdom. For example:

Blessed are the merciful, for they will be shown mercy. (Matt. 5: 7)
I tell you that anyone who is angry with his brother will be subject to judgment. (Matt. 5: 22)
Forgive us our debts, as we also have forgiven our debtors. (Matt. 6: 12)
For if you forgive men when they sin against you, your heavenly Father will also forgive you. But if you do not forgive men their sins, your Father will not forgive your sins. (Matt. 6: 14–15)
Do not judge, or you too will be judged. For in the same way you judge others, you will be judged, and with the measure you use, it will be measured to you. (Matt. 7: 1–2)
In everything, do to others what you would have them do to you. (Matt. 7: 12)

The Sermon on the Mount is about practical Kingdom living, about practical holiness which, in its simplest terms, is living like Jesus. This sermon is a moral ideal impossible to attain, unless those who seek to live it know they are children of the Kingdom with the life of God's Holy Spirit within them to enable them to do so.

In this particular parable Jesus makes it clear that to be an inheritor of the Kingdom is not sufficient; to have such a privilege involves the Christian in the responsibility of living Kingdom life, learning to react as Jesus would in each situation.

This will be demanding in many respects, for it is not possible for part of a believer to be in the Kingdom and another part outside. The Holy Spirit is watering the seed of the Kingdom placed within the believer so that the positive life of that Kingdom can replace all the negative areas. This is a process of sanctification, of making the believer holy in person and behaviour like Jesus. The more the Christian's life corresponds to that of the King, the more fruitful he will be as a witness of the Kingdom in the world. He will be more positive in faith, attitudes, thoughts and actions and less negative in his response to difficult situations.

If he is living as a child of the Kingdom, the Christian will bear witness by his actions as well as his attitudes, that he has been freed from the negative and is no longer in bondage to the world, the flesh and the devil. In Christ he has been set free!

Chapter 16

FACING THE COST

There is cost for those who would be true to Jesus, the cost of willingly and daily taking up a personal cross to follow Him: 'If anyone would come after me, he must deny himself and take up his cross and follow me. For whoever wants to save his life will lose it, but whoever loses his life for me will find it.' (Matt. 16: 24–5)

This cross does not represent what is imposed on the Christian against his will, like sickness or fear. It is what he willingly takes upon himself in order to be obedient and faithful to the King of kings. Nothing must come before Him, or the life and work of His Kingdom, in the order of his priorities. God and His Kingdom come first.

THE COST OF GIVING

Whatever is sacrificed for the Kingdom will be repaid many times over in this life, with the reward of eternal life as well! To take the gospel of the Kingdom into the world has always involved cost. It cost Jesus His human life. The disciples left their occupations and had to experience long periods of separation from their families to follow Him.

Physical comfort and worldly security often have to be sacrificed so that others can receive the good news of the Kingdom. It is costly to take needy people in your home in order to share Kingdom life with them. It is demanding to live for others rather than yourself. And yet those who love the King are devoted to the extension of His Kingdom, and are prepared to face the inconveniences that the demands of love often make and the sacrifices required to make Him known.

There is no greater joy than knowing the King and serving the cause of His Kingdom, seeing others receive the revelation that they are forgiven, made acceptable to God, have received the gift of the Kingdom, have been set free from their bondages and can love and worship the King in the beauty of His holiness. There is no greater joy than knowing you have fulfilled His command to feed the hungry and serve the needs of the destitute, both spiritually and physically:

> Is not this the kind of fasting I have chosen: to loose the chains of injustice and untie the cords of the yoke, to set the oppressed free and break every yoke? Is it not to share your food with the hungry and to provide the poor wanderer with shelter – when you see the naked, to clothe him, and not to turn away from your own flesh and blood? (Isa. 58: 6–7)

All this is costly to do in practice and yet it is rewarding, not only for the individual believer or for the recipients of his love, but for the whole cause of the Kingdom in the nation:

> Then your light will break forth like the dawn, and your healing will quickly appear; then your righteousness will go before you, and the glory of the Lord will be your rear guard. Then you will call, and the Lord will answer; you will cry for help, and he will say: Here am I. (Isa. 58: 8–9)

Obedience to the Lord releases His activity and provision into our lives. He literally multiplies back what is given to Him. Desire for more is not the motive behind the giving, but the desire to serve the King and express the life of His Kingdom. That involves expressing Him in the people we are, and therefore in the things we do:

> If you do away with the yoke of oppression, with the pointing finger and malicious talk, and if you spend yourselves on behalf of the hungry and satisfy the needs of the oppressed, then your light will rise in the darkness, and your night will become like the noonday. The Lord will guide you always; he will satisfy your needs in a sun-scorched land and will strengthen your frame. You will be like a well-watered garden, like a spring whose waters never fail. (Isa. 58: 9–11)

The measure you give is the measure you receive back! And yet there can be no comparison between the two. We give ourselves in our frail, human weakness and sinfulness; He gives Himself in His majesty and glory. We seek to serve the spiritually oppressed and hungry, taking to them the good news of the victory of Jesus and the freedom available through Him; and we receive the eternal gift of His Kingdom. We feed the physically poor and hungry, and He promises that we shall lack nothing ourselves.

The cost is in giving before you see the reward. Our willingness to give depends on how much self-love there is in us, whether we love ourselves more than Jesus and those He gives us to love. We need to be dead to that love of self. He said: 'I tell you the truth, unless an ear of wheat falls to the ground and dies, it remains only a single seed. But if it dies, it produces many seeds.' (John 12: 24)

Look how productive the death of Jesus has been. The Son of God gave His life that many sons might be drawn into the Kingdom. The principle is the same in our lives; 'the man who hates his life in this world will keep it for eternal life. Whoever serves me must follow me; and where I am, my servant also will be. My Father will honour the one who serves me.' (John 12: 25–6)

Jesus is emphatic: 'Anyone who does not carry his cross

and follow me cannot be my disciple.' (Luke 14: 27) So it is as well for those who want to serve the King to count the cost of doing so. He points out that if a man wants to build a tower he first calculates the cost of doing so. He will be ridiculed if he completes the foundations and then runs out of money. 'In the same way, any of you who does not give up everything he has cannot be my disciple.' (v. 33) Everything is available to the King and the work of His Kingdom.

The rich man wanted to enjoy his wealth in self-indulgence and was blind to the needs of the poor man at his gate. It is possible to close our eyes to the needs of those around us when the Lord has made material and spiritual things available to us to share with others. That is an essential part of Kingdom life: to share whatever we have with others. And it is Kingdom faith to believe that we shall not be the losers by doing so. We shall receive back what we have given many times over in this life, and in the age to come we shall rejoice eternally with our heavenly King.

PAUL'S CROSS
Paul's own testimony bears this out:

> As servants of God we commend ourselves in every way: in great endurance; in troubles, hardships and distresses; in beatings, imprisonments and riots; in hard work, sleepless nights and hunger; in purity, understanding, patience and kindness; in the Holy Spirit and in sincere love; in truthful speech and in the power of God; with weapons of righteousness in the right hand and in the left; through glory and dishonour, bad report and good report; genuine, yet regarded as imposters; known, yet regarded as unknown; dying, and yet we live on; beaten, and yet not killed; sorrowful, yet always rejoicing; poor, yet making many rich; having nothing, and yet possessing everything. (2 Cor. 6: 4–10)

This amazing testimony demonstrates how the positive power of God's Kingdom overcomes all the negatives. Throughout the history of the Church, other Christians have experienced similar trials with similar fortitude and victory. No matter how negatively the world treats those living in righteousness, their positive testimony wins through. The purity, understanding, patience, kindness and sincere love given by the Holy Spirit endures through all the troubles, hardships and distresses. The truthfulness and genuineness of those who remain faithful withstand all the lies and false accusations against them inspired by the enemy. Out of their poverty of spirit, many are made rich in the Lord. Nothing can take away their joy and their inheritance. Having nothing, they possess everything.

We have the treasure of the Kingdom in earthen vessels. The power of God can shine through our lives to give Him glory, and to demonstrate that He is the source of that power, and not us. And so Paul can say: 'We are hard pressed on every side, but not crushed; perplexed, but not in despair; persecuted, but not abandoned; struck down, but not destroyed.' (2 Cor. 4: 8–9)

Perseverance in the face of opposition was a feature of Paul's life. At Ephesus, for example, he spoke boldly in the synagogue for a period of three months 'arguing persuasively about the kingdom of God.' (Acts 19: 8) Some obstinately refused to believe and maligned his teaching before he left them. When he summoned the elders of the Ephesian Church while on his way to Jerusalem, he reviewed his time of ministry with them.

He preached the gospel of the Kingdom to them, he says, and in so doing did not hesitate to preach anything that would be helpful to them. No compromise for Paul in order to please the people! He did not hesitate 'to proclaim to you the whole will of God.' (Acts 20: 27) He did not pick and choose the attractive parts of the gospel at the expense of the more demanding things Jesus taught.

When he leaves them he commends them 'to God and to the word of his grace, which can build you up and give you an inheritance among all those who are sanctified.' (v. 32) It is only by facing the gospel in its entirety that they would be prepared for the inheritance that awaits those who are sanctified, made holy in God's sight through the cleansing blood of Jesus and the indwelling of the Holy Spirit.

DISCIPLINE
Perhaps there is no area where we try to excuse ourselves more than that of prayer. A Christian seeking first the Kingdom and God's righteousness will be a praying person. Yet we often excuse ourselves by delaying our prayer times or only praying in a superficial or cursory manner. We claim we are so busy or too tired.

Our God is a Lord of order and He wants to bring spiritual order, as well as physical, emotional, financial, political and social order into our lives. Spiritual order is rooted in discipline. We need a life of discipline if we are going to prevail in prayer, learning how to pray through to a victorious answer, setting our sights clearly on our objective and praying until that target is achieved.

Jesus anticipated that those who received the revelation that they were part of the Kingdom would give their lives to see the Kingdom extended. This would become their reason for living. To profess love and honour for the King without being concerned about the cause of His Kingdom, would be hypocrisy.

This was certainly the emphasis throughout the earthly ministry of Jesus and also in the life of the early Church. When Jesus appeared to His disciples in His risen body, it might have been anticipated that He would have taken the opportunity to teach them the principles of church planting, structure and organisation. But instead He continued to teach them about the Kingdom: 'He appeared to them over a period of forty days and spoke about the kingdom of God.' (Acts 1: 3)

The apostles followed their Lord's example. In Samaria Philip 'preached the good news of the kingdom of God and the name of Jesus Christ'. (Acts 8: 12) At Lystra, Iconium and Antioch, Barnabas and Paul warned: 'We must go through many hardships to enter the kingdom of God'. (Acts 14: 22) Here they refer to the full manifestation of the Kingdom that lies in the future. To live as Kingdom people now will involve obedience, sacrifice, persecution and hardships before the heavenly reward can be enjoyed. However, no disciple is ever without the Lord's presence or power, and the resources of heaven are available to him no matter what his situation or need.

Chapter 17

FOLLOWING JESUS

All those who are children of the Kingdom of God are called to be disciples of Jesus. A disciple is one who puts the claims of Jesus first in his life, regardless of the cost to himself. He lives, not to serve himself, but the King of Heaven. He enjoys the privileges of the Kingdom, but also faces the responsibilities that are his as a child of God.

Because Jesus Christ is his Lord, everything in his life is to be submitted to the authority of Jesus. The disciple is called to be holy, to be like Jesus. The more he submits to the Lordship of Jesus, the more Christ-like he becomes both in character and actions; and the more he is then able to enjoy his privileges.

'Whatever you do, whether in word or deed, do it all in the name of the Lord Jesus, giving thanks to God the Father through him.' (Col. 3: 17) The name in Scripture denotes the person. To speak and act in the name of Jesus is to speak and act in the person of Jesus: to say what He would say, or do what He would do in your position. That is made possible because God has given us His Kingdom life and has empowered us with the Holy Spirit. We have within us the same life that indwelt Jesus; and we have available to us the same Kingdom resources.

When Jesus called His disciples to follow Him, He wanted them to follow His example, both in life and ministry. They were to proclaim the Kingdom in word and power. And He was uncompromising in teaching what He expected of disciples.

Today many Christians have settled for a level of discipleship that bears little resemblance to the teaching and expectations of Jesus. Would He even recognise as true disciples many of those who claim to follow Him? His words are often compromised by believers either out of expediency, or to avoid personal cost.

As a result, many Christians fail to be the witnesses God wants them to be and, in many places, the Church is regarded as weak, ineffective or irrelevant.

God's children are to demonstrate the life-transforming presence of Jesus in the world. He calls them to face the implications of true discipleship, to be obedient and faithful to the Lord irrespective of personal cost to themselves. There are many privileges to being children of the Kingdom; there are also great responsibilities.

Out of love for Jesus, disciples are willing to apply His standards to their lives. A discipleship without cost is not true discipleship. Christians are called to deny themselves and take up their cross daily in order to follow Christ. That cross is not a burden imposed upon them, but what they willingly undertake for the sake of the gospel.

God comes first in their lives, before consideration of self; His will matters above all else. To put God first before either personal considerations, or even loved ones, is best both for the disciple and all those he loves.

It is one thing knowing what we ought to do; it is another thing actually to do it. How can we apply the principles of the Kingdom to our lives so that we might live in the good of them?

We can ask ourselves the question: What would Jesus do in my position? How would He think? What would His attitude be if placed in similar circumstances? What would He believe and how would He pray about a particular matter? What does Jesus want of me at this moment? If He was standing by me, what would I do? Would I be ashamed of doing some things I do normally, if I was so aware of His presence?

In most situations the disciple would be able to answer such questions easily, through his knowledge of Scripture and by listening to the witness of the Holy Spirit. There may be some occasions when he would be genuinely perplexed. That would encourage him to seek the Lord for clear guidance; he would not want to step outside God's purposes.

Even when he perceives what Jesus would do, he will still be tempted to disobey if obedience would prove costly. That would be to place love of self above love for the Lord. Jesus said that those who love Him obey Him.

The Christian is not going to face up to the demands of true discipleship unless he sets his heart on doing so. He will need to make a firm decision that he is going to walk as Jesus did. This is God's calling on his life and there is no lesser calling for any Christian. John says: 'Whoever claims to live in him must walk as Jesus did.' (1 John 2: 6) This is a must for all Christians. When a person becomes a Christian he is placed in Christ and he is to live accordingly. Jesus Himself said: 'Whoever serves me must follow me; and where I am, my servant also will be. My Father will honour the one who serves me.' (John 12: 26)

The flesh does not like obedience or cost. It is futile to settle for a level of discipleship acceptable to us, and imagine that it will be acceptable to God. Our decision to follow Jesus is not an emotional response to the gospel, but a definite act of the will. There is little point in making decisions that are not implemented.

THE VITAL QUESTION
In every situation ask yourself the question, WHAT WOULD JESUS DO? – and then do it! Your life will come more into line with what He desires of you. Don't be put off by the expectation of failure. God can use your failures

positively to show you when you do not want to obey Him, or fail to trust Him.

You must decide for yourself what the Christ-like action would be in any particular situation. Even if you pray with others, or talk over a certain matter with them, the ultimate decision is yours. That is your responsibility as a disciple of Jesus. You need to decide what you believe in conscience Jesus would do in your position, and then do it!

You are not making decisions about anyone else's conduct, only your own. You have no right to judge others for the decisions they make.

There will be occasions when you need to submit significant decisions to those who are in spiritual authority over you. You need not fear to do that, if you genuinely want the will of God for your life. Disciples do not act in independence; they are, however, to be personally responsible for their actions.

You need to agree to apply this principle to every area of your life, otherwise you will avoid the question when you want to avoid cost. You agree to do what Jesus would do regardless of the cost to yourself, even if this involves loss of position or prestige in the eyes of the world. Financial loss could result if you are compromising your Christian principles by being involved in dubious business practices. Better to walk with Jesus in righteousness than to walk with the ungodly.

There will be times when you fail to follow Jesus; but these will be because of errors of judgment rather than deliberate disobedience. Once you have made the decision to walk as Jesus did, it will grieve you to grieve Him. When you make mistakes, or fail to take the necessary action because of human weakness, you can receive God's forgiveness. There is no condemnation for you because of that passing failure. Allow that failure to increase your desire for obedience in the future.

The fear of failure should not prevent you from making a firm decision to follow Jesus. You are simply agreeing to put the teaching of Jesus into practice, regardless of what others do or say. Some may accuse you of taking your discipleship too seriously, or will claim that it is impracticable to follow Jesus so closely in modern society. Stand firm against such suggestions and lovingly and graciously make it clear that you will not compromise your obedience to the Lord Jesus Christ.

BENEFITS OF OBEDIENCE

To set your heart on doing what Jesus would do will produce many positive benefits in your life. Obviously, some of your attitudes towards people, money, business practices and social responsibility are likely to change. Any changes will be for the better, if they bring your life into a closer conformity to the life of Jesus Himself.

God gives you both His Word and His Spirit to help you understand His will for you. You will become more sensitive to the voice of the Holy Spirit and more willing to respond to His leading. You will experience God's refining out of your life many negative thoughts, attitudes and actions, inconsistent with the life of Jesus.

When you desire to act like Him, He will give you the faith to do so. Faith and love will be the governing principles of your actions, words and attitudes. You will become more patient and tolerant of others, more willing to forgive them. You will have a greater compassion for those in need and a greater concern for the lost.

All these changes will be positive and will make you a more whole person. The more like Jesus you are, the healthier you will be in every way. You inherit everything from God that He inherits, if you are willing to share His suffering now so that you may also share in His glory. Even when obedience proves costly you will not be the loser, for God will always give back to you infinitely more than you have given to Him, both in this life and, eternally, in heaven.

Changes will take place in you because God wants to see

those changes. Many of the old habits will go! Submit willingly to these changes and resist the temptation to return to those old habits and so compromise your discipleship.

By taking your discipleship seriously you will be seeking first the Kingdom of God and His righteousness. You can be confident that God will keep His promise to you and meet your every need, as He did with Jesus.

You will pray with greater purpose and faith, for you will want to pray as Jesus would, meeting every situation with His faith, gaining His perspective on the various circumstances in which you are placed. Remember that Jesus promises to do anything you ask in His name.

When others challenge you as to why you make the decisions you make, do not deny your Lord or avoid the issue. State simply that you have decided to act as you believe Jesus would have acted in your position. Trust that God will use that as both a witness, an inspiration and a challenge to others.

You can make this simple covenant, or agreement, with the Lord, realising that this states in simple terms what it means to be a disciple, one who seeks to live as a child of the Kingdom of God:

I will ask myself the question: what would Jesus do?
I will then do what He would do in my position.
I will apply this question to all my actions.
I will do what Jesus would do regardless of the cost to myself.
I will ask for God's help by the Holy Spirit to enable me to walk as Jesus did.
I understand that I shall not be under any condemnation when I fail, but it is my honest intention to seek God's will in every situation. I want to be a true disciple and live as a child of the positive Kingdom.

It would be good to copy this agreement, sign it and keep it in your Bible. On the first day of every month you can reaffirm your decision to walk as Jesus did and pray for God's continued help to enable you to do so.

Chapter 18

THE HEAVENLY REWARD

To live Kingdom life *now* is to do what Jesus would do in your position, regardless of the cost. Your citizenship is already in heaven. But it is not enough to rejoice in your inheritance; God expects your life to be lived in a manner worthy of such an inheritance. He expects a life of faith and love as evidence that He is your life.

Paul tells the Thessalonians that they will be counted worthy of the Kingdom (for which they were then suffering persecution), because both their faith and their love of one another was increasing. (2 Thess. 1: 3–5) Obviously the Holy Spirit was watering the seed of the Kingdom in their lives, so that they were increasingly fruitful even in adverse circumstances. Paul prays that God may count them worthy of His calling, and by His power He may fulfil every good purpose of theirs and 'every act prompted by your faith.' (v 11) He wants to see Jesus glorified in them and for them to be glorified in Him, by the grace of God the Father and His Son.

To live a life of Kingdom faith will require perseverance. Jesus said: 'No-one who puts his hand to the plough and looks back is fit for service in the kingdom of God.' (Luke 9: 62) There will be constant pressure from the world, the flesh and the devil, to compromise your obedience to Him.

We can be adept at finding excuses for not putting Jesus first. When some tried to delay following Him, He retorted 'Let the dead bury their own dead, but you go and proclaim the kingdom of God.' (Luke 9: 60)

Christians are made holy, to be holy. They are to be like Jesus. That will never be accomplished by trying to imitate Him in their own strength, but only through His life being expressed through them. The seed of the Kingdom is planted within them so that, watered by the Spirit, that seed will grow to maturity. A life of submission to the authority of the King is evidence of this.

The eternal life, the fullness of God's life, given him in Jesus, will result in more of the Lord shining through the believer's life; more of Jesus will be seen in him.

Paul persevered until the end of his life in fulfilling the commission given him by God. Even when in detention in Rome: 'From morning till evening he explained and declared to them the kingdom of God.' (Acts 28: 23) For two whole years 'Boldly and without hindrance he preached the kingdom of God and taught about the Lord Jesus Christ.' (v. 31) The result was that even in Caesar's household there were those who had accepted the gospel and had received the inheritance of the Kingdom.

Jesus makes it clear to His disciples that to live the life of the Kingdom in an ungodly society will prove costly. Being part of the Kingdom does not mean they will be spared troubles and difficulties: 'In this world you will have trouble. But take heart! I have overcome the world.' (John 16: 33)

The children of the Kingdom can live in the victory of the King, even though they may suffer persecution and rejection. Tribulation, persecution and rejection are inevitable if God's children are to live in this negative world.

Jesus says: 'Blessed are those who are persecuted because of righteousness, for theirs is the kingdom of heaven. Blessed are you when people insult you, persecute you and falsely say all kinds of evil against you because of me. Rejoice and be glad, because great is your reward in heaven, for in the same way they persecuted the prophets who were before you.' (Matt. 5: 10–12)

Living the life of the positive Kingdom of light amid the

negative kingdom of darkness, is clearly not going to be easy. Jesus Himself did not have an easy time, experiencing much opposition especially from the religious traditionalists, who were more concerned about the outward performance of their rites and ceremonies than about spiritual rebirth.

To live a life of righteousness amid unrighteousness or self-righteousness, is inevitably going to produce conflicts. Because Satan's kingdom is one based on lies and deception, it is inevitable that those seeking to live in the truth and righteousness of Jesus, will be on the receiving end of slander and insult.

The people are reminded by Jesus that, no matter what opposition is encountered because of their faith in Him, those who are part of His Kingdom can afford to rejoice and be glad amid all their difficulties, for their heavenly reward is assured. Beyond their life and witness in this world, they will be able to enjoy all the privileges of the Kingdom without any such opposition.

INCREASING OPPOSITION

Jesus speaks, not only of the presence of the Kingdom, but also of its future manifestation, when the sovereignty of Jesus will be established everywhere as He returns in triumph.

Before that event the children of the Kingdom can expect to suffer an increase in opposition and persecution. There will be many false Christs, wars and rumours of wars, famines and earthquakes. But there will be no need for them to be alarmed. 'For I will give you words and wisdom that none of your adversaries will be able to resist or contradict.' (Luke 21: 15) Such things must happen and are the beginning of birth pain heralding the coming of the new order. 'When you see these things happening, you know that the kingdom of God is near.' (v. 31)

'Then you will be handed over to be persecuted and put to death, and you will be hated by all nations because of me. At that time many will turn away from the faith and will betray and hate each other'. (Matt. 24: 9–10) False prophets will deceive and there will be an increase in wickedness. Many people's love for God will grow cold in this time of severe testing, 'but he who stands firm to the end will be saved.' (v. 13)

Christians in some nations have been through times of testing, but it seems that Jesus is warning there will be greater trials ahead. These will demonstrate who truly are the children of the Kingdom. They will not fall away, because they will not deny the King who reigns over them.

It is natural to wonder if you would be able to endure such testing yourself. That is not a proper question. To the faithful God will always supply the grace to remain faithful. In a time of severe testing, you would have all the resources of the Kingdom available to you. Through faith in Jesus you could draw on these resources, knowing that He would not leave you, fail you or forsake you.

Jesus promises: 'And this gospel of the kingdom will be preached in the whole world as a testimony to all nations, and then the end will come.' (v. 14) There will be a world-wide proclamation of the truth, of God's offer of the Kingdom to those who acknowledge His sovereignty.

The Son of man will come 'on the clouds of the sky, with power and great glory. And he will send his angels with a loud trumpet call, and they will gather his elect from the four winds, from one end of the heavens to the other.' (vv. 30–1) The elect are the children of the Kingdom!

Jesus urges His disciples to 'keep watch, because you do not know on what day your Lord will come.' (Matt. 24: 42) They are to be prepared like the faithful and wise servant who was trusted to give his household food at the proper time while the master was away. Such a servant will be put 'in charge of all his possessions.' (Matt. 24: 47) He will enter into the full inheritance of the Kingdom he has experienced only partially, but has served faithfully.

By contrast, the wicked servant beats his fellow servants and eats and drinks with drunkards. The master of that servant will come when he least expects him. 'He will cut him to pieces and assign him a place with the hypocrites, where there will be weeping and gnashing of teeth.' (v. 51)

THE TEN VIRGINS

The alternatives seem clear! To emphasise the point Jesus gives the parable of the Ten Virgins. The Kingdom of heaven will be like ten virgins who took their lamps and went out to meet the bridegroom. Five were wise and five foolish. The foolish ones took their lamps, but no oil; the wise took flasks of oil as well as their lamps.

The bridegroom was a long time in coming and they all fell asleep. When they were awoken at midnight by shouts heralding his imminent arrival, the foolish asked the wise for some of their oil as their lamps were going out. The wise refused as they did not have enough for all. The foolish ones would have to go and buy fresh supplies of oil.

While they were gone, the bridegroom arrived. The wise virgins went with him into the banquet, and the door was shut. When the foolish returned and asked for the door to be opened, they were told by the bridegroom: 'I tell you the truth, I don't know you.' (Matt. 25: 12)

The lesson to learn is clear: 'Therefore keep watch, because you do not know the day or the hour.' (v. 13)

The bridegroom is Jesus, the wise virgins the faithful children of the Kingdom. In Scripture, oil is used to describe the Holy Spirit. It is by His Spirit that God, not only teaches what resources of the Kingdom are available to us; He also enables us to understand the signs of the times, to be prepared for the coming of Jesus. How important, therefore, that our lamps are full and we have oil to spare. If we are found wanting, there will be no point in turning to others for help, no time to acquire fresh oil. His fullness is always available to us and it is in that fullness that God intends us to live. 'And I pray that you, being rooted and established in love, may have power, together with all the saints, to grasp how wide and long and high and deep is the love of Christ, and to know this love that surpasses knowledge – that you may be filled to the measure of all the fullness of God.' (Eph. 3: 17–19)

FAITHFUL TO THE END

In the early chapters of Revelation God addresses letters to seven churches. In these He talks of overcoming the opposition and difficulties that each is confronted with, so they may receive their reward. The Spirit says: 'To him who overcomes, I will give the right to eat from the tree of life,' (Rev. 2: 7) meaning that we will enjoy eternal life in the final consummation of the Kingdom.

'Be faithful, even to the point of death, and I will give you the crown of life.' (v. 10) He who overcomes will not be hurt by the second death; he will not experience eternal death or separation from God.

Those who overcome will have authority over the nations; they will share the Messiah's kingly reign. They will receive hidden manna, be given entrance to the heavenly banquet. They will be dressed in white, the symbol of purity, and their names will never be erased from the book of life.

Each will be acknowledged by name before the Father and His angels. Jesus had promised: 'Whoever acknowledges me before men, I will also acknowledge him before my Father in heaven. But whoever disowns me before men, I will disown him before my Father in heaven.' (Matt. 10: 32–3)

He who overcomes will be a pillar in God's temple, another assurance of being part of the final, victorious manifestation of the Kingdom. 'Never again will he leave it.' He will even have the Lord's name written on him as a sign both of His possession and protection. And he will be given 'the right to sit with me on my throne, just as I overcame and sat down with my Father on his throne.' (Rev. 3: 21)

Such promises are immense in their implications, but do point to the need to be faithful; that as children of the Kingdom nothing will be allowed to hinder us from entering into our full inheritance.

The man who abides in Jesus has nothing to fear. He seeks first the Kingdom and is concerned to walk in holiness and righteousness with the Lord, loving, giving and serving faithfully. These are not to be seen as conditions to entering the Kingdom of heaven, but as the natural consequence of already being part of that Kingdom. There needs to be no fear of judgment for anyone who lives to please the Lord.

THE TALENTS

A man entrusted his property to his servants while away on a journey. To one he gave five talents of silver, to another two and to another one, 'each according to his ability.' (Matt. 25: 15) 'The man who had received the five talents went at once and put his money to work and gained five more. So also, the one with the two talents gained two more. But the man who had received the one talent went off, dug a hole in the ground and hid his master's money.' (vv. 16–18)

It was a long time before the master returned and settled accounts with them. The first said: 'Master, you entrusted me with five talents. See, I have gained five more.' (v. 20) His master was delighted: 'Well done, good and faithful servant! You have been faithful with a few things; I will put you in charge of many things. Come and share your master's happiness!' (v. 21)

The man with the two talents had gained two more and received the same commendation from his master. The third said: 'Master, I knew that you are a hard man, harvesting where you have not sown and gathering where you have not scattered seed. So I was afraid and went out and hid your talent in the ground. See, here is what belongs to you.' (vv. 24–5)

The master was furious with him. He should at least have

deposited the money with bankers to gain interest on it. 'Take the talent from him,' he commanded, 'and give it to the one who has the ten talents. For everyone who has will be given more, and he will have an abundance. Whoever does not have, even what he has will be taken from him. And throw that worthless servant outside, into the darkness, where there will be weeping and gnashing of teeth.' (vv. 28–30)

If God entrusts us with His riches, spiritual and material, He expects them to be used faithfully and fruitfully. If He has planted the seed of His Kingdom in our lives, He expects us to produce Kingdom fruit.

In the parable of the Sower, the seed planted in good soil could produce good fruit, but in varying quantities. Jesus makes a similar point in the parable of the Talents: different people have different capacities. God does not expect a man to produce fruit beyond his capacity; but He does desire that each bears fruit to the full extent of his capacity.

The fruit is the reproduction of the seed or of the talents. The seed sown is the seed of the Kingdom. The talents represent the gifts and rich resources God makes available to the children of His Kingdom.

The master is delighted with those who are fruitful according to their respective abilities, and they are promised great responsibility and a share in his joy – a promise of inheritance in the Kingdom of heaven, where they will be able to know God's joy eternally.

The third servant suffers a different fate. Once again we are faced with evidence of God's wrath that will be vented in judgment on the disobedient. The servant had received from the master, but wasted his inheritance; he was unfruitful, he was unfaithful. The judgment: he would lose what he had.

Again Jesus reiterates an important spiritual principle; 'For everyone who has will be given more, and he will have an abundance.' When we are fruitful, seeking first God's Kingdom and righteousness, He lavishes His provision on us. We want for nothing. He demonstrates His love and care for us. When we give to Him in any way, He always gives more back to us; He always outdoes us in giving.

When we are unfruitful or hold back from giving, we thereby impoverish ourselves. It is not that God wants to withhold His blessings and abundance from us; we are not fulfilling the spiritual principles of the Kingdom that Jesus taught. The more of His resources we put to fruitful use, the more He gives.

On the other hand: 'Whoever does not have, even what he has will be taken from him.' The man who is unfruitful will lose even what he appears to have. We must not side-step the things that Jesus said because we do not like them, or because they do not fit in with concepts of the kind of Lord we want Him to be. There is no point in trying to spiritualise the message of this parable out of existence. What Jesus says is simple: the man with one talent proved unfruitful, the talent was taken from him, he was judged as worthless and ordered to be cast into outer darkness.

This is in full accord with what Jesus teaches elsewhere. When describing Himself as the True Vine, He described the disciples as branches. No branch can bear fruit by itself; it must remain in the vine. The man who does so will bear much fruit. He does not have to produce the fruit himself or be anxious about the level of fruitfulness in his life. By abiding in Jesus he will be fruitful. The sap of the Holy Spirit will flow through his 'branch' and produce the fruit.

The Father will prune the fruitful branches to make them more fruitful still. But Jesus also says; 'He cuts off every branch in me that bears no fruit'. (John 15: 2) What happens to such branches? 'If anyone does not remain in me, he is like a branch that is thrown away and withers; such branches are picked up, thrown into the fire and burned.' (v. 6)

Jesus is not afraid of warning people of the eternal consequences of rejecting Him, of their unbelief or unfruitfulness.

Does this mean that those who have received the gift of the

Kingdom from God should fear losing their inheritance? Not at all. The Father does expect them to remain faithful to the end; and he will keep them faithful, if their hearts are set upon pleasing Him. 'May God himself, the God of peace, sanctify you through and through. May your whole spirit, soul and body be kept blameless at the coming of our Lord Jesus Christ. The one who calls you is faithful and he will do it.' (1 Thess. 5: 23–4)

BEFORE THE THRONE

After the parable of the talents, Jesus talks of His second coming; 'When the Son of Man comes in his glory, and all the angels with him, he will sit on his throne in heavenly glory. All the nations will be gathered before him, and he will separate the people one from another as a shepherd separates the sheep from the goats. He will put the sheep on his right and the goats on his left.' (Matt. 25: 31–3) This is consistent with what Jesus taught when explaining the parable of the Weeds.

The King will say to those on the right, 'Come, you who are blessed by my Father; take your inheritance, the kingdom prepared for you since the creation of the world.' (v. 34) They are invited to be part of the great consummation of the Kingdom because they have proved faithful and fruitful. By their correctness of liturgical practice or doctrine; by their strict observance and loyalty to tradition? No! By the practical outworking of Kingdom principles in their lives, reaching out into the world with the love and resources of the King. 'For I was hungry and you gave me something to eat, I was thirsty and you gave me something to drink, I was a stranger and you invited me in, I needed clothes and you clothed me, I was sick and you looked after me, I was in prison and you came to visit me.' (Matt. 25: 35–6)

The righteous ones, the sheep, the Kingdom people, are amazed at this assessment of their lives and ask when they did such things for the Lord; to which the King replies: 'I tell you the truth, whatever you did for one of the least of these brothers of mine, you did for me.' (v. 40)

Why their perplexity? Because their hearts were full of the love God had given them it seemed only natural and right to do such things, as the opportunities were presented to them. They responded quietly to God's call to express His love in these ways, without any thought of reward. They did them because they loved the Lord and desired to walk in right ways with Him. Because they loved Him, they loved people and welcomed the opportunities to love and serve in His name.

The goats are given a very different judgment: 'Depart from me, you who are cursed, into the eternal fire prepared for the devil and his angels.' (v. 41) They had received similar opportunities to love and serve, but had not responded to them. They too are taken aback by the judgment, but for different reasons. There is a sense of bewilderment, of resentment and indignation in their reply: 'Lord, when did we see you hungry or thirsty or a stranger or needing clothes or sick or in prison, and did not help you?' (v. 44) The implication is that if they knew it had been the Lord Himself they would have given to Him; but it was only people!

The King replies to them: 'I tell you the truth, whatever you did not do for one of the least of these, you did not do for me.' (v. 45) And Jesus sums up by saying: 'Then they will go away to eternal punishment, but the righteous to eternal life.' (v. 46)

This shows how intensely practical Kingdom living is, bringing love and service to those in need, expressing the compassion and mercy of God. How easy to have the wrong motives, expecting to be thanked, praised, recognised, admired even!

Kingdom children quietly get on with the job, not for any appreciation or reward, but simply out of love. They not only have a position of righteousness before God because of all that Jesus has done for them; they seek to live in righteousness, doing in each situation what He wants them to do, what He would have done Himself in the days of His humanity.

What a warning for the super-spiritual, those who are full
of the right-sounding religious jargon, but who fail to
produce the fruit of the Spirit in their lives! What a warning
for those who do not want the quiet comfort of their lives
invaded by the needs of others!

Jesus had said to the religious leaders: 'Woe to you,
teachers of the law and Pharisees, you hypocrites! You give a
tenth of your spices – mint, dill and cummin. But you have
neglected the more important matters of the law – justice,
mercy and faithfulness.' (Matt. 23: 23)

Who, then, are the righteous? Those who have come to
Jesus in repentance and faith. They are washed in His blood
and made righteous in God's sight. They are the children of
His Kingdom by His grace and mercy. They have new hearts
and have been given new life. The Holy Spirit lives in them
and bears fruit in their lives. Because they have submitted to
the sovereignty and authority of Jesus, they want His will
above their own, to express His love and compassion to those
in need, loving their brethren as He has loved them, and
reaching out into the world with the truth and power of the
positive Kingdom.

And who are the goats? Those who have rejected the King
and demonstrate that rejection by the way in which they treat
His brethren. That does not mean they are devoid of good
works. But no amount of good works can justify a person in
God's sight!

Jesus is pointing out that true righteousness, borne out of a
true experience of new birth, will be expressed in practical
ways. Faith will produce good works; but good works will not
produce faith – and without faith it is impossible to please
God.

The righteous need not fear judgment. The unrighteous,
on the other hand, face the eternal punishment of which Jesus
warns. Christians cannot afford to be complacent. The
believer, who has assurance in his heart of his salvation, is full

of zeal to share his faith with others, to see the lost drawn into the Kingdom, to express his love for Jesus in practical ways by loving others.

Chapter 19

KINGDOM GLORY

There is glory to come for all the children of the Kingdom, for their King will return to the earth in triumph. They are to prepare for that time, not knowing when it will be, but living as if it is to be today.

Whenever there has been revival in the Church's history, there has been expectancy of Christ's return, accompanied by a sense of urgency in the preaching of the Kingdom. His return will be a glorious event for the saved, but will involve judgment for the lost. Renewed faith in the great hope that God's Kingdom will be established and recognised everywhere, brings with it the sense of urgency in reaching as many of the lost as possible with the truth, so that they may have opportunity to repent of their sins and be born again into the Kingdom of God.

'In the presence of God and of Christ Jesus, who will judge the living and the dead, and in view of his appearing and his kingdom, I give you this charge: Preach the Word; be prepared in season and out of season; correct, rebuke and encourage – with great patience and careful instruction.' (2 Tim. 4: 1–2)

Jesus did not wait until His disciples were theologically trained before sending them out with the good news of the Kingdom. They had a divine commission; they were being sent out in the name of the King of heaven. If people received them, well and good; if not, they had clear instructions: 'But when you enter a town and are not welcomed, go into its streets and say, "Even the dust of your town that sticks to our feet we wipe off against you. Yet be sure of this: The kingdom of God is near." ' (Luke 10: 10–11)

REVIVAL

We live in exciting times. A spiritual revival has begun in some parts of the world, and with it the expectation that the Second Coming of the King is imminent. There is an increasing sense of urgency in reaching the lost with the gospel, a realisation that there can be no answer to the dilemmas of modern society, except a spiritual one. Jesus Christ is the only answer to men's needs, individually and socially. He is the Way, and the gospel of the Kingdom the means, by which a spiritual revolution is to take place in the coming generation.

We can only marvel at being chosen by God, not only to be alive at such a time as this, but to be included in His divine purpose. We can rejoice that our names are written in heaven and that we are sent out to heal the sick, spiritually, emotionally, physically and socially; to declare that 'The Kingdom of God is near.' We have the divine commission and He is ready to anoint all who will go in obedience to His command.

It is encouraging to see many young people, especially men, being called to full-time ministry. Some are being called to ordination in the historic denominations, but by no means all. The variety of New Testament ministries are being restored to the Church. God is firing the hearts of many with a new enthusiasm and zeal for the Kingdom, and is equipping them with the power of His Spirit for His service. It seems God is raising up an army, and is appointing officers to be trained to lead a great march against the powers of darkness that reign rampant over many places, holding the lives of multitudes in spiritual, moral and even physical bondage.

This is not wishful thinking, it is happening; and the

spiritually discerning see that it is happening. God is calling for faith among His children, for they are to proclaim not a Kingdom of words but of power. With the verbal proclamation there is to be evidence of signs and wonders. What we have seen in recent years, great as that has been, is only the prelude to the greater things we are about to see.

The Lord is not only asking His people to pray for revival, but to be themselves revived. Out of that will come the urgent desire to reach the lost, to be faithful witnesses; and still more will hear God's call to lay aside all other considerations of personal gain and ambition, to be available totally to the King.

WITNESSES

Others will sense the importance of their Kingdom witness in their prevailing circumstances at work, with neighbours, friends and especially among their own families.

God is wanting not only faith, but an increase of love among His children. The closer they draw near to Him who is love, the more they will sense His love for them; the more they will know love for Him and for others, and the more willing they will be to live Kingdom life. For they will acknowledge how their love of sin has not only deprived them of enjoying many of the Kingdom riches God has made available to them, but has also had a negative effect on their witness to others. It is difficult for the world to believe that the Kingdom is at hand, if it is difficult to see evidence of the Kingdom among Christians.

'Love the Lord your God with all your heart and with all your soul and with all your strength and with all your mind', (Luke 10: 27) and your neighbour as yourself, is still God's purpose.

God is calling His children back to holiness, to be like Jesus, to be people full of His Spirit, men and woman of faith and love; those who recognise that God has set them apart for

Himself. He has separated them from sin so that they can live in righteousness, living lives pleasing to Him.

God is confronting His children with the areas of compromise in their lives. He is showing them that they cannot please both God and men. In pleasing God they will be able to minister more effectively to men. It is a time, not to be conformed to the pattern of this world, but to be transformed by having our minds renewed, by having them set on things above, on pleasing the King and living as Kingdom children.

REAPING

It is a time of reaping. The fields are white and ready for harvest. It is God's moment when we will see the greatest harvest of souls the world has ever seen, as the gospel of the Kingdom is faithfully lived and proclaimed. This is true already in several nations in different parts of the world; it will be more widely the case in the coming years.

This does not mean that the way ahead will be easy. Wherever there is a major thrust forward of the gospel, the forces of darkness gather to oppose the spread of the Kingdom. Those who exercise their Kingdom faith and authority are not daunted by opposition, because they know already the outcome of the conflict.

It is God's time to possess the land, to see a return to faith in God's Word and the demonstrations of His power; to see His love shed abroad in the way lives are manifestly transformed. Instead of selfishness and waste, there will be selfless giving to others. Instead of pride, men and women will humble themselves under the mighty hand of God.

It is a time for righteousness to be restored:

If your hand causes you to sin, cut it off. It is better for you to enter life maimed than with two hands to go into hell, where the fire never goes out. And if your foot causes you to sin, cut it off. It is better for you to enter life crippled than to have two feet and be thrown into hell. And if your eye causes you to sin, pluck it out. It is better for you to enter the kingdom of God with one eye than to have two eyes and be thrown into hell. (Mark 9: 43–7).

God's timing for revival is linked with His children's willingness to seek Him, with their desire to be godly and to be used by Him in prayer and action to reach the lost. Revival is costly. Those that have wanted nothing to do with the renewal we have seen in recent years, certainly will not want to face the cost of revival.

And yet when hearts are set aflame with love for God, the cost does not seem important. It is never too costly to please the one you truly love. When we want to satisfy ourselves in some way, we leave nothing undone that could contribute to the success of our aims. When we want to please the King, we will not count obedience too costly; we will be more aware of the honour accorded us from heaven.

It was so out of place for the mother of James and John to ask Jesus that they might sit on either side of Him in His Kingdom. (Matt. 20: 21) We do not serve Him for any honour to be accorded to us either on earth or in heaven. Neither are we obedient to His commands to gain entrance into His Kingdom. We serve, love and obey because we have been given such a wonderful inheritance and want others to share in the joy of the Lord. 'Blessed is the man who will eat at the feast in the kingdom of God.' (Luke 14: 15)

To His disciples Jesus said: 'And I confer on you a kingdom, just as my Father conferred one on me, so that you may eat and drink at my table in my kingdom and sit on thrones, judging the twelve tribes of Israel.' (Luke 22: 29–30) Not all of us will judge in that way, but all who are faithful to the King are invited to the marriage supper of the Lamb of God. 'Here I am! I stand at the door and knock. If anyone hears my voice and opens the door, I will come in and eat with him, and he with me.' (Rev. 3: 20)

HIS MAJESTY REVEALED

When the Lord announces His return to John, He says: 'Behold, I am coming soon! My reward is with me, and I will give to everyone according to what he has done.' (Rev. 22: 12) Those who have availed themselves of His redeeming love will enjoy that heavenly reward: 'Blessed are those who wash their robes, that they may have the right to the tree of life and may go through the gates into the city. Outside are the dogs, those who practise magic arts, the sexually immoral, the murderers, the idolaters and everyone who loves and practises falsehood.' (Rev. 22: 14–15)

Throughout Scripture there is the contrast between the faithful who humble themselves before God, and the proud who set themselves up against Him by the flagrant disobedience in their lives.

Not only will the Kingdom children feast at the heavenly banquet; they will reign on the earth; 'with your blood you purchased men for God from every tribe and language and people and nation. You have made them to be a kingdom and priests to serve our God, and they will reign on the earth.' (Rev. 5: 9–10)

The provisional manner in which the Kingdom can be manifested now, its secret hidden from many, will give way to the open manifestation of the majesty of Jesus when all will be revealed. Satan and his demons will be condemned to their eternal torment. They have tormented men for centuries and will receive their just reward for their rebellion against God.

Satan will be cast down and the saints of God, the children of the Kingdom, will receive their full inheritance. 'The kingdom of the world has become the kingdom of our Lord and of his Christ, and he will reign for ever and ever.' (Rev. 11: 15)

The elders who surround the throne worship the Lord

because He has taken His great power and has begun to reign universally. This is the time for judgment and for rewarding 'your saints and those who reverence your name, both small and great – and for destroying those who destroy the earth.' (Rev. 11: 18)

Satan's defeat is final. No longer will he be able to accuse the brethren: 'Now have come the salvation and the power and the kingdom of our God, and the authority of his Christ. For the accuser of our brothers, who accuses them before our God day and night, has been hurled down. They overcame him by the blood of the Lamb and by the word of their testimony'. (Rev. 12: 10–11)

Jesus saw His own death as a release into the glory of the Kingdom from which He had come. The whole passion narrative is pregnant with the significance of what is happening in relation to the Kingdom. As Jesus is greeted with cries of 'Hosanna' on His triumphal entry into Jerusalem, some of the crowd shout: 'Blessed is the coming kingdom of our father David!' (Mark 11: 10)

When He blesses the cup at the Last Supper, He says: 'I tell you the truth, I will not drink again of the fruit of the vine until that day when I drink it anew in the kingdom of God.' (Mark 14: 25) He tells the disciples that He will not eat the Passover again until 'it finds fulfilment in the kingdom of God.' (Luke 22: 16) He will not drink of the fruit of the vine 'until the kingdom of God comes.' (v. 18)

The penitent thief crucified alongside Jesus asks Him to 'remember me when you come into your kingdom.' (Luke 23: 42) For the Christian, death is not a defeat but release in the full manifestation of God's glory.

The Christian has both entered the Kingdom and awaits its coming. Meanwhile he lives to praise and exalt the King. Psalm 145 is a great hymn exalting the majesty of God and the glory of His Kingdom.

Each generation will be able to tell of His mighty acts and 'speak of the glorious splendour of your majesty'. (v. 5) The saints, those redeemed by Jesus, 'will tell of the glory of your kingdom and speak of your might, so that all men may know of your mighty acts and the glorious splendour of your kingdom.' (vv. 11–12)

These are prophecies that relate to this, as to every other, generation. It is we who are to extol the promises of our heavenly King and tell men of the glory of His Kingdom, because we have experience of that ourselves. We cannot speak of what we do not know. If we know the Kingdom as a reality, we know not only of its future hope, but of its present power. We can tell, therefore, of the mighty acts our God performs in demonstration of His Kingly presence among men.

And yet the greater revelation of His glory awaits us. 'Your kingdom is an everlasting kingdom, and your dominion endures through all generations.' (v. 13)

Jesus says that a kingdom divided against itself will fall. Satan's dominion is divided and his ultimate demise together with all who gain their authority from him, is assured.

Those who honour King Jesus will in turn be honoured by Him. Meanwhile we have the opportunity and the responsibility to declare to this generation by word and power the glorious good news of the gospel of the Kingdom. Our faith needs to rise to embrace the purposes of God that, before the great and final conflict, many will embrace the King as they respond to His offer to give them the Kingdom.

And may He continue to remove from our hearts and lives every negative thought, desire, motive and intention that hinders the growth of Kingdom life within us. As He takes out the negative, may He continue to pour into our hearts and lives all the positive power of His Holy Spirit to enable us to live in Kingdom faith, expressing Kingdom love and exercising Kingdom power and authority.

'Thank you, heavenly Father, for your positive Kingdom.'

PERSONAL VICTORY

Personal Victory

Colin Urquhart

HODDER AND STOUGHTON
LONDON SYDNEY AUCKLAND

Personal Victory

To all those who want to live
a victorious Christian Life

Contents

Acknowledgments

My thanks to all who have worked with me in the preparation of this book, especially to Rose-Mary who has laboured diligently on the word processor and has assisted in preparing the material for publication. She has been helped by Alison and Heather.

I am also thankful to all at Kingdom Faith Ministries for their love, prayer and encouragement.

My wife and daughter, Andrea, have been able to rejoice that I could be based at home while writing; a real treat for all of us!

My prayer is that the Lord Jesus will use this little book to point the way to a victorious Christian life for many who have found the way difficult.

C.U.

1

Living in Victory

The way to victory:
   God's purpose is for you to live in personal victory.
   This is possible by faith in Jesus who has *already*
   overcome the world and is reigning in triumph.

Your victory scripture:
   Without faith it is impossible to please God. (Heb. 11:6)

Many Christians find it difficult to believe they can live in
victory! Yet God's purpose is for them to overcome their
difficulties, not be defeated by them.

Jesus does not promise His followers an easy life.
Neither does He offer trite answers to people's needs.
Instead He makes it clear that God's power and resources
are available to those who believe in Him.

Those who appropriate these resources will be victorious.
They will overcome their problems through faith in Jesus
Christ. **This is possible for you because it is God's will for you**.

He has not called you to be defeated or to fail. **He has
called you to a life of victorious faith**.

THE LORD'S PURPOSE

Faith overcomes the world

Christians talk about the victory of the Cross, the resurrection and the ultimate victory of Jesus when He comes again

in glory. Why do they hesitate to speak of living in personal victory? Is this because of unbelief? Do they have the kind of faith which believes the right doctrines, but makes little difference to their daily lives?

'This is the victory that has overcome the world,'even our faith,' says John (1 John 5:4).

Men and women of faith will live in victory. They *have* overcome the world. 'Who is it that overcomes the world? Only he who believes that Jesus is the Son of God' (1 John 5:5). **If you believe Jesus is the Son of God you can overcome whatever problems confront you**. God has already given you a faith which overcomes. Jesus is greater than any problem or need. He proclaimed boldly, 'I have overcome the world' (John 16:33).

As He has overcome the world so He anticipates that those who believe in Him will overcome.

Paul was a realist, as well as a man of great faith. He faced many seemingly impossible situations, and suffered both rejection and frequent physical punishment for the sake of the gospel. Yet he could say:

> We are hard pressed on every side, but not crushed; perplexed, but not in despair; persecuted, but not abandoned; struck down, but not destroyed. (2 Cor. 4:8–9)

He maintained this positive attitude because, although he lived with a constant awareness of his own weakness, he knew the treasure of God's 'all surpassing power' within him.

As a Christian   **you have this same power within you;
you have the person of God Himself, the
Holy Spirit, living in you;
you have Christ in you.**

And it is His purpose to lead you in His triumphant procession.

It is not by determination nor your own strength that you will triumph; but by faith in Jesus working within you through His Spirit.

IF YOU TRUST IN YOURSELF, YOU WILL FAIL;
IF YOU TRUST IN HIM, HE WILL ENABLE YOU
TO OVERCOME.
**God does not want you to fail; He wants you to be
victorious**.

REWARDS OF FAITH

Great promises are given to those who overcome. To them
God 'will give the right to eat from the tree of life, which is
in the paradise of God' (Rev. 2:7). They will not be hurt in
any way by the second death and their names will never be
erased from the book of life. Jesus will acknowledge them
before His Father and His angels. They will be given the
right to sit with Jesus on His throne, just as Jesus overcame
and sat down with His Father on His throne.

**These wonderful promises are for you. This is God's will
and purpose for you. He wants you to overcome, to live in
victory and triumph through Jesus Christ. He wants you
reigning with Him in glory.**

First you need to learn to reign in this life through faith.
For 'without faith it is impossible to please God, because
anyone who comes to him must believe that he exists and
that he rewards those who earnestly seek him' (Heb. 11:6).

As a Christian how can you overcome the world, the
flesh and the devil? How can you live in the victory Jesus
has won for you on the cross and demonstrated in His
resurrection? How can you be victorious in prayer, believing God's promises and seeing them fulfilled? How can you
know victory in the conflicts within you and the difficult
circumstances around you?

CONCENTRATION ON PROBLEMS

Many Christians make the fatal mistake of concentrating
on the problem instead of the answer. To speak of victory

is unrealistic, they suggest. Instead they speak endlessly of their needs, difficulties and sicknesses.

Isn't this a great temptation? It is so easy to spend your prayer time thinking about your problems, instead of expecting Jesus to deal with them. It is tempting to keep telling others about your difficulties because you want them to understand your situation or feel sorry for you. It seems so natural, and yet such conversations can seriously hinder faith.

How different this is from the way Jesus taught His disciples to live! **For Jesus, faith is the only realistic way of living**. Faith in God's love. Faith in God's power. Faith in God's mercy and grace.

Jesus said: 'Come to me, all you who are weary and burdened, and I will give you rest' (Matt. 11:28). I was taught to do this every time I prayed and it was impressed on me that it did not take long to pass a burden over, once I was prepared to let go of it.

You do not have to go into an immense amount of detail; the Lord knows more about your situation than you do. It is like handing the burden of a full suitcase to someone else. You do not set the case on the ground, open it and describe all its contents. If somebody offers to carry the burden, you simply hand over the suitcase, together with everything in it.

And you do not keep hold of one corner when you hand the burden to Jesus. He is able to carry the entire weight.

This is one of the first elementary acts of faith for you to learn. **Jesus loves you so much He wants to carry your burdens**.

He encouraged His disciples to live in faith, and His greatest disappointments over them were on the occasions when they failed to exercise that faith: 'O unbelieving and perverse generation, how long shall I stay with you? How long shall I put up with you?' (Matt. 17:17).

Many situations will challenge your faith. Jesus was not afraid to confront problems. He teaches that anyone who speaks to a mountain of need in faith, will see that mountain moved if he 'believes that what he says will happen' (Mark 11:23). Jesus says this of 'anyone', **and that includes you!**

You do not please the Lord by carrying burdens He wants to lift from you. He is honoured, not by the passive acceptance of problems, but by the faith which confronts and overcomes them.

You will live in victory if you live by the principles of faith Jesus taught.

Faith in Jesus trusts Him instead of self.

Faith in Jesus believes Him to change the circumstances instead of submitting to problems.

Faith in Jesus believes what He says, instead of doubting His Word.

Faith in Jesus acts on the Word instead of being disobedient.

You may love the Lord Jesus sincerely and desire earnestly to be true to Him, and yet still experience much failure and frustration.

God confronts all of us with our shortcomings, including those of faith, only that He might teach us to trust Him more fully. He wants to teach you to be victorious in your daily life.

This is to become your experience, not simply a pious hope. **Jesus wants you to overcome your circumstances not to be overcome by them. He does not want you to be the victim; but the victor. He does not want you to be trampled underfoot; He wants you to triumph!**

Your key to a victorious life:
FAITH IN JESUS ENABLES YOU TO OVERCOME.

2

The Victory of the Cross

The way to victory:
    **The victory of the Cross over every human need and
    every spiritual power is available to *you* through faith.**

Your victory scripture:
    **The message of the cross is foolishness to those who are
    perishing, but to us who are being saved it is the power
    of God. (1 Cor. 1:18)**

To live by faith is to live in the victory Jesus has already won
for you on the Cross.

During His pastoral ministry Jesus overcame sin, sickness and even death. What He did then has been made
available to those of any generation who put their faith in
Him. The Cross has eternal value for every believer.

Death is God's just and holy judgment on sin. Because
He never sinned, Jesus did not deserve to die. He fulfilled
completely His Father's will, being obedient to Him in
every way, regardless of the cost.

He offered His life as a sacrifice on behalf of sinners. All
who grieve the Lord by their sins can know His forgiveness
and complete deliverance from guilt. Jesus also took upon
Himself all the suffering, affliction and rejection we can
experience. He was even oppressed and 'crushed' for us,
experiencing complete dereliction on the Cross: 'My God,
my God, why have you forsaken me?'

At that moment, Jesus was totally identified with the needs of every human being. He knew the separation from the Father which is the direct consequence of sin, not His own sin, but yours and mine.

IT IS DONE

There was nothing sentimental about the Cross. Jesus bore on His body the marks of betrayal and severe disfigurement, caused by the torture to which He was subjected. As He hung there He was without any beauty or attraction, despised, rejected and hated.

This was the cost of giving His sinless life as an offering for sinners, His righteous life for the unrighteous, His perfect life for the imperfect, His obedient life for the disobedient, His successful life on behalf of failures. All who have sinned can find their identity in Christ on the Cross. He died for all.

The disfigured, the ordinary, the despised, the rejected, the oppressed, all had their needs met by Jesus at that moment. He experienced oppression from the devil, religious leaders, temporal authorities and through physical suffering. Yet He emerged triumphant.

God's love for you took Jesus to the Cross, so you might be set free from sin, oppression, rejection, sickness and every other need. Because of what He suffered He is able to lead you through the difficulty to a place of victory.

Like you, I am often aware of my total unworthiness before God. I wonder how He could have chosen me out of the mass of humanity, to be His child. It seems inconceivable that the Holy God should want to have anything to do with me in any way. He must be aware of my ungodly thoughts and desires. And how I must hurt Him every time I sin or disobey His Word.

And yet I have had to come to terms with the truth. In

Jesus, He has demonstrated His love for me. **The Cross is personal for *me*. Jesus died for *me*.** And when I ask Him to forgive my sins, His blood cleanses me from all that is unholy in His sight. He makes me worthy in God's Presence. I can stand before His throne clothed in the white garment of righteousness which He puts on me.

I deserve none of this. It is the work of His grace. And what He has done for me, He has done for you.

As Jesus triumphed on the Cross, you can triumph in faith as you appropriate what He did for you there.

THE MESSAGE OF THE CROSS

Jesus warned His followers they would have trouble in this life, but reminded them He had overcome the world. He promised to be with them always. No matter what their difficulties, He would never leave them. His physical presence with them would give way to His living presence within them through the Holy Spirit. And He promised to answer their prayers of faith. Whatever they ask in His name will be given to them – if they believe!

Paul recognises, 'The message of the cross is foolishness to those who are perishing, but to us who are being saved it is the power of God' (1 Cor. 1:18). **The Cross is the power which enables you to overcome. For Jesus met your need there. He did everything necessary:**

> **to ensure forgiveness of your sins,**
> **to free you from every spiritual bondage,**
> **to make possible the healing of any emotional or physical need.**

No wonder Paul said: 'For I resolved to know nothing while I was with you except Jesus Christ and him crucified' (1 Cor. 2:2).

Paul testified: 'I have been crucified with Christ and I no

longer live, but Christ lives in me. The life I live in the body, I live by faith in the Son of God, who loved me and gave himself for me' (Gal. 2:20). At the time of the crucifixion Paul was Jesus' enemy. He came to realise that the old Saul of Tarsus with all his pride and misplaced religious and legalistic fervour, was put to death on the Cross, so that a new man could be brought to life, Paul the apostle. He became a man of faith, because he understood **he could only receive this new life through faith in Jesus crucified, and he could only live the new life by continuing to live by faith.**

THE EXTENT OF THE VICTORY

The Cross marked the beginning of a new covenant, a new relationship, between God and men. It marked the end of trying to please God by formal, religious observances, and heralded a new era of faith.

When you surrendered your life to the Lordship of Jesus:

> God made you alive with Christ. He forgave us all our sins, having cancelled the written code, with its regulations, that was against us and that stood opposed to us; he took it away, nailing it to the cross. (Col. 2:13–14)

The law gives way to faith in Jesus. **Now by faith you can share in His triumph**.

This victory not only meets every human need; it is also the means by which all the spiritual powers of darkness are overcome:

> And having disarmed the powers and authorities, he made a public spectacle of them, triumphing over them by the cross. (Col. 2:15)

All your needs have been met in the crucified Jesus. He is now risen in triumph. And the promise of God's Word to you is this: 'And my God will meet all your needs according to his glorious riches in Christ Jesus.' (Phil. 4:19). **These glorious riches are yours in Christ Jesus.**

In Him your old life is crucified.
In Him you are raised to a new life.
In Him your needs are met.
In Him you can triumph.

Your key to a victorious life:
ALL YOUR NEEDS HAVE BEEN MET IN THE CRUCIFIED JESUS.

3

Victory in the Name of Jesus

The way to victory:
Jesus' name has power and authority over everything material and spiritual. You will not fail if you do things in His name.

Your victory scripture:
And whatever you do, whether in word or deed, do it all in the name of the Lord Jesus. (Col. 3:17)

Jesus was victorious on the Cross, overcoming sin, sickness and every form of evil. His name is above every other name. He is supreme. He is Lord.

Therefore God exalted him to the highest place and gave him the name that is above every name, that at the name of Jesus every knee should bow, in heaven and on earth and under the earth, and every tongue confess that Jesus Christ is Lord, to the glory of God the Father. (Phil. 2:9–11)

THE NAME THAT SAVES

The Father exalted Jesus because of His perfect obedience in fulfilling His purpose on earth. Now His name is above every name in heaven and earth. He has power and authority over everything spiritual or material. 'He became as much superior to the angels as the name he has inherited is superior to theirs' (Heb. 1:4).

In scripture the name denotes the person. The name of Jesus signifies all that He is and everything He has done. You cannot separate the name of Jesus either from the words He spoke, or from the things He accomplished.

Jesus is the Way, the Truth and the Life. There is no other way to heaven except through Jesus. There is no other name by which a man can be saved, 'Salvation is found in no-one else, for there is no other name under heaven given to men by which we must be saved' (Acts 4:12). It is by the power of the name of the crucified and victorious Jesus that **you have been accepted and forgiven by God. Through Him you have received new life and the gift of God's Kingdom.**

If you confess with your mouth, 'Jesus is Lord,' and believe in your heart that God raised him from the dead, you will be saved. (Rom. 10:9)

Jesus is the name of salvation. Salvation means healing and deliverance. So this is the name by which you can know victory in every circumstance of your life.
Through Jesus you have been:

saved from sin;
saved from sickness and rejection;
saved from poverty and despair;
saved from Satan and the powers of darkness;
saved from the curse of the law and the demands of legalistic religion;
saved from yourself and your complete helplessness without a Saviour.

EVERYTHING IN HIS NAME

No wonder you are encouraged to do everything in the name of Jesus! **'And whatever you do, whether in word or** deed, do it all in the name of the Lord Jesus, giving thanks to God the Father through him' (Col. 3:17).

It brought a revolution in my own life and ministry to realise that I was called by God to do everything in the name of Jesus. At first it seemed a daunting prospect. How could I possibly live up to such a high calling? Then I began to see something of the principle of speaking on Jesus' behalf, and being invited to pray what He would pray.

Would the Father really listen to me as He listens to His Son? Then came the recognition that God has made me a son and has put His own name upon me. I was not to waste the privilege the Lord had given me.

The more I dared to believe, the more He would do. The more bold I became in faith, the greater the faith God could honour. The more I understood that I am in Christ and He in me, the more thankful I became that He both heard and answered me.

My first steps in faith seemed tentative, and yet God honoured them. Answers to prayer are a great encouragement!

I learnt to thank the Lord for allowing me to fail at times, for then I had trusted in myself and not in Him. I had viewed my situation through purely human eyes, without the perspective that Jesus would bring.

Slowly I began to make more use of the privilege of praying in His name. 'If this is how Jesus would view the situation, then this is how I will view it. If that is what He would pray, that is what I will pray.'

Often I had to admit I did not believe what He would believe, or expect the answers He anticipated. But as I humbled myself before the Lord, confessing my unbelief, so then I could receive the words of faith with which He wanted to encourage me.

It is inconceivable that Jesus should ever fail. If you act in His name you act on His behalf, saying or doing what He would say or do in that situation. You will look at your circumstances through His eyes, praying what He would pray, believing what He would believe. Like Him, you have available to you the riches and resources of heaven.

When you act in your own strength, or do what is opposed to God's purpose, you will experience failure, frustration and defeat. You have to acknowledge the far-reaching power that faith releases into your life.

> I tell you the truth, if you have faith as small as a mustard seed, you can say to this mountain, 'Move from here to there' and it will move. Nothing will be impossible for you. (Matt. 17:20)

NOTHING WILL BE IMPOSSIBLE FOR YOU. This is the result of faith working in your life. Again Jesus affirms: **'Everything is possible for him who believes'** (Mark 9:23).

PRAY IN HIS NAME

Every time you say the Lord's Prayer you acknowledge that God's holy name is to be praised. And Jesus makes a series of amazing promises of what God will do when you pray in His name:

> And I will do whatever you ask in my name, so that the Son may bring glory to the Father. You may ask me for anything in my name, and I will do it. (John 14:13–14)

> You did not choose me, but I chose you and appointed you to go and bear fruit – fruit that will last. Then the Father will give you whatever you ask in my name. (John 15:16)

> I tell you the truth, my Father will give you whatever you ask in my name. (John 16:23)

What a privilege to be invited by Jesus to use His name in prayer as a guarantee you will be heard and answered! What a privilege to be given such wonderful promises by the One who has never broken His word! What encouragement to learn how to pray in the name of Jesus!

But He makes it clear that the one who truly prays in His name, will not pray with doubt, or be double-minded about the outcome. He will believe he has received the answer.

> **You are saved by the name of Jesus.**
> **You can act in the name of Jesus.**
> **You can speak in the name of Jesus.**
> **You are to pray in the name of Jesus.**
> **You have authority through the name of Jesus.**
> **You have power in the name of Jesus.**
> **You can heal in the name of Jesus.**
> **You are protected by the name of Jesus.**

All this because: **You have faith in the name of Jesus.**

This is your calling as a child of God, and we shall see how you can fulfil such a calling. Understand that this is possible for you. Because you are saved by His name, you can say and do everything in His name, on His behalf, expecting victory.

Before going to the Cross Jesus prayed that the disciples would be protected by the power of His name:

> Holy Father, protect them by the power of your name – the name you gave me – so that they may be one as we are one. While I was with them, I protected them and kept them safe by that name you gave me. (John 17:11–12)

That same protection is yours because you belong to Jesus. You are protected by the power of His name, as you seek to walk in faithful and loving obedience to His word.

BY FAITH IN THE NAME OF JESUS

After the resurrection and the coming of the Holy Spirit at Pentecost, the disciples saw the fruit of acting in the name of Jesus. When Peter and John healed the crippled beggar at the gate of the temple, they told the crowd:

> By faith in the name of Jesus, this man whom you see and know was made strong. It is Jesus' name and the faith that comes through him that has given this complete healing to him, as you can all see. (Acts 3:16)

When later they had to give an account to the Jewish council as to why the man had been healed, the High Priest asked them, 'By what power or what name did you do this?' The answer that Peter gave reiterated what he and John had told the crowd, 'It is by the name of Jesus Christ of Nazareth, whom you crucified but whom God raised from the dead, that this man stands before you healed' (Acts 4:10).

Is the name of Jesus as powerful now as then? Of course. Is faith in His name the same? That is the crucial question. Where such faith exists people today are healed in the name of Jesus, and their needs are met.

The name of Jesus brings salvation. Everything is possible to those who believe in Him. His name protects all who belong to Him. By His name the sick are healed and those in bondage are set free. The name of Jesus is above every other name in heaven or on earth.

As you learn to speak out and pray in His name, you will experience personal victory.

Your key to a victorious life:
  THE WAY OF VICTORY IS TO SPEAK, ACT AND
  PRAY IN THE NAME OF JESUS.

4

Victory in the Holy Spirit

The way to victory:
You can experience victory by submitting your human spirit to the Holy Spirit. He will lead you into victory, not failure and defeat.

Your victory scripture:
The Spirit gives life; the flesh counts for nothing. (John 6:63)

GOD'S PLAN FOR YOUR LIFE

Jesus has been victorious on the Cross. In His name you can be victorious. Now you need to see how this victory can be applied to your life. Paul prays:

May your whole spirit, soul and body be kept blameless at the coming of our Lord Jesus Christ. The one who calls you is faithful and he will do it. (1 Thess. 5:23–24)

The Lord wants you to live in faith and victory. His purpose is to sanctify you, to make you holy, like Jesus in spirit, soul and body. These are not two separate purposes, but different parts of one overall plan He has for your life:

He wants you to live by faith in Jesus.
He wants you to live in victory.
He wants you to live in love for God and others – faith working through love.

He wants to sanctify you in spirit, soul and body, making
you holy like Jesus.
He wants to keep you blameless in His sight.

This is God's plan for every Christian. He calls us to
different ministries, but all within the same plan. To see
how this plan will be effected in your own life, it is
important to understand the different functions of your
spirit, soul and body.

BEFORE YOUR NEW BIRTH

Before you became a Christian you lived 'according to the
flesh', your soul and body acting independently of God.
The soul consists of three main areas:

a) the mind, including your reason and intellect
b) the emotions or feelings
c) the will, your ability to make decisions and choices.

Before you were a Christian you had your own ideas about
everything, including God. These ideas formed the foundation of what you believed as a person, and therefore
influenced the way you chose to act. There may have been
no reference to God at all in your thinking even though you
might have believed in His existence. Or you may have
attended some form of worship, but without enjoying a
personal relationship with Jesus. Until your new birth,
your mind was not submitted to the Spirit of God and could
not be informed by Him as to His will and purpose.

The different functions of the soul interrelate and
influence one another. So, for example, whatever goes on
in the mind influences the emotions. If someone thinks
negatively about himself, he will feel negative and make
negative decisions with his will. Then his behaviour will be
negative.

Before your new birth you probably lived on your
feelings to a great extent. You did what you felt like doing,

and tried to avoid what you did not want to do. You were the victim of the way in which others spoke to you and treated you. You may have harboured feelings of bitterness, resentment and hurt. You may have lived an immoral life seeking the fulfilment of your fleshly desires. You may have been involved in dubious business practices. You may have tried to live a 'good' life, but with very independent attitudes.

Because your mind was conditioned by your own ideas and way of thinking, and because your life was influenced greatly by your feelings, you used your will to please yourself, or to do what you thought right according to your own wisdom. You acted independently of any direction from God.

This is the way that most people live. However it is not the way God intends His children to behave.

THE NEW BIRTH CHANGES THINGS

When you were born again you became a Christian through your faith in Jesus Christ. At that point something dynamic happened in your human spirit. The Spirit of God came into your spirit and brought you to life spiritually. Before your new birth you had a human spirit, but it was to all intents and purposes dead. It did not influence your life in a positive direction. You lived a soulish, rather than a spiritual life.

Jesus said, 'God is spirit, and his worshippers must worship in spirit and in truth' (John 4:24). God communicates with you spiritually. You can hear His voice and receive revelation from Him in your spirit rather than in your mind.

With your mind you can appreciate and understand what God has said to you. But it is in your spirit you receive revelation. There are several ways in which this can happen. Often it occurs as you read the Bible. It can also take place when reading a spiritual book, listening to a sermon or in conversation. Suddenly something lights up inside you and you know you have heard the Lord.

So when you came alive spiritually, God could begin to produce in you His order for your life. The Holy Spirit could work through your human spirit to influence your soul.

THE SOUL AND SPIRIT

The Lord wants your mind to be submitted to His thinking.
The Lord wants your feelings ruled by His Spirit.
The Lord wants your will submitted to His will.

If your soul is submitted to the Lord, His Spirit is able to flow out of your body like rivers of living water. This is how Jesus described the activity of His Spirit in believers.

In the Figure the diagram on the left describes this process:

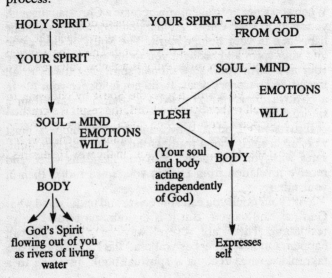

HOLY SPIRIT

YOUR SPIRIT

SOUL – MIND
EMOTIONS
WILL

BODY

God's Spirit
flowing out of you
as rivers of living
water

YOUR SPIRIT – SEPARATED
FROM GOD

SOUL – MIND

EMOTIONS

FLESH   WILL

(Your soul
and body   BODY
acting
independently
of God)

Expresses
self

This submission does not come easily to any of us. We often want our own way. We want to receive God's blessings and live in obedience to Him, but without too much cost. We can feel aggressive about our own views. We want to impress others with our knowledge. It matters immensely how we feel about things, and we expect others to be considerate about our feelings.

We think it sufficient to desire God's will, but without doing it. We are quick to notice others' faults and failings, but expect them to be gracious, forgiving and understanding about our own inadequacies. We certainly do not readily view others the way we want them to view us.

Submission does not come naturally or easily, but it is vitally necessary if we are to see God glorified in our lives.

The Holy Spirit cannot direct your body without the willing co-operation of the soul. When the soul is submitted to the Spirit, you can express the new life in your body. Without this co-operation you will act according to your natural inclinations and senses, and inevitably grieve the Lord.

The term 'flesh' in the New Testament does not refer to the physical body alone, but to the way in which the soul and the body act independently of God. This is the way you lived before your new birth, but it is not how you are to live now.

If you raise your soul above the Spirit by choosing to please yourself rather than the Lord, the result is a crushed spirit. Your spirit feels weighed down. God has not taken His Spirit away from you, but He cannot function within you, or express His life through you, in the way He desires.

GOD'S ORDER

This is God's order for your life: your soul submitted to His Spirit, so that rivers of living water flow out of your life.

Your mind submitted to the Spirit, **which means you live according to God's Word.** Your thinking is informed by His truth revealed in the scriptures.

Your emotions submitted to God's Spirit. Because you want to please Him, *you do not allow your feelings to rule you; you allow the Spirit to rule your feelings.* You will not allow feelings which oppose God's purposes and so influence your decisions.

Your will is submitted to His purposes **as revealed in His Word. You want to see His Word expressed in your life.**

God's Spirit cannot influence your thinking, your feelings and your will unless they are surrendered to Him. Only then will you make the right choices and give the correct directions to your body.

If there is not this submission of soul and body to the Spirit, God's order for your life is disrupted (as in the right-hand diagram). This does not infer that you are not a Christian, or that God has removed His Spirit from you. It simply means that you cannot function in the way God intends without this submission to His Spirit.

The Holy Spirit can only be victorious in your life, if you are prepared to be submissive to Him. You will never be victorious in your own strength, but only through submission to the Lord. Faith cannot operate properly without this submission.

This is not a submission to men, but to the Lord Himself and to the integrity of His words of truth.

Jesus walked in constant victory because He lived in perfect faith. This faith was expressed in a life lived in total submission to His Father's will. 'For I have come down from heaven not to do my will but to do the will of him who sent me' (John 6:38).

You will only live a life of faith and be victorious if you follow Jesus. He will lead you along a way of submission to God's will, and obedience to His Word. Only in this way can

your spirit, soul and body be kept under the Lordship of Jesus and the influence of His Holy Spirit.

Those who attempt to live by faith, without such submission, are likely to be disappointed – no matter how many times they claim the promises of God.

Your key to a victorious life:

SUBMIT YOUR SOUL (YOUR MIND, EMOTIONS AND WILL) TO THE HOLY SPIRIT.

5

Victory through God's Word

The way to victory:
   A life of faith is based on obedience to God's Word. To
   live according to His Word is to live in victory.

Your victory scripture:
   The words I have spoken to you are spirit and they are
   life. (John 6:63)

JESUS IS THE WORD

Jesus is the Word of God. By this Word He created. This
Word became a man and lived among us. So when Jesus
speaks, the Father speaks through His Son, revealing
eternal truth to us. Jesus' words are spirit, life and truth:

   Man does not live on bread alone, but on every word that
   comes from the mouth of God. (Matt. 4:4)

If you are to live by faith you will not base your decisions on
your own intellect or rational thought, nor on your senses,
but on what God says in His Word. **His words will be a
constant source of life for you and the foundation upon
which you structure your life.**

ROCK AND SAND

Jesus told the parable of the man who built his house on

rock and another who built on sand. The one who built on rock heard God's words and put them into practice. The other heard God but did not do what He said.

The obedient one experienced victory when the storm came. He was able to withstand all the pressures that came against him.

The one who had built on sand had heard what God said, but had not obeyed. He suffered the loss of his house in the storm.

If you are to be a man or woman of faith, you will need to apply God's Word to your life. There is no point in possessing a Bible, reading it and even saying that you believe what is written there, if you are not prepared to put the Word into action. **The one who lives the Word will be victorious.**

Faith is not knowing a series of promises which you claim for yourself. These promises are part of the covenant God has made with His children. He will certainly keep His side of the agreement and will bless you abundantly.

He expects you to live your side of the agreement: to live according to His Word and by the power of His Spirit. This can only be done by faith.

The man of faith realises that the whole revelation of God's Word is for him. He cannot pick and choose what he fancies. There are words to obey and promises to believe. Both belong together.

God intends you to be able to withstand whatever storms batter you, whatever difficulties confront you. **Faith and obedience form the way of victory: hearing God, believing what He says and doing it.**

LIVE THE WORD

The words of Jesus are the answer to every need. It is through His words that believers are set free:

If you hold to my teaching, you are really my disciples.
Then you will know the truth, and the truth will set you
free. (John 8:31–32)

Many Christians try to find liberty and freedom from their
needs and problems in other ways, through techniques in
ministry or prayer. It is only the truth of Jesus' words and
what He has accomplished, that will actually liberate people.

Jesus says that the Holy Spirit will guide us into all the
truth. 'He will not speak on his own; he will speak only
what he hears, and he will tell you what is yet to come. He
will bring glory to me by taking from what is mine and
making it known to you' (John 16:13–14). The Holy Spirit
'will teach you all things and will remind you of everything I
have said to you' (John 14:26).

Even God's Spirit does not act in independence. His
purpose is to reveal Jesus' words to us so they become
revelation in our hearts. Only then can faith be created
within us. Only then can we be motivated to obey Him.
Then we are able to act upon His words. When we do so, we
experience peace. Failure to live God's Word leads to
conflict. We then have no confidence before God. When
we pray we doubt what the outcome will be. And such
doubt prevents both faith and victory.

FAITH AND REASON

There will be many times when you will want to contradict
His words with your reason. There will be other occasions
when your feelings seem utterly opposed to what God says.
At such times you will have to choose whether you will trust
your feelings, or believe the truth.

This is one of the most important aspects of a life of faith.
The temptation to believe the natural reason rather than
the supernatural power of God, will always be with you.
Reason limits the Lord in your life; faith releases His
activity in your experience.

It is easier to believe reason than revelation.
It is easier to believe feelings than the Word.
It is easier to listen to your doubts than to the Lord.

Easier – but not right.

This is the point of struggle for many Christians. It is so much more reasonable to believe what you can see, touch or feel. **But faith is believing what you do not see.** Are you going to adopt the easy way, or live by faith?

For a whole generation the children of Israel wandered around the wilderness because, when Moses sent the spies ahead into the Promised Land, ten of the twelve believed what they saw rather than the promises God had given them. **They listened to their fears instead of to their faith.**

Only Joshua and Caleb listened to the Lord, believing His words. To Joshua was given the privilege of leading the people into their inheritance. But those who listened to their fears perished in the wilderness. For them the promises and their own ambitions remained unfulfilled.

God is not opposed to reason; He is beyond reason. His thoughts and ways are much higher than your thoughts and ways. **Do not limit the Lord by your reason.**

If God says one thing and you say another, someone has to be wrong! Whenever you contradict the Lord you can be sure He is right. He will not change His Word to accommodate your reason or feelings. **It is your ideas and attitudes which will need to change and be brought into line with His truth.**

Many do not walk in victory and experience triumph in their Christian lives because they choose to believe themselves; to believe what they think or fear, rather than to agree with God's revelation of truth and the promises He gives in His Word. You have to make the decision whether you believe what God says or whether you trust your own wisdom instead.

For the man or woman of faith, there can be no

compromise on this point. You cannot mix a little of the Word with your own wisdom and expect to see great things from God. Your mind will need to be submitted to His Spirit. And He will reveal the truth to you.

Hear the truth.
Believe the truth.
Obey the truth.

The wise man built on rock. If you are wise you will listen carefully to the Lord and put His words into practice. If on the other hand you choose to be foolish, you may hear what He says but trust in your own 'wisdom' instead. Then you will build your house on sand and it will not be able to withstand the storms of life. Are you going to be wise or foolish?

Your key to a victorious life:
  PUT GOD'S WORD INTO PRACTICE.

6

The Victory of Your King

The way to victory:
   If Jesus is your King, He will reign in your life, then you
   will have confidence before God and be assured of the
   victory He alone can give.

Your victory scripture:
   Not everyone who says to me, 'Lord, Lord,' will enter
   the kingdom of heaven, but only he who does the will of
   my Father who is in heaven. (Matt. 7:21)

YOUR LORD AND KING

If Jesus is your Lord and King your life is to be submitted to
His authority; you want Him to rule and reign over you.
   This means He is your boss. He is number one in your
life. You yield the control of your life to Him, and nothing
is allowed to be more important than Him. Nor do people,
no matter how much you love them, have any higher place
in your priorities or any greater claims upon you than Jesus.
   For Him to effect His reign in you, your soul needs to be
in submission to His Spirit; your mind, emotions and will
submitted to Him. The Spirit directs you to His Word. To
live under the authority of Jesus as His disciple, is to live
according to His Word.
   God's promises are linked to obedience and faith. The
Christian who seeks to obey Jesus' words but does not

believe His promises, will not live in the revelation of God's abundant grace and generosity. The one who believes the promises but does not obey the Word will not be able to appropriate the riches of the inheritance which he claims.

If you are tempted to disobey, the Holy Spirit within you will warn you. If you do not heed His warnings you will find it exceedingly difficult to walk in faith and victory.

FAITH AND OBEDIENCE

Faith within you is inspired by hearing God's words in your heart. The Holy Spirit takes the words of scripture and speaks them to you, so you know you have heard directly from God.

The Holy Spirit will not convict a believer of sin and promise blessing at the same moment. What the Lord does, both in scripture and in the Christian's experience, is to give promise of blessing if there is repentance first.

All these blessings will come upon you and accompany you if you obey the Lord your God. (Deut. 28:2)

To recognise Jesus as your Lord is to respect His authority over you. When your soul and body are submitted to the influence of His Spirit you will be mightily blessed, and will have confidence before God when you pray. You will be able to believe the wonderful promises Jesus gives you.

This is not to be a begrudging submission coming from a rebellious heart, but a willing response to His love. It is love answering love. **In His love God gives; in your love you submit willingly to His authority and obey**. After fifty years of seeing how Jesus' promises worked in practice, John wrote:

Dear friends, if our hearts do not condemn us, we have confidence before God and receive from him anything we ask, because we obey his commands and do what pleases him. (1 John 3:21–22)

Allowing Jesus to be Lord in the daily circumstances of your life gives you confidence before Him. You want to obey Him and do what pleases Him. In response, He wants to bless you and grant the desires of your heart. 'Delight yourself in the Lord and he will give you the desires of your heart' (Ps. 37:4).

Those living a victorious life walk in obedience to Jesus. This is true fellowship. He is the Victor. He is the Answer to every need. And you can live in close harmony and fellowship with Him.

Not only will you be blessed as a result, but others will be blessed because of you. When your life is submitted to Jesus, His Spirit flows out of your life as rivers of living water. And others are blessed with God's love and power because of you.

DISOBEDIENCE BRINGS CONFLICT

If self is raised above Jesus, in effect He is dethroned in your life. He is not allowed to be Lord and King in practice. Several things can cause this: self-concern, fear, worry, anxiety, selfishness, pride, greed, and so on. When you give way to these fleshly things the natural soul life, or 'self', opposes the Spirit and the Word.

This is not necessarily the Christian's desire or intention, but what effectively happens.

Conflict comes from not accepting what God says. The Spirit is leading in one direction, self in another (see figure).

You have confidence in your relationship with Jesus when you are at peace with Him. If there is a conflict of wills, you cannot know that peace, until you are ready to submit to Him. So Jesus says:

> If anyone would come after me, he must deny himself and take up his cross and follow me. For whoever wants to save his life will lose it, but whoever loses his life for me will find it. (Matt. 16:24–25)

WRONG

SOUL – Fear
        Worry
        Anxiety
        Negative feelings
        Selfish motives
        Wrong attitudes
        Weak will

CRUSHED SPIRIT

Cannot function properly

the Lord is grieved

BODY – Expresses fear,
        man-pleasing,
        selfishness

RIGHT

YOUR SPIRIT INFORMED
BY THE HOLY SPIRIT

SOUL – Faith in Word,
        not reason
        Listening to Holy
        Spirit not feelings
        Determined to obey

BODY – Expresses faith,
        obedience,
        love

'The measure you give is the measure you receive' is a principle of God's Kingdom. You give your life to Him, He gives His life to you! You give yourself in loving obedience to Him, and He gives the abundance of His riches to you.

This inheritance is yours by faith, and appropriated through obedience. Does this mean you can only receive the Lord's blessing when you have achieved a certain degree of obedience? Not exactly, for **everything you receive from Him is a gift, the result of His grace and mercy.**

However, Jesus expects obedience to what He speaks into your life at any given time. As you grow in spiritual maturity it seems He expects more of you. But the blessings that accompany a growth in obedience also increase. He expects much of those to whom He gives much. **You can be confident in faith when you know you are seeking to fulfil God's will in your life. When you are submitted to Him, His**

Spirit inspires faith within you to believe His promises of victory.

As you submit your life to the sovereignty of Jesus, recognising His rule and reign over you, so you will discover you can then rule and reign over your circumstances in His name. As you acknowledge His authority over you, so you are able to exercise authority yourself.

THE CRUCIAL DECISION

You have to make the crucial decision: Is Jesus going to be on the throne of your life, or do you still want to be in control? He will never force Himself upon you, nor make you do His will. In His Word He shows you His purpose; your obedience is to come from your love for Him. 'If anyone loves me, he will obey my teaching,' Jesus said (John 14:23). **Your love is a response to His love for you. And in His love He wants to provide for you!**

Your key to a victorious life:
    WALK IN OBEDIENCE TO JESUS.

Victory in the Mind

The way to victory:
Fill your mind with the positive truth of God's Word and you will be able to refuse, resist and reject all negative input, and will experience victory in your thought life.

Your victory scripture:
Be transformed by the renewing of your mind. Then you will be able to test and approve what God's will is – his good, pleasing and perfect will. (Rom. 12:2)

God wants to influence your thinking by declaring His Word to your heart by the Holy Spirit.

At the same time your mind is battered by three negative influences:

> the world
> your own flesh
> and the devil.

The world around you is full of negative attitudes, ideas and beliefs totally alien to the Christian faith. You have to counter these, so that you are not influenced by them.

Your negative attitudes oppose faith, whether negative attitudes towards problems or people.

When people react negatively towards problems they expose their unbelief:

they worry about the problem
they fear the outcome
they resent the situation
they submit to the need
they accept the sickness.

When reacting negatively to people:

they refuse to forgive them
they judge and criticise them
they resent them
they are jealous of them
they may accuse and condemn them.

The negative situation has not caused these reactions. The difficult problem or person exposes what is already there within the Christian. To the same situation:

A negative Christian will react negatively
A positive Christian will act positively.

The negativity is an absence of faith in that particular situation.
The positive attitude is a demonstration of faith in Jesus.

THE WORLD

Every Christian has to learn how to counter the negative influences in the world around him by refusing to accept them into his thinking. He resists living with the world's values by submitting to those of Jesus. He refuses to think as wordly people do, becoming despairing or despondent. He refuses to be caught up in the desire to outdo his neighbour in material possessions. He refuses to be seduced by the world's dubious business practices and its love of position and esteem.

The best answer to the negative is the positive. It is easier to resist the negative if your life is offered positively to God. If this is the case the use of your time, money and abilities will be firmly under the Lordship of Jesus.

THE FLESH

You have to learn how to counter the negatives within yourself. Although at new birth your thinking changed about many aspects of your personal life and relationships, yet you are not yet perfect in your thinking, just as you are not yet perfect in behaviour. You have the mind of Christ both in the written word of scripture and by the inspiration of the Holy Spirit; but you can still choose to believe your own thinking. This is often negative, because of the negative patterns of thought that have existed in your life over many years.

These may be negatives about yourself, about the kind of person you are and what you can or cannot do. If you consider yourself a failure you will inevitably think negatively in particular situations. If you do, you will not be able to walk in positive faith until your thinking is renewed.

Because you desire to live by faith, **resist all thoughts which accuse you of being unacceptable, unloved, rejected or a failure.**

You are accepted in Christ Jesus.
You are loved by God. He has lavished His love upon you by making you His child and by filling you with the Holy Spirit.
You are not rejected, for there is no condemnation for those who belong to Jesus.
You are not a failure, even though sometimes you fail. Everybody fails at times, but you are not to think you are doomed to persistent failure. You are learning to live by faith with all God's resources at your disposal.

Resist your fleshly desires, not allowing your mind to dwell on proud or selfish thoughts. Resist lustful fantasies, temptations to indulge greed and any unwillingness to forgive. **As soon as you are conscious of such thoughts reject them immediately in the name of Jesus.**

The positive is the best answer to the negative; light dispels darkness. Set your mind on the positive truth and praise God for His victory within you.

THE DEVIL

The enemy tries to bombard the mind of every Christian. But the shield of faith God has given you is able to quench all the fiery darts of the evil one. He wants to undermine your faith in God's Word and encourage you to centre your thoughts on yourself instead. If he can persuade you to believe your own thinking, you will act in your own strength and not in God's supernatural promises.

The devil wants you to act independently of God. This is the way he attacked Jesus in the wilderness. He suggested that He should turn stones into bread to satisfy His hunger. But His Father had not told Him to do this. To obey Satan would be to act independently of His Father's will and direction. Any such action is sinful. If Jesus had yielded to such temptation He would have become imperfect and could not have been our Saviour. Jesus always refused to act independently of His Father.

The devil will try to entice you by encouraging worldliness and stirring up your flesh life. He does not announce his presence, but likes to work subtly. Often his attack is a single negative or enticing thought. But if accepted by the Christian, Satan will follow the first negative with another and then another.

Refuse to accept the first negative thought every time the enemy attacks.

NO CONFUSION

Some express concern because they are not sure whether particular thoughts are from God, the enemy or 'self'. Here the scriptures are your yardstick. **You can safely reject anything that does not conform to the teaching of the New Testament, no matter how reasonable or beautiful the thought may appear to be.**

A good example of this is the statement that everybody will go to heaven when they die. Many worldly people believe this, but it is also a fleshly temptation for the Christian to think in such a way, especially in relation to people he knows and loves. The devil encourages such thinking because it is not true; it conflicts directly with what Jesus and the whole New Testament revelation tells us. Jesus says:

> Whoever believes in him (God's Son) is not condemned, but whoever does not believe stands condemned already because he has not believed in the name of God's one and only Son. (John 3:18)

He says this immediately after making it clear that He did not come to condemn but to save. In His love God the Father has provided us with a Saviour. **But to reject the Saviour is to reject the salvation He offers.** And Jesus clearly states that those who are not with Him are against Him. There is no neutral ground, no fence to sit on and no compromise with the truth.

Faith is undermined by bitter and resentful attitudes towards others, especially those who have caused hurt. This is why Jesus said, 'And when you stand praying, if you hold anything against anyone, forgive him, so that your Father in heaven may forgive you your sins' (Mark 11:25).

If you do not forgive others God will not forgive you. And if you are not forgiven you cannot have confidence before the Holy God, even though He is your Father.

So the enemy will try to persuade you that you are justified in your resentful attitude. You were in the right. It is for the other one to apologise. You ought to feel sorry for yourself for being treated in such a way.

You can recognise easily that such attitudes conflict directly with Jesus' teaching to forgive. So do not listen to anything which conflicts with His will.

FILL THE MIND

The best method of defence is attack. **If the mind is filled with the positive truth of God's Word it will not play host to the negative influences of which we have spoken.** Knowledge of the Bible, and the New Testament in particular, will enable you to discern whether something is right or wrong. The Holy Spirit also helps in this, even when you are ignorant of what the scriptures teach about a particular matter.

There will be times when you sense something is not right even though you may not know why. **Listen carefully to the intuitive warnings of the Holy Spirit.** He will guide you into all truth; He will take what belongs to Jesus and declare it to you.

Remember, God's thoughts are higher than your thoughts. He takes into account the spiritual dimension in every situation. He is supernatural; His power is greater than the natural.

Jesus taught His disciples to think spiritually, to take account of the supernatural resources available to them. An obvious example of this is the miracle of the feeding of the five thousand. When told to feed the crowd, the disciples looked at the situation with the natural eyes of reason and thought the task impossible.

But Jesus knew what He would do to meet the people's need, because He looked with spiritual eyes. He took the supernatural power of God into account. He thought with faith attitudes.

It is not that God wants you to be a non-rational being. He has created you with the ability to reason. **He wants you to expand your thinking, not reduce it. He wants you to think in supernatural, not natural terms, to take into account what God can do by His Spirit when you trust Him.**

Jesus' first disciples did not find it easy to make the necessary adjustments in their thinking; neither will you always find it easy. Making such adjustments is essential to a life of faith, fighting the temptation to limit God by your natural thinking. Your natural thinking will defeat you. **Your supernatural thinking will point you to victory.**

In many situations you will have to decide whether you are going to believe the revelation of God's Word, or your own ideas:

Are you going to accept what the Lord says, or listen to the negative doubting attitudes of your own mind?
Are you going to listen to God or men?
Are you going to believe the truth, or the lying deceptions of the enemy?

As a man or woman of faith you are going to believe God; not yourself, or the world, or the devil – but Jesus!

Your key to a victorious life:
RESIST THE NEGATIVE THOUGHTS WHICH OPPOSE FAITH; FILL YOUR MIND WITH THE POSITIVE TRUTHS OF GOD'S WORD.[1]

[1] See Colin Urquhart, *In Christ Jesus* (Hodder, 1981), for a more detailed explanation of your inheritance in Christ.

8

Victory in the Emotions

The way to victory:
  The Lord's love is not dependent on feelings. He wants
  you to live in the power of His Spirit rather than to be
  controlled by your emotions.

Your victory scripture:
  There is no fear in love. But perfect love drives out fear.
  (1 John 4:18)

It is possible to exalt the mind above the Spirit, living by
your own rational ideas instead of through revelation of the
truth in God's Word. Likewise you can listen to your own
feelings instead of the Lord's voice.

Everybody is emotional because everybody has emotions. God has created us with the ability to feel.

A person may be free in his emotions, free to express
love and joy. A fearful person will appear to be frozen
emotionally. He feels as deeply as anyone else but because
of his fear tries to hide his emotional response to people
and events.

The Lord wants you to have a healthy mind, filled with
His thoughts. Similarly **God wants you to be emotionally
healthy.** Just as your mind must not rule your spirit, so
you must not allow your feelings to dominate or rule
you.

NOT FROZEN

The perfect love of Jesus casts out all fear. No statement in scripture is repeated more often than the simple command, 'Fear not.' Fear demonstrates a lack of faith. If your trust is in the Lord, there is no need to fear.

To fear God is to be in awe of Him, not emotionally frightened of Him.

God's love for you is spiritual, not emotional. Your love for Him comes from your spiritual birth, not an emotional response to Him.

However, your love for God cannot be complete unless it touches your emotions. His Spirit is to flow through your soul. Therefore His love is to be expressed in the way you think with your mind and feel with your emotions. **God's love for you is not born of emotion, yet it is to touch the emotions.**

The Christian should not be afraid to feel God's love for him, or to feel love for God. Your relationship with the Lord is neither dependent on nor complete without feelings.

Similarly you can think rationally about God's love for you and your love for Him. But this love is not born of reason; it is born of the Spirit.

If a person has never felt God's love for him, or felt love for God, something is deficient in his relationship with the Lord. Many a 'frozen' person has begun to thaw out emotionally once he or she has received the Holy Spirit. For the first time there is real experience of God's love. There is a release in love, joy, praise and a willingness to witness. What has happened in the human spirit touches the senses, including the emotions.

Emotional insecurity caused by a sense of rejection, failure or inadequacy will make a person fearful of feelings. He fears even God touching those sensitive areas of his life, although His touch is the touch of love which heals and binds up the broken-hearted.

I was an extremely fearful person myself and know what it is to be acutely self-conscious and embarrassed. I would never have chosen a public ministry for myself, especially one in which I had to travel so much, constantly meeting new people.

Feelings of inadequacy dominated my life. So it was wonderful when I experienced Jesus' love for me and knew He had accepted me. But still I needed to be set free to love others and allow them to love me. I did not want people to get too close to me or know too much about me. I must have expended much nervous energy in building and maintaining my defences.

Then the Lord showed me that He loved *me*, not an image of myself that I wanted others to accept. He loved the real me, with all my feelings of inadequacy and failure. He lived in me, not some image of myself. He could work through me despite my weakness.

I needed to forgive those who had contributed to these feelings of inadequacy. I had to ask the Lord to forgive me for living by fear instead of faith. When I truly wanted to be set free, He spoke the word to my heart that set me free and I experienced a fresh release of the Spirit's love in my life.

From that time I have been able to relate far more freely, and have been able not only to love others, but also to allow myself to be loved. Still there are occasions when my natural reaction is to withdraw or hold back. But I have learned that if I listen to my fears I will be paralysed into inactivity. If I listen to words of faith, I can go forward confident of the Lord's enabling:

'Fear not, for I am with you always.'
'I will never leave you, nor forsake you.'
'God has not given you a spirit of fear, but a spirit of power, of love and a sound mind.'

It is certainly not the Lord's purpose that any Christian be rendered inactive through fear. Apart from any other consideration, fear is sin. 'Everything that does not come from faith is sin' (Rom. 14:23). And the Lord always wants to do something about a person's sin!

The Lord wants to heal frozen emotions, but the believer concerned needs to acknowledge:

the sin of his fear
his need of forgiveness
his need of the Spirit
a willingness to be set free.

NOT OVER-EMOTIONAL

A frozen or fearful person is over-emotional, although that is the very thing he or she would deny. Any person whose life is governed by feelings is over-emotional, whether those feelings are negative or positive.

So there are two kinds of over-emotional people:

the frozen, who withdraw behind a shield of silence;
the over-exuberant, whose faith fluctuates with feelings.

Unless the believer submits his emotions to the Spirit they will rule his life. Without this submission he will be dependent on feelings rather than the Lord and His Word.

The one who depends on feelings rather than the Lord, only believes the presence of God if he 'feels' His presence. He believes His love, only if he 'feels' that love. He obeys the Word, if he 'feels' it right to do so. When his feelings are negative because of problems, he quickly panics or even falls into despair. He can easily be made to feel condemned by the enemy's false accusations.

It is impossible to live by faith when so dependent on feelings. **Often the emotional response to a situation will be the opposite to a faith response. The Christian is called to believe the Lord, not his feelings.** Every day of my life I have to walk in victory over emotional feelings. So do you!

When the soul is submitted to the Spirit, the feelings are influenced by the Lord but do not control the believer's decisions. The over-emotional frequently place the soul above the Spirit.

The emotionally insecure are usually spiritually insecure, because they pay so much attention to feelings. Those who are prone to feel rejected may well have problems believing the Lord has accepted them. Those who have felt the need to be self-dependent because they have found it difficult to trust others will find it difficult to trust the Lord. Those who have tried to manipulate others will try to manipulate the Lord.

The Lord does not want your emotions to govern you; He wants you to govern your emotions.

This is possible, even if you have been over-emotional either through fear or an over-dependence on experience. Your emotions are influenced by your thinking. **Right attitudes will lead to right feelings, which in turn will lead to right actions.**

Those with emotional difficulties usually need a renewal in their minds. To seek healing of the emotions is to try to treat the symptom, not the cause.

You can experience victory in your emotions as part of the total victory God wants you to have in your soul.

Your key to a victorious life:
DO NOT ALLOW YOUR FEELINGS TO CONTROL YOU.

9

Victory in the Soul

The way to victory:
Neither your reason nor your feelings are the truth. Jesus is the truth. Believing what He says sets you free in your soul – in your mind and emotions.

Your victory scripture:
If you hold to my teaching, you are really my disciples. Then you will know the truth, and the truth will set you free. (John 8:31–32)

MIND AND EMOTIONS

The emotions are influenced greatly by the mind. Negative thinking leads to negative feelings, which in turn lead to negative actions.

NEGATIVE ATTITUDES
about self, others or situation.

POSITIVE ATTITUDES
about self, others or situation
through faith in the Word.

NEGATIVE FEELINGS
about self, others or situation.
Self-pity and self-concern.

POSITIVE FEELINGS
Confidence through trust in the
Lord. Compassion. Concern
for others. Meets problems
with faith.

NEGATIVE ACTIONS	POSITIVE ACTIONS
governed by fear, unworthiness, low self-esteem, lack of confidence. Criticism, anger or jealousy towards others. Resigned attitude to problems.	Personal boldness in faith. Encourages, forgives, expresses God's love. Attacks problems in Jesus' name.

Ask yourself: Are my feelings in line with God's Word? Are they conditioned by the truth or am I being deceived?

Nobody wants to believe he or she could be deceived. 'The heart is deceitful above all things and beyond cure' (Jer. 17:9). The heart refers to the seat of the emotions and it is here that Christians can be deceived unless they beware. They can be deceived by:

Believing negative feelings to be the truth even though they contradict the Word.
Believing positive feelings based on an emotional response to events. Such responses easily lead to unreality. **An enthusiastic attitude is not necessarily a faith attitude.**

Obviously negative feelings are opposed to the love, joy and peace of God. But religious feelings which may appear to be good are no substitute for the genuine work of the Spirit in the heart and life of the believer. People often mistake soulish experiences, aesthetic experiences of music and drama, for example, as being genuine spiritual experiences. Many non-believers, even those utterly opposed to the Christian faith, have such experiences. They are of the soul, not the spirit. The genuinely spiritual is that which is initiated by God's Spirit. It comes from God, not the soul. Soulish enjoyment and experiences, pleasant though they may be, are no substitute for the true work of God.

It is not going too far to say some forms of worship are aimed directly at the soul, at making people feel good. It is possible to escape reality into a kind of euphoric praise which does not necessarily touch the spirit, but only makes people feel better for a short period of time. Genuine worship in the Spirit leads to an encounter with God which leaves its mark on the worshipper. He knows he has met with the Lord and something has happened in his spirit as a result.

Jesus said, 'God is spirit, and his worshippers must worship in spirit and in truth' (John 4:24). Not in the emotions; in the spirit. What is conceived in the spirit can touch the emotions; but rarely does that which is conceived in the emotions touch the spirit.

THE RIGHT KIND OF MINISTRY

Much ministry that is popular today is aimed at the soul rather than the spirit. Those who receive ministry for their feelings are receiving the wrong kind of ministry. To trifle with people's feelings is only to confirm them in a pattern of behaviour that has already led to failure, defeat or to some bondage of fear and insecurity. To minister to the feelings encourages the person to persist in a life which is based upon feelings.

If you want to build genuine faith into people's lives and help them to experience personal victory, you will need to teach them:

to walk in the Spirit, not in soulish ways:
to depend on God's Word rather than their own feelings.

THE TRUTH SETS THE BELIEVER FREE. **The truth about what Jesus has done for him,** not the facts about all the hurts he has experienced.

What Jesus has made him – he is God's child, a new creation, accepted, forgiven, loved. Negative feelings and dwelling on past experiences tempt the emotional believer to deny the truth.

What Jesus promises him. Ministry directed at the soul concentrates on the self, not the rich inheritance which belongs to every believer.

FREEDOM FROM HURT

Everybody experiences hurt in their lives. Those who we think of as damaged personalities have not necessarily suffered more hurt than others. Often they have not known how to cope with the hurt.

When someone becomes a Christian, he needs to understand he does not have to carry the hurts of his old life into his new life in Christ.

Jesus sets people free from hurt when they forgive those who have caused the hurt. He never used the phrase 'inner healing', but he spoke often of the need to forgive others. A refusal to forgive results in bitterness, resentment and self-pity. These are like spiritual cancer eating away inside the person.

To concentrate on the hurt is to be stuck with it. Jesus met every need on the Cross. He suffered rejection, betrayal, false accusation. He was attacked, beaten and ridiculed.

He took your hurt upon Himself to set you free. All He asks you to do is to forgive those who caused your wounds, even as He forgave those who caused His.

Then you can look to Him for the touch of His healing love. 'It is for freedom that Christ has set us free' (Gal. 5:1)!

Jesus not only wants to set people free; He wants to build them up in the knowledge of His truth, enabling them to walk by faith. Then they will meet future opposition and hurt with forgiveness, not resentment.

If the Christian forgives immediately, he will not be eaten away inside by bitterness or resentment. If he is merciful, he can depend on the Lord's healing mercy.

When you turn to the Lord you expect and receive instant forgiveness, providing you are prepared to forgive others. In the world people want revenge. They like to see those who have caused them hurt suffering in turn. Jesus tells His followers not only to forgive but to love and pray for those who have caused them hurt. What a difference in the two attitudes! Obeying Jesus will prevent future hurts festering and affecting you deeply.

Some very hurt and damaged people may not find it easy to forgive immediately. Forgiveness is not an emotion; it is an act of the will. The Christian decides to forgive. **The right feelings will follow the right decision.**

Receiving God's forgiveness does not depend on feelings, but believing the truth of God's Word: 'If we confess our sins, he is faithful and just and will forgive us our sins and purify us from all unrighteousness' (1 John 1:9). The right feelings will follow the forgiveness, not precede it. When you are forgiven, then you have peace with God. In other words, the emotions respond to what is happening in the spirit.

The same is true with emotional healing. It is not the right feelings that will give the healing, but the activity of God by the Holy Spirit. I would never have received my healing if I had listened to my feelings. Instead I listened to God's words to my heart: 'You are free.'

Later he showed me that if I had not believed what He said I would not have been set free. Accepting that what He said was true led to freedom from emotional bondage.

You do not have to be bound by hurts from the past. You do not have to live in resentment and bitterness any longer. You can choose to forgive all those who have hurt you now. You can come to the Lord with your hurt and be set free. This is God's will and purpose for you. He will minister His truth and His life into your spirit and your whole soul will be liberated by the activity of God's power.

Hear Him speak His words of deliverance to your heart: 'You are free, for the Lord Jesus has set you free.' I have seen countless numbers of people set free through these or similar words.

Do not listen to your feelings; they are not the truth, even though they appear to be the truth at times. Jesus is the truth. What He says is truth. What He has done to meet your need is the real truth. **'And the truth will set you free.'**

THE TRUTH THAT KEEPS YOU FREE

To receive the gift of the Holy Spirit is to receive His power and love for a dynamic life of discipleship. The Christian who is born again and has received the Holy Spirit can rejoice in many truths.

From the very first day of your new birth:

You are forgiven all your past sins.
You are now a child of God.
You are accepted by your heavenly Father.
You belong to God.
You have eternal life.
You have received the gift of God's Kingdom.
You are a new creation.
The old has passed away; the new has come.
You are no longer in bondage to the devil.
God lives in you by the presence of the Holy Spirit.
You have been placed 'in Christ Jesus'.
Every Spiritual blessing in heaven is already yours in Christ.
You have received fullness of life.
You have been given everything you need for life and godliness.
The Lord promises to meet every need of yours because of the glorious riches you have in Christ Jesus.

For the rest of your life you are to live in the truth of the inheritance you received the day you first believed in Jesus. It is these truths which will enable you to live in freedom and faith, not in bondage to your own feelings or fears.

Your key to a victorious life:
BELIEVE WHAT THE WORD TELLS YOU ABOUT YOURSELF – NOT YOUR OWN REASON OR FEELINGS.

10

Victory in the Will

The way to victory:
> When you submit your will to God's will you can live in
> victory. Choosing your own will instead will only lead
> to frustration, failure and defeat.

Your victory scripture:
> Not as I will, but as you will. (Matt. 26:39)

YOUR WILL IS YOUR OWN

God has given you free will. You have the ability to make
choices. Your decisions will depend largely on the other
aspects of your soul life. **If your mind and emotions are in
submission to the Spirit, you will choose to do what God
wants.** The alternative is to act independently of the Lord.

An independent person makes independent decisions.
His mind is not controlled by God's Word, but by his own
natural thinking.

The emotions are conditioned largely by the person's
thinking. Negative thinking produces negative feelings and
negative decisions. **Positive thinking produces positive
feelings and positive decisions.**

There is a certain amount of truth about the power of
positive thinking. But we are not concerned here with
'mind over matter'. The Lord wants to see His Spirit ruling
over mind and matter. He wishes to influence every aspect

of your soul – your mind, emotions and will. Then the activity of God's Spirit can be expressed more fully in your character and behaviour.

If your mind is set on things above, on the words of truth, your emotions will more readily be brought in line with God's purposes, **and you will make the right decisions with your will.**

God will never interfere with your will. He will not force you to obey Him. He reveals His will to you; but in every situation you have the choice to obey or disobey, to please Him or grieve Him.

Neither can anyone else make your decisions for you. When a child you were placed under certain laws at home and school. You were expected to obey. You reacted to your circumstances either willingly or rebelliously. Nobody could determine your response for you.

Now in adult life law is not imposed on you in the same way. You are expected to make responsible decisions. You have to respect the civil laws of the society in which you live; but you can choose to be a law-breaker.

Nobody else can interfere with your ability to choose, and to believe. They can exert pressure and try to influence you. However, you have to choose whether to believe men or God, whether to submit to circumstances or God's Word.

A CRISIS OF LOVE

At times you experience conflict. You know what God is saying to you by His Spirit, either through the scriptures or by direct revelation. But your personal wishes may differ from the Lord's purposes. You know God's will, but do not want to do it. Perhaps you would like to avoid the cost of obedience; or you may hold back because of fear. You may be concerned about the way others will react if you are obedient to the Lord!

Your determination to do God's will is dependent on your

love for the Lord. 'If you love me, you will obey what I command,' said Jesus (John 14:15). The conflict you experience arises out of a conflict of love. Is your love for self greater than your love for the Lord – at that moment, in that situation? If so, you will choose to please self because it is more convenient to do so. **If your love for the Lord is greater than love for self, you will deny yourself, take up your cross and follow Jesus.**

Your love for the Lord is not theory. You may be asked whether you love the Lord more than yourself and answer affirmatively. But the true answer is seen in your choices.

None of us loves the Lord perfectly. Every time we choose self instead of others we show how persistent our love of self can be. And all of us experience the conflict between flesh and spirit.

We learn that making the wrong decisions which deny God's Word and grieve Him never leads to happiness or fulfilment – only to conflict and frustration. Yet in our foolishness we continue to choose self again and again.

The Lord's patience with each of us is truly remarkable. What love was shown by the Prodigal Son's father. He watched the son leave and squander his inheritance through the misuse of his free will, and could only wait for his return. And yet he welcomed his return with open arms embracing him in love and wanting everyone to share in his joy. That boy learned his lesson the hard way and knew he did not deserve his father's patience or forgiveness.

JESUS' EXAMPLE

Life is a series of decisions. Every day you are faced with choices. Many of these are made without much reflection. Some choices are automatic because of the kind of person you are or the nature of the relationship you have with the Lord.

The difficult decisions are those which involve a conflict

of interests. It may be easier to please self, but that does not make it right to do so. Jesus experienced conflict in the Garden of Gethsemane. He sweated blood as He faced the decision before Him, 'My Father, if it is possible, may this cup be taken from me. Yet not as I will, but as you will' (Matt. 26:39).

Humanly He did not want the pain of crucifixion or to suffer separation from the Father, which would be the inevitable consequence of taking our sins upon Himself. But His soul was submitted to His Father at all times. It is His Father's will that matters, not His own. His decisions must not conflict with His Father's purposes. You see in Jesus the act of perfect submission: 'Yet not what I will, but what you will' (Mark 14:36).

Jesus lived in constant submission to His Father and that was the secret of His authority. Although He was the Word of God made flesh He spoke no words of His own, only the words His Father gave Him to speak. He could do nothing by Himself, but did only what He saw the Father doing. All believers need to emulate this example of submission to the Father's will and authority, a submission that comes from love for Him.

FAITH AND AUTHORITY

Jesus saw a close relationship between faith and authority. He commended the Roman centurion for his faith because he trusted in the authority that Jesus displayed. **The man of faith will be a man of authority.**

You are only able to exercise authority if you know how to submit to authority. **The more a Christian recognises and submits to God's authority, the greater the authority he will be able to manifest in his own life and ministry.** And the man of faith needs to exercise authority if he is to be victorious – authority over the enemy, and the mountains or problems which confront him, over his own flesh.

There is a chain reaction which begins with love and which God wants to see operating in your life:

You love the Lord.
Because you love Him, you are willing to submit to His authority and do His will.
This obedience gives you confidence before God.
This confidence is expressed in the authority you manifest as a believer.
This authority is an essential element in your ability to live by faith.
This faith results in victory.

So there is a direct link between your love for the Lord and the victory you experience. That victory is dependent on your expressing your love for the Lord by willingly submitting to His authority over you.

THE RIGHT DECISIONS

You make the right decisions with your will because of your love for the Lord. Submit your mind to the mind of Christ and do not allow your natural emotions to rule and govern your life, particularly in the important decisions you have to make. Do not be surprised when you experience a conflict of interests; that is only to be expected. **By His grace you will make the right choices if your desire is to please Him.**

Should you make wrong decisions choosing to please self instead of the Lord, you will not be condemned. Through His grace and mercy He is willing to forgive as soon as you repent.

This is not an excuse to treat God's will lightly. Before you were a Christian sin had dire consequences in your life as it separated you from the Lord. Sin is no less important now. It may not have the eternal consequences it had before your salvation; but it deeply grieves God and prevents His Spirit from flowing through you in the way He desires.

Jesus waged war on sin. Every believer is to do likewise, first in his own life, then in the world around him. **It matters to God that you please Him by obeying His will.** But still He will not force you to do so.

You grieve Jesus when you consciously or deliberately sin against Him, choosing self rather than the cross of self-denial. Jesus warned that the way would be narrow and difficult. It is so tempting to choose the broad and easy way, especially once you are secure in your salvation.

If your heart is set on pleasing Jesus, you will obey Him. Nothing matters more to you than doing His will.

He will use the disobedient times to show you the self-love which persists within you. But even when you stumble temporarily, He still works within you to bring you back to obedience.

The way of peace is
the way of love, which is
the way of obedience, which is
the way of submission, which is
the way of authority, which is
the way of faith, which is
the way of victory, which is
the way of Jesus.

Your key to a victorious life:
WILLINGLY SUBMIT YOURSELF TO THE AUTHORITY OF JESUS.

11

Victory in the Body

The way to victory:
Victory in the use of your body is a reflection of the victory in your spirit and soul. Your body does not need to rule you; you can rule your body.

Your victory scripture:
Live by the Spirit, and you will not gratify the desires of the sinful nature. (Gal. 5:16)

YOUR BODY IS A TEMPLE

Your body houses your soul and spirit. When you received the gift of God's Holy Spirit your body became a temple of the Holy Spirit. Now God lives in you; His holy presence is within you.

Your body is not only to contain God's life; it is to express that life. The light of Jesus is to shine through your behaviour, attitudes and relationships, in what you say and how you say it. Even your face and general appearance can radiate the joy and peace of God within you.

The human body reflects what is happening in the soul. This was true about Jesus in His humanity as it is true for you. God's Spirit worked perfectly through His soul and body. Because your soul is not perfectly submitted to the Father's authority, His life is expressed only imperfectly in you.

Paul's testimony was clear:

I have been crucified with Christ and I no longer live, but Christ lives in me. **The life I live in the body, I live by faith in the Son of God,** who loved me and gave himself for me. (Gal. 2:20)

The life He lives in the body is a life of faith. So two important truths have to be put together.

1   **The life of God's Spirit will only be expressed through your body if there is the right submission to His will and authority.**
2   **This is only possible if you live by faith.**

To God your body is precious because it is a temple of the Holy Spirit. It is not to be misused or abused.

Satan tempts people to gratify their physical desires in lust and greed because he wants to see the temple defiled. He wants Christians to be lazy so their bodies are not put to proper use.

Whatever happens in the mind and emotions governs the will and this in turn directs the body. In the diagram overleaf the diagram on the right indicates that the sinful use of the body points to a spiritual problem. If the soul is submitted to the Spirit, the believer will not be ruled by his bodily appetites but will deny the cravings of his body in order to glorify God. Without this submission he will be ruled by his desires and will grieve the Lord.

This is not only true in the sexual area of life. The body can express many other ungodly attitudes. Paul mentions hatred, discord, jealousy, fits of rage, selfish ambition, dissensions, factions and envy – to name but a few! But he is quick to point out:

Live by the Spirit, and you will not gratify the desires of the sinful nature. For the sinful nature desires what is contrary to the Spirit, and the Spirit what is contrary to the sinful nature. (Gal. 5:16–17)

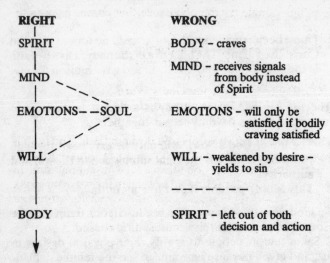

RIGHT	**WRONG**
SPIRIT	BODY – craves
MIND	MIND – receives signals from body instead of Spirit
EMOTIONS– –SOUL	EMOTIONS – will only be satisfied if bodily craving satisfied
WILL	WILL – weakened by desire – yields to sin
BODY	SPIRIT – left out of both decision and action

When you act independently you walk in the flesh, not the Spirit. That is how you lived before you were a Christian. Now you can live dependent on the Lord, trusting to the leading and empowering of His Spirit. Then the fruit of the Spirit is manifested in you: 'Love, joy, peace, patience, kindness, goodness, faithfulness, gentleness and self-control' (Gal. 5:22–23).

The misuse of the body is an ugly thing in God's sight; but its proper use is glorious to Him. **For it is with the body that you do His will, proclaiming the gospel of the Kingdom in word and action.**

> Whatever you do, whether in word or deed, do it all in the name of the Lord Jesus, giving thanks to God the Father through him. (Col. 3:17)

To do everything in the name of Jesus is to do what He would do in your situation. John says, 'Whoever claims to live in him must walk as Jesus did' (1 John 2:6).

Obedience is seen in action. Faith is expressed in action. Once again we see the two together. Paul saw his ministry as calling people 'to the obedience that comes from faith' (Rom. 1:5).

Faith is: **Hearing God's Word**
                Believing what He says
                Acting upon it
Obedience is: **Hearing God's Word**
                    Believing what He says
                    Acting upon it.

Obedience can only be expressed through faith. And faith is expressed in obedience. What you do in your body will express both faith and obedience, if you submit soul to Spirit. Your love for Jesus will be seen in the way you speak and act. 'Dear children, let us not love with words or tongue but with actions and in truth' (1 John 3:18). If you say you love, perform the actions of love.

RESIST TEMPTATION

Jesus tells us to watch and pray that we may not fall when tempted, for though the spirit is willing, the body is weak. The enemy will try to exploit this weakness through bodily appetites.

Christians do not readily admit to living in a fleshly or soulish manner. They excuse themselves by saying what they did was 'only natural'. They felt it right to 'express themselves'. They remind you that 'nobody is perfect' and suggest that God 'understands their little ways' and makes allowances.

Whenever you are about to sin the Holy Spirit will warn you. If you choose not to heed His warnings and yield to temptation you will lose your peace with God until you have turned back to Him in repentance.

We can praise God for His patience, His grace and His mercy towards us. When we sin He does not cast us off but gently brings us back to the place of obedience, where we rightly belong.

Paul speaks of the enticement of sin that comes to us

through the body; but he also points us to how to live in victory over such temptations.

> For we know that our self was crucified with him so that the body of sin might be done away with, that we should no longer be slaves to sin – because anyone who has died has been freed from sin. (Rom. 6:6–7)

You do not have to be ruled by the body and its appetites any longer. If your soul and body are truly submitted to the Lord, if Jesus is your King and is reigning in your life, you want to please Him. So do not compromise with sin. Paul continues:

> Therefore do not let sin reign in your mortal body so that you obey its evil desires. Do not offer the parts of your body to sin, as instruments of wickedness, but rather offer yourselves to God, as those who have been brought from death to life; and offer the parts of your body to him as instruments of righteousness. (Rom. 6:12–13)

Although you are a new creation, it is still possible to obey evil desires. Your body can be an instrument of either righteousness or wickedness. Before your conversion you pleased yourself and served Satan. Now you can please the Lord and serve Him.

CONSECRATE YOUR BODY

Because you have been brought to life spiritually, you are to offer the parts of your body to the Lord as instruments of righteousness. **Your body is to be consecrated to Him, set apart for His holy purposes.**

There is no limit to the power of God's Spirit within you but His Spirit is housed within the weakness of your mortal flesh. Paul says, 'I put this in human terms because you are weak in your natural selves. Just as you used to offer the parts of your body in slavery to impurity and to ever-increasing wickedness, so now offer them in slavery to righteousness leading to holiness' (Rom. 6:19).

The only way to know victory in the body is to consecrate it to the Lord. To live 'in slavery to righteousness' is only possible if you recognise your body is not your own to do with as you please. **'You are not your own; you were bought at a price. Therefore honour God with your body.'** (1 Cor. 6:19–20) Now you are no longer to bear fruit for death, you are to bear fruit for God!

YOU HAVE DIED

Paul was aware of conflict within himself:

> But I see another law at work in the members of my body, waging war against the law of my mind and making me a prisoner of the law of sin at work within my members. What a wretched man I am! Who will rescue me from this body of death? Thanks be to God – through Jesus Christ our Lord! (Rom. 7:23–25)

There is only one way to overcome the conflict; through Jesus Christ our Lord! 'But if Christ is in you, your body is dead because of sin, yet your spirit is alive because of righteousness. And if the Spirit of him who raised Jesus from the dead is living in you, he who raised Christ from the dead will also give life to your mortal bodies through his Spirit, who lives in you' (Rom. 8:10–11).

To let your life be ruled by your body is spiritual death; to let your life be ruled by the Spirit is life and victory. Each one of us has the choice to make.

Your body is not to rule you; you are to rule your body. Submit your soul to the Spirit and do not be drawn away from God's will by your physical and bodily appetites. To gratify the flesh is only to grieve God and to cause great conflict within yourself.

The way of victory is not to deny the body and its appetites in your own strength, but to **reckon yourself dead to the principle of sin that lives in your body.** This is where faith has to operate.

There have been many occasions when I have fought

battles with myself. I have been aware of desires that oppose God's will for me and have wanted to yield to temptation. The more I have struggled the more intense the battle has become.

Sometimes I have cried out to God to help me, to take the pressure away somehow. I have asked him to change my desires. I have felt such a failure for wanting what displeases Him, even though not always yielding to the temptation.

All these tactics have met with very little success. But time and again the Lord has answered my need by bringing me back to the simple truth: 'You have died.'

Oh, the joy of revelation when the truth comes to your heart afresh! **That's it! I have died!** I do not need to fight the flesh; that only stimulates its activity. I have died. I have been crucified with Christ. It is no longer I who live. Christ lives in me. I have died – and do not have to fight what has died. **Instead of fighting the flesh I can turn away from it and walk in the Spirit.** This is the truth; and the truth works!

You have died and your life is now hidden with Christ in God. That is a statement of truth. Believe it! You do not have to be ruled by your bodily passions. You can obey the leading of God's Holy Spirit, fulfilling His will and His Word.

A NEW BODY

It is not the physical appearance of the body that matters. Irrespective of physical beauty or a lack of it a person can radiate the love, the joy and the peace of Jesus Christ. His beauty can shine through the most ordinary face. The peace and joy of the Lord Jesus flows out of a person's words, attitudes and actions. There is no greater compliment that can be paid to a Christian than for someone to say, 'I can see the Lord Jesus in you.' You can look forward to the time when you will have a new resurrection body that will perfectly reflect the glory of the Lord.

The body that is sown is perishable, it is raised imperishable; it is sown in dishonour, it is raised in glory; it is sown in weakness, it is raised in power; it is sown a natural body, it is raised a spiritual body. If there is a natural body, there is also a spiritual body. (1 Cor. 15:42–44)

Until that time you have to express the life of Jesus in your earthly body. Paul says we are to 'purify ourselves from everything that contaminates body and spirit, perfecting holiness out of reverence for God' (2 Cor. 7:1).

NO NEED TO WORRY

Jesus tells us not to worry about the body's needs:

Therefore I tell you, do not worry about your life, what you will eat or drink; or about your body, what you will wear. Is not life more important than food, and the body more important than clothes? (Matt. 6:25)

If we seek first God's Kingdom and righteousness, He promises He will meet every need. We will not have to worry about the body's material and physical needs.

In other words, if things are in their right order (spirit, soul, body) you can depend on God's faithful provision. Satan seeks to reverse that order, denying God's authority and will. The devil's order is body, soul and forget the Spirit!

You have died.
Your life is now hidden with Christ in God.
You are not your own.
You were bought by Jesus.
He paid the price that you might belong to Him.
Your body belongs to the Father.
He wants to be glorified in the way you see it.

Your key to a victorious life:
CONSECRATE YOUR BODY TO THE LORD.

12

Victory of the Heart

The way to victory:
  If you continually yield your new heart to Jesus, you will express His thoughts, words and actions. A victorious life is a reflection of a victorious heart.

Your victory scripture:
  God has poured out his love into our hearts by the Holy Spirit, whom he has given us. (Rom. 5:5)

THE HEART

The word 'heart' is used in a variety of ways in scripture. At times it is used of the human spirit; the innermost part of the person's being. At other times it refers to the soul, or one particular function of the soul. And there are occasions when it signifies the spirit and soul together.

And yet it is a word used often in scripture and in contemporary Christian terminology. By heart we mean 'man's entire mental and moral activity, both the rational and the emotional elements' (*Vine's Dictionary*). In other words we use this word 'heart' to signify what is going on in us, without trying to analyse too precisely the functions of the 'heart'.

Before you knew Jesus your heart was your own, but when you came to Him you gave your heart to Him. He came to live within your heart, so He can express His life through your life.

As the heart is to be the governing centre of your whole being, it is from there, within you, that Jesus wants to exercise His reign in your life. The heart makes a person what he is and governs his actions. It is within the heart that your true character is formed.

So Jesus said: 'Love the Lord your God with all your heart and with all your soul and with all your mind' (Matt. 22:37). Every part of your being is to be given to the Lord in love. For in scripture, to love is to give.

OLD HEART

Before you were born again, your heart was 'corrupt' because of its self-motivation. Jesus said:

> But the things that come out of the mouth come from the heart, and these make a man 'unclean'. For out of the heart come evil thoughts, murder, adultery, sexual immorality, theft, false testimony, slander. (Matt. 15:18–19)

Whatever exists within the heart will be expressed in a person's words and deeds. If the heart is corrupt or unclean, then he will speak and act in ways unacceptable to God.

Jesus goes beyond the Jewish thought of His day. Under the Law it was clear what contravened the Lord's commands. However, Jesus teaches that the contemplation of sin in the heart is as bad as the deed itself.

> You have heard that it was said, 'Do not commit adultery.' But I tell you that anyone who looks at a woman lustfully has already committed adultery with her in his heart. (Matt. 5:27–28)

Jesus was not imposing a new law, the tenets of which were even more demanding than those of the old covenant. In all His preaching He aimed at the heart. **If the heart is pure and consecrated to God, the person's thoughts, attitudes, words**

and actions will be pure and so glorify God. 'Blessed are the pure in heart, for they will see God' (Matt. 5:8).

Because of the sinful nature of the heart in natural man, it proved impossible to keep all the commandments. The Law demonstrated that men would never be able to please God, or make themselves acceptable to Him, through their own determined efforts.

Under the promises of the new covenant, the Lord says He will give His people 'a new heart'.

> I will give you a new heart and put a new spirit in you; I will remove from you your heart of stone and give you a heart of flesh. And I will put my Spirit in you and move you to follow my decrees and be careful to keep my laws. (Ezek. 36:26–27)

A new heart will bring new motivation, a new desire to please the Lord; and the gift of the Holy Spirit will provide the ability to effect His will.

Under the terms of the new covenant the Lord says: 'I will put my law in their minds and write it on their hearts. I will be their God, and they will be my people . . . they will all know me, from the least of them to the greatest' (Jer. 31:33–34).

THE NEW HEART

Because you are part of the new covenant, God has given you a new heart. 'God has poured out his love into our hearts by the Holy Spirit, whom he has given us' (Rom. 5:5).

You are now a son of God with God's Spirit in your heart. 'Because you are sons, God sent the Spirit of his Son into our hearts, the Spirit who calls out, "*Abba, Father*"' (Gal. 4:6).

Jesus has 'set his seal of ownership on us, and put his Spirit in our hearts as a deposit, guaranteeing what is to come' (2 Cor. 1:22). Paul prays that 'Christ may dwell in your hearts through faith' (Eph. 3:17).

That is the prayer for all who want to live by faith! A prayer for those who were already believers! Without a new heart in which Jesus lives, it is impossible to please God.

Jesus spoke against the religious leaders of His day, because their legalistic observances could not bring about a change of heart, either in their own lives or in those they led. They refused to turn to Jesus to receive the new heart He alone could give them.

> Isaiah was right when he prophesied about you hypocrites; as it is written: 'These people honour me with their lips, but their hearts are far from me.' (Mark 7:6)

A new heart is given to those who surrender the old one to Him. Until that act of surrender, a person can try to serve God through religious zeal – like Saul of Tarsus. He was exceedingly zealous, but blind to the truth. Instead of submitting to Jesus he persecuted those who did so. He must have closed his ears to their testimonies, preferring to hold on to the religious law and traditions of the past. In doing so he genuinely thought he was serving God.

Religious zeal cannot create a new heart. Only God can give that to those who turn to Jesus.

THE OVERFLOW OF THE HEART

Whatever is in a person's heart will be expressed in his words and actions.

> The good man brings good things out of the good stored up in his heart, and the evil man brings evil things out of the evil stored up in his heart. For out of the overflow of his heart his mouth speaks. (Luke 6:45)

A new heart, filled with the life of Jesus, will produce good things. A good heart cannot produce bad fruit, neither can a bad heart produce good fruit.

God has given you a new heart.
Christ lives in your heart by faith.
The overflow of that new heart will produce good fruit.

So do not be drawn back to the past, the old life in which you displeased God. Set your heart on pleasing Him. 'Since, then, you have been raised with Christ, set your hearts on things above' (Col. 3:1).

It is possible for you to set your heart on pleasing self, even though you are a new creation, with a new heart. Or you can daily surrender your heart to the Lord, living to please Him. To '**set**' the heart on things above implies a determination to keep looking to the Lord in dependence on Him.

Victory in your heart comes from continual surrender. To turn your heart away from the Lord is to invite failure and defeat, for then you have to depend upon yourself or others; 'See to it, brothers, that none of you has a sinful, unbelieving heart that turns away from the living God' (Heb. 3:12). Paul prays: 'May the Lord direct your hearts into God's love and Christ's perseverance' (2 Thess. 3:5).

I find it important to remind myself that whatever I do or say is a reflection of what is happening in my heart. I can confess sins to the Lord but I will only repeat them, unless I want Him to deal with the heart of the matter. A change of heart will lead to a new attitude, which in turn will affect my behaviour. I need to ask Him to search my heart and show me what is wrong.

Likewise I can only act in faith and experience victory if there is faith in my heart. Many try to put on a performance which they think expresses faith, but without any true revelation of God's Word in their hearts. Then they wonder why things have not happened in the way they wanted.

Jesus went straight for the heart when He taught the people. And when they came to Him for healing, He asked them telling questions which would indicate what they believed in their hearts.

A VICTORIOUS HEART

A victorious heart is one *set* on the Word of God, a heart full of faith. With your new heart you want to be like Jesus and see His life flowing out of you. Jesus wants to reproduce Himself in you. The Holy Spirit makes this possible. You cannot be like Jesus without a heart like His and without expressing victorious faith. For none of His words or actions were superficial; they came from the overflow of His heart, a heart submitted to the will of His Father, a heart which believed His Father could always honour His Words and answer His prayers – a gentle and humble heart.

By contrast the unredeemed heart is aggressive and proud. The evils in the world around us are a demonstration of this. When unredeemed men express what is in their hearts, violence, vice and other atrocities are inevitable.

Those who try to live 'good' lives may manage to contain the more obviously evil traits of their unredeemed nature; but they can never create within themselves the love and presence of Jesus. Nor can they produce His life.

The Holy Spirit is working in you to do just that. He will show you the things which are inconsistent with your new life in Jesus, the pride and selfishness which persist and are evident when your heart is not set on things above.

And He will encourage and create within you the aspects of the personality of Jesus which will please Him. He was never defeated. Because His heart was pure He had confidence and in every situation could exercise the authority His Father had given Him. He was victorious because He had a victorious heart, a clean heart, full of faith – yet He was 'gentle and humble in heart'.

Here is the paradox. **The more humble you are, the more of God's authority you can exercise, just like Jesus.** Even though He is God's Son, He came as a servant, but lived in the fullness of divine power and authority.

Many find it difficult to see that **our confidence before God comes from humbling our hearts before Him and choosing to walk in His ways:**

> Dear friends, if our hearts do not condemn us, we have confidence before God and receive from him anything we ask, because we obey his commands and do what pleases him. (1 John 3:21–22)

Confidence before God will always give you victory, because then you know God hears and answers your prayers. You can pray to Him from your heart, a clean heart, knowing He always answers the prayer of the heart.

God has given you a new heart. But the heart becomes dirty with use, for we live in a dirty world and are not yet perfect in our living of the Jesus life. We can identify with David when he cries out to God: 'Create in me a pure heart, O God, and renew a steadfast spirit within me' (Ps. 51:10).

This He is pleased to do, constantly working within us to refine us. Every branch of the Vine of Jesus is pruned, 'that it will be even more fruitful' (John 15:2).

This is what you want: to be more fruitful for God. This is what glorifies Him, that you bear much fruit, proving yourself to be His disciple. **As a branch of this Vine, with His Spirit within you, you can set your heart on pleasing Him.**

This will involve saying 'No' to those things you perceive to be offensive to His Word and will. When you confess your sin and failure to the Lord, He cleanses you again. He knows you cannot serve Him effectively without regular cleansing of the heart.

The victorious believer is quick to humble himself before the Lord, and is prepared to walk humbly before others in his daily life. He desires earnestly that the Spirit will convict him of any impurity in his heart, any deception or wrong attitude.

His heart is set on the Lord's truth, not on his own ideas or opinions, nor on fulfilling his own desires. He puts his faith in what God says.

Jesus Christ lives in his heart by faith, leading him in His victorious procession. The Christian follows the Man of faith and authority, the Man.who lived with a perfect, a gentle and humble heart.

Let Jesus cleanse and refine your heart!

Your key to a victorious life:
  SET YOUR HEART ON PLEASING GOD.

13

Victory in Prayer

The way to victory:
You can experience victory in prayer as you pray in the
Holy Spirit, believing Jesus' promises and persisting in
faith and obedience.

Your victory scripture:
I tell you the truth, my Father will give you whatever
you ask in my name. (John 16:23)

PRAYER WITH FAITH

Jesus expects His disciples to be victorious in prayer:

You did not choose me but I chose you and appointed
you to go and bear fruit – fruit that will last. Then the
Father will give you whatever you ask in my name. (John
15:16)

The Lord has chosen you.
He has called you by name, and you are His.
He has appointed you as one of His disciples to be fruitful.

As you fulfil this purpose He gives you this wonderful
promise: 'The Father will give you whatever you ask in my
name.'
This is in line with a series of similar promises Jesus gives.

But we need to take careful note of the context in which He makes these sweeping statements. He promises:

> And I will do whatever you ask in my name, so that the Son may bring glory to the Father. You may ask me for anything in my name, and I will do it. (John 14:13–14)

The word 'And' obviously links this promise to what has been said immediately beforehand: 'I tell you the truth, anyone who has faith in me will do what I have been doing. He will do even greater things than these, because I am going to the Father' (John 14:12).

This must rank as one of the most remarkable of all the statements Jesus made. Anyone (and that includes you!) who has faith in Him will do the same things as He did, and even greater things.

Jesus was about to return to His Father. Then the Holy Spirit would be given to His followers. He would enable them to do the same things as Jesus.

The even greater things are possible because the Spirit has now been given. During the time of Jesus' ministry even He did not pray for people to be baptised in the Spirit, for He makes plain that the Spirit would not be given until He had been glorified. Now He is glorified there are no such limitations. You can pray with others to be filled with the Holy Spirit and God will honour your prayers.

God living in us is even greater than having Him living among us!

We will only do as Jesus did if we act in faith and pray in His name. To pray in Jesus' name is to pray in the way He would pray. There is no set formula of words to use; you pray with the same faith and expectation Jesus would exhibit in your situation.

This is not as impossible as at first it may sound. Because He lives within you by the power of His Spirit, He is present in your situation. **He can show you what to pray and inspire your prayer with faith.**

> But you, dear friends, build yourselves up in your most holy faith and pray in the Holy Spirit. (Jude 20)

Use the gifts of the Holy Spirit, for even when you do not know how to pray, He does. He will not only inspire faith and bring revelation to your heart about the Father's purposes, He will even give you the words which express what is in His heart. The words may be in your own language or in the 'tongue' God gives you by His Spirit. Use that tongue and let the Holy Spirit pray through you.

Faith and prayer belong together in Jesus' thinking. You cannot imagine Him praying without the faith that His Father would answer Him. He not only taught this; He demonstrated it. Standing before Lazarus' tomb He prayed, 'Father, I thank you that you have heard me. I knew that you always hear me' (John 11: 41–42).

Jesus promises He will do whatever we ask in His name when we operate by faith, expecting to do the things He did and even greater things.

This is His word to 'anyone who has faith'. Do you see this as God's purpose for you? As you move out in faith so you will see the Lord honouring your prayer.

WHATEVER YOU WISH

Jesus also said:

> If you remain in me and my words remain in you, ask whatever you wish, and it will be given you. (John 15:7)

This seems an even more sweeping statement: 'Ask whatever you *wish*, and it will be given you.' But there is a condition – 'If you remain in me and my words remain in you.'

When you became a believer God took hold of your life

and placed you 'in Christ'. You have fullness of life in Him. **God blesses you with every spiritual blessing in Him. He will meet your every need in Him. Your life is now hidden with Christ in God.**

Jesus tells you to continue to live in Him. The verb in Greek has a continuous meaning. **Go on living where God has put you – in Christ. Do not live as if separated from Him. Do not walk in your own independent ways; live in Jesus.**

And let His words continue to live in you. Have faith in God and what He says, rather than in the problem or need. Let your life be an example of one who is not only hearing, but putting the Word into practice, with your heart set on doing His will.

Jesus is safe in saying you can then ask anything you wish, and it will be done for you. If you are abiding in Him and His words are living in you, you will not want what is alien to His purposes.

Personal blessing is certainly included in this promise. Jesus is saying: **if you give your life to me in this way, you can be confident I will give you whatever you want.** 'The measure you give is the measure you receive.' He promised:

I tell you the truth, my Father will give you whatever you ask in my name. (John 16:23)

THE FATHER AND THE SON

Some people are confused as to whether to address their prayers to the Father or Jesus, and whether it is the Father or Jesus who will respond. In these prayer promises Jesus says you can ask the Father or Him, and either will answer. So do not fret over this detail. 'I and the Father are one,' said Jesus (John 10:30). Often you will find yourself praying one moment to the Father and then to Jesus. The formula of words does not matter, but what you believe in your heart.

Whether we pray to the Father or Son, we ask in the name of Jesus. This is the name above every name, the name of the victorious and glorified One. Are you getting the picture? **If you live in His name, you can truly pray in His name** and 'my Father will give whatever you ask in my name'.

Jesus gives these great prayer promises to those who:

Know they are chosen and appointed to bear lasting fruit.
Live in Christ.
Have His words living in them.
Are living by faith, doing the same things as Jesus and greater things through the Holy Spirit.
Pray in the name of Jesus, with His expectations.

Victory in prayer comes from a life of faith and obedience.

AGREEING TOGETHER

Again, I tell you that if two of you on earth agree about anything you ask for, it will be done for you by my Father in heaven. (Matt. 18:19)

Jesus does not mean we are to agree to a formula of words when we pray. We are to agree in faith. There is to be a heart agreement.

It requires only two who live in Jesus, and have His words living in them, to agree in prayer. If they agree, both will have the same expectations as to what the Lord will do in response to their prayer. Both will have the same witness of the Spirit in their hearts.

It is possible for someone to pray a prayer and others to respond with the 'Amen', but there is no indication as to what people actually believe. Is there an agreement of faith? Are their lives in agreement with the Word?

Jesus gives this particular promise when talking of

believers' authority to bind and loose, exercising authority over other spiritual powers which can influence lives. We have seen how the exercise of authority is a consequence of submission to Jesus.

He promises that where two or three are gathered in His name He is with them. Clearly He is present to hear and respond to the agreement of faith between His followers. If we pray in His name, then He will agree with the prayer, and it is done.

It may seem that more and more conditions are being made if we are to see those amazing prayer promises fulfilled. We must remember that the fruit of answered prayer is produced in a life of faith and obedience.

This does not mean that only those who have reached a certain standard of discipleship can expect answers to their prayers. EVERY ANSWER IS AN ACT OF GOD'S GRACE AND MERCY. Even the newest Christian can experience mighty answers in prayer. He is fresh but expectant in his faith, and his new heart prompts obedience to the Lord.

Both faith and obedience are essentially simple and are possible for any Christian at any time.

Faith believes God to answer.
Obedience does what God says.

Any Christian can do either at any time.

However, disobedience saps the Christian's confidence. Instead of expecting the Lord to answer, the disobedient are prone to think of reasons why the Lord would be justified in not answering their prayers.

Jesus encourages us in a life of faith and obedience, promising that such a life produces much fruit for the Father's glory and the reward of answered prayer.

Many have lived selfish lives and have been disappointed in prayer and then wondered why. Many have lived disobedient, unbelieving lives and have then complained bitterly because God has not done what they asked. They point to such promises and say they are untrue, or unrealistic, or not for today. But Jesus' message is clear:

If you believe, you will receive whatever you ask for in prayer. (Matt. 21:22)

You could not ask for a more simple, straightforward statement.

FAITH AND AUTHORITY

Faith is the chief element in prayer. And those who live by faith speak not only to the Lord, but to the problem also.

I tell you the truth, if you have faith and do not doubt, not only can you do what was done to the fig-tree, but also you can say to this mountain, 'Go, throw yourself into the sea,' and it will be done. If you believe, you will receive whatever you ask for in prayer. (Matt. 21:21–22)

The exercise of faith involves authority. The man of authority will not only speak to the Father, he will address the situation in the name of Jesus. This is how Jesus operated in faith, authority and prayer; He addressed the need:

'Be opened.'
'Your sins are forgiven.'
'Get up and walk.'
'Peace, be still.'
'Lazarus, come forth.'

To give only a few examples!

You can speak to your problems and needs and see them moved. You can have victory 'if you have faith and do not doubt'.

What if such faith does not exist? Humbly submit

yourself to Jesus, confess your unbelief and ask Him to forgive you. Then ask Him to speak a word of faith into your heart, a word relevant to your situation.

Faith comes from hearing God.

When I teach about these prayer promises, the unbelief which persists in the heart of many Christians is readily exposed. Sometimes I am verbally attacked by those who suggest I should not make such outrageous statements. But the promises do not come from me; they were given by Jesus. Like everybody else I find them both challenging and faith-building.

I know that when I do not see the answers to prayer that are needed the fault does not lie with God. He has not withdrawn His promises, neither has He broken His Word.

Frequently I have to ask myself what I truly believe He will do in answer to my prayer. I ask:

'What do I believe God will certainly do in answer to this prayer?'
'Do I believe I have received the answer, or am I only hoping something will happen?'
'Am I only saying the right words, or do I believe in my heart that He has done it?'

The Lord honours our honesty, but He hates hypocrisy. If I know faith is lacking, I have to ask Jesus to forgive me and then pray the Holy Spirit will speak a word of faith to my heart. Only faith the size of a mustard seed is needed – the faith of God, which He gives.

THE PRAYER OF FAITH

When teaching the disciples how to pray with faith (Mark 11:22–25), Jesus makes four points:

1 **Have faith in God** – not the problem, not yourself, not your fear nor in others – in GOD.

2 **Speak to the mountain of need** – but do not doubt in your heart; believe that what you say will happen. It is the faith of the heart that is victorious, not the form of words.

3 **'Whatever you ask for in prayer believe that you have received it, and it will be yours.'** You receive by faith immediately, when you pray, even though there may not be anything to show at once for such confidence. You receive the answer in your spirit, and know it is only a matter of time before you see the outworking of it.

4 **Forgive any who have wronged you** or God will not forgive you. And nothing hinders the receiving of answers more than unforgiven sin.

FAITH PERSISTS

Ask and it will be given to you; seek and you will find; knock and the door will be opened to you. For everyone who asks receives; he who seeks finds; and to him who knocks, the door will be opened. (Matt. 7:7–8)

Again there is a continuous meaning to the verbs 'ask', 'seek' and 'knock'. This shows us there needs to be a persistence in prayer. We continue to ask, seek, find, believing the promise, 'everyone who asks receives'.

Do not look at your past experience or at the experiences of others. Consider the Word. Listen to Jesus. Believe His promises. He will not reduce the words and promises to the level of your experience. He wants to raise your experience to the level of His Word.

Faith persists and does not give up because the answer is not immediately visible. 'Believe that you have received it, and it will be yours.' If Jesus says it will be, it will be! Believe Him!

Jesus told the parable of the persistent widow (Luke 18:1–8) 'to show them that they should always pray and not give up.'

If you believe, you will receive whatever you ask in prayer. Jesus says so!

This is victorious prayer. Remember it is as possible for the newest Christian as for the mature believer. Any disciple, young or old, can choose to live by faith and in obedience.

FAITH is hearing God.
believing what He says and acting upon it.
OBEDIENCE is hearing God,
believing what He says and acting upon it.

Your Key to a victorious life:
VICTORIOUS PRAYER COMES FROM A LIFE OF FAITH AND OBEDIENCE.[1]

---

[1] For further reading on the subject of prayer see Colin Urquhart, *Anything you Ask* (Hodder, 1978) and *Listen and Live* (Hodder, 1987).

14

Victory over the Devil

The way to victory:
  Jesus has already won the victory over the devil and all
  his angels. He has given you authority over the enemy.
  You can share in His victory.

Your victory scriptures:
  The reason the Son of God appeared was to destroy the
  devil's work. (1 John 3:8)
  I have given you authority . . . to overcome all the
  power of the enemy; nothing will harm you. (Luke
  10:19)

RESCUED

Jesus' victory is complete. The spiritual powers of darkness
have been overcome by the Light of the World.

  The devil is described as the god of this age, who blinds
the minds of unbelievers. He is 'the prince of this world'
(John 14:30). This does not imply he has any power,
authority or status above that of Jesus. Satan can rule only
where he is allowed to rule. Because the world is opposed
to God's purposes, Satan appears to hold sway. His
influence is seen in many political and social areas of
life, for example. But all have sinned and, like the devil,
have fallen short of God's glory. So every person is in
spiritual darkness until he or she comes to personal faith in
Jesus.

At that point the new believer is rescued from the devil's clutches by the Lord:

For he has rescued us from the dominion of darkness and brought us into the kingdom of the Son he loves. (Col. 1:13)

Satan's power is transitory. Jesus is both Lord and King eternally. He has already overcome Satan. The time will come when all the enemy's power will be taken from him, and there will be a new heaven and a new earth.

DELEGATED AUTHORITY

Meanwhile those who exercise authority in the name of Jesus discover they have power over the devil and all his minions. Those who belong to the Kingdom of God have authority over the powers which belong to the dominion of darkness. Jesus told His disciples:

I have given you authority to trample on snakes and scorpions and **to overcome all the power of the enemy; nothing will harm you.** (Luke 10:19)

'Snakes and scorpions' refer to the evil powers which acknowledge Satan. **Jesus gives authority to disciples to overcome *all* the power of the devil. The man of faith does not need to fear defeat from him or any of his forces. Faith in Jesus is more powerful, for His is the name above *every* name.**

Jesus confirmed that He had given such authority to His followers after saying, 'I saw Satan fall like lightning from heaven' (Luke 10:18).

Satan was originally the archangel Lucifer, who led worship in heaven. All that God made was good, including Lucifer. Worship is a response of love to the Lord, and the angels were created as spiritual beings able to love. Lucifer abused this love. Instead of leading others to worship the Lord, he determined that others should worship him.

This one act of rebellion led to his immediate expulsion from heaven, together with one third of the angels who followed him in his rebellion. Jesus witnessed the event.

Satan was given leave to go to and fro over the earth. Now, through temptation, he is used to test men's hearts to see whether they truly remain steadfast to the Lord, or turn away from God in rebellion – like the devil himself.

He even had leave to tempt Jesus in the wilderness at the outset of His ministry. But he could find no way of making Jesus rebel against His Father's will and authority.

LIGHT AND DARKNESS

In him was life, and that life was the light of men. The light shines in the darkness, but the darkness has not overcome it. (John 1:4–5 mgn.)

There is no way that the darkness could overcome the Light. When you shine a torch into a dark room, the darkness has to give way to the shaft of light. The darkness can do nothing to repel the light.

The tragedy is that so many, having naturally rebellious hearts, have followed Satan in rejecting the Light of Jesus. They have refused to repent and turn to Him. So Jesus says:

This is the verdict: Light has come into the world, but men loved darkness instead of light because their deeds were evil. Everyone who does evil hates the light, and will not come into the light for fear that his deeds will be exposed. (John 3:19–20)

Repentance and faith in Jesus deliver you from spiritual darkness. 'Put your trust in the light while you have it, so that you may become sons of light' (John 12:36).

Those who have received the Light of God's truth in

Jesus are to walk in the light. They are to live in light, not darkness.

> I am the light of the world. Whoever follows me will never walk in darkness, but will have the light of life. (John 8:12) I have come into the world as a light, so that no-one who believes in me should stay in darkness. (John 12:46)

Because you live in the light of Jesus, you do not need to fear the darkness. You are no longer separated from Jesus. You live in Him and He lives in you. You live in the Light and the Light lives in you.

You have become light to the world. Light can shine from your life into the darkness. What belongs to the light is positive, while the darkness is full of negatives. God's Kingdom is positive; the dominion of darkness is negative.

You are a child of God's positive Kingdom.
You can reign over the negative.
You are a child of light.
You do not need to fear the darkness.
You can overcome evil in the name of Jesus.
You have authority over the devil and his works.

EXERCISE YOUR AUTHORITY

You need to exercise authority over the devil. There is little point in having such authority if you do not use it!

The devil cannot touch those who are walking in light. Sin and disobedience make Christians vulnerable. While they walk in the light they have no fellowship with the devil and are able to resist him.

Isaiah describes the Way of Holiness:

> The unclean will not journey on it . . . wicked fools will not go about on it. No lion will be there, nor will any ferocious beast get up on it; they will not be found there. But only the redeemed will walk there. (Isa. 35:8–9)

The devil is described as a roaring lion who prowls around looking for someone to devour (1 Pet. 5:8). But no lion can get on to the Way of Holiness. Neither can wild beasts, the demonic forces.

It is as if these animals are on either side of this Way of Holiness. While you walk along the Way of Holiness, living in the light, they cannot touch you. Should you stray from the way, you make yourself vulnerable to their influence.

THE THIEF

Satan has refused to repent, to submit to the Lordship of Jesus, and has been judged for his rebellion. He refused to put faith in Jesus and is condemned for his sin and disobedience. Sentence has already been passed and he will be cast into the Abyss.

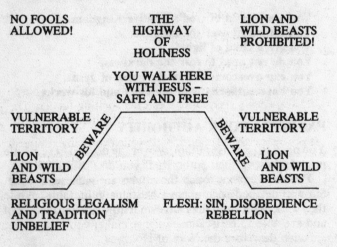

Because he is your enemy, you need to understand his tactics. He is the 'deceiver of the brethren', and can appear as an 'angel of light'. He is a liar, the father of lies and has 'sinned from the beginning'.

Jesus describes Satan as the thief who 'comes only to steal and kill and destroy'. By contrast Jesus came that men 'may have life, and have it to the full' (John 10:10).

The thief comes ONLY to be destructive. This is his purpose – to destroy. He would like to destroy your faith, your health, your relationships, your peace, your life. **But he cannot undo what Jesus has done for you. He cannot take away your eternal inheritance.** But he will try to stop you living in the goodness of that inheritance now.

There is little point in having authority over the enemy if you do not exercise that authority. Why let the thief steal what is yours? **The effect of using your authority is clear: he will flee from you.**

> Submit yourselves, then, to God. Resist the devil, and he will flee from you. (Jas. 4:7)

There is a clear order of events here:

1 **Submit yourself to God;**
2 **Resist the devil;**
3 **He flees from you.**

The Christian who submits to God's authority is able to resist the devil's temptations and his spoiling tactics. The devil flees from the one who lives in obedience and faith.

> Take up the shield of faith, with which you can extinguish all the flaming arrows of the evil one. (Eph. 6:16)

The devil will never relax his efforts to undermine your Christian life. But you have the shield of faith which overcomes all his attacks when put to use. Because you have this shield, use it! Disobedience makes you vulnerable and saps your confidence. So:

> Be self-controlled and alert. Your enemy the devil prowls around like a roaring lion looking for someone to devour. Resist him, standing firm in the faith. (1 Pet. 5:8–9)

Resist the enemy in faith.

Paul says we are not unaware of his schemes (2 Cor. 2:11). He loves to cause division and strife, even among Christians. He appeals to people's pride and encourages unforgiving attitudes towards others. He knows that if you do not forgive others, God will not forgive you, and then you are vulnerable to his devices.

> Do not let the sun go down while you are still angry, and do not give the devil a foothold. (Eph. 4:26–27)

A person is deceived when he believes he is right, but is not. How important to test the things we believe and do against God's Word. If they do not agree with His revelation, have nothing to do with them, no matter how good they may appear to be.

Many have been sucked into false religions and cults through such deceptions. Many Christians have fallen into sinful relationships through deception; what appeared to be good at first can end in grievous sin. Why believe Satan or any demon, when he is the father of lies.

SATAN'S MOUTHPIECE

Even a disciple can be used as Satan's mouthpiece, as Peter discovered to his cost. One moment he was used to speak mighty revelation from the Father, stating that Jesus is the Christ, the Son of God. Soon afterwards he hears these stinging words from Jesus: 'Get behind me, Satan! You are a stumbling block to me, you do not have in mind the things of God, but the things of men' (Matt. 16:23).

Why should Jesus speak such words to him? Because Peter had dared to contradict Him when He spoke of His coming rejection and crucifixion. This did not fit in with Peter's views of Messiahship, or his desires for the Master he loved. But who was he (or any man) to argue with God's Son, or to disagree with His words?

Christians today can be used by the enemy to speak against the truth, if they listen to their own ideas or traditions which are a contradiction to the revealed truth of the scripture. That is like the clay telling the Potter that he doesn't know his business.

This is real deception. Anything which opposes the truth is a lie. And we know the identity of the father of lies! Jesus told those who opposed His teaching that their father was the devil.

John says: 'He who does what is sinful is of the devil, because the devil has been sinning from the beginning.' But immediately points out:

> The reason the Son of God appeared was to destroy the devil's work. (1 John 3:8)

He has done just that.

Jesus has destroyed deception by revealing the truth.
Jesus is the true Light of the world. He does not appear as a false angel of light.
Jesus is righteous. He does not lie like Satan.
Jesus came to give abundant life, not to steal love, faith, health and happiness.
Jesus gives eternal life. He does not want any to be condemned.
Jesus overcame the devil on the cross, that you might overcome him in your life.
Jesus came to destroy the devil's work to give you victory over him.

WHOSE CHILD ARE YOU?

The one who is born of God will not continue to sin, says John. And so it is apparent 'who the children of God are and who the children of the devil are' (1 John 3:10). The one who is truly born of God will do what is right and will

love his brother. When he sins the Holy Spirit will convict
him and lead him back to obedience.

Some of the parables Jesus taught show that God's
children and those of the devil grow up together. But when
the Day of the Lord comes there is to be a glorious sort out!
In the parable of the weeds, for example, 'the weeds are the
sons of the evil one, and the enemy who sows them is the
devil' (Matt. 13:38–39). They will be sentenced to 'the fiery
furnace'.

By contrast, 'the righteous will shine like the sun in the
kingdom of their Father' (v. 43).

You are not a child of the evil one; **you are God's child.
His plan for you is that you will shine like the sun in His
Kingdom. He wants you to live as a righteous one,** resisting
every attempt of the devil to encourage you to live
unrighteously.

Above all, the enemy wants to steal the revelation of
God's Kingdom from people. He wants to eat the seed
spread by the Sower, for he knows that once a Christian has
received the revelation of the Kingdom, he is able to exercise
the authority of the King over the powers of darkness. **He
will not steal this revelation from you. 'Whatever you bind
on earth will be bound in heaven, and whatever you loose on
earth will be loosed in heaven'** (Matt. 18:18).

God has given you His Kingdom.

You are a child of God.

You do not need to continue to sin.

**You do not want to contradict Jesus, or serve the devil in any
way.**

**You do not need to be afraid of him; if you resist him he will
flee from you.**

He cannot steal your inheritance.

He is no longer your father; God is now your Father.

**So do not give any opportunity to the devil. As you follow
Jesus, submitting yourself to Him, you can take the shield of**

faith and overcome all the devil's attacks on you. As you walk the Way of Holiness, he cannot touch you. As you exercise your Kingdom authority over him, nothing can harm you.

Your key to a victorious life:
YOU HAVE AUTHORITY OVER THE DEVIL AND ALL HIS WORKS.[1]

---

[1] For further teaching on the victory you have over the enemy, see Colin Urquhart, *The Positive Kingdom* (Hodder, 1985).

15

Victory in Spiritual Warfare

The way to victory:
Exercise the authority over the enemy Jesus gives you
as a child of His Kingdom.

Your victory scripture:
Do not rejoice that the spirits submit to you, but rejoice
that your names are written in heaven. (Luke 10:20)

DEMONS

Some Christians have over-emphasised the significance of
demons, holding them responsible for every negative thing
in a person's life, believer or non-believer. Others have
underestimated their importance or have denied they have
any influence at all.

Jesus believed in the existence of both the devil and
demons. To explain away the gospel references to the
demonic by saying that Jesus was using the thought forms
of His day, is nothing short of blasphemous. This is to
accuse Jesus of deception. He constantly put right other
contemporary misconceptions. It is unthinkable that He
would speak to the devil and demons if they did not exist!

We see the right balance in Jesus' ministry. There were
occasions when He commanded demons to come out of
sick people. At other times He spoke a simple word of
healing. He exercised discernment, knowing when the

problem was a specifically demonic one. Jesus freed a demonically possessed and very violent man. 'He had often been chained hand and foot, but he tore the chains apart and broke the irons on his feet. No-one was strong enough to subdue him' (Mark 5:4).

Jesus spoke to the demonic presence with authority: 'Come out of this man, you evil spirit!' The evil spirits were given leave to enter a herd of pigs, which 'rushed down the steep bank into the lake and were drowned' (Mark 5:13).

This demonstrated the destructive nature of these demonic powers, but also the authority of Jesus over them. And this was by no means an isolated event.

> When evening came, many who were demon-possessed were brought to him, and he drove out the spirits with a word and healed all the sick (Matt. 8:16).

These demonic powers can cause physical impediments: 'Then they brought him a demon-possessed man who was blind and mute, and Jesus healed him, so that he could both talk and see' (Matt. 12:22). He knew when the demonic powers were the direct cause of the sickness and therefore had to be confronted. It seems that Jesus did not pray to the Father on such occasions; He addressed the demons.

AUTHORITY OVER DEMONS

Jesus gave His disciples authority over evil spirits and power to heal the sick:

> He called his twelve disciples to him and gave them authority to drive out evil spirits and to heal every disease and sickness. (Matt. 10:1)

This authority was not confined to the twelve. When the seventy-two returned from their mission they were overjoyed, 'Lord, even the demons submit to us in your name' (Luke 10:17).

Of all the things they had seen happen, this impressed them the most. Jesus immediately pointed them to the reason why they had such authority: **'Do not rejoice that the spirits submit to you, but rejoice that your names are written in heaven'** (Luke 10:20).

Because they belonged to the Kingdom of heaven, they had authority over the spirits which belonged to the dominion of darkness. The real cause of joy is the fact that they belong to the Lord's Kingdom; their names are written in heaven.

This is also true for you. **Your name is written in heaven; you are a child of God's Kingdom. You have the same authority as those first disciples.** If you doubt that, consider what Jesus said next.

> At that time Jesus, full of joy through the Holy Spirit, said, 'I praise you, Father, Lord of heaven and earth, because you have hidden these things from the wise and learned, and revealed them to little children. Yes, Father, for this was your good pleasure'. (Luke 10:21)

Do you consider yourself a little child in spiritual things? You qualify. Do you feel foolish before those with worldly wisdom? You qualify. Do you feel weak in yourself? You qualify. It has been the Father's good pleasure to choose you, to redeem you and invest in you the authority of His Kingdom!

> But God chose the foolish things of the world to shame the wise; God chose the weak things of the world to shame the strong. (1 Cor. 1:27)

You do not need to fear demons if you recognise you have authority over them. You simply need to know how to deal with them so that they do not influence your life in any way. Jesus said:

> How can anyone enter a strong man's house and carry off his possessions unless he first ties up the strong man? Then he can rob his house. (Matt. 12:29)

Jesus has bound the strong man and defeated him. In his name you can do likewise. 'I tell you the truth, whatever you bind on earth will be bound in heaven, and whatever you loose on earth will be loosed in heaven' (Matt. 18:18).

There was a time when I did not believe in the existence of demons. Involvement in the healing ministry changed my thinking. I saw the Lord healing many people, performing mighty miracles. But there were the stubborn cases that did not seem to respond to prayer in the usual way.

'Address the evil.' This was a command the Lord gave me when praying with someone. When I obeyed, the person was set free from a long-standing condition.

That prompted me to look at the gospels with fresh insight and to be open to the Holy Spirit to show me when such prayer was necessary. If Jesus needed to take authority over demonic powers, we will certainly need to do likewise.

DISCERNMENT

You do not have to allow the enemy to harass you. It may seem that one thing after another goes wrong or you seem to come under attack from sickness regularly. As you pray about the situation little seems to happen. When you take authority over the enemy the harassment ceases.

The discerning of spirits is one of the gifts of the Holy Spirit. The use of this gift will enable you to recognise the nature of the opposition, whether it is demonically inspired or not. Do not fear to use this gift. The demonic problems are simple to deal with because of the authority you have as God's child.

This does not imply that demons 'possess' you. They can certainly attack you, but you have power and authority over them.

Every Christian should be alert to the need to rebuke the enemy at times. Remember, the best method of defence is attack. This does not give you a 'deliverance ministry'. I am not speaking about ministering to others, but walking in victory yourself.

You do not need a formula. **You have authority and faith in the name of Jesus. Exercise that authority and use that faith.** Do not anticipate a battle, but complete victory.

There will be times when you need to bind the enemy in prayer; when praying for non-believers to be converted, for example. Remember, the god of this age has blinded their minds. They cannot understand the truth even though you may have tried to persuade them on many occasions. You need to pray for them, but also to pray against the enemy who has blinded them. When he is bound it becomes possible for the person to *hear* the gospel, although he will still need to come to a place of personal response.

There will also be occasions when you will need to bind the spirits of infirmity which can cause sickness.

> Jesus rebuked the demon, and it came out of the boy, and he was healed from that moment. (Matt. 17:18)

You can do this in prayer, using the name of Jesus. Remind yourself and the enemy that you are under the protection of the blood, and that nothing can harm you.

I am not advocating that you undertake personal ministry with those who you think may have a demonic problem. That is best left to those with pastoral responsibility and experience.

It also needs to be said that many think their problem is demonic when it is not. It is convenient to blame the enemy for sin and disobedience which are the responsibility of the individual Christian. If the father of lies can persuade a believer he is 'possessed' or in bondage to the devil, he has been allowed a victory which should never have been given to him. He is a liar.

Refuse to accept any of his lying accusations. Live in personal victory, not allowing the enemy to bring you into any false bondage, condemnation or confusion. Remember, neither the lion nor any wild beasts can walk in the Way of Holiness.

Keep walking along that Way!

Your key to a victorious life:
YOU HAVE AUTHORITY OVER DEMONS BECAUSE YOUR NAME IS WRITTEN IN HEAVEN.

16

Victory over Opposition

The way to victory:
    Rejoice in the face of opposition. Maintain an attitude
    of love, mercy and forgiveness towards those who
    oppose you.

Your victory scripture:
    Love your enemies, do good to those who hate you,
    bless those who curse you, pray for those who ill-treat
    you. (Luke 6:27–28)

FAITH OVERCOMES THE WORLD

Jesus does not promise His followers an easy life. 'In this
world you will have trouble,' He says (John 16:33).
However the verse continues: 'But take heart! I have
overcome the world.'
    Because you live in Jesus, you can live in His victory. John
says:

This is the victory that has overcome the world, even our
faith. Who is it that overcomes the world? Only he who
believes that Jesus is the Son of God. (1 John 5:4–5)

To whom are these words addressed? **'Everyone born of
God.' That includes** *you*.
    Because you are a Christian, born again of the Holy
Spirit, **you have overcome the world. You can be victorious
no matter what the world does to you.**

John talks about the exercise of such faith within the context of obedience. God's commands are not burdensome to those who love Him. The one who obeys has overcome the world, which is opposed to faith and God's Word because of the rebellion that pervades fallen mankind.

YOU ARE BLESSED

The believer can expect opposition because those of the world live by an entirely different set of values to his own. In fact, the Christian is blessed when he meets with opposition, even of an unjust kind:

> Blessed are you when people insult you, persecute you and falsely say all kinds of evil against you because of me. Rejoice and be glad, because great is your reward in heaven. (Matt. 5:11–12)

> Blessed are you when men hate you, when they exclude you and insult you and reject your name as evil, because of the Son of Man. Rejoice in that day and leap for joy, because great is your reward in heaven. (Luke 6:22–23)

When confronted with such opposition it takes a man of faith to react by leaping for joy! Paul was such a man, which was why he could sit in prison and write to the Philippians telling them to rejoice in the Lord always. He teaches that we are to give thanks in all circumstances, because this is the will of God for us in Christ Jesus.

To respond to opposition with such joy and thanksgiving is evidence of faith. The believer keeps his eyes not on the opposition, but on the Lord. It does not matter what he has to suffer for the sake of the Kingdom. He cannot expect understanding, or even justice, from a fallen world. But he knows Jesus has perfect understanding of every predicament in which he can find himself. The Lord will always treat him with justice, love and mercy.

LOVE YOUR ENEMIES

So Jesus tells us to go further still in our attitudes towards opposition:

> But love your enemies, do good to them, and lend to them without expecting to get anything back. Then your reward will be great, and you will be sons of the Most High, because he is kind to the ungrateful and wicked. Be merciful, just as your Father is merciful. (Luke 6: 35–36)

In all these scriptures Jesus emphasises that the believer's reward will be great in heaven. Why worry about the way the world treats you now? No one can steal your heavenly inheritance, and when in heaven, you will receive no further opposition from the world.

Jesus tells us to love our enemies and be merciful towards them.

> **Love your enemies, do good to those who hate you, bless those who curse you, pray for those who ill-treat you.** (Luke 6:27–28)

Love, do good, bless and pray! What a contrast to the way people usually react to opposition and hate. The natural reaction is to complain, return the hate, feeling bitter and resentful, demanding revenge and punishment for those who have caused the problems. All such reactions belong to the world, not to God's Kingdom, and are destructive of faith if they are found in a Christian. He will have to repent of such reactions, no matter how justified they may seem to be.

What a contrast; and what a witness it can be to the world when a Christian acts in love and forgiveness. I think of a Christian couple being interviewed on television following the murder of their daughter. They expressed only sorrow for the one who had perpetrated such a crime, stated clearly that they had forgiven him and even wanted to visit him in prison to share Jesus with the murderer.

What a contrast with those of the world who in similar circumstances scream out for vengeance and retribution.

Opposition can hurt, especially when untrue things are said about you. Jesus knows we cannot be shielded from hurt; it is part of the inevitable cost of living the gospel in a fallen world. But He shows us how to react to such opposition.

When you rejoice in the face of opposition, any hurt is short-lived. Your heart goes out to those who have caused the hurt. You realise that much of the opposition comes from a lack of spiritual understanding.

What really hurts is opposition from other Christians, often through jealousy or prejudice. You know such opposition is ungodly and it is not always easy to maintain a loving, forgiving attitude.

JESUS' EXAMPLE

You only have to look at the example Jesus gave to see how to cope with opposition. He was not passive when issues of truth were at stake, pointing out the hypocrisy of much of the religious legalism of His day. The religious leaders were determined to kill Him, because he was a threat to their traditions, their positions of esteem and their system of religious conformity. They hated Him and were plotting to murder Him long before the crucifixion. But they were unable to have their way before God's appointed time.

When He was arrested it was out of jealousy, not justice. The charges were false and the witnesses did not agree. But whenever falsely accused, Jesus refused to reply to the charges.

Here is an important principle for every Christian. **You do not have to justify yourself, for God ensures the truth is vindicated,** even if this takes time. In Jesus' case it took three days. The resurrection was total vindication; but even so His opponents did not want to believe.

The only time Jesus answered Pilate was when He was directly challenged as to who He was. To remain silent then would have been to hide the truth. But He did not have to answer false accusation.

What a difficult lesson this is for many Christians to learn! This is the true meaning of turning the other cheek.

It is your faith which HAS OVERCOME the world. The power of the Kingdom is greater than that of the world. The former is spiritual, the latter is temporal. The first is supernatural, the second natural. The Kingdom is eternal, the world finite. So keep your eyes on Jesus and the victory He has already won!

You do not have to behave like others around you. You do not have to conform to worldly values and patterns of life. You do not have to allow yourself to be sucked into the world's negativity: bitterness, resentment, hatred, malice, greed, envy, and so on.

The victory of faith in Jesus overcomes all the worldly attitudes with which you can be confronted.

When you are insulted, rejoice.

When you are persecuted, you are blessed.

When you are falsely accused, remain silent; the Lord will vindicate you.

When you are rejected for your faith in Jesus, remember your reward is great in heaven.

When you are faced with continual opposition, be thankful that Jesus is with you.

When you are opposed by enemies of the gospel, love them.

When you are treated ungratefully, continue to be kind and merciful like Jesus.

When you are hated, do good to those who hate you.

When you are cursed, bless those who curse you.

When you are ill-treated, pray for those who cause the hurt.

When your faith is challenged, speak boldly in the name of Jesus.

You can rejoice in the face of all opposition, knowing you are blessed and that the Lord will reward you for remaining true to Him. You can answer opposition with the love and forgiveness Jesus demonstrated.

This is the gospel of Jesus. He died to make it possible for you to react in such ways. He took all your negativity to the Cross that you might be filled with the positive virtue of His love.

Your key to a victorious life:
   YOUR FAITH OVERCOMES THE WORLD AND
   ALL THE WAYS YOU CAN BE OPPOSED.

17
Victory Attitudes

The way to victory:
    As you believe what God says about you in His Word, you will be able to live in faith and victory. You are more than a conqueror, able to reign in life.

Your victory scripture:
    No, in all these things we are more than conquerors through him who loved us. (Rom. 8:37)

MORE THAN A CONQUEROR

Do you approach problems negatively or positively, with unbelief or faith? **You are more than a conqueror.** This is not a statement to make you feel better when you feel low; it is the truth about you because you live in Christ and can never be separated from His love. **God wants you to have a faith attitude as a way of life.** You cannot turn faith on and off like a light switch.

'Who shall separate us from the love of Christ?' asks Paul. 'Shall trouble or hardship or persecution or famine or nakedness or danger or sword?' (Rom. 8:35). He then proceeds to answer his own questions:

No, in all these things we are more than conquerors through him who loved us. For I am convinced that neither death nor life, neither angels nor demons, neither the present nor the future, nor any powers, neither height nor depth, nor anything else in all creation, will be able to separate us from the love of God that is in Christ Jesus our Lord. (Rom. 8:37–39)

Do you believe this? Do you accept what the scriptures say about you?

I was not brought up with faith attitudes in my early Christian experience. When I was first ordained the Lord told me that He would teach me to believe His words instead of questioning everything He said. My mind and reason had to become submitted to His truth.

Little did I realise the full implications of this at first. Over the years my faith has been enlarged as I have applied one truth after another to my own life.

I would certainly not have thought of myself as being 'more than a conqueror'. But then I did not expect to see mighty miracles or dynamic answers to prayer either. Such things were for a bygone age, or for people of great spiritual stature. They were certainly not for the likes of me.

How wrong can you be! For I came to understand that the truths of scripture are for every Christian, including me. It is true for everyone who is born again that nothing can separate him or her from the love of God revealed in Christ Jesus. Any believer can be 'more than a conqueror' in his daily walk with God – even me!

I began to apply the truths of the Word to myself in very direct and personal ways, realising God was speaking to me about me. From these verses in Romans 8, I learned:

In all things God works for my good, because I love Him and have been called according to His purpose.
God knew me even before I was born.
He predestined me to be conformed to the likeness of His Son.
He called me.
He justified me, making me acceptable in God's sight.

He has glorified me. He already sees me in the ultimate
victory of His glory.
If God is for me, who can be against me?
He will graciously give me all things.
Jesus is interceding for me at God's right hand.
Nothing can separate me from the love of Christ.
In the face of any difficulty I am more than a conqueror
through Him who loves me.

I did not always understand the full implications of what I
read. But this was God speaking to me about me! Who was
I to argue with Him? I had to learn to see things as He did,
for He would never deceive me.

**Nothing, absolutely nothing, can separate you from
God's love because your heavenly Father has placed you in
Christ Jesus. This is the basis of your confidence. You are 'in
Christ' no matter what your situation or problem. You are
more than a conqueror through Him who loves you.**

PERSEVERANCE

Jesus has already conquered. You are more than a
conqueror because you can enjoy His victory without
having to fight His battle! Do not resent your problems; see
them as challenges which can lead to the strengthening of
your faith.

Consider it pure joy, my brothers, whenever you face
trials of many kinds, because you know that the testing of
your faith develops perseverance. Perseverance must
finish its work so that you may be mature and complete,
not lacking anything. (Jas. 1:2–4)

Resentment is negative; joy is positive. Just as one who is
persecuted needs to 'leap for joy', so you can rejoice in the
trials of your faith. **Jesus has not abandoned you; He is with
you in the middle of what might appear to you to be mess,
muddle and confusion.**

Your faith will not develop, neither will you grow in spiritual maturity, without having to face trials of many kinds. **Do not expect to be overcome by your difficulties. Anticipate that Jesus will carry you through. Do not become preoccupied with the problem. Do not allow the need to become bigger in your vision than the One who is able to meet that need. And know you will be blessed as you persevere in faith.**

> Blessed is the man who perseveres under trial, because when he has stood the test, he will receive the crown of life that God has promised to those who love him. (Jas. 1:12)

Every problem is a challenge to trust Jesus and see how He will lead you through to victory.

NEGATIVE AND POSITIVE

The one who approaches problems without positive faith is doomed to failure. Faith works negatively as well as positively. You anticipate disaster or sickness and it will come upon you. When Job experienced a series of disasters at Satan's hands, he said: 'What I feared has come upon me; what I dreaded has happened to me' (Job 3:25).

Fear is negative faith. This is why the Lord says again and again: 'Fear not.'

The negative person expects the worst and when problems arise accepts them with resignation. He may even believe this to be the right spiritual response, humbly accepting whatever happens as God's will.

This conflicts seriously with Jesus' attitudes. He taught His disciples to speak to the mountains and command them to move. This is going on to the attack, rather than receiving passively whatever happens.

A faith person is a positive person.
He resists the negatives.

He affirms the positive truths of his life in Jesus.
He believes God's promises.
He attacks problems.
He anticipates victory.
He knows nothing can separate him from Jesus' love.

REIGN IN LIFE

Repentance is the answer to the problems you cause yourself. You can learn to react joyfully to persecution, and to exercise authority over the enemy. There are times when you need to confront your circumstances for you perceive clearly that what is happening is not according to God's Word, and is therefore inconsistent with His will.

You have received God's abundant provision of grace and of the gift of righteousness. Therefore you are to reign in life through Jesus (see Rom. 5:17). You are to rule over your circumstances instead of allowing them to control you.

This requires a complete change of attitude for some Christians. They do not realise that God has given them the capacity to possess a faith that can rule. Yet this was God's intention for all men.

Then God said, 'Let us make man in our image, in our likeness, and let them rule over . . . all the earth.' (Gen. 1:26)

Man's ability to rule was lost when he sinned. But Jesus came with the gift of the Kingdom. Those who have faith in Him and receive His gift have the ability to rule restored to them.

You have received God's Kingdom.
The Kingdom is within you.
You are to reign in life.
YOU ARE NOT THE VICTIM; YOU ARE THE VICTOR.

You will be surprised to discover how readily God rewards your militant faith attitude.

The military analogy does not come easily for some, but is certainly biblical. You are to 'fight the good fight of faith'. And when you fight do not anticipate failure and defeat!

There will be times when you feel indignant with the devil for the sickness, chaos or confusion he has created in people's lives. Come against him in righteous indignation.

It is not only the major problems which test your faith. You will need to be victorious in numerous seemingly trivial matters. **React to every situation with faith, not with fear, despondency or expectation of failure.**

If you do not learn to deal with the foothills, you won't fare very well with the mountains! Jesus wants to train you to have the right faith attitudes in every situation.

> **You are not to switch faith on and off when it suits you.**
> **It is to be a way of life.**
> **You are to live in victory.**

Your impulsive natural response to a crisis may be negative; but if you are sensitive to the Word and Spirit, your negative reaction will be immediately obvious to you. Without delay you can ask Jesus to forgive the negative response and begin to affirm the positive answer to the situation. This is something that you have to do. Nobody can do it for you. Faith is not a matter of sitting back and waiting for something to happen.

You have faith; put it into operation. Believe the positive answer to the negative problem.

In your particular situation, what would Jesus do? How would He think? What would His attitude be? Would He passively accept the problem? Would He speak to the mountain? Would He take authority over the enemy? Would He believe His Father to give Him complete victory? How would He pray? What results would He expect from His prayer?

You will be surprised how readily you will be able to answer such questions. And when you are perplexed you can look to the Holy Spirit to show you what Jesus would have said and done.

If you do everything in the name of Jesus, you will emulate His example. When faith is lacking, you can confess your unbelief and ask the Lord to speak a Word of faith to your heart. For there will certainly be occasions when you know what Jesus would have believed and done, but have to recognise a lack of similar faith in your own heart.

Faith involves determination. You are not prepared to accept any answer; only the right answer. And that is the way Jesus answers those who trust Him.

When answers come which only partially resolve a situation, you need to question seriously whether they are given by God, or whether you have responded fully to what He has said. **Do not accept the mediocre when He wants to give you the best.** In Christian things, the good is the enemy of the best.

JESUS IS KING
He is reigning.
You are reigning in Him.

Your key to a victorious life:
MAINTAIN A POSITIVE, FAITH ATTITUDE AT ALL TIMES.

18

Victory through Forgiveness

The way to victory:
  The way of victory is the way of love. The way of love is
  the way of forgiveness – always!

Your victory scripture:
  In everything, do to others what you would have them
  do to you. (Matt. 7:12)

PEOPLE CAN BE PROBLEMS

At times life seems full of problems. Some of these may be
of our own making. We have disobeyed and our sin has
created difficulties we would not have had otherwise.

Other problems arise from the enemy's attacks on us.
These may be times when we yield to temptation he which
places before us. Or we may experience opposition as we
seek to live truthful, righteous and godly lives in an unrighteous world. Sometimes there is no apparent reason for
the difficulties we face. But nearly all our problems involve
people!

Problems are often people and people are often problems.
We live in an imperfect world among imperfect people.
The sins of others can influence our lives, sometimes in
significant and even disastrous ways.

By the same token our sins can have serious repercussions in others' lives especially those who are close to us at
work, in church or at home.

Some say their sins are a private matter between God and themselves. This is not the case, for **sin is a social disease with social consequences.**

Problems arise because we live in a fallen world among fallen people. But even in the Christian community we are dealing with others, who like ourselves, are in the course of being refined and perfected, but have not yet attained that goal. Jesus says:

> My command is this: Love each other as I have loved you. Greater love has no-one than this, that he lay down his life for his friends. You are my friends if you do what I command. (John 15:12–14)

LOVE EXPRESSED IN FORGIVENESS

Love conquers all. This is the Christian message. Jesus' love on the Cross overcame sin, sickness and even death. He sends His disciples into the world with the message of love.

This is not some sentimental kind of cosiness, but the practical way of overcoming the problems people cause, while at the same time reaching out to them in the name of Jesus.

At the heart of love is forgiveness. You could not know God's love for you without experiencing His forgiveness. **You are to extend that forgiveness to others, whoever they may be, regardless of what they have done.** The fellowship Christians enjoy together should be marked by love, forgiveness and acceptance of one another.

The one who refuses to forgive has surrendered to defeat in that particular situation and this can have serious repercussions in his life. The one who forgives experiences spiritual victory and knows he is at peace with God, others and himself.

How often have people prayed, 'Forgive us our sins, as

we forgive those who sin against us', while harbouring grudges or even feelings of hatred towards others. Jesus explained:

> For if you forgive men when they sin against you, your heavenly Father will also forgive you. But if you do not forgive men their sins, your Father will not forgive your sins. (Matt. 6:14–15)

To forgive is to be victorious. To resent is to accept defeat until you are prepared to forgive.

> Do not judge, or you too will be judged. For in the same way as you judge others, you will be judged, and with the measure you use, it will be measured to you. (Matt. 7:1–2)

As a Christian wanting to live by faith, adopt the attitude that you are not going to accept failure and defeat. You want to be victorious in every situation in life. And life is made up of people, and the relationships you have with them. You are going to be victorious by maintaining loving, forgiving, merciful attitudes.

Jesus died to free you from the judgment you deserved. Why put yourself back under judgment by judging others? The way in which you judge them will be the way you are judged. No wonder, then, that Jesus encourages you to 'Be merciful, just as your Father is merciful' (Luke 6:36).

THE GOLDEN RULE

In everything do to others what you would have them do to you (Matt. 7:12).

Do you want to be judged?
Do you want to be criticised?
Do you want to be condemned by others?
Do you want to be hated?
Do you want to be resented?

Of course not. **So do not judge, criticise, condemn, hate or resent others. Every time you resist the temptation to do so, you are victorious.**

> Do you want to be forgiven?
> Do you want to be accepted?
> Do you want to be loved?
> Do you want to be encouraged?
> Do you want to be blessed?

Of course you do. **Then forgive, accept, love, encourage and bless others. Every time you do so, you are victorious.**

CORRECTING OTHERS

There will be occasions when it is right to correct others. Jesus gives clear direction as to how to do this:

> If your brother sins against you, go and show him his fault, just between the two of you. If he listens to you, you have won your brother over. (Matt. 18:15)

That is indeed victory and is far more likely to be gained this way than by openly criticising and speaking against him. Jesus continues:

> But if he will not listen, take one or two others along, so that 'every matter may be established by the testimony of two or three witnesses'. If he refuses to listen to them, tell it to the church; and if he refuses to listen even to the church, treat him as you would a pagan or a tax collector. (Matt. 18:16–17)

Jesus wants the man to have plenty of opportunity to repent of his sin before more stringent measures are taken against him. **But notice that the man is judged by the Church, not by the individual.** This leaves no room for personal animosities or vendettas.

The time to go to a brother or sister you believe has sinned, is when you know you can go in love and not judgment, in a spirit of forgiveness not resentment.

BE MERCIFUL

Jesus gives us the parable of the unmerciful servant to reinforce this teaching on mercy and forgiveness. He tells the story in response to Peter's question as to how often he should forgive his brother. He suggests seven times as being appropriate. But Jesus responds: 'I tell you, not seven times, but seventy-seven times' (Matt. 18:22), signifying an infinite number.

A servant owed his master an enormous amount. The servant's master took pity on him, cancelling the debt. But the servant refused to forgive a fellow-servant a petty amount and had the man thrown into prison.

The master was furious when he heard what had happened: 'Shouldn't you have had mercy on your fellow-servant just as I had on you?' he asks (Matt. 18:33). In anger, the master had the servant thrown into prison until he had paid his debt. 'This is how my heavenly Father will treat each of you unless you forgive your brother from your heart,' concludes Jesus (Matt. 18:35).

Jesus is not asking for some token, formal act of forgiveness, but a heart-felt letting go of anger and resentment, treating the brother as if the sin no longer existed.

This parable has serious implications, for it is clear the unmerciful servant had his debts restored, not removed!

God has put His love into your heart by the Holy Spirit. You have the grace to forgive, to know you are at peace with others, that you harbour no bitterness, neither do you hold on to any resentment. Praise God for being free of such negative attitudes.

As the Lord has had mercy on us, so His mercy can be seen

in you day by day, as you maintain an attitude of forgiveness towards anyone who may inadvertently or even deliberately hurt you.

Do not wait for their apologies before you forgive. In your heart forgive immediately the deed is done, so that no root of bitterness can grow in you.

Your key to a victorious life:
LIVE WITH AN ATTITUDE TOWARDS OTHERS OF LOVE, FORGIVENESS AND MERCY.

19

Victory in Relationships

The way to victory:
   Love is your way of life, giving as well as forgiving.

Your victory scripture:
   Do everything in love. (1 Cor. 16:14)

CALLED TO PRACTICAL LOVE

You are to forgive others. You are also to encourage them
and build them up in love. Paul gives clear, practical
instruction about relationships:

Love must be sincere.
Hate what is evil; cling to what is good.
Be devoted to one another in brotherly love.
Honour one another above yourselves . . .
Share with God's people who are in need.
Practise hospitality.
Bless those who persecute you; bless and do not curse.
**Rejoice with those who rejoice; mourn with those who
   mourn.**
Live in harmony with one another . . .
Do not repay anyone evil for evil . . .
**If it is possible, as far as it depends on you, live at peace
   with everyone.**
Do not take revenge . . .
Do not be overcome by evil, but overcome evil with good.
                                        (Rom. 12:9–21)

Many other passages could be quoted with similar instructions.

The best answer to the negative is to be full of the positive. It is far easier to maintain an attitude of mercy and forgiveness towards others when you are full of love yourself.

Love is the fulfilment of the law. You are to love with all your heart, mind, soul and strength. You are to love your neighbour as yourself. And Jesus has given the new command: to love one another as He has loved us.

> Let no debt remain outstanding, except the continuing debt to love one another, for he who loves his fellow-man has fulfilled the law. (Rom. 13:8)

When Jesus baptised you in His Holy Spirit, He flooded your heart and life with His love. You now have His resources to enable you to fulfil these commands of love.

If you know you lack such love, ask Jesus to fill you with His Spirit. He promises that everyone who asks receives.

AGAPE – LOVE IN ACTION

God is love. The nature of His love is expressed in giving. Jesus demonstrated this love in action. He showed that love is at the heart of God's purposes. He did not speak often about love; He simply did it!

Paul describes the nature of God's love, the same love He gives to you through the Holy Spirit.

In place of the word love, you can put the word 'Jesus' and know that every statement rings true. It is a humbling exercise to substitute 'I' instead of 'love'. You are immediately conscious of the inadequacy of your love.

This is not a negative exercise. These statements about love describe the life God is forming in you. He wants you to see yourself living in such love. This is the faith picture He wants you to have about yourself. If you anticipate failure you will certainly fail, but as you realise the Holy Spirit within you is the Spirit of love, so you will understand He can express this quality of love through you.

Love is	Jesus is	I am	patient
Love is	Jesus is	I am	kind
Love does not	Jesus does not	I do not	envy
Love does not	Jesus does not	I do not	boast
Love is not	Jesus is not	I am not	proud
Love is not	Jesus is not	I am not	self-seeking
Love is not	Jesus is not	I am not	easily angered
Love	Jesus	I	keep(s) no record of wrongs
Love does not	Jesus does not	I do not	delight in evil
Love	Jesus	I	rejoice(s) with the truth
Love	Jesus	I	always protect(s)
Love	Jesus	I	always trust(s)
Love	Jesus	I	always hope(s)
Love	Jesus	I	persevere(s)
Love	Jesus	I	never fail(s)

(1 Cor. 13:4–8)

This is an exercise I do personally from time to time, checking my relationships against this description of love, seeing in what ways my attitudes fall short of God's purposes. I find it humbling, but rewarding. The Lord forgives my failure and I can see clearly the areas where I need to bring my life more fully into line with His will, by the grace and power of His Holy Spirit.

Faith without love is worth nothing. 'The only thing that counts is faith expressing itself through love' (Gal. 5:6). Set your heart on expressing such love in your life.

'Do everything in love', says Paul (1 Cor. 16:14). If you ask the Holy Spirit to help you, He will enable you to act in love.

Be imitators of God, therefore, as dearly loved children and live a life of love, just as Christ loved us and gave himself up for us as a fragrant offering and sacrifice to God. (Eph. 5:1)

This love is a response to God's love for you. Just as you can see the need to be merciful to others, because of the way the Lord has been merciful to you, see also your need to love others because of the great love He has for you.

This is how we know what love is: Jesus Christ laid down his life for us. And we ought to lay down our lives for our brothers. (1 John 3:16)

This has to be done in practical ways, seeking to meet each other's need, whether of a spiritual or material nature. The one who loves is born of God and knows God, and He wants to see you living in the victory of love. 'If we love one another, God lives in us and his love is made complete in us' (1 John 4:12).

Jesus demonstrated a victorious life through love. It is for us to learn how to meet every situation with love. It is not enough to know this is what we ought to do; we need to do it in practice. It does not honour the Lord if you have faith without love. He wants to see faith in love being expressed in your life.

Every day the Lord puts before you opportunities to reach out to others in love, or to speak words of faith and encouragement to them. Empty platitudes are meaningless. **It is no use telling people you love them unless your words are supported by appropriate action.**

What does it mean to 'be devoted to one another in brotherly love' (Rom. 12:10)? Such a statement cannot be fulfilled if you have a casual attitude towards relationships.

If a brother has a need, you are victorious when you provide for that need. And you will experience a deep sense of satisfaction that God could use you to express His love to another.

To refuse to meet the need when the Spirit is urging you to do so is failure. Such disobedience disappoints the Lord.

He loves you so much. He wants to see you sharing His love with others. You cannot take every burden on yourself and the Lord does not intend you to do so. But God places certain people and needs before you and His Spirit prompts you to take action. 'Share with God's people who are in need' (Rom. 12:13).

FAILURE TO LOVE

Pride and selfishness are the most common causes of failure in love. Some think certain tasks are beneath them, forgetting they are to prove faithful in small things. Jesus came as a Servant, and the greatest in the Kingdom are those who regard themselves as least of all.

Some want recognition, appreciation, applause and praise from others instead of obeying the injunction to 'honour one another above yourselves'!

There are those who will find excuses if an act of love would prove inconvenient or demanding. They are content to leave the costly tasks to others, perhaps claiming this particular job is not their ministry, or they have no specific word about it from God. They will only 'practise hospitality' when it suits them, and will be very careful about who should be the recipients of their hospitality.

Some are happy to rejoice with those who rejoice, but avoid those who mourn. They are content to slap them on the back with what they consider a suitable platitude: 'Cheer up!' 'The Lord loves you.' 'Look to Jesus.' 'Praise the Lord – anyway.'

All truth has to be communicated in love! There are those who are more interested in being right than in expressing love. With such people the truth comes across in a cold, harsh manner – not at all the way Jesus communicated with the people. They seem to speak more in judgment than love, and easily make people feel condemned rather than convicted.

Then they wonder why they are not victorious in

communicating the truth. The fault cannot be in themselves, of course! It must be the hardness of heart and rebellion of the others. More condemnation!

What is the point of telling people there is no condemnation in Christ, when your whole manner and approach only makes people feel condemned?

There are those whose idea of love is to keep themselves to themselves. 'I don't want to bother anyone,' they say. 'My religion is a personal matter between God and myself.'

Perhaps they fear relationships, imagining they will be rejected or considered unacceptable. At the same time they are likely to be inwardly angry that they are not loved and appreciated.

FREE TO LOVE

The way to receive is to give. This is true of love, as of every other aspect of life. It is a spiritual truth of God's Kingdom. Until a person is willing to give himself in relationships, he will always feel a failure.

He will become victorious only when he allows himself to be set free by the truth. In Christ he is loved, accepted, forgiven, appreciated and liberated. In love Jesus sets him free to enable him to love others.

Make every effort to add to your faith goodness; and to goodness, knowledge; and to knowledge, self-control; and to self-control, perseverance; and to perseverance, godliness; and to godliness, brotherly kindness; and to brotherly kindness, love. For if you possess these qualities in increasing measure, they will keep you from being ineffective and unproductive in your knowledge of our Lord Jesus Christ. (2 Pet. 1:5–8)

You are free to love.
God has put His own Spirit of love within you.
He does not want you to think of yourself as a failure in
relationships, for love never fails.

It is not by striving or self-effort that you will grow in love.

Look to the Holy Spirit every day.
Call on Him for help whenever your love seems shaky.
Remember the One who lives within you is patient and kind.
He is ready to work through you.
He will enable you to protect, hope, persevere – and not fail!

Your key to a victorious life:
 EXPRESS YOUR LOVE FOR OTHERS IN GIVING TO THEM IN PRACTICAL WAYS.

20
Victory in Giving

The way to victory:
　　Give generously and joyfully and you will prosper. This
　　is God's will for you.

Your victory scripture:
　　Give, and it will be given to you. A good measure,
　　pressed down, shaken together and running over, will
　　be poured into your lap. For with the measure you use,
　　it will be measured to you. (Luke 6:38)

A PROSPEROUS PEOPLE

God intends His children to prosper financially and materially. The Old Testament evidence is clear: He promises
prosperity when His people are obedient, living in the
holiness which is His purpose for them. This contradicts the
misconception that equates holiness with poverty.

　　The Lord will establish you as his holy people, as he
　　promised you on oath, if you keep the commands of the
　　Lord your God and walk in his ways. Then all the peoples
　　on earth will see that you are called by the name of the
　　Lord, and they will fear you. **The Lord will grant you
　　abundant prosperity.** (Deut. 28:9–11)

Israel's 'abundant prosperity' is evidence to other nations
that they are the Lord's people, singularly blessed by Him.

However, this prosperity is dependent on their obedience and holiness.

If they became complacent and rebelled in their prosperity (as they did), they were warned they would return to poverty. **Poverty is a curse for the nation's disobedience.** So the alternatives were clear.

> See, I set before you today life and prosperity, death and destruction. (Deut. 30:15)

If His people love the Lord, walk in His ways and keep His commands, they will prosper.

Has God changed? Are not the promises of the new covenant even greater than those of the old? Is not Jesus the 'Yes' and 'Amen' to all of God's promises?

> Walk in all the way that the Lord your God has commanded you, so that you may live and prosper and prolong your days in the land that you will possess. (Deut. 5:33)

If the people obeyed the covenant between God and themselves they would prosper in everything they did.

David was an anointed man with an inspired perception of spiritual truth. The man who fears the Lord, he says, 'will spend his days in prosperity' (Ps. 25:13). **The righteous will flourish** (Ps. 72:7). And he prays:

> Remember me, O Lord, when you show favour to your people, come to my aid when you save them, that I may enjoy **the prosperity of your chosen ones.** (Ps. 106:4–5)

Has the Lord not saved you? Are you not one of His chosen ones? Then He wants you to enjoy prosperity. David says that 'blessings and prosperity will be yours' (Ps. 128:2) if you fear the Lord and walk in His ways.

AN EXPRESSION OF HIS HEART

Several of the Proverbs speak clearly of the Lord's desire to see His people prosper.

> My son, do not forget my teaching, but keep my commands in your heart, for they will prolong your life many years and bring you prosperity. (Prov. 3:1–2)

Once again, prosperity is linked with obedience, this time of the individual, rather than the nation.

The Lord gives prosperity because He is the Lord of prosperity: 'With me are riches and honour, enduring wealth and prosperity' (Prov. 8:18). His purpose is to make us as He is, because we are made in His image. If He prospers, He wants His children to prosper.

'A generous man will prosper' (Prov. 11:25). This is in line with Jesus' teaching that the measure you give is the measure you receive. 'Prosperity is the reward of the righteous' (Prov. 13:21). He has made us righteous in Jesus, that we might live in righteousness and enjoy the rewards of the righteous!

> Whoever gives heed to instruction prospers, and blessed is he who trusts in the Lord. (Prov. 16:20)

> **Faith is hearing the Word,**
> **believing what God says and**
> **acting upon it.**

If you do this you will prosper. By contrast, 'A man of perverse heart does not prosper' (Prov. 17:20).

'He who cherishes understanding prospers' (Prov. 19:8)! 'He who pursues righteousness and love finds life, prosperity and honour' (Prov. 21:21)! 'He who trusts in the Lord will prosper' (Prov. 28:25)!

The message is clear. **The man who walks in faith, love**

and obedience, will prosper. He will prosper in practical, material ways, as well as prospering spiritually.

The believer's prosperity comes from the Lord. 'I bring prosperity and create disaster, I, the Lord, do all these things' (Isa. 45:7). He does not want to bring disaster on His people; that is only a last resort when they are deliberately and persistently rebellious. His purposes are good:

'I know the plans I have for you,' declares the Lord, 'plans to prosper you and not to harm you.' (Jer. 29:11)

Although there are times when He needs to punish them, He promises He will restore prosperity to His people as soon as they return to His ways.

When the Lord speaks prophetically to His people of what He will do when the new covenant is established, He says:

You will be my people, and I will be your God. I will save you from all your uncleanness. I will call for the corn and make it plentiful and will not bring famine upon you. I will increase the fruit of the trees and the crops of the field. (Ezek. 36:28–30)

This speaks very definitely of a material prosperity. And this is indeed what we see in the New Testament.

GIVING AND RECEIVING

Jesus teaches you to give, for this is the outworking of love. But He makes it clear that God will outdo you in giving. The measure you give will determine how much you are able to receive from the Lord. This does not imply that you can buy blessing. The freedom and generosity with which you give is an indication of what is in your heart.

It is not the amount you give, as Jesus made clear when the rich were putting their gold into the Temple treasury, while the poor widow could only give her last two small coins. This was a far greater offering because it represented all she had. It demonstrated faith, that she would trust the Lord to provide for her. Paul explains the principle:

> Remember this: Whoever sows sparingly will also reap sparingly, and whoever sows generously will also reap generously. Each man should give what he has decided in his heart to give, not reluctantly or under compulsion, for God loves a cheerful giver. (2 Cor. 9:6–7)

> **Sow generously,**
> **You will reap generously.**
> **Do not give reluctantly.**
> **Give cheerfully.**

How will the Lord respond to generous, cheerful giving? With abundant grace. He gives to the undeserving. We cannot purchase or earn His gifts. All He gives comes by His grace.

> **And God is able to make all grace abound to you, so that in all things at all times, having all that you need, you will abound in every good work.** (v. 8)

This is indeed prosperity: in All things,
at all times,
having ALL that you need.

Why should God be prepared to give so abundantly?

> **You will be made rich in every way so that you can be generous on every occasion.** (v.11)

Made rich IN EVERY WAY. Then 'you will abound in every good work'; 'you can be generous on every occasion.'

It was while telling about 'this grace of giving' which results in such generosity from God, that Paul said:

> **For you know the grace of our Lord Jesus Christ, that though he was rich, yet for your sakes he became poor, so that you through his poverty might become rich.** (2 Cor. 8:9)

Obviously Jesus has made us rich in *every* way, and that includes financial and material blessing, as the context makes clear. Jesus Himself said:

> And everyone who has left houses or brothers or sisters or father or mother or children or fields for my sake will receive a hundred times as much and will inherit eternal life. (Matt. 19:29)

You cannot outdo the Lord in giving. He calls you to a sacrificial life of yielding yourself completely to Him, obeying His Word and walking in righteousness. He calls you to express your love and faith in giving to Him and to others. But look what He promises in return!

> **Give, and it will be given to you. A good measure, pressed down, shaken together and running over, will be poured into your lap. For with the measure you use, it will be measured to you.** (Luke 6:38)

The principle applies to every area of life including forgiveness, mercy, love, money. The same principle works negatively too. Judge and you will be judged. Refuse to forgive and you will not be forgiven.

The message is simple. **In whatever area of life you honour God, He will honour you. In whatever ways you are generous, He will be far more generous in return.**

If you want to be victorious in the financial department of your life the message is clear:

> **Keep the commands of the Lord your God as one of His holy people.**
> **Walk in His ways and obey His Word.**
> **Give yourself in love to the Lord and others.**
> **Honour the Lord in your resources.**

Do not be deceived: God cannot be mocked. **A man reaps what he sows** (Gal. 6:7).

I would need to write a whole book to give adequate

testimony about how I have seen these principles work in practice. Both in my personal life and in the ministry of which I am a part, I have experienced God's amazing generosity. He has supplied tens, and sometimes hundreds of thousands of pounds in answer to prayer, without any money-raising activities.

But He has impressed on us the need to be faithful in giving, expecting Him to measure back His abundance. There have been times when I have given away thousands of pounds, usually when we have needed even greater sums for ministry projects.

To the reason it seems crazy to give away when you need. But we are living according to the principles of God's Kingdom. And I know the truth of God's Word. We always receive His 'good measure, pressed down, shaken together and running over'. Then we will have more to give away where it is needed.

This is faith in action.

FAITH, OBEDIENCE AND PROSPERITY

So the Bible does not speak of a material prosperity detached from a life of faith, love and obedience, but of a prosperity that will be the outcome of such a life. We are not taught to seek material blessing apart from our life in the Kingdom, but as a witness to others of the goodness of the Lord expressed to those who belong to His Kingdom.

> The one who sows to please his sinful nature, from that nature will reap destruction; the one who sows to please the Spirit, from the Spirit will reap eternal life. (Gal. 6:8)

So we are not to become weary in doing good, in loving and in giving. We will reap the harvest at the proper time if we do not give up.

To believe certain promises is not a passport to instant financial riches. To give your life to Jesus, in whatever society, nation or situation you may be, enables Him to give Himself to you in the fullness of life. And you can experience His love and care in abundance, so that you are able to demonstrate His generosity to others, financially and in other ways.

The worst thing you can do when in need is to stop giving. Remain faithful, honouring the Lord and His Word, and He will honour His promises in your life. Like Paul you may experience times of plenty and times of need. God will use both. **In the times of plenty you can bless others. In the times of need you can listen attentively to what God is saying to you.** Nothing encourages us to listen more than need.

The Lord wants you to believe in His grace and generosity.
He wants you to give freely – in every way.
He wants to give to you generously – in every way.

Your key to a victorious life.
WALK IN FAITH, LOVE AND OBEDIENCE AND YOU WILL PROSPER.

21

Victory over Selfishness

The way to victory:
  Never become weary of giving to others.

Your victory scripture:
  A man reaps what he sows. (Gal. 6:7)

LOVE IS GIVING

God is love. The nature of His love is expressed in giving in every area of life. His purpose for us is expressed in love; to love the Lord whole-heartedly, to love our neighbours as ourselves, to love one another as He has loved us.

This purpose can only be expressed in giving: giving to God, to your neighbour, to your fellow Christians. This giving can involve any and every part of your life, making your time, abilities and money available for His use. Above all, making yourself available to Him.

Selfishness is the opposite to giving. It is wanting to receive rather than give; it is holding on to what you have instead of making it available to the Lord and to others.

Do not be deceived: God cannot be mocked. **A man reaps what he sows.** The one who sows to please his sinful nature, from that nature will reap destruction; the one who sows to please the Spirit, from the Spirit will reap eternal life. (Gal. 6:7–8)

'A man reaps what he sows.' This is a spiritual principle, which Jesus applies in several different areas of teaching:

> Blessed are the merciful, for they will be shown mercy. (Matt. 5:7)
> For if you forgive men when they sin against you, your heavenly Father will also forgive you. (Matt. 6:14)
> So in everything, do to others what you would have them do to you. (Matt. 7:12)
> Do not judge, and you will not be judged.
> Do not condemn, and you will not be condemned.
> Forgive, and you will be forgiven.
> Give, and it will be given to you . . .
> For with the measure you use, it will be measured to you. (Luke 6:37–38)

You do not want to sow to please your sinful, selfish nature. You want to sow to please the Spirit, to give cheerfully, lovingly, generously, faithfully.

To give in such a way is to experience victory over your naturally selfish instincts. Failure to give is defeat in that particular situation.

The selfish one does not want to give and may refuse to do so. If he does give and gains some advantage, he is likely to be content and not allow himself to be stretched in further giving.

Some years ago I found it necessary to ask the Lord to give me a generous heart, which would reflect something of His own generosity. He answers such prayers when He knows this is what is desired seriously, and is not just a sentiment being expressed because it seems a good thing to pray.

CONTINUAL GIVING

The life of the Christian is one of continual giving, being content to serve in whatever way the Lord asks irrespective of how menial the task may seem. For Jesus makes it clear it is only when you have proved faithful in little things, giving yourself wholeheartedly to the Lord, that you will then be put in charge of greater Kingdom responsibilities. So Paul encourages us:

> **Let us not become weary in doing good, for at the proper time we will reap a harvest if we do not give up. (Gal. 6:9)**

There are times when you give so continuously it is tempting to stop giving. It may be you receive little in return at first. Your giving may be rejected, taken for granted, abused or misused. But the promise is that if you continue to give, you will reap the harvest in due course.

My life and ministry involves a constant giving out to others. I do not begrudge that at all because it is a privilege to serve the King of kings, and humbling to be used by Him to speak into others' lives. But I cannot deny there are times when I become exceedingly weary. There are so many demands, even when I feel there is nothing left to give.

And yet the Lord always supplies the resources of energy necessary under the anointing of the Holy Spirit. I hear this word in my own heart, never to become weary in doing good. There will be ample time to rest in heaven – I trust!

The message is clear. **Do not give up. Do not compromise in the matter of expressing your love in giving to God and to others.** Give time to prayer and study of the Word. Faith will be enlarged and you will reap the rewards of faith.

> Therefore, as we have opportunity, let us do good to all people, especially to those who belong to the family of believers. (Gal. 6:10)

You can have victory over selfishness by taking the opportunities to give which God places before you. Sometimes this will require an act of faith because you feel inadequate or fear that you will lose rather than gain. At such times you have to believe God's Word – not the world, your own flesh or the devil.

Your key to a victorious life:
  KEEP GIVING TO THE LORD AND OTHERS.

22

Victory in Sickness

The way to victory:
   Allowing God to use sickness creatively for His purpose gives victory *in* sickness.

Your victory scripture:
   Surely he took up our infirmities and carried our sorrows. (Isa. 53:4)

GOD'S ANSWER TO SICKNESS

There is a difference between victory *in* sickness and victory *over* sickness.

Without sin there would be no sickness; both are consequences of man's fallen nature. In the Old Testament it is clear that God does not want His people to be ill, although He allows plagues and sickness to overtake them if they are persistent in their disobedience and rebellion. For the same reasons He allows their enemies to defeat them. Any amount of suffering and hardship would be worthwhile to bring them back to obedience to His covenant with them. Then He would bless them mightily and abundantly, which is what He desired.

The Lord wants to bless His people, not to curse them. Satan is the agent of sickness, as we see in the book of Job. It was the enemy, not the Lord, who attacked Job in many ways, including sickness.

The prophecy of Isaiah looks forward to what God will effect through the Cross, when the new covenant would be ratified with the blood of His Son. Jesus dealt with every spiritual, emotional and physical condition.

> Surely he took up our infirmities and carried our sorrows . . . and by his wounds we are healed. (Isa. 53:4–5)

He suffered, spirit, soul and body, to bring salvation, or health, to spirit, soul and body.

THE CROSS AND SICKNESS

Below are phrases from the prophecy of Isaiah 52:13–53:12 describing the various ways in which Jesus suffered. The righthand column shows how people can identify with different aspects of Jesus' work of total salvation.

WHAT JESUS SUFFERED	THOSE WHO IDENTIFY WITH HIM
His appearance was so disfigured beyond that of any man and his form marred beyond human likeness.	Those who are born with physical defect, or who are maimed.
He had no beauty or majesty to attract us to him, nothing in his appearance that we should desire him.	Those who consider they lack any beauty or attraction – either physically or as people.
He was despised and rejected by men.	All who feel despised and have been rejected by others.
A man of sorrows.	All who have experienced personal sorrow.
Familiar with suffering.	Those who have continual suffering.

WHAT JESUS SUFFERED	THOSE WHO IDENTIFY WITH HIM
He was despised.	Those who know what it is to be hated.
Surely he took up our infirmities.	Any who experience sickness, emotional or physical.
And carried our sorrows.	All who are grief-stricken.
We considered him stricken by God, smitten by him, and afflicted.	All in the prime of life who are struck down with sickness.
He was pierced for our transgressions.	All who sin.
He was crushed for our iniquities.	All those who feel crushed by the weight of their sin and guilt.
The punishment that brought us peace was upon him.	All who deserve to be punished and judged by God.
By his wounds we are healed.	Any who are sick can receive the healing which He accomplished.
He was oppressed.	All who are oppressed can be set free.
Afflicted.	All who suffer affliction, no matter what its nature.
By oppression and judgment he was taken away.	All who are oppressed and judged falsely.
For the transgressions of my people he was stricken.	All who deserve punishment for their sins.
He was assigned a grave with the wicked.	All who deserve death can now receive the gospel of eternal life.
It was the Lord's will to crush him.	What love the Father must have for you, to crush His Son on your behalf!

WHAT JESUS SUFFERED	THOSE WHO IDENTIFY WITH HIM
And cause him to suffer.	To deliver you from suffering.
The will of the Lord will prosper in his hand.	His will is that you should have life in all its fullness.
He poured out his life unto death.	Through His death you have received that life.

VICTORY IN JESUS' MINISTRY

Healing of physical disease played a major part in Jesus' ministry. These healings were seen as signs that Jesus had come with the good news of God's Kingdom. They demonstrated that His Kingdom is more powerful and has greater authority than anything that can be perpetrated by the dominion of darkness.

Matthew clearly states that healing of sickness and deliverance from demons were a fulfilment of the Isaiah prophecy:

> When evening came, many who were demon-possessed were brought to him, and he drove out the spirits with a word and healed all the sick. This was to fulfil what was spoken through the prophet Isaiah, 'He took up our infirmities and carried our diseases' (Matt. 8:16–17)

How could Matthew apply these verses to what happened in Jesus' ministry *before* the Cross? **What Jesus did in a limited time during the three years or so of His human ministry was made eternally available to all men of all ages of all nations, who put their faith in Him, when He went to the Cross.**

Jesus took away the infirmities and diseases of those who came to Him in faith during His earthly ministry.

Jesus takes away the infirmities and diseases of those who come to Him now in faith, because He has dealt with their need on the Cross.

By the power of His Spirit we can therefore see and experience the same works as Jesus did. He came and waged war on sin and sickness and was victorious over both. In the name of Jesus that victory is made available to all.

VICTORY IN SICKNESS

In an ideal, perfect world there would be neither sin nor sickness. Until Jesus comes again such a perfect world will not exist. Every person sins and it is possible for anyone to be sick.

This does not mean God *wants* you to be sick, just as He never *wants* you to sin.

As you are in Christ, there is no condemnation for you if you sin. You can receive forgiveness through the Lord's grace and mercy.

There is certainly no condemnation for you if you become sick. Although some sickness is the direct result of sin, this is by no means always the case. The enemy often attacks with sickness, as he did with Job.

Healing for any and every disease is possible through Jesus. With God nothing is impossible, and 'Everything is possible for him who believes' (Mark 9:23). And yet it needs to be clearly stated that **a Christian who does not receive healing is not condemned.**

Many have testified to how God has met them in sickness. They speak of important refining and spiritual developments taking place in their lives in times of sickness. There can be no doubt that such testimonies are genuine. However there is no lesson God teaches us in sickness that He would not rather teach us in health. The

Lord does not want to make us sick in order to teach us. What kind of a father would do that to his children?

When ill, people have time to reflect, to be still, to listen and respond to what the Lord may have been saying for some time. The person may have been unwilling or unable to hear because of his ceaseless activity or preoccupation with other things. There is nothing like pain to encourage repentance and a crying out to God. In such times people become aware of their need to re-order the priorities in their lives.

If the time of illness is used creatively for God's purposes, then it could certainly be claimed that the Christian has experienced spiritual victory *in* sickness. He has come to a renewed repentance and submission of his life to God.

CRIPPLING DISEASES

And yet there is another way of understanding victory *in* sickness. Prolonged sickness, disfigurement, crippling diseases and maiming accidents can all cause deep emotional hurt, resentment and bitterness, mixed with a sense of non-acceptance by others. In other words, instead of the sickness being creative it is destructive, not only of the body but of the person. This may be an understandable reaction among non-Christians, but should not be the case among God's redeemed people.

Sickness must not be allowed to overcome the personality; the person must overcome the sickness. Many Christians have been brought through to such victory. They may be paralysed, bedridden or confined to a wheel-chair, they may have been born with crippling disfigurement, but they show no sign of resentment, bitterness or hatred even towards those who may have caused the disaster. They bear no malice towards God who is well aware of their predicament. Instead their lives are shining examples of those who know the love and acceptance of Jesus. They are an encouragement to other Christians because, despite their disfigurement, His love and graciousness shine out of their lives.

The sickness has not triumphed over their human spirits. In their spirits they have triumphed over the sickness. This in itself is a great work of God's Spirit within them and we can be thankful for their witness and example.

Having experienced this much, some are content to accept the sickness as being God's will for them. They appear to have no faith that they could, or should, be completely restored physically, even though they know such things are possible and do happen today. They have victory *in* their sickness, but not *over* the sickness itself.

COMPLETE HEALING

Others are not content with victory in their sickness. They are reaching out to God for complete healing and deliverance from their need. They believe for this and nothing less. They may need first to be set free from any sense of bitterness or resentment for their situation, or receive victory *in* their sickness. **But they look to God for the Word of faith which will restore them to complete health.**

The Lord honours such faith today and many mighty miracles take place as a result. The fact that they occur more readily in Third World countries may be significant. Perhaps there is a simplicity of faith in Jesus to effect the miracle. Perhaps it is not enough to know victory *in* sickness if there is no welfare state to care for you. There is no greater incentive to faith than to know the Lord is the only answer, rather than being one course among a number of different options.

Jesus certainly brought people victory over sickness. He was not content to comfort people in their need; He met their need. This is surely His purpose today.

We can praise God for those who experience victory *in*

sickness. But we can reach out to God with the faith which will bring victory *over* sickness.

However, do not belittle the work of God's grace in those who have met with Him in their sickness. And do not imagine you will need to become sick for God to teach you.

You are a disciple of Jesus.
Sit at His feet and learn from Him.
Respond readily to His Word and the leading of His Spirit.
Be quick to learn and respond, in health or sickness.

Your key to a victorious life:
SICKNESS WILL NOT TRIUMPH OVER YOU.

23

Victory over Sickness

The way to victory:
  Understand that the Lord does not want you to be sick;
  He wants you to be whole in spirit, soul and body.

Your victory scripture:
  By his wounds we are healed. (Isa. 53:5)

HEAL THE SICK

Because the Cross of Jesus embraced every healing need, He wants you to experience healing *over* sickness as well as other adverse circumstances.

In the New Testament, there is a clear distinction between suffering and sickness. We are called to suffer for the sake of the Kingdom. This may involve persecution, rejection, even physical deprivation and torture. We are called to suffer the cost of self-denial, to take up our personal crosses day by day and follow Jesus.

We are not called to be sick.

Jesus would not have given His disciples power and authority to heal the sick if His Father had caused the sickness or willed it. God is not divided against Himself in this way.

Healing goes with the proclamation of the good news of God's Kingdom. As disciples of Jesus today we have inherited this commission.

He called his twelve disciples to him and gave them authority to drive out evil spirits and to heal every disease and sickness . . . As you go, preach this message: 'The kingdom of heaven is near.' Heal the sick, raise the dead, cleanse those who have leprosy, drive out demons. Freely you have received, freely give. (Matt. 10:1,7–8)

The Acts of the Apostles makes it clear that these men continued to fulfil this commission after Jesus' death and resurrection, when the Holy Spirit had come upon them.

RESIST SICKNESS

It is God's plan for His Church to extend healing to the sick in the name of Jesus. Likewise, **He desires His children to stand against sickness, as they are called to stand against sin.**

God's best purpose is that you should not be sick. If sickness attacks you He wants you to stand against it in the name of Jesus, refusing to accept it. This is a very different attitude from quietly submitting to sickness as being God's will for you.

You may need to speak to the sickness. Jesus tells you to speak to mountains commanding them to be moved, not doubting in your heart that they will be moved.

You can accept and believe symptoms or you can come against them in faith. When you resist them, the early symptoms disappear and the disease does not take hold of you. The best method of defence is attack! You may experience a period of conflict, as if a battle is going on within you. But as you persist in faith you come through to victory.

The medical profession today confirms what the Bible has affirmed for centuries. The majority of physical sicknesses are psychosomatic; they begin in the mind. The Christian can go further and say that the mind is often in turmoil because the person's spiritual life is in turmoil.

Keep your mind clear of thoughts of sickness, of fears of becoming ill. Those who dread sickness are not surprised when they become ill. Their expectations are fulfilled. Those who dwell on symptoms will see them intensify. Often physical pain is the result of emotional and mental anguish.

Often people seek healing of a physical complaint, and discover that God wants first to deal with the anguish and tension within them. There is little point in removing the symptoms if the cause remains.

WHOLENESS

Jesus met your every need on the Cross, spiritual, emotional, psychological and physical. When coming to God with faith you need to appreciate that He wants you to have victory over the sickness. **He has not created you to be sick, but to be made whole through Jesus.**

He usually starts with the heart and works outwards, even though there are many occasions when you would like Him to do the reverse. But He is concerned with your total well-being, with 'wholeness', health of spirit, soul and body. **In coming to Him for healing come with your whole being, not part of yourself. It is *you* He wants to heal, not only some part of your body.**

Above all He wants you to live in peace, to have faith in Him and walk in His ways so that you do not become vulnerable to sickness because of fear, tension and worry.

Disobedience can lead to sickness. The obvious examples are certain sexually-related diseases, and those caused by overwork and over-indulgence. So Christians need to see that their lives are regulated according to God's Word.

If heart strain is caused by overweight, which is caused by greed, it is obvious that the Lord will want to deal with the greed and whatever causes the greed. This may be the sin of over-indulgence; it may be that the person is eating in an attempt to provide some emotional compensation.

Because of His love for the person, Jesus wants to deal with the root cause so there can be true victory over every area of dis-ease.

RECEIVE YOUR HEALING

There are many ways in which the believer can receive healing. This is not the place for a lengthy discussion of this subject, but we can take note of a few important principles.

1 Do not allow the sickness into your heart. If you believe in the sickness you will not have faith to see it removed from your body. This does not mean that you refuse to acknowledge the existence of the sickness. But you do not regard the illness as the ultimate truth, which is the healing that is part of your inheritance in Christ.

2 Your faith is in the victory of Jesus: 'By his wounds you are healed.'

3 As you pray, see your healing as an established fact. You are taking hold of that which is already done in Christ.

4 Do not be double-minded about the subject. It is the Lord's will to heal you.

5 Speak to the sickness in the name of Jesus, commanding it to leave you. He tells you not to doubt the outcome.

6 As you pray, believe you have received your healing. 'Whatever you ask for in prayer, believe that you have received it, and it will be yours' (Mark 11:24).

7 Having prayed with faith, you are walking in God's healing not in sickness.

8 Before asking the Lord to deal with the physical condition, be sure you are right with Him spiritually. Ask Him to forgive your sins, and be specific when you do so.

9 Be sure that you have forgiven others, that you are not holding on to any hurt, bitterness or resentment.

10 If necessary, ask others to pray with you in the name of Jesus. Believe such times as being occasions when you actually receive from God, whether or not you are conscious of any particular sensation.

It is important to have the right faith attitudes. The method by which you receive the healing is unimportant. **Do not look to men,** even those with a reputation for being used in healing. **Look directly to the Lord Jesus.**

> **Put your faith in Him.**
> **You will receive your healing in His name.**

Jesus has won the victory over sickness; so Jesus can give you that victory in your circumstances.

Faith comes from hearing God's word in your heart. Even if faith does not exist at first, God can speak His Word to your heart by His Spirit. Such a word does not lead to a general sense that the healing will happen sometime in the future. The Lord may give such a promise that it is His will to heal. **But promises have to be appropriated by faith. A specific word from God leads to specific action. When He speaks that Word, believe what He says.**

When you know in your spirit it is done, the matter is resolved. The physical sickness may disappear immediately, or begin to go at that moment. Sometimes there can be a time delay in the manifestation of healing. However, **at that moment of faith you know the matter is resolved.** You are in the Lord's hands and He does not fail.

You can appropriate emotional healing in the same way.

Appreciate that Jesus has met your need. It is His desire and intention to free you from that need.

He has taken your sin.
He has suffered your sorrow and rejection.
He has carried your sicknesses to the Cross.
By His wounds you are healed.

Your key to a victorious life:
RESIST SICKNESS IN THE NAME OF JESUS.[1]

---

[1] For a fuller treatment of the subject of healing, see Colin Urquhart, *Receive Your Healing* (Hodder 1986).

24

Victory over Oppression

The way to victory:
Do not allow your spiritual ear to be dulled to God's voice because you listen instead to the enemy's lies.

Your victory scripture:
It is for freedom that Christ has set us free. (Gal. 5:1)

BELIEVING YOUR INHERITANCE

'The devil is oppressing me.' Certainly the devil will try to oppress God's people. But if believers exercise the faith and authority they are given he will not be successful in his attempts.

Everything in God's Kingdom is positive. In His Kingdom there are certain clearly defined principles by which God works.

The devil is unprincipled and attempts to contradict the positive with his negatives.

The Spirit gives freedom. The devil tries to steal this from the believer by tempting him to disbelieve his inheritance or focus his attention on his fears, feelings and failures instead of on the truth.

The mind is usually his first line of attack. He sows a negative thought. If this is received he follows it with another and another. The Christian is accepting a negative line of thought which affects his whole attitude to some aspect of his life.

Take sickness as an example. The first thought may be: 'You have cancer.' If this is received it will not be long before the devil points to any unusual bodily sensation as being the first evidences of the disease. He may continue his subtle tactics by suggesting: 'There is a history of cancer in your family, isn't there?' 'This is the age your cousin died of cancer.' And so on.

He will say anything to encourage fear and cause the person to believe he is really going to die of this disease. His business is destruction.

Of course, the devil will do similar things in many other areas of life besides sickness, encouraging you to fear the future, to believe the worst is going to happen, that you will inevitably fail in whatever lies ahead of you.

His most destructive attacks are those made on the principles of your faith, contradicting the truth of God's word.

Through His blood you are accepted by Jesus. Satan will suggest you are unacceptable and will point to your sins and inadequacies as evidence of his contention.

Where you repent the Lord forgives your sins. Satan will want you to think that forgiveness cannot be that simple, that you deserved to be punished for your sins.

You live in Christ. The enemy will point out your failures again and again, suggesting you are so unworthy you could not possibly live in Jesus.

Christ lives in you. The devil will encourage you to believe the Lord would not come to live in someone so unholy. It cannot be true.

Christ leads you in His triumphant procession. Satan suggests this is the biggest joke of the century with your record of failures.

You are made worthy in God's sight. The enemy points to every sin as evidence of your unworthiness. And so on.

Every attack is calculated to cause unbelief, confusion, condemnation and failure, by denying the truth.

Never is the devil more active, it seems, than when you need to hear directly from God about a certain matter. How many people admit to finding it difficult to discern the voice of God from the deceptions of the evil one?

The answer to these attacks is simple and obvious. **You hold on to the truth and refuse to accept any of the lying deceptions of the enemy.** This requires constant vigilance, for he is likely to strike like the serpent he is, at the most unlikely moment.

PERSONAL ATTACK

Oppression can take different forms. There are the times when your personal worth and faith seem under attack. The devil wants you to believe you are a no-good, spiritual failure, that God does not want anything to do with you. He suggests you have failed so miserably even your ultimate salvation is far from certain or secure.

If you listen to him you lose all your confidence before God and then feel trapped by your circumstances. Everything seems hopeless, you feel helpless and the Lord seems far removed from your concerns.

An extreme form of this state causes depression. The person has believed so many lies, and has thus become so negative in his thinking, he no longer knows how to be positive. His eyes are not on the truth of the Word, but on himself and his feelings. **He loses sight of the victory because his eyes are on himself instead of the Victor.**

The one who has become depressed by believing so many lies will need to recognise the folly of what he has been doing in listening to the enemy. He will have to repent of this, claiming God's forgiveness and the freedom He alone can give.

Then he will also need to have his mind renewed. This is a process rather than something which happens in a moment of time. He will need to fill his mind with the positive truth of the Word. **Listening to the enemy will have made his spiritual ear dull to the voice of the Holy Spirit.**

I find I have to be constantly vigilant, so that the enemy is not allowed to establish a negative foothold anywhere in my thinking. I know that I cannot be sensitive to what God is saying if I allow my mind to be filled with Satan's lies.

THE FATHER OF LIES

The other way in which the enemy will try to undermine your faith is by pointing to the difficult circumstances in which you are sometimes placed. He will suggest every problem is an indication that God cannot truly love you, or He would not have allowed such things to happen. The irony is that the devil has been responsible for the very things for which he wants to blame God. But Satan always seems to play the same tunes; so they are easily recognisable.

'Why should this have happened to you if God really loves you?'
'This must be punishment for your sins.'
'Faith may work for others, but it would never work for you.'
'How can a God of love allow you to be sick?'
'How can God possibly love you, when you suffer so much pain?'
'He cannot be much of a God if he is with you always and yet you experience so much rejection and confusion.'

He nags away persistently with such lies. So you have to deny them just as persistently.

Hold on to the truth.
If you resist the devil, he will flee from you.
Refuse to accept any of his negative lies or accusations.
Take the shield of faith, which repels all his attacks.

It is easy to tell the voice of the devil if you remember:

He accuses you; Jesus does not.
He tries to condemn you; Jesus does not.
He undermines faith; Jesus gives faith.
He diverts your attention on to the problems; the Holy
   Spirit directs you to Jesus.
He blames God; Jesus offers help.
He is negative; the Father, Jesus and the Holy Spirit are
   positive.

YOU ARE FREE

You can expect the devil to oppose you, but you do not
need to allow him to oppress you, to make you feel that
either he or your circumstances are on top of you.

Another way in which you can experience the enemy's
attempts to oppress is through a sense of spiritual heaviness
coming on you. You may feel very tired and restless,
unable to concentrate for no accountable reason, especially
when you have important Kingdom business in hand. You
may find it difficult to look to the Lord in prayer, and praise
is exceedingly difficult.

**At such times take authority in the name of Jesus over the
devil and all his works. Claim the victory that is yours and
praise Jesus.** This may require a real act of the will at first,
but as you persevere so you will break right through to the
glory of Jesus' majesty.

Oppression is like ropes with which the devil wants to
bind you. You are created to be free in Christ Jesus, not
bound. So do not let yourself be bound.

**It is for freedom that Christ has set us free. Stand firm,
then, and do not let yourselves be burdened again by a
yoke of slavery. (Gal. 5:1)**

The enemy even tries to oppress through religious activity.
He wants to limit the freedom of the Holy Spirit among

God's people, through tradition, conformity and legalism. Paul's message to the Galatians is clear and is certainly relevant today.

The cause of the gospel is damaged severely by religious prejudice, self-righteousness, denominationalism and judgmental attitudes towards other believers. It is not always understood who is stoking the fires of division or who encourages attitudes which oppose the liberty of God's Spirit in churches.

Do not listen to the enemy's attempts to encourage a return to religious conformity and tradition.

Do not allow him to put you back under the bondage of the law.

He will do anything to take away the freedom you have in Jesus.

It is for freedom Christ has set you free in every area of your life.

Your key to a victorious life:
CHRIST HAS SET YOU FREE TO LIVE IN FREEDOM.

25

Victory over Error

The way to victory:
   Check against God's Word your ideas and reason, your feelings and decisions, and what others teach you.

Your victory scripture:
   I tell you the truth, if anyone keeps my word, he will never see death. (John. 8:51)

THE TRUTH

The enemy wants to distort the truth. The greatest danger for Christians comes from ignorance of the truth.

Many admit they need a better knowledge and understanding of God's Word. Intention or desire is not enough. The only way to combat error is with the truth.

   You need to know the truth of what God has done for you in Jesus.
   You need to know who you are as a child of God.
   You need to know the rich inheritance you have through His grace.
   You need to know God's purpose for your life and what He expects of you.

The Lord speaks to you personally through His Word and by His Spirit. The Holy Spirit is the Spirit of truth who will guide you with the truth.

Just as light penetrates and overcomes darkness, so truth overcomes error. **Truth is not a matter of debate or discussion. Truth is truth and never changes.** The truth of God and His Son, Jesus, is eternal. This is why Jesus says that heaven and earth will pass away, but His words will never pass away.

To live by faith is to live by the truth. And the truth is often stranger than the facts we experience with our senses.

I TELL YOU THE TRUTH

Everything Jesus says is truth. But sometimes He used the phrase 'I tell you the truth' because He knew the statement that followed would meet with unbelief. Jesus is saying that this is definitely the truth whether you believe it or not.

As we look at some of these statements from John's gospel, we can appreciate that such truth is rejected by many today, even by some who call themselves Christians. They argue against these truths with their reason, or question what Jesus says because the truth offends their own ideas of what they want to do with their lives.

I tell you the truth, no-one can see the kingdom of God unless he is born again. (John 3:3)

I tell you the truth, no-one can enter the kingdom of God unless he is born of water and the Spirit. (John 3:5)

Many of these statements relate to who will receive the gift of eternal life and go to heaven. These truths cut right across popular misconceptions that everyone will go to heaven.

I tell you the truth, whoever hears my word and believes him who sent me has eternal life and will not be condemned; he has crossed over from death to life. (John 5:24)

Note the emphasis on personal faith in Jesus; he who believes has eternal life.

You have received the gift of eternal life.
You will not be condemned.
You have crossed over from death to life.
You have been born again.
You have repented and come to personal faith in Jesus.
You know Him as your Lord and Saviour.
You are born of water and the spirit.

Without Jesus you could not have God's life within you. Because you know and love Him you can feed on His words, for He is the living Bread which has come down from heaven.

I tell you the truth, unless you can eat the flesh of the Son of Man and drink his blood, you have no life in you. Whoever eats my flesh and drinks my blood has eternal life, and I will raise him up at the last day. (John 6:53–54)

The blood of Jesus cleanses you from your sins. You belong to Him; and He is the resurrection and the life. And so you have His assurance that you will not die eternally, but He will raise you up to be with Him in triumph.

I tell you the truth, everyone who sins is a slave to sin. Now a slave has no permanent place in the family, but a son belongs to it for ever. So if the Son sets you free, you will be free indeed. (John 8:34–36)

You are no longer a slave but a son, by faith in Jesus Christ.
You have the rights and privileges of a Son of God's Kingdom.
You also have the responsibility of a son, not to be ruled by sin but to walk in loving and faithful obedience to your heavenly Father.

The Son has set you free from sin, from your past, from hurt, rejection and bitterness.

It is His truth that has set you free –
from the devil
from yourself
from every bondage.

'If you hold to my teaching, you are really my disciples. Then you will know the truth, and the truth will set you free' (John 8:31–32).

Jesus gives you mighty promises as you live His Word:

I tell you the truth, if anyone keeps my word, he will never see death. (John 8:51)

Jesus is the only way to the Father. No one can receive the gift of the Kingdom except through Him:

I tell you the truth, I am the gate for the sheep. All who ever came before me were thieves and robbers, but the sheep did not listen to them. I am the gate; whoever enters through me will be saved. (John 10:7–8)

The cost of belonging to the Kingdom is that you follow Jesus' example. Like a seed you must fall into the ground and die to self, to what you have been, in order that you might be fruitful for God and enjoy His eternal reward.

I tell you the truth, unless a grain of wheat falls to the ground and dies, it remains only a single seed. But if it dies, it produces many seeds. The man who loves his life will lose it, while the man who hates his life in this world will keep it for eternal life. (John 12:24–25)

As true disciples we are to be like our Master, not having exalted ideas about ourselves, but walking humbly before Him and others.

I tell you the truth, no servant is greater than his master, nor is a messenger greater than the one who sent him.

Now that you know these things, you will be blessed if you do them. (John 13:16–17)

Jesus submitted to the principle of dying to Himself, and He came the Servant of all. We are sent out and commissioned in His name, and Jesus makes this amazing statement about us as His representatives or ambassadors.

I tell you the truth, whoever accepts anyone I send accepts me; and whoever accepts me accepts the one who sent me. (John 13:20)

You go in Jesus' name, to proclaim His truth in the power of His Spirit, in the face of the error, misunderstanding and unbelief which abound in the world around you.

Even more amazing is what Jesus tells us is possible when we go in faith:

I tell you the truth, anyone who has faith in me will do what I have been doing. He will do even greater things than these, because I am going to the Father. (John 14:12)

THE EFFECTS OF THE TRUTH

These are only a small number of the challenging things Jesus said as He revealed the truth.

The truth opens the way for you to eternal life and God's Kingdom.

The truth frees you from condemnation and leads you to fullness of life.

The truth leads to resurrection and glory.

The truth proclaims your Sonship through God's grace.

The truth points you to the only Saviour and Lord, showing you all He has done for you to set you free from every bondage.

The truth shows you the cost of discipleship and the way to be fruitful in God.

The truth gives you your commission and God's promises.

The truth is Jesus Himself.

The truth sets you free.

It is not the truth of yourself that will give you victory, but the truth of all Jesus has done for you, and what God has made you now you belong to Him.

This truth will correct any error about the way you view yourself, your circumstances or your future. The truth will keep you from error concerning the nature of God Himself or His purpose for you.

Anyone who runs ahead and does not continue in the teaching of Christ does not have God; whoever continues in the teaching has both the Father and the Son. (2 John 9)

Check your ideas and reason against the Word of God. Do not accept anything that is not in line with the scriptures.

Check what others teach against God's revealed truth. Do not accept anything which is a contradiction to His Word, no matter how plausible or even 'loving' it may seem.

Check your feelings and decisions against the truth. When inconsistent with the Word, deny the feelings and reject the thoughts you have. **Make choices in line with God's words and then you will walk in His way and fulfil His will.**

Your key to a victorious life:
LIVE BY THE TRUTH OF GOD'S WORD.

26

Victory over Temptation

The way to victory:
　　Jesus can help you to be victorious over every temptation.

Your victory scripture:
　　Because he himself suffered when he was tempted, he is able to help those who are being tempted. (Heb. 2:18)

TEMPTATION IN JESUS' MINISTRY

No matter what temptation you experience, Jesus is present with you. He knows what it is like from His own experience to have to stand firm under similar temptation.

Because he himself suffered when he was tempted, he is able to help those who are being tempted. (Heb. 2:18)

This is the extent to which the Son of God identified with your situation. With the Lord on your side and His Spirit within, you are able to resist and overcome the temptation.

For we do not have a high priest who is unable to sympathise with our weaknesses, but we have one who has been tempted in every way, just as we are – yet was without sin. (Heb. 4:15)

Jesus was always victorious and He can enable you to resist temptation in whatever form it occurs. He understands your weaknesses; He knows your vulnerability and the things you find difficult. This does not imply that He condones sin, but He is present to enable you to withstand the temptation and demonstrate your faithfulness and love for Him by your obedience to His will.

> Blessed is the man who perseveres under trial, because when he has stood the test, he will receive the crown of life that God has promised to those who love him. (Jas. 1:12)

During his manhood, Jesus was tempted in every way, yet remained sinless because He resisted all temptation. Before His public ministry began, the devil tempted Him to act independently of His Father, to take the initiative for His life into His own hands. This Jesus refused to do.

He underwent many further attacks, but none greater than the conflict He experienced in the Garden of Gethsemane. We cannot imagine the spiritual and mental anguish He experienced which caused Him to sweat blood. We can only be thankful that He made the decision He did. Lovingly and humbly He submitted His will to that of His Father, 'Not my will, but yours be done' (Luke 22:42).

TEMPTATION IN YOUR LIFE

It is not a sin to be tempted. What you do in response to the temptation is what matters. It can come at any time, even when you least expect it:

> If you think you are standing firm, be careful that you don't fall! No temptation has seized you except what is common to man. And God is faithful; he will not let you be tempted beyond what you can bear. But when you are tempted, he will also provide a way out so that you can stand up under it. (1 Cor. 10:12–13)

Paul is making a number of important points here:

1 **'Pride comes before a fall'** often proves true. For pride leads to complacency and a lack of watchfulness. Then a person is vulnerable to temptation. Even when you are standing firm you need to be on the watch.

2   Whatever temptation you suffer is experienced by many others. It may seem unique to you, but the devil plays the same cards again and again, because he knows the weak, vulnerable points at which to attack.

3   You can be sure the Lord will never allow you to 'be tempted beyond what you can bear'. He does not want to see you fall from grace. He is the Lord who is able to keep you from falling and present you blameless before His throne.

4   No matter what the temptation, the Lord will always provide you with an escape route. So it is not right to say: 'I couldn't help it. I felt I had to do it.' The honest truth is that you chose to sin. It is a sign of God's faithfulness to you as His covenant child that He will not allow Satan to attack you in such a way that you have to yield to his demands.

5   You are able to withstand the temptation; you can be victorious. Why give Satan the satisfaction of even a minor victory?

James gives us further truths:

When tempted, no-one should say, 'God is tempting me.' For God cannot be tempted by evil, nor does he tempt anyone; but each one is tempted when, by his own evil desire, he is dragged away and enticed. Then, after desire has conceived, it gives birth to sin; and sin, when it is full-grown, gives birth to death. (Jas. 1:13–15)

6   The devil is the tempter, not God. He allows the enemy to tempt because temptation exposes your vulnerable areas. You see the ways in which you need to trust God, and be built up in His strength. But God Himself does not tempt you. He wants you to stand firm in faith against the temptation.

7   Temptation does not create sin; it simply exposes the sinful desires which exist within you. It exposes what is in your heart; those things which are alien to God's purposes but which you still desire; your 'own evil desires'.

8   If you allow evil desires to entice you away from God's purposes, you will inevitably sin. Satan offers all kinds of temporary pleasures, many of which are illusory. **Jesus offers eternal rewards to those who remain faithful to Him.**

SPIRIT AND FLESH

Your flesh will always be flesh, and can never be anything other than flesh. Satan wants you to go back to the flesh. Jesus wants you to walk in the Spirit. You have authority over the devil; so do not allow him to seduce or deceive you.

It is important therefore to nip the problem in the bud. **Resist the first sinful thought or desire. Do not dwell on the matter. The more you concentrate on it, perhaps enjoying the mental anticipation of the sin, the more difficult it will be to resist.**

You may not want to resist because you desire the object of the temptation so much. If you yield you may be temporarily satisfied in the flesh, but you will suffer spiritual defeat. **If you resist the temptation, you will experience victory over the flesh, reckoning yourself dead to your own desires and able to please the Lord.**

To dwell on the thought of the sin is to invite the sin itself. The thought is as bad as the deed, Jesus tells us. But He does not imply there is any condemnation in the fact that we are tempted. He was tempted in the wilderness, but did not sin because He immediately rebuffed the devil.

Even when you do yield to temptation, deliberately or unintentionally, the Lord is still ready to restore you through His forgiving love. But remember He is 'able to keep you from falling and to present you before his glorious presence without fault and with great joy' (Jude 24).

Remember: **temptation is not sin.** Do not be surprised

that you are tempted, or imagine that you will ever reach a point beyond temptation.

Satan's appeal is to the flesh, to the natural self-life. He suggests you satisfy your bodily appetites through sexual immorality, greed or laziness. He tempts you to satisfy yourself, to exalt self, to be self-sufficient and independent. He wants you to lie, deceive, cheat. In other words he wants to reproduce his own distorted character in you because he is utterly opposed to God's purpose of forming Himself in you.

Remember the simple test: Satan will want you to be negative – to refuse to forgive, to judge, condemn, ridicule, destroy. **Jesus will produce the positive nature of His Kingdom life in you by the power of His Spirit.**

It is obviously foolish to put yourself in situations where you know you will be open to temptation. Your flesh will always be flesh and can never become spiritual. **The way to deal with the flesh is to reckon it dead, crucified with Christ.**

Instead of getting worried about fleshly desire, you can adopt the attitude: 'That's my flesh. Praise God I have died to all that nonsense and do not have to yield. My trust is in the Lord. Glory be to Jesus.' You will find that such tactics are far more effective than being full of concern because you have detected some ungodly desire.

When others fall into sin, do not adopt a judgmental attitude, no matter how grievous the situation may seem. Rather than be critical of others, you are warned to 'watch yourself, or you also may be tempted' (Gal. 6:1).

Never become complacent. You are not beyond temptation, which can come in unexpected ways at unexpected times. When it happens, **resist and walk in victory.**

Your key to a victorious life:
    WALK IN THE SPIRIT; SAY 'NO' TO EVERY TEMPTATION TO INDULGE THE FLESH.

27

Victory over Pride

The way to victory:
  Submit yourself to God, delighting to do whatever He
  asks of you, no matter how insignificant.

Your victory scripture:
  God opposes the proud but gives grace to the humble.
  (Prov. 3:34; Jas. 4:6; 1 Pet. 5:5)

JESUS' HUMILITY

Jesus said: 'I am gentle and humble in heart' (Matt. 11:29).
It is difficult to imagine the love which lay behind the
Creator of the universe choosing to be born in the weakness
of human flesh as a fragile child.

Imagine God walking on earth, tending the needs of His
people, teaching them the truth, encouraging them to
receive His gifts and inherit His promises! The Son of God
even washes His disciples' feet, doing the work of a humble
slave.

Jesus came to reveal the Father, not to glorify Himself.

  My food is to do the will of him who sent me and to finish
    his work. (John 4:34)

  I tell you the truth, the Son can do nothing by himself; he
    can do only what he sees his Father doing, because
    whatever the Father does the Son also does. (John
    5:19)

> By myself I can do nothing; I judge only as I hear, and my
> judgment is just, for I seek not to please myself but
> him who sent me. (John 5:30)

**Here is the secret of Jesus' success, of His ability to manifest
perfectly the love, power, and authority of God. He was not
interested in doing what He wanted for Himself. His delight
was in pleasing His Father and fulfilling His purpose.**

> For I have come down from heaven not to do my will but
> to do the will of him who sent me. (John 6:38)

> I do nothing on my own but speak just what the Father
> has taught me. (John 8:28)

> The one who sent me is with me; he has not left me alone,
> for I always do what pleases him. (John 8:29)

The Anointed One submitting himself to rejection, humi-
liation, torture and crucifixion, all in obedience to His
Father's will. What love! What humility!

YOUR ATTITUDE

Your attitude should be the same as that of Christ Jesus:
Who, being in very nature God, did not consider equality
with God something to be grasped, but made himself
nothing, taking the very nature of a servant, being made
in human likeness. (Phil. 2:5–7)

He sowed His life, letting the seed fall into the ground and
die, that there might be a mighty harvest of souls in God's
heavenly Kingdom. Without that sowing there would not
be the reaping.

'Your attitude should be the same,' says Paul. Being
prepared to die to self, to be made nothing in the world's
eyes, in order that you might be fruitful for God.

This is the death and resurrection principle that has to be
seen in our lives. There is no glory without the Cross.

The Lord gave me a picture of packets of seeds on a shelf.

The packets represented churches and the seeds the Christians who belong to them. The seeds in these packets were praying for revival. They wanted to see God's glory in the land, with many turning to Him in repentance and faith. It seemed their prayers were having little effect.

These packets needed to be taken from the shelf. The seeds had to fall to the ground and die. Then they could bear fruit. Then there could be a harvest of righteousness in the land.

Can we expect to receive all God wants to give us without being prepared to respond to His Word? The self-life does not want to fall into the ground and die. It will do anything to resist such total commitment, which is why the Church does not experience continual revival.

Pride challenges God.

Pride wants to please self rather than Him.

Pride leads many to contradict God's Word, preferring their own reason and ideas.

Pride ignores the need for spiritual discipline and exalts self.

Pride draws attention to the Christian rather than his Lord, when witnessing or testifying.

Pride causes the believer to want recognition, position, thanks and praise from others.

Pride wants others to know of the Christian's virtues, accomplishments, revelations, healings and miracles.

If the glory is not taken from the Lord at least it is shared by the proud believer, instead of being given exclusively to Jesus. The works of flesh are worth nothing. And the works of the Spirit are just that, the works of the Spirit; and therefore all the glory for them belongs to the Lord.

How many tense and broken relationships in the Church are caused through pride? Through people wanting things to be done according to their personal preferences? Through seeking position, authority, control even, instead of recognising that the Church is the Lord's and only what He wants matters.

Even Jesus said: 'If I glorify myself, my glory means nothing. My Father, whom you claim as your God, is the one who glorifies me' (John 8:54).

And so James tells us: **'Humble yourselves before the Lord, and he will lift you up'** (Jas. 4:10). Instead of exalting yourself, seeking prestige and applause, humble yourself before God. **'God opposes the proud but gives grace to the humble.'**

Submit yourself to God and resist the devil's attempts to stimulate pride. **The way to be victorious over pride is not to fight the pride but submit yourself to God.**

'Come near to God and he will come near to you' (Jas. 4:8). The arrogant cannot draw near to God. But you can come into the glory of His holy presence through the Cross. And the Cross spells the death of the self-life. 'It is no longer I who live.'

The humility so obvious in Jesus' attitudes comes from the fact that He knows His right position in relation to the Father. You can rejoice that you are His child, with all the attendant privileges and authority. Nevertheless you are to be a humble and obedient child.

It is necessary to experience the breaking of your pride. Only by humbling yourself before God, submitting to His pruning knife, can He cut out of your life what is proud and vain. He alone can give you the right spirit to be humble before men.

> The sacrifices of God are a broken spirit; a broken and contrite heart, O God, you will not despise. (Ps. 51:17)

Peter also quotes the proverb: **'God opposes the proud but gives grace to the humble'** (Prov. 3:34; 1 Pet. 5:5). Peter urges his readers to clothe themselves in humility, to humble themselves under God's mighty hand that he may lift them up in due time.

This is a strange way to be victorious. The way up is the

way down! Down on your knees before the mighty and holy one. **The humble one will be more likely to resist temptation, trust God, and be able to exercise His authority and power – like Jesus.**

God actually opposes the proud. You do not want to be in a position where God opposes you. He gives grace to the humble; He gives His everything to those who know they deserve nothing.

Again and again God's Word encourages us to walk humbly before God and man.

> **The greatest among you will be your servant. (Matt. 23:11)**
> **Whoever exalts himself will be humbled, and whoever humbles himself will be exalted. (Matt. 23:12)**
> **Whoever humbles himself like this child is the greatest in the kingdom of heaven. (Matt. 18:4)**
> **Do not be conceited. (Rom. 12:16)**
> **Clothe yourselves with . . . humility. (Col. 3:12)**
> **Be completely humble and gentle. (Eph. 4:2)**
> **Show true humility towards all men. (Tit. 3:2)**

EXALTED IDEAS

Many want to be raised up in ministry, often having exalted ideas about themselves. They say their calling is to be evangelists, although they bring no one to the Lord. They want to be prophets, but no one recognises their anointing. They want to be healers, out of a genuine desire to help people or perhaps to have a publicly acclaimed ministry; but they do not see healings taking place. They even call themselves apostles when this is a calling that can be given only by God, not by a church organisation.

By contrast, others say I am called to serve, called to help, called to quietly give myself.

Those whom God does raise up and use in national and international ministries are those who know His dealings in their lives. They have been humbled and refined, and recognise the need to stay humble before Him. Should pride raise its ugly head and should they ignore the warnings of the Spirit, their ministries can come crashing down about their ears. For those God raises up, He is certainly able to pull down should that prove necessary. He pulls down the proud and haughty but lifts up the humble.

God's dealings with individuals cannot normally be seen. But the fruit is obvious by the people they are and the ministries they have. There are no short cuts to fruitfulness, and no way of avoiding the truth which is so plainly taught in His Word. It is the humble whom God exalts and raises up.

Do you aspire to greater things in God? Do you want to be more fruitful? Do you wish to glorify the Lord more fully in your life?

Then walk in victory over pride, rejoicing that you can prove faithful in little things. The Lord knows you and your deeds. He knows what He can entrust into your hands.

The Father glorified Jesus when He had obediently and faithfully obeyed His commission. Aspire to such humility and obedience. **Your reputation is to be that you are a man or woman of God, that people see Jesus in you – His love, humility and graciousness.** Whatever works of power, the healings and the miracles, you do in His name as a result of His dealings with you, will certainly give Him glory.

If you have any ambition in God, let it be that you grow in true humility. The truly humble man walks in the presence of God, not attempting to do things by His own inspiration or strength, for He recognises the truth of what Jesus says: 'Apart from me you can do nothing' (John 15:5).

Your key to a victorious life:
WALK HUMBLY BEFORE GOD AND OTHERS.

28

Victory over Death

The way to victory:
If you have died with Christ, you can share in His victory over death and live in resurrection power, with assurance of eternal salvation.

Your victory scripture:
I am the resurrection and the life . . . whoever lives and believes in me will never die. (John 11:25–26)

RAISED WITH CHRIST

The resurrection demonstrated Jesus' victory over death. He submitted Himself to death that we might have salvation; but death could not hold Him! This was the outworking of His claim before going to the Cross:

I am the resurrection and the life. (John 11:25)

He took all mankind to the Cross that salvation could become possible for any who put their trust in Him. **But it is only those who believe in Him as God's Son who are raised to new life with Him now, and to eventual glory with Him in heaven eternally.**

I am the resurrection and the life. He who believes in me will live, even though he dies; and **whoever lives and believes in me will never die. (John 11:25–26)**

The believer will experience a physical death but will not die spiritually. He will share in the victory of Jesus over death. He is in Christ crucified; he is also in Christ risen from the dead. There is a sense, therefore, in which the believer is already seated in heavenly places:

> And God raised us up with Christ and seated us with him in the heavenly realms in Christ Jesus. (Eph. 2:6)

He has done this, Paul tells us, to show 'the incomparable riches of his grace' that He has expressed in His kindness to us in Jesus.

Notice the tense of the verb. 'God raised us up.' It is something that He has done, that is already accomplished because we are 'in Christ Jesus'. So Paul also says:

> If we have been united with him like this in his death, we will certainly also be united with him in his resurrection. (Rom. 6:5)

It is this certainty which takes away from the believer the fear of death, a fear which afflicts many other people. What happens to them beyond death is a big question mark. For the Christian, there is no doubt. **His salvation is assured because of the amazing grace God has shown him.**

I have to fight feelings of jealousy when a believer is promoted to glory! What a comfort to know my turn will come at God's appointed time. Hallelujah!

RESURRECTION

Belief in the resurrection is vital to the whole Christian cause: 'And if Christ has not been raised, our preaching is useless and so is your faith' (1 Cor. 15:14). For if Jesus is not raised, we cannot be raised and therefore would not have salvation.

> But Christ has indeed been raised from the dead, the firstfruits of those who have fallen asleep. (v.20)

Christ is the firstfruits; then 'those who belong to him' (v.23) will be raised with Him. He must reign until He has put all His enemies under His feet. The last enemy to be destroyed is death.

Paul explains something of the nature of our resurrection and the difference between the natural and the risen body:

> The body that is sown is perishable, it is raised imperishable; it is sown in dishonour, it is raised in glory; it is sown in weakness, it is raised in power; it is sown a natural body, it is raised a spiritual body. (1 Cor. 15:42–44)

We shall bear the likeness of 'the man from heaven'. This final transformation will happen 'in a flash, in the twinkling of an eye, at the last trumpet' (v.52).

Meanwhile 'we, who with unveiled faces all reflect the Lord's glory, are being transformed into his likeness with an ever-increasing glory, which comes from the Lord, who is the Spirit' (2 Cor. 3:18).

The final transformation will take place when we see the Lord face to face; then we shall be like Him. This will be the glorious fulfilment of His purposes for us and every believer. We shall finally be like Him!

> May God himself, the God of peace, sanctify you through and through. May your whole spirit, soul and body be kept blameless at the coming of our Lord Jesus Christ. The one who calls you is faithful and he will do it. (1 Thess. 5:23–24)

So the Christian does not need to fear death. For him this is merely the gateway to the ultimate victory. For beyond death there is resurrection, a new risen body and glorious transformation into the likeness of Jesus.

THE FINAL VICTORY

God wants to heal His children of sickness that robs them of their health and effective witness as the children of His

Kingdom, that takes them prematurely from the ministries He has for them now. But the believer is not afraid of going to be with the Lord. He or she will join the great company of the redeemed around God's throne:

> They are before the throne of God and serve him day and night in his temple; and he who sits on the throne will spread his tent over them. Never again will they hunger; never again will they thirst. The sun will not beat upon them, nor any scorching heat. For the Lamb at the centre of the throne will be their shepherd; he will lead them to springs of living water. And God will wipe away every tear from their eyes. (Rev. 7:15–17)

Glory to God! You are among that number. How could you ever doubt that you are called to personal victory? You have the Lord's presence with you, His power within you and His promise of eternal glory!

Your key to a victorious life:
WHEN YOU SEE THE LORD FACE TO FACE, YOU WILL BE LIKE HIM.

Appendix 1
Key Scriptures

1 Without faith it is impossible to please God. (Heb. 11:6)
2 The message of the cross is foolishness to those who are perishing, but to us who are being saved it is the power of God. (1 Cor. 1:18)
3 And whatever you do, whether in word or deed, do it all in the name of the Lord Jesus. (Col. 3:17)
4 The Spirit gives life; the flesh counts for nothing. (John 6:63)
5 The words I have spoken to you are spirit and they are life. (John 6:63)
6 Not everyone who says to me, 'Lord, Lord,' will enter the kingdom of heaven, but only he who does the will of my Father who is in heaven. (Matt. 7:21)
7 Be transformed by the renewing of your mind. Then you will be able to test and approve what God's will is – his good, pleasing and perfect will. (Rom. 12:2)
8 There is no fear in love. But perfect love drives out fear. (1 John 4:18)
9 If you hold to my teaching, you are really my disciples. Then you will know the truth, and the truth will set you free. (John 8:31–32)
10 Not as I will, but as you will. (Matt. 26:39)
11 Live by the Spirit, and you will not gratify the desires of the sinful nature. (Gal. 5:16)
12 God has poured out his love into our hearts by the Holy Spirit, whom he has given us. (Rom. 5:5)

13 I tell you the truth, my Father will give you whatever you ask in my name. (John 16:23)

14 The reason the Son of God appeared was to destroy the devil's work. (1 John 3:8)
I have given you authority . . . to overcome all the power of the enemy; nothing will harm you. (Luke 10:19)

15 Do not rejoice that the spirits submit to you, but rejoice that your names are written in heaven. (Luke 10:20)

16 Love your enemies, do good to those who hate you, bless those who curse you, pray for those who ill-treat you. (Luke 6:27–28)

17 No, in all these things we are more than conquerors through him who loved us. (Rom. 8:37)

18 In everything, do to others what you would have them do to you. (Matt. 7:12)

19 Do everything in love. (1 Cor. 16:14)

20 Give, and it will be given to you. A good measure, pressed down, shaken together and running over, will be poured into your lap. For with the measure you use, it will be measured to you. (Luke 6:38)

21 A man reaps what he sows. (Gal. 6:7)

22 Surely he took up our infirmities and carried our sorrows. (Isa. 53:4)

23 By his wounds we are healed. (Isa. 53:5)

24 It is for freedom that Christ has set us free. (Gal. 5:1)

25 I tell you the truth, if anyone keeps my word, he will never see death. (John 8:51)

26 Because he himself suffered when he was tempted, he is able to help those who are being tempted. (Heb. 2:18)

27 God opposes the proud but gives grace to the humble. (Prov. 3:34; Jas. 4:6; 1 Pet. 5:5)

28 I am the resurrection and the life . . . whoever lives and believes in me will never die. (John 11:25–26)

Appendix 2

Your Key to a Victorious Life

1 Faith in Jesus enables you to overcome.
2 All your needs have been met in the crucified Jesus.
3 The way of victory is to speak, act and pray in the name of Jesus.
4 Submit your soul (your mind, emotions and will) to the Holy Spirit.
5 Put God's word into practice.
6 Walk in obedience to Jesus.
7 Resist the negative thoughts which oppose faith; fill your mind with the positive truths of God's Word.
8 Do not allow your feelings to control you.
9 Believe what the Word tells you about yourself – not your own reason or feelings.
10 Willingly submit yourself to the authority of Jesus.
11 Consecrate your body to the Lord.
12 Set your heart on pleasing God.
13 Victorious prayer comes from a life of faith and obedience.
14 You have authority over the devil and all his works.
15 You have authority over demons because your name is written in heaven.
16 Your faith overcomes the world and all the ways you can be opposed.
17 Maintain a positive, faith attitude at all times.
18 Live with an attitude towards others of love, forgiveness and mercy.

19 Express your love for others in giving to them in practical ways.

20 Walk in faith, love and obedience and you will prosper.

21 Keep giving to the Lord and others.

22 Sickness will not triumph over you.

23 Resist sickness in the name of Jesus.

24 Christ has set you free to live in freedom.

25 Live by the truth of God's Word.

26 Walk in the Spirit; say 'No' to every temptation to indulge the flesh.

27 Walk humbly before God and others.

28 When you see the Lord face to face, you will be like Him.